THE ONLY KANGAROO
AMONG THE BEAUTY

KARL KELLER

THE ONLY KANGAROO
AMONG THE BEAUTY

EMILY DICKINSON AND AMERICA

THE JOHNS HOPKINS UNIVERSITY PRESS

BALTIMORE AND LONDON

FOR KINGSLEY WIDMER

Mines in the same ground meet by tunneling.

EMILY DICKINSON, 1882

CONTENTS

Six

THE UNUSED UNIVERSE

Seven

GOD BE WITH THE CLOWN

Eight

THE HOPELESS DITCH

Nine

THE SWEET WOLF WITHIN

Ten

WHEN THE SOUL IS AT PLAY

A CODA

ACKNOWLEDGMENTS

Four people gave the most encouragement for this kind of study—Sacvan Bercovitch, Charles H. Foster, David S. Wilson, and Everett Emerson.

One man's work was an almost perfect example to follow—Kingsley Widmer.

Still other persons gave me ideas and language and kept me within conceivable limits—David Bergman, James Rother, Cherie Harley, James Hinkle, Carl Dolmetsch, Alice Swayne, and Ruth Keller.

Anyone who studies Emily Dickinson is greatly in the debt of Thomas H. Johnson, George Whicher, Charles Anderson, William Sherwood, Jay Leyda, and Richard B. Sewall, who found her first and knew her best. I try to build here on their remarkable case for her.

THE ONLY KANGAROO
AMONG THE BEAUTY

AN INTRODUCTION

THE AFFINITIES OF A VERNACULAR POET

Creator – Shall I – bloom?

[#442]

Jorge Luis Borges gives us a parable, "Everything and Nothing," in which he pictures Shakespeare appearing before God and begging to know who he is:

> No one has ever been so many men as this man, who like the Egyptian Proteus could exhaust all the guises of reality. . . . History adds that before or after dying he found himself in the presence of God and told him: "I who have been so many men in vain want to be one and myself." The voice of the Lord answered from a whirlwind: "Neither am I anyone; I have dreamt the world as you dreamt your work, my Shakespeare, and among the forms in my dream are you, who like myself are many and no one."

A description of Emily Dickinson poses much the same difficulty: there are ways in which she too is everything and nothing. The greatest woman poet—and one of the great poets in the history of American literature—has therefore often escaped us.

To a great extent she *is* unknowable. Those students of hers who have not learned this have been, with few exceptions, fooled by their certainties. Mine is an attempt to restore her multiplicity, ambiguity,

1

complexity, even as I hold out for something intrinsic—perhaps a self, a will, an "iron string"—behind her unknowability. I am fascinated and defeated; yet I hope I have helped to save a life—or at least a mind and an art.

Saving a life like Emily Dickinson's from that hall of tortures called biography while saying something accurate and moving perhaps means leaving her silences and slips alone—not the unknowns, but the white spaces where we have little or no ability to look with *our* eyes. It also means learning from her how to believe in the possibility of knowing her and living *without* it. The rest it is necessary to report, if without total reconstruction or total coherence. To forewarn us, she wrote:

> if this little flower
> To Eden, wandered in –
> What then? Why nothing,
> Only, your inference therefrom!

[#180]

There *is* a life in her poems, but it is a life she fragmented for us, and that is what one has—not pieces of a figure but sides, each one imagined or real as she understood it or as we do. The sides outline a figure without making it whole or fully satisfying. What went on in her life and mind moment by moment is unfathomable. No one can possibly relate the whole story, no matter how limited a fragment of Emily Dickinson's life and art he chooses to dwell on. "Who can say how many [the women] were, or who they were," Rilke said of a group of writers, phrasing the uncertainty of his own Malte Laurids Brigge. "It is as if they had destroyed beforehand the words with which one might grasp them."

What *is* graspable makes up, I believe, the fascinatingly large mind of a panoramist painting miniatures. She was so good and so large—perhaps a great deal like what she admired the most: the Bible, Shakespeare, Emerson, George Eliot, though with her own good and large difference—that I think we could say she was multifarious, multiform, multiple. That is her dimension. She liked to talk about herself (a little grandly, a little divinely) in terms of circumference.

But at the same time we must recognize that Emily Dickinson is a great tease. Her life, like her poetry, seduces without offering complete satisfaction. For all the expansiveness, there is always something lacking, insufficient, incomplete, tentative, not really finished at all. Little that she did or wrote seems to have a whole world to it. Perhaps it is her own fault that she invites so many conjectures and theories and that she moves one to doubt so easily one's own critical judgments of her poems.

But perhaps that hardly matters. The tease in her goes well beyond mere attractiveness and invites, I believe, Borgesian historical simulations: you take her influence on you as a way of looking at others (we can read Hawthorne, for instance, because Kafka has changed us, and Shakespeare because we have been remolded by Nabokov); or you take what you know about others as a means of looking at her (thus, creating a Puritan environment for her, or a Transcendentalist milieu, or a playful Frostean frame of mind brings out that side of her without distorting hypotheses). The affinities help one know her, without the pretense that one will know her whole. Her connections with some of the more attractive features of the world around her, along the whole range of American literary history, give us some fairly bold features of her to think about and test out.

"There are very few important American poets either before or after her," writes H. H. Waggoner, "whose work is not suggested somewhere in hers, whose images she did not try out, whose insights she did not recapitulate, criticize, or anticipate. She not only bridged the gap between Edward Taylor and Emerson, she bridged the one between Emerson and Frost—and even more rarely but distinctly enough—between Emerson and Eliot and Stevens."[1] But, as Richard Sewall has pointed out in his somewhat fulsome biography of her, while pinpointing influences on/of Emily Dickinson is an extremely precarious undertaking, since she covered most of her tracks well, her affinities are another matter entirely. "Much has been accomplished, . . . but . . . much still needs to be done. How close was she to Emerson in certain ways, how far from him in others? And Thoreau, Hawthorne, Whitman, and the English Romantics, especially Keats and Wordsworth? The way is open for some important studies."[2] Emily Dickinson's poetry was, I would like to argue, an important piece in what André Malraux calls the Museum without Walls: "Certain works of genius can look across the centuries and whisper to one another— ideally existing in the mind."

Much of my method here is to play with what I—teased—know about Emily Dickinson, which means also playing with what others know about her. Play seems to me the true function of the critic anyway. But mine is not a dance around a monument, as John Gardner recommends for one's relationship to memorable writings of a past era. It is closer to a tease of my own, to see what life a subject may yet yield. In the past three-quarters of a century, admirers have produced upward of forty-five books about Emily Dickinson, most of

1. H. H. Waggoner, *American Poets: From the Puritans to the Present* (New York, 1968), p. 213.
2. Richard B. Sewall, *The Life of Emily Dickinson* (New York, 1974), p. 679.

them awful and a few awfully good. In almost all of them the seriousness has been deadly, as if Emily Dickinson herself were. So perhaps
she has been admired to death.

My own teases here explore some possibilities for enjoying her
critically by talking about her in a substantially different way: playing
her off against some American writers with whom we know she had
some rather definite intellectual relations or with whom we may rea-
sonably imagine she shares some rather definite intellectual characteristics. These are her American affinities. My intent is to set her
squarely in the center of American literary history and see how far out
the illuminations go, then to enjoy the different color each of the
affinities takes. Silly even to feel that the confines of American history
and culture delimited her as they defined her.[3] Instead, they reveal
how wide a world her circumference took in.

Yet there are so many affinities in the mind and life of Emily
Dickinson that the critic who elects some for her may reveal his own
interests over hers. I confess that I find the acquired Puritan New
England past, for example, not merely dominant but overwhelming
to her; and, in large part because she refreshed it considerably, I
therefore find it overwhelming to us. It is represented here by her
affinities with Anne Bradstreet the Proud Puritan Woman, Edward
Taylor the Experimental Frontiersman, Jonathan Edwards the Inventive Hell-raiser, and Harriet Beecher Stowe the Obsessed Utopian.

I find, on the other hand, that her times baffled Emily Dickinson, and so her attention to them was divided and defensive. They are
represented here by her affinities with Hawthorne the Lost Ambiguist, Emerson the Secure Aphorist, her highly erratic Circle of
Literary Friends, her sister reformers in New England, and Walt
Whitman the Beautiful, Failed American. All of these are my foils for
talking about neglected sides of Emily Dickinson. My hope is that the
selection somehow describes her, places her, promotes her.

I admit, to be more specific, that one of my main intentions in
this trial of Emily Dickinson is to define Puritan esthetics—because I
feel *she* did—not by staring down the writers of the seventeenth century and early eighteenth century for their revelations, but rather by
watching the esthetics flower at a later time when a "Puritan" was free
to have them *as esthetics*. Whereas one can get at the esthetics of

3. I argue as strongly as I can against Inder Nath Kher's thesis in *The Landscape
of Absence: Emily Dickinson's Poetry* (New Haven, 1974) that any emphasis on Emily
Dickinson's Americanness only "minimize[s] the range of her poetic sensibility" (p. 5).
And against Ellen Moers's position in *Literary Women* (New York, 1976): "The real
scandal of Emily Dickinson's life is . . . her embarrassing ignorance of American Literature" (pp. 60–61). The affinities with American thinking and American writing do exist
and reveal much about her.

American Puritanism only inadvertently—through, say, the awkward, hidden spiritual exercises of Edward Taylor or the democratic-ecclesiastical jargon of Thomas Hooker and Solomon Stoddard or the coded sensationalism of Jonathan Edwards, in all of whom, with others, the theology *is* essentially esthetic—with Emily Dickinson one has theology-produced/-induced esthetics separated off from the theology and therefore Puritan esthetics in purer, observable form. In time the crude ore yielded its true mettle. New England Puritanism *was* the American past to Emily Dickinson—the only one she knew.

Another intention is to try to fix Emily Dickinson's presence among her American contemporaries a little more firmly. Here she does not hold still very well for a portrait, for she is largely uncomfortable with the company. Though they got a kind of hold on her, she did not have a very solid hold on Hawthorne or Emerson, her two most noticeable contemporaries. And those in her more immediate circle of literary friends—both good and bad indicators of popular culture to her—were simply annoying; she did not grasp them very well because they could not grasp *her* very well. She was not significantly at odds with public reform movements of women in her time, to single out a particular type of contemporary, and not really very much out of step with the times' literary Jesus, Walt Whitman, but simply often *better* (in her own way) at what they meant to do and at what they have been made to stand for in our literary histories. She could not "see to see" what we would try to see if we were her *then.* Yet there she stands now, as good at reform, at ambiguity and aphorism, and at being an American (though in her own way) as some of her contemporaries. The century was also *hers.*

Still another intention (though developed more tentatively and temptingly) is to show her teaching the twentieth century how to write. She is still almost as avant-garde as when she was first published (though how palely then and how wildly now!) in the 1890s. She has been used to get a lot of modern poetry going, from Stephen Crane and Amy Lowell to Robert Frost and Richard Wilbur. I suspect that is in part because she did not always know exactly what she was doing, but that a number of twentieth-century poets, needing her, *have* known. They have thus made her their precursor, though I think she would have denied and orphaned them all. The Fall gave her fairly narrow vision amid an abundant creation; she did more than she knew she did.

Decidedly missing from my elected affinities for her, I admit, is Emily Dickinson's interest in writers outside the United States—interest in George Eliot and Emily Brontë, John Keats and Elizabeth Barrett. That is not to underrate their importance to her at all but to underscore the fact that they have already been of more interest to her critics than American writers have. What's more, I relate her to Americans in order to explore the problem of an American writer's juxtaposition to mainstream culture. She is traditionally the one most remote from it. I try to show that she *is* it—she is *also* it. American literature cannot be defined without her. We cannot go on defining centrist America without its eccentrics. And this is my final and most important intention.

America is named only once in Emily Dickinson's poetry. Yet, along with Whitman, she is America's great early radical, the radical as poet. She is at the roots. An America is not so much assumed behind her life and poems, however, and not so much subsumed in them either, as *made by them*. Hers is *an* America, an America as a woman, Emily Dickinson, had it.

Just think: Where else but in America do we have a woman torturing herself with such puritanical flash? Where else do we have a poet presenting herself/himself quite so unfinished—deliberately unfinished? Where else do we have someone demanding that the Other bless her and her protest against It, bless her personal antinomian heresy? Where else do we have someone who is forever talking about herself but cannot ever talk *to* herself—a voice in a space, singing in a beautiful wilderness, making a place, a locale, a location for herself in time, making a portable life? Where else do we have someone who desperately wanted to be a poet and yet felt no obligation to be learned and could therefore take her own experience in her own place and time as her greatest accomplishment? Where else do we find poetry constructing a politics of refusal? Where else is a loner so involved?

It is important to work to bring off this affinity between Emily Dickinson and America, because once and for all I would like to demolish the stereotype of E. D. the Recluse, Emily D. the New England Nun, Emily Dickinson as "*the* Emily Dickinson?" Erica Jong, like many others, bemoans Emily Dickinson's traditional lonely lot—but awfully blindly, I feel:

> decorous Jane Austen . . .
> & Sappho leaping,
> & Sylvia in the oven . . .
> & pale Virginia floating like Ophelia,
> & Emily alone, alone, alone.

Sometimes lonely, perhaps, but not always so very much alone, except in the quite opposite sense of being alone with (to use Richard Howard's idea of being unconsciously but definitely affined with) a world she was connected to, or can be connected with—but hardly totally alone, hardly unassociated, hardly dissociated. Though anomalous, she "knew."

Emily Dickinson the recluse, the isolata, the individual. How the image sticks! Even when Julie Harris is on stage as the Belle of Amherst, she is *alone;* there is only a very small and very silent world that she moves around in; there are no others. Perhaps the late twentieth century needs such an example—the Example of Emily Dickinson—as aloofness from society becomes more difficult and as one's self becomes harder to see. But this insistence leaves any portrait of her merely a still life, with precious little world for her to move around in and precious little life for her to live.

Emily Dickinson's American affinities, however, are more than parallels or similarities and imply some foundation in history, in the culture, in biography, even in *use.* "I . . . never consciously touch a paint," she disclaimed to T. W. Higginson in 1862, "mixed by another person."[4] Consciously or unconsciously connected, the means and methods of other American writers and thinkers were also *her* media, *her* median. The paradigms they bring to American culture I use as epistemes in her art; some of their designs are some of her possibilities.

Although Emily Dickinson is not entirely knowable (while still perhaps salable), her forms are not unknowable. She left an incomplete image of herself, but the forms she worked in and with are virtual revelations. The revelations are not entirely surprising, however, for we should have known all along, as this study tries to show, that she was a post-Puritan woman standing up, that she bent Puritan conventions to meet her own needs, that she used Puritan teleology as ground to dance on, that the Puritan-projected American future could not faze her, that she found the ambiguous universe a tease, that certain language structures were for her a measure of security, that she was vulnerable to criticism, that she was deliberately myopic about society's forms, that she went wild, that she found poetry fun and funny. These are the arguments I make about her as I relate her to American life.

Nabokov (in *Transparent Things*) compares human life to a person dancing in a variety of forms around one's own self. This discussion is an attempt to describe some of those forms. I think Emily Dickinson might have recognized all of them herself. But more than that, I think she might have enjoyed the dance here orchestrated for her to dance around herself by.

4. Thomas H. Johnson, ed., *The Letters of Emily Dickinson* (Cambridge, Mass., 1955), p. 415.

# One

THE ELFIN/GAMIN

Emily Dickinson and Anne Bradstreet

I pray for the tenants of that holy chamber, the wrestler, and the wrestled for.

[*Letters*, p. 356]

When Samuel Eliot Morison chose the builders for his Bay Colony, he inadvertently canonized (if a little chauvinistically) two Puritan women as the patron saints of the beginnings of a form of liberated womanhood in America. He first gave them anxiously desirous if suppressed roles to play—

> As I turn the pages of Anne Bradstreet's poems, and try to project myself into her life and time, I catch the merest hint of that elfin, almost *gamin* attitude of Emily Dickinson to God. Even Emily in the nineteenth century would so express herself only to her dearest friends. Anne, in the seventeenth century, would hardly have dared admit as much even to herself.

—and then he mythologized them as women given poetic powers by the dynamics of Puritan piety:

> [Anne Bradstreet's] life was proof, if it were needed, that creative art may be furthered by religion; and that even the duties of a housewife and mother in a new country cannot quench the sacred flame. It was another question whether that flame could be passed on to others in an

8

isolated frontier commonwealth, where material life clutched greedily at all that spiritual life relinquished. This question was not answered for two centuries, when the genius of Anne Bradstreet was reincarnated in Emily Dickinson.[1]

In Morison's hands they are examples of the ways Puritan woman-hood is selfhood, the ways woman became creative under a religious code—something the Puritan libertarian in Milton understood; something the New England apologists (from Winthrop to Edwards) understood; and something both Anne Bradstreet and Emily Dickinson understood as a crucial factor in their well-realized lives.

One of early Puritanism's best legacies to the modern world is the promise of the elevation of women.[2] If Anne Hutchinson was not exactly the age's ideal, neither was the wife-as-servant nor the lady-as-platonic-ideal. Anne Bradstreet more nearly fits the Puritan hope. And Emily Dickinson added to the role Anne Bradstreet originally made. Intellectually, women held a more privileged place in American culture during its formative centuries than in European culture because it was shorthanded; Emily Dickinson is the one female author to stand with the foremost males. Within the Puritan pattern, both of them accept their womanhood, recognize that as women they have claims on attention, and find their concern for themselves as women turning them into creative people. In the history of the search to understand Emily Dickinson's origins, it is possible to assert that the fullest appreciation of her as a writer begins at those points where Anne Bradstreet's begins. Their shared concept of self-fulfillment for both men and women is entirely within Puritan hopes. We know it was Puritanism that gave American literature its only two important women poets before the twentieth century. In it we have one source of what they accomplished.

I suggest, however, that the liberated Anne Bradstreet is not the one who read Sidney and Herbert and DuBartas and would have enjoyed Donne, or the one whose heart kept rising against settlement and against religious confinement, or the one who dared to write and complain against sexism, but the one elevated as a woman by her

---

1. *Builders of the Bay Colony* (Boston, 1930), pp. 323, 335–36. Morison's attempt to link the two as elfin/gamin figures grows out of a hopeful historiography: they were both women poets, both doubters/seekers/rebels, both witty and deviant, both Massachusetts women.

2. Arno Karlen, *Sexuality and Homosexuality: A New View* (New York, 1971), pp. 126–30, has the boldest argument in support of Puritanism's claim to the advancement of women. For Karlen, the only significant revolution in sexual mores in the modern world has been the changing position of women, and the influence of Puritanism in that revolution he finds helpful.

Puritan faith to the position of self-sufficient responsibility for her soul.

Likewise, the liberated Emily Dickinson is not the one who read Emerson and George Eliot and would have known how to read Kierkegaard, or the one who looked out of her window in Amherst occasionally to write about sex and trains and to criticize ministers and high-society ladies, but the one pushed by her Puritan background into substantiality.

The lives of both women had the tone of self-conscious, independent conformity as much as that of eccentricity, deviance, and rebelliousness. To be sure, both of them cried out against their condition and station, both played mockingly at female stereotypes, both had moments when they had the conviction that, as Emily Dickinson put it, "Faith is *Doubt.*" But in the main they show how early Puritanism had within it the seeds (if never the social means) for the elevation and liberation of women like themselves. It is no paradox that in the discipline of her Puritan inclination, Emily Dickinson found one of the sources of herself as a poet.

Hawthorne, for one, saw Puritanism as a primary source of a woman's equal capabilities, though declining with its decline:

> The [Puritan] age had not so much refinement, that any sense of impropriety restrained the wearers of the petticoat and farthingale from stepping forth into the public ways. . . . [These women] stood within less than half a century of the period when the man-like Elizabeth had been the not altogether unsuitable representative of the sex. . . . Morally, as well as materially, there was a coarser fiber in those wives and maidens of old English birth and breeding, than in their fair descendants, separated from them by a series of six or seven generations; for throughout the chain of ancestry, every successive mother has transmitted to her child a fainter bloom, a more delicate and briefer beauty.[3]

Emily Dickinson might have surprised Hawthorne as a partial reincarnation of the kind of Puritan woman he admired.

For the Puritan woman of the early seventeenth century, the Puritan cosmic order was dignifying. She was called to salvation, not to keep house or have children—though that was, as it turned out, the socially preferred way. In theory, she was no more limited to wifely/motherly routines than a man was to his work. Fortunate for her call to salvation, men's authority over her was strictly limited by early New England concepts of love and duty; the duty of family governance and instruction gave her a common status at home with men; she was

3. Nathaniel Hawthorne, *The Scarlet Letter,* Centenary edition (Columbus, Ohio, 1962), p. 50.

expected to assert her worth even as she joyfully submitted to men's will; and she gained dignity from the "tender respectiveness" men owed her. The devotion of marriage raised her above subservience, and her Puritan self-consciousness led her to discover in duty (and here is another of Puritanism's paradoxes) a kind of liberation. Emily Dickinson capsulated the mode:

'Twas my one Glory
Let it be
Remembered
I was owned of Thee –

[#1028]

The theoretical priesthood of all believers, though ambivalent and dishonest in many of its promises, made a certainty amid a woman's worldly uncertainties. If independence was not possible, an individual security was—a distinction, no doubt, that satisfied both the positive demands of the theology and the negative demands of society. A woman would make herself good even when the society of men could not make good on the priesthood of all (women) believers.[4]

Her calling was everyone's calling, to discern her inherent possibilities; and so the part she played in the religious life was active and autonomous, even if private and self-conscious. It was most certainly a stimulus to her to be able to think well of the possible worth of her spiritual self. For which Bunyan's Christiana was the model: woman *too* had to make her way to eternal salvation independently. Sex was no hindrance, no advantage. More than such conventional Puritan opportunities as the dependable marriage, the principle of "religious sharing," and the respect for woman as moral and religious personality, woman's "emancipation" under early Puritanism lay in *her respon-*

4. See Ben Barker-Benfield, "Anne Hutchinson and the Puritan Attitude toward Women," *Feminist Studies* 1 (fall 1972): 65–96. The argument here is a wholly partisan one: when Anne Hutchinson was not allowed her antinomian enthusiasm, America committed itself to a chauvinist pattern. Overlooked is what was happening *within* women themselves under orthodox Puritan pressures.
I very much like Elsa Green's comment on the burden of being a Puritan woman; it applies equally well to both women:

Emily Dickinson *was* a female. She knew it and we know it. She did not, in fact, inhabit the same milieu which influenced Ralph Waldo Emerson and his puritan male forebears; and it is a deadly favor to assume she did. Emerson was not raised to celebrate piety, purity, submissiveness, and domesticity as divinely-commanded attributes of himself. He was not taught that God would punish men who preferred the pen (or the scalpel, or the balance sheet, or anything else) to the broom. In simply *choosing* the vocation of poetess, Emily Dickinson risked psychic and social penalities unknown to her masculine predecessors.

["Emily Dickinson Was a Poetess," *College English* 34 (1972): 63–70]

sibility for herself. The fundamental emphasis on individual salvation—and its accompanying loneliness, self-sufficiency, self-reliance, and risks (all of these important, dominant qualities in the lives and works, as far as we can assess them, of both Anne Bradstreet and Emily Dickinson)—elevated her. Though the logic may escape us today, her piety was her freedom.[5]

The age was not ready for her secular autonomy; yet its dignifying (and perhaps also cruel) cosmic demands on the individual soul rather automatically assured woman considerable elevation within the covenants of the faith over her status in any comparable contemporary culture. "Due to religious beliefs and the economic and social conditions in the colonies," write Leonard, Drinker, and Holden, "married women acquired definite rights and privileges that had not been theirs in England or on the continent."[6] To be sure, the Puritan code for women was repressive: "He for God only, she for God in him." Yet the range of possibilities for women was very quickly expanding, running from a position like that of William Whately's ("Every good woman must suffer herself to be convinced in judgment that she is not her husband's equal") to that of William Gouge ("[There is but] small inequality which is betwixt the husband and the wife: for of all degrees wherein there is any difference betwixt person and person there is the least disparity betwixt man and wife").[7] We should therefore never conclude that Puritan women became subservient or browbeaten; the precise opposite was likely as not the case. "There is, indeed, one respect," writes William Haller, "in which the two are on the same level."

5. Puritan woman is not a very well-known figure. She has often been avoided as a nonentity in the culture (one of the few sins of Perry Miller and his students), and she has often been looked for in the wrong places. See Carroll Camden, *The Elizabethan Women* (Houston, 1952), for example, where the "somewhat new woman of the Renaissance" is sought in the antifeminist belles lettres of the period. Or see Elizabeth Anthony Dexter, *Colonial Women of Affairs* (Boston, 1931), where religious pressures on women are disregarded altogether. At times she has been sentimentalized out of sight and at times made the butt of flippant polemics. Only two studies have seen her in the light of her own beliefs: Edmund Morgan, *The Puritan Family* (New York, 1944), and Levin L. Schücking, *The Puritan Family* (New York, 1970), both arguing the advancement of women (however slow and limited) in Puritan society, though both preferring the evidence from the age's apologists over sociological information, and both concerned solely with the Puritan wife/mother, not the Puritan woman otherwise. A survey of the criticism is in Joan Wilson's notes to "Dancing Dogs of the Colonial Period: Women Scientists," *Early American Literature* 7 (winter 1973): 231-35.
6. Eugine Andruss Leonard, Sophie Hutchinson Drinker, and Miriam Young Holden, *The American Woman in Colonial and Revolutionary Times, 1565-1800* (Philadelphia, 1962), p. 28.
7. William Whately, *A Bride-Bush; or, A Direction for Married Persons* (London, 1619), p. 189; William Gouge, *Of Domesticall duties* (London, 1622), p. 273.

Since they are equal in sin and alike in their appointed inheritance of death, therefore they are the heirs together of the grace of life. The husband, that is to say, not withstanding his superiority in other respects, had no better title to salvation than the wife who submitted to him, and she, conversely, had as good a claim to the means and assurance of grace as any he alive. Hence the godly wife, no matter how hard her earthly lot, could be certain that the balance would be righted in heaven, and in that assurance there was an advantage which many a woman must have enjoyed without waiting for heaven. . . . Woman was inferior to man in nature but equal and, in given cases, superior in grace. Her soul was as worth saving as his, and its experiences had equal significance.[8]

When ministers preached on godliness in wives, they were calling women to an intensely active existence on all levels, emotional and spiritual, physical and practical. There was no such thing as a dull, weak, idle *Puritan* woman. On its cosmological scale of souls, therefore, early Puritanism promised woman an authentic existence. In large measure, Emily Dickinson wrote because of that promise.

Anne Bradstreet saw, as Emily Dickinson was to experience two centuries later, that under the Puritan covenants emphasized in the early decades of the seventeenth century, woman was given a creative stimulus. Being a woman gave her possession of an inner space, and to be a woman was to gain power by turning inward. A man may conquer the world, but, like a man, a Puritan woman already had a world (in the Puritan, meditative sense of the word) *within*. Within Puritanism womanhood *is* selfhood. Anne Bradstreet appears to have understood this possibility better than the men who watched and commented on her, and she became a poet as an expression of her Puritan womanhood. Much later, Emily Dickinson turned the same Puritan possibility into an ethical urge to affirm her personal existence, not as a woman but as a being: the solitary woman with an aggressive creativity whose self-fulfillment as a woman was the earthly form she could make the grace of God take.

First, we have in Anne Bradstreet's poetry an example of Puritanism as an esthetic. In Anne Bradstreet the self-sufficiency encouraged by Puritan womanhood (the cosmic necessity of concern for one's own soul, whether male or female, high-placed or oppressed)

8. William and Malleville Haller, "The Puritan Art of Love," *Huntington Library Quarterly* 5 (1942): 250–51, 256. For other studies on the subject of the Puritan woman and her religious calling, see Louis B. Wright, *Middle-class Culture in Elizabethan England* (Chapel Hill, N.C., 1935) and Chilton L. Powell, *English Domestic Relations, 1487–1653* (New York, 1917).

took the form of a spunky humility—an elfin/gamin role, as Morison calls it to underscore the witty, teasing, taunting, Puritan vigor and shrewd manner in his two canonized women. Anne Bradstreet wrote, upon having to settle at Boston at seventeen (the statement now a classic):

> I . . . came into this country, where I found a new world and new manners, at which my heart rose. But after I was convinced it was the way of God, I submitted to it and joined to the church at Boston.[9]

This rising heart is not a woman's presumptuousness but simple participation in duty; she must know on her own if it is the right thing for her. It may sound to us like protest only if one initially expects, in our own stereotype of a puritanized woman, an abject submissiveness and holy silence. "The way of God" has made her, she feels, a participant in the covenant, and so she "joins."

Similarly, it is easy to locate too much worldliness and rebelliousness—and too little Puritan preparationism—in Anne Bradstreet's "many times hath Satan tempted me" statements. It is rather conventional (and hyperbolic) soul-searching; compare her tone with Edward Taylor's in his First Series of Meditations and with Jonathan Edwards's in his "Personal Narrative." If she could confess, "Yet have I many times sinkings and droopings," we should understand not a lapse but a self-consciousness of her participation in her spiritual worth. This is what Perry Miller calls "the expanding limits of human ability": each individual, regardless of sex and station, involving himself/herself, however tentatively and weakly, in the issue of his/her own salvation. In the decisive program of predestinarian psychology, creating a self-consciousness was what there was left to do. Anne Bradstreet's was not the "quiet rebellion" that some of the best modern apologists rudimentarily assign her. She is at no point working passionately against her allegiances. Her allegiances themselves give her, I argue, her independence of effort and mind and her womanly self-assertiveness.[10] In her, as later in Emily Dickinson, there

---

9. "To My Dear Children," in *The Works of Anne Bradstreet*, ed. Jeannine Hensley (Cambridge, Mass., 1967), p. 241.

10. Ann Stanford writes of Anne Bradstreet: "Rebellion and a struggle for or against conviction form a pattern which runs through her writing. . . . In her determination to write and in her defense of the capability of women to reason, to contemplate, and to read widely, she showed herself capable of taking a stand against the more conservative and dogmatic of her contemporaries. It was a quiet rebellion, carried on as an undercurrent in an atmosphere of conformity" ("Anne Bradstreet: Dogmatist and Rebel," *New England Quarterly* 34 [September 1966]: 373–89). The attempts to make her an example of variance from Puritan orthodoxy have not been entirely satisfying. She is lively-minded but a true believer. In her own words, she is a dutiful, dignified

is, if we are willing to hover over its qualities with correct Puritan sympathies, a form of substantiality—even grace.

Throughout Anne Bradstreet's religious life, her relationship to her God appears often to have been close to that of a challenger. The proximity and energy (elfin/gamin) are a sign of her feel of her worth. "After some time I fell into a lingering sickness like a consumption together with a lameness," she wrote to her children, "which correction I saw the Lord sent to humble and try me and do me good, and it was not altogether ineffectual." They are doing battle and God has won, but she has won by *letting* him win, though not too willing to award him the victory. She insists (spunkily) the victory is hers.[11] Such challenges sometimes take the form of assigning to God's will her illnesses and the deaths of members of her family, blaming him. Yet it is a lover's quarrel. She, a woman, is a copartner with God in the covenant, and he has agreed that she should work his will, having children and teaching them his way.

In a poem of 1632, "Upon a Fit of Sickness," written when nineteen, she again insists on getting the upper hand, having the last word, winning:

> The race is run the field is won,
>   the victory's mine I see;
> Forever know, thou envious foe
>   the foil belongs to thee.[12]

There is a participatory tone in such a relationship with her God, as there is when she writes:

> It pleased God to keep me a long time without a child, which was a great grief to me and cost me many prayers and tears before I obtained one, and after him [God] gave me many more.[13]

This is not contentious, but insistent: it is her duty—and God's—for her to have children. In fulfillment of that duty, she wants coopera-

---

participant in her own salvation when she speaks of "my straying soul": "I have been with God like an untoward child, that no longer when the rod has been on my back (or at least in sight) but I have been apt to forget Him and myself too. Before I was afflicted I went astray, but now I keep Thy statutes" (*Works,* p. 242). When she describes the "blocks" in her life—doubts about the truth of the Scriptures, about belonging to the true church, and about religious security in the world—we must remember that she is telling exemplary stories to her children, not warning them of her tendency to heresy. See Stanford's arguments further in "Anne Bradstreet," in *Major Writers of Early American Literature,* ed. Everett Emerson (Madison, 1972), and her *Anne Bradstreet: The Worldly Puritan* (New York, 1974).

    11. *Works,* p. 241.
    12. *Works,* p. 222.
    13. *Works,* p. 241.

tion from him. There are certain things she wants as a dutiful participant in a divine plan. She has an important part to play and will not be denied her role. The tone of such comments is that of covenant theology: dutifulness. God has promised and must carry out his bargain.

She is selling herself to us in such poems and anecdotes as the ideal Puritan woman: duty has promised to raise her to a dignifying status. It is therefore not her flirtation with doubt that shows her spiritedness but her ability to conquer her "sitting loose from God," her "block." She is celebrating not her ability to raise questions but her ability to be strong in overcoming them. Faith makes her a real woman, a personage in a divine scheme. No such volatile, homuncular persona as one might like to find sticking out from the oppressions of early New England culture, she is a *participant*.

It is not so much that her spirited attitude represents a thaw of the early rigid Puritan ethos[14] or that she is made alive by the conflict of the worldly and otherwordly in her,[15] but rather, as she has it in her poem "In Reference to Her Children, 23 June 1659," that she has self-fulfillment through children, home, husband, love, duty. "The first step on the way to Emily Dickinson," writes George Whicher, "was to turn away from large impersonal subjects and to find poetry in personal and domestic matters. That step Mrs. Bradstreet took."[16] This is liberation via piety, via Puritan allegiance. She rejoices in "the duties I owe to [God] and the work of my family." She has discovered an energy inherent in Puritanism: every man *and woman* struggling toward the Celestial City. We have the small eschatology of Christiana rather than that of a Faustina.

In her long poem "Contemplations," Anne Bradstreet makes a comparison of Adam and Eve as the male and female archetypes. Adam she makes out to be inherently "lord of all" and "sovereign," and Eve is pictured "in a retired place," sighing "how she lost her bliss to be more wise." Woman in the Fall is, to Anne Bradstreet, made mature by accepting her duty as mother and wife. Through religious duty she is made "more wise." In this she is raised above the effects of the Fall—only a small step toward today's woman, perhaps, as defined by male dependency and female presumptuousness, but a substantial remove from the woman of the late Middle Ages and Renaissance.

The Puritan way that both Anne Bradstreet and Emily Dickin-

14. The argument of Elizabeth Wade White, *Anne Bradstreet: "The Tenth Muse"* (New York, 1971), pp. 306–7. That Anne Bradstreet possessed "a sort of mental rage" that could have done "irreparable damage" to herself is merely speculative.

15. The argument of Robert D. Richardson, Jr., "The Puritan Poetry of Anne Bradstreet," *Texas Studies in Literature and Language* 9 (1967): 320–22.

16. George F. Whicher, *Alas, All's Vanity* (New York, 1942), pp. 27–28.

son inherited expected of women, as I am attempting to underscore, the same independence of mind toward their salvation and the same learning and understanding of themselves as it did of men—though all the while failing to provide the *social* means for achieving such. It was Anne Bradstreet's Puritan orthodoxy that encouraged what independence we find in her, not her independence that made her wayward, unlike her unhappy, obnoxious, and ultimately rejected sister Sarah. Puritanism liberated Anne Bradstreet not to heresy, but to duty.

This is especially so in her attitude toward writing. In writing she found not a control of her rebelliousness or a defiance of religious conventions, but a means of fulfilling herself. It was a solution Emily Dickinson also hit on as a means of fulfillment in her early thirties when all other womanly possibilities seemed to have failed her or to have passed her cruelly by. In each instance the Puritan emphasis on fulfillment through faith gave a woman her poetry.

Often in her best poems Anne Bradstreet links being mother and wife with being a poet. It is a twinned motif in many of her private verses. She is not at all shy or ashamed about being a woman-poet. In her apologia "The Author to Her Book" she appropriately characterizes her role as writer in domestic terms: she is a woman/mother whose duty it is to make her verse/children good. For her, under the covenant of duty, being mother and being artist are the same thing. She is expressive in both roles. The Puritan ethic for a man and woman becomes a Puritan esthetic.

Her humble disclaimer "My muse . . . calls me ambitious fool, that durst aspire" is not an apology, not a fear of being a challenge to men, but the beginning of a warning to others that she has the duty to fulfill herself: "Good will, not skill, did cause me bring my mite." She speaks of "th'aspersion of her sex," not defensively, but assertively:

> Now say, have women worth? or have they none?
> O had they some, but with our Queen is't gone?
> Nay masculines, you have thus taxed us long,
> But she, though dead, will vindicate our wrong.
> Let such as say our sex is void of reason,
> Know 'tis a slander now but once was treason.
> ["In Honour of That High and Mighty Princess Queen Elizabeth . . ."]

Such an independence of mind is not an aberration—though no doubt thought so by the cavalier and reactionary of her time—but a fulfillment of Puritan covenants; it is to Anne Bradstreet slander and treason against God to attempt to deny a woman her duty, her self-fulfillment, her effort to discover her abilities and worth.

Theoretically (that is, doctrinally) Puritanism made it possible for a woman to publish as no other ideology of the time could. Only high-born/high-blown ladies like the Countess of Pembroke entered the field, and then only while leaning on men of literary reputation. It was perhaps unusual for Anne Bradstreet to be published only because the position to which Puritanism raised women was fairly new. All the dedicatory verses to her *Tenth Muse* pretend to wonder at the author as a woman (thus John Woodbridge, "What you have done . . . for a womans Work 'tis very rare," and Nathaniel Ward, "I muse whither at length these Girls will go"); but it is in a congratulatory way, not at all denigrating. To be sure, Puritanism led her *not* to address herself to a female audience or to try to sell herself as a female writing for (as she represents) females. Though she herself says in her poem "The Prologue" she "dare not go beyond [her] Element," she champions a world where women are called to fulfill themselves as well:

> Let Greeks be Greeks, and women what they are . . .
> Preeminence in all and each is yours [i.e., man's];
> Yet grant some small acknowledgment of ours.

Her writing was not a rebellious act but an organic outgrowth of a faith that was increasingly encouraging women like her to think in terms of their worth.

Anne Bradstreet's assertion of her promised worth, especially her need and desire to write, is a Puritan correction of the cult of the time that made a convention of the dispraise of women through overpraise. In her first poems, those long ones of *The Tenth Muse,* she plays a role that is distinctly non-Puritan and a little annoying. She overreaches her real life; she is not herself. In her more personal verses, the ones no doubt more satisfying to her (as to us), she is Puritan, woman, authentic, fulfilled. For the most part she fails in *The Tenth Muse* poems at being a new woman of the Renaissance. She tried her hand at it and gained a small reputation for it in New England and abroad. The Puritan woman was already a new phenomenon: in that role Anne Bradstreet was already at home, turning womanly duty into poetic power.

How she thought of herself in this womanly creative/poetic role is interesting to watch. In an early poem she states that she is envious of Demosthenes because

> By art he gladly found what he did seek,
> A full requital of his striving pain.

This has been overlooked in Anne Bradstreet, as I think it has in Emily Dickinson: the fact that art (her poetry) was a medium she discovered to requite her "striving pain," her desire for identity and individuality. She confesses to having "A weak or wounded brain" yet one that has a "striving pain" in it; that is, a desire to strive, achieve, assert, emerge, risk, see.[17] It also suggests that, like Edward Taylor after her, writing itself satisfied her. We can take her protests against its initial publication as genuine: working with language in private was in itself to some extent a sufficient "requital of [her] striving pain."

In this same poem, immediately after the pleasant confession of her discovery of the secret service writing does her, she criticizes a public not yet ready for a woman as a poet:

> I am obnoxious to each carping tongue
> Who says my hand a needle better fits,
> A poet's pen all scorn I should thus wrong,
> For such despite they cast on female wits:
> If what I do prove well, it won't advance,
> They'll say it's stol'n, or else it was by chance.

There are those, she says of the critical public she feared somewhat paranoidly (and, as it turned out, wrongly), who are unprepared to appreciate what service writing provides for the "striving" woman. They would not know that she wants only to express herself, however "weak and wounded." The Greeks, she argues, were "more mild" in allowing writing as a means of "striving" for a woman. Her Puritan religion she represents in Greek terms: just as in *their* religion woman had an important place, so does she, she knows, in *Puritan* Christianity, by virtue of the covenant of womanhood-as-self-conscious-participation.

She does herself no good, however, when she gives up her Puritan claim to recognition and turns instead to begging for attention, as she does in a few of her poems ("Yet grant some small acknowledgment of ours") or when she plays the servant-girl game with her masculine readers ("This mean and unrefined ore of mine / Will make

---

17. John Berryman sees Anne Bradstreet as a woman of strong ambition:

John Cotton shines on Boston's sin—
I am drawn, in pieties that seem
The weary drizzle of an unremembered dream.
Women have gone mad
at twenty-one. Ambition mines, atrocious, in.

But he also pictures her imagining herself almost completely fulfilled as wife and mother:

Beloved household, I am Simon's wife,
and the mother of Samuel. . . .

[*Homage to Mistress Bradstreet*, 15, 22]

your glist'ring gold but more to shine"). She is funny and a little abrasive in the ways she calls attention in a few of her poems to her being a woman; she stamps her foot and demands attention—she would use sex as a weapon if she could. But ultimately she knows this does not work, and at times she seems to be laughing at herself for acting this way. Knowing, however, that she has no chance of competing with the masculine world, except by their gracious condescension, she can fall back on a more devotional esthetic, as Emily Dickinson was to do: writing still helps to satisfy her "striving pain."

Perhaps this is why there is an obsession throughout her poems, as there is in Emily Dickinson's, with the Puritan question of *worth*. What is it that makes a person of worth? she is constantly asking. How can she gain worth by association (in her poems) with worthies such as Sir Philip Sidney, DuBartas, Queen Elizabeth? Perhaps she experiences vicarious fulfillment—and, conventionally, via men. Yet there is a significant disparity between her poems about what she calls the "manly life" and those about the happy domestic woman: envy versus acceptance. Her elegy on Sidney, for example, is a piece of envy: the qualities she attributes to him correspond to the "striving pain" of a woman—fame for excellence, skill in many areas, envy from others. Her identification of herself with him represents, however, her desires for herself more than her worship of the lot of men. She is most interested in "his worthiness"; and by writing about such an eminence, she can imagine a state and status which society prevents her from having but which her Puritanism has encouraged her to desire, if almost entirely on the plane of the soul.

It is much the same in her poem on Elizabeth; again she is concerned with (in this case, a woman's) fame. She is particularly taken by the fact that "From all the kings on earth [Elizabeth] won the prize." This encourages Anne Bradstreet: it is indeed possible for a woman "to play the rex." To her, a part of "the heaven's great revolution" at some point in the future is the emergence of women like phoenixes out of Elizabeth's ashes. It is, to her, part of religious destiny that this should be so. She thus sees in Elizabeth's example a vindication of her desires for a life of ability, if not also authentic recognition.

The character in her "Contemplations" she envies most is the free "sweet-tongued Philomel," who "charted forth a most melodious strain / Which rapt me so with wonder and delight." Anne Bradstreet wishes she had wings "with her a while to take my flight." This is her desire to be free of conventional work and cares and to express herself freely as she wishes. But this is a romantic illusion she entertains only momentarily. She knows that turning inward to contemplate her earthly/heavenly duties is what has made it possible for her to express herself the most genuinely. Her inner world, not her flights of fancy, makes her poetry. As Emily Dickinson was to know two centuries later, this inwardness is a search for importance.

Anne Bradstreet's conviction that her faith gave worth to her life as a person—on a spiritual scale, a worth equal to a man's—may be thought of as a pattern into which both she and Emily Dickinson fit (and many other women made creative in that stretch of years by the pressures of Puritan responsibility, from Eliza Pinckney to Harriet Beecher Stowe): the myth of Puritan Woman Raised to Creativity through Duty. The characteristic would have been therefore not a matter of history or evolution or influence, but of an undercurrent in the culture, an assumption for two hundred years that woman too had to do something about her salvation—and on her own and within the range of her inherent possibilities and according to her physical and mental inclinations.

But I fear that myth is too simplistic a way for realizing how a poetic role became part of a womanly role in Anne Bradstreet and Emily Dickinson. There is more involved than an unconscious infrastructure of cultural phenomena. We can only know that the initial means for becoming what they became was provided by a Puritan humanism to which both of them (having similar functions but different expression, the same security but different lengths of tether) gave allegiance.

The connection between being a woman, being a Puritan, and being a poet must be viewed with more respect to their individual complexity than phenomenology allows if it is to help us locate the source of Emily Dickinson's emergence as a poet, the stimulus of her writing. Anne Bradstreet serves the study of Emily Dickinson in that, while herself complex and not entirely accessible to us, she is exemplary of the power of Puritan psychology on a woman writer. Emily Dickinson creates in her a precursor: there is a side of Emily Dickinson that is Anne Bradstreet. She is, by virtue of her largeness and her complexity, like Anne Bradstreet struggling to realize part of the Puritan promise to women.

Emily Dickinson fulfilled the Puritan requirements for womanhood, which were considerable, though not very many of the requirements, I think, of "a woman of the nineteenth century." She was not any sort of a Victorian dry run for the Steinem Follies. She has little allegiance to women as a social class or group, and only occasionally does it occur to her to concern herself with the otherness, the alterity of woman. Where nineteenth-century libertarianism would have taught her such concerns, Puritanism could not. Her poetry is, instead, the result of a *Puritan*-liberated role. The liberated Emily Dickinson is the woman who regards the self as the essential. She cares little about the situation in which she is the *in*essential. Her otherness was where Puritanism told her it was—in herself. A private poetry could therefore become Emily Dickinson's way of fulfilling herself (in perfect Puritan model) *as a woman*.[18] To understand this about her, as in understanding Anne Bradstreet, one should begin not at the extreme points of her rebellious epiphanies, where her biographers and critics have often found material for their stereotype of her as wild-minded, wild-worded woman, but at the base from which she springs—her understanding of herself and her understanding of how her sex was a stimulus to her art. Because unsure of election, neither woman could be as thoroughly antinomian as our own century might like. Without presuming that the woman in her was her only base or that she understood which was her base and which her divergence, we might find her trying to know the relation between being woman, being believer, and being poet. From her woman poems (some of those in which her voice is that of a woman concerned about the qualities of her voice as a woman) we see something of the relationship as she saw it.[19]

In a poem of 1861, written when she was thirty-one and seeking to reconcile herself to poetry as a sufficient authentic fulfillment of herself as a woman, Emily Dickinson celebrates womanhood as a "blameless mystery":

> A solemn thing – it was – I said –
> A Woman – white – to be –
> And wear – if God should count me fit –
> Her blameless mystery –
>
> A timid thing – to drop a life
> Into the mystic well –

18. I hope that this argument might provide a corrective to the position of John Cady, *After Great Pain: The Inner Life of Emily Dickinson* (Cambridge, Mass., 1971), a climactic study in a series of attempts to psychoanalyze Emily Dickinson. To Cady her poetry came from her psychological abnormality, her eccentricity. It was not inherent in her but was made by family tragedy and sexual response. It is an old saw: she was abnormal, therefore a poet, since poetry is not normal. Madness is creativity. Perhaps Anne Bradstreet teaches us how to read Emily Dickinson's poetry better than the psychiatrists do.

19. My argument would modify the position of Albert J. Gelpi, *Emily Dickinson: The Mind of the Poet* (Cambridge, Mass., 1966), a position inherited from Allen Tate, to the effect that Emily Dickinson was possible only with the thaw of Puritanism in New England, that her sensibility could not function within the Puritan context.

Too plummetless - that it come back -
Eternity - until -

I pondered how the bliss would look -
And would it feel as big -
When I could take it in my hand -
As hovering - seen - through fog -

And then - the size of this "small" life
The Sages - call it small -
Swelled - like Horizons - in my breast -
And I sneered - softly - "small"!

[#271]

Amid the usual aspersions that a woman is "a timid thing" with a "'small' life," she says she finds a "hallowed" quality within herself capable of "bliss," her essential worth, which, like a woman's pregnancy, "Swelled - like Horizons - in my breast." The religious terms are joined with sexual terms to argue her productivity. She has by nature a world within that can be used to prove that a woman is not small but full of life. The "mystery" has "Horizons." This pattern was one she developed often: a religious definition of herself as a woman leading to her creativity.

In a similar poem written the same year (#290), she admits that she has, within a man-dominated/God-dominated world, merely a "simple spirit," but claims for it "Taints of Majesty" that encourage her to "take vaster attitudes." Her sure concept of herself, at the same time feminine and religious, leads her to "strut upon my stem," like a flower, "Disdaining Men, and Oxygen, / For arrogance of them." As a woman she exults, "My Splendors, are Menagerie." In her concept of womanhood at this early point in her work as poet, she feels she achieves what a man may not: instead of struggle and activity, an amazing abundance.

In a poem of 1865 (#1058) she discusses what it takes for a woman to bloom. Woman is symbolized for the occasion by a flower "Assisting in the Bright Affair" of nature. She has her flowerly (womanly) duties: "To pack the Bud - oppose the Worm - / Obtain it's right of Dew - / Adjust the Heat - elude the Wind - / Escape the prowling Bee." She does these so as "Great Nature not to disappoint / Awaiting Her that Day." The covenanted duties of her sex bring her to full flower: "To be a Flower, is profound / Responsibility." Responsibility leads to her own flowering. Her phrase "the Bright Affair" has in it the three elements of her concern: religion, sex, and fulfillment. "Bloom - is [the] Result."

In still another on womanhood, she links a Puritan duty ("the honorable Work / Of Woman, and of Wife") with immense possibilities ("Fathoms"):

> She rose to His Requirement – dropt
> The Playthings of Her Life
> To take the honorable Work
> Of Woman, and of Wife –
>
> If ought She missed in Her new Day,
> Of Amplitude, or Awe –
> Or first Prospective – Or the Gold
> In using, wear away,
>
> It lay unmentioned – as the Sea
> Develope Pearl, and Weed,
> But only to Himself – be known
> The Fathoms they abide –

[#732]

Terms of betterment ("rose, "Her new Day," "Develope") inform her dutiful life. The woman in her (for this poem certainly) has a productive depth. She exchanges "Playthings" for "Fathoms" in being the dutiful woman. The covenant of grace makes womanhood "honorable."

It must be stressed that the issue of womanhood for Emily Dickinson is seldom one of equality with men, as it might well have been in a less puritanized world than hers,[20] but a matter of woman's inherent worth. On relations of the sexes she is standard, even backward, with some of the intersexual games she reports. She cannot imagine many ways of living with a man. When the issue of equality does come up in her poems, she finds a woman's inwardness (her rationalization!) sufficient to a man's ampleness.

---

20. But see her complaint in #493:

> A doubt – if it be fair – indeed –
> To wear that perfect – pearl –
> The Man – upon the Woman – binds
> To clasp her soul – for all –

And see her stereotype (#354) of a woman of leisure enjoying nature, as opposed to men working:

> Her Pretty Parasol be seen
> Contracting in a Field
> Where Men made Hay –
>
> . . . .
>
> Where Parties – Phantom as Herself –
> To Nowhere – seemed to go
> In purposeless Circumference –

Exhiliration - is within -
There can no Outer Wine
So royally intoxicate
As that diviner Brand

The Soul achieves - Herself -
To drink - or set away
For Visiter - Or Sacrament -
'Tis not of Holiday

To stimulate a Man
Who hath the Ample Rhine
Within his Closet - Best you can
Exhale in offering.

[#383]

Her inner "Exhiliration," divine in its achievement, is a sufficient offering.

The pattern becomes a familiar one wherever Emily Dickinson tries to define the productive woman: religious imagery giving way to her expressiveness, herself given a voice by inward obligation. She has religious faith as a stimulus to her self-reliance and independence as a woman. Self-sufficiency, self-reliance, and individual conscience were the promise of covenant theology, as she asserts in one of her most exclamatory, explicitly theological poems:

Mine - by the Right of the White Election!
Mine - by the Royal Seal!
Mine - by the Sign in the Scarlet prison -
Bars - cannot conceal!

[#528]

This demonstrates her strong assertion of the right to individuality ("in Vision - and in Veto") secured for her by her faith. The Puritan system ("Titled - Confirmed - / Delirious Charter!") has secured rights for her as a woman that nothing else could do. Liberation is private rather than social, a matter of self-sufficiency rather than a matter of movements.

There are many women in Emily Dickinson's poems—the range, a not entirely convincing one, from sweet child ("I hope the Father in the skies / Will lift his little girl") to crude seductress ("He strove - and I strove - too - / We did'nt do it - tho'!"). This is the crux of Emily Dickinson's "Exhiliration"—her amazing talent for "putting on the world" as mimic, as poseuse. The portraits of her ladies—almost all of them *herself*, of course—are in extreme colors. One gallery goes in the direction of the winner-nun:

Given in Marriage unto Thee
Oh thou Celestial Host –
Bride of the Father and the Son
Bride of the Holy Ghost.

Other Betrothal shall dissolve –
Wedlock of Will, decay –
Only the Keeper of this Ring
Conquer Mortality –

[#817]

The other gallery is in the direction of the lovely, lost vamp:

Did the Harebell loose her girdle
To the lover Bee
Would the Bee the Harebell *hallow*
Much as formerly?

Did the "Paradise" – persuaded –
Yield her moat of pearl –
Would the Eden *be* an Eden,
Or the Earl – an *Earl?*

[#213]

She can even play the daring virgin inviting seduction, foreplay and penetration:

Come slowly – Eden!
Lips unused to Thee –
Bashful – sip thy Jessamines –
As the fainting Bee –

Reaching late his flower,
Round her chamber hums –
Counts his nectars –
Enters – and is lost in Balms.

[#211]

But as I am suggesting, the one she finds the most secure and creative is the Puritan woman she plays.[21] In a justly famous but much over-psychoanalyzed poem, #754, she is the woman fulfilled in her wifely devotion to the man:

My Life had stood – a Loaded Gun –
In Corners – till a Day

21. In Elsa Green, "The Splintered Crown: A Study of Eve and Emily Dickinson" (Ph.D. diss., University of Minnesota, 1968), we have a very different view: all of Emily Dickinson's poems about man-woman relations show her to have been a violent rebel against all relations that were not equal or in which the woman would not win.

The Owner passed – identified –
And carried Me away –

When she has a man for "Master," she says, she can "speak": she then has "power" and "art." The Puritan arrangements for man and woman, as she outlines them in still another poem, are to her a sufficient religion:

The Sweetest Heresy recieved
That Man and Woman know –
Each Other's Convert –
Though the Faith accommodate but Two –

The Churches are so frequent –
The Ritual – so small –
The Grace so unavoidable –
To fail – is Infidel –

[#387]

In one of her most revealing poems on the subject, she is a housewife with power and security within, being tempted by another kind of life, the life of an empress that would be public, pretty, and static:

The Soul selects her own Society –
Then – shuts the Door –
To her divine Majority –
Present no more –

Unmoved – she notes the Chariots – pausing –
At her low Gate –
Unmoved – an Emperor be kneeling
Upon her Mat –

I've known her – from an ample nation –
Choose One –
Then – close the Valves of her attention –
Like Stone –

[#303]

The active verbs in the poem are all hers ("selects," "notes," "choose," "close"), hers the religious terms ("The Soul," "her divine Majority"), hers the better rhymes (successful feminine rhymes on first and third lines but failing masculine rhymes on the others), hers all the rich possessiveness ("her own Society," "her divine Majority," "Her low Gate," "her mat," "her attention"), and hers the sexual security ("her low Gate," "her [Rush] mat," "the Valves of her attention"). From the secure position of a world within, she moves into the productive forms of the language itself: the poem is a woman enlivened *in* language by virtue of her self-sufficient, self-reliant, conscientious religious security.[22]

In such a role, Puritan privacy gives her her security and aggressiveness:

> For largest Woman's Heart I knew –
> 'Tis little I can do –
> And Yet the largest Woman's Heart
> Could hold an Arrow – too –
> And so, instructed by my own,
> I tenderer, turn Me to.
>
> [#309]

Interiority is superiority. "Option is within," she wrote her sister in 1864. "That is why I prefer the Power, for Power is Glory, when it likes, and Dominion, too." "Within, . . ." she wrote in a letter to Maria Whitney in 1883, "is so wild a place."[23]

> You cannot take itself
> From any Human soul –
> That indestructible estate
> Enable each to dwell –
> Abundant as the Light
> That every man behold. . . .
>
> [#1351]

Pushed by the devotional need to discover her self, she advances to her glory, which (ultimately) is a glory of language. The devotional preparationism she inherited (though with much of the theological backbone gone out of it) led her to the acceptance that, at the base, her self was secure. "There is always one thing to be grateful for," T. W. Higginson says she told him in 1873, "that one is one's self and not somebody else."[24] The path inward ends at her self and upon emerging finds expression. The route/distance/perspective gives her both a stage and a voice. The uncompromised vitality of her tensions becomes poetry. Self-contained, she explodes.[25]

22. It is significant that she addresses her famous love letters of 1860–61 to a "Master." Because she finds fulfillment in the controlled situation—the Puritan woman in her—she begs to be "mastered": "Master – open your life wide, and take me in forever, I will never be tired - I will never be noisy when you want to be still. I will be your best little girl - nobody else will see me, but you - but that is enough - I shall not want any more" (*Letters*, p. 392). Note the role of masterable woman she also plays in her letters to T. W. Higginson ("Preceptor, I shall bring you - Obedience") and Otis Lord ("Love is a patriot now Gave her life[,] for its country Has it[s] meaning—Oh nation of the soul thou hast Thy freedom now") (*Letters*, pp. 412, 615).
23. *Letters*, p. 432.
24. Jay Leyda, *The Years and Hours of Emily Dickinson* (New Haven, 1960), 2:213.
25. Though there is reason to believe that Emily Dickinson reveals herself much

Emily Dickinson's Puritan view of womanhood is particularly striking in the daring with which she pictures herself as a woman who is the minion (at least the partner, the cohort, certainly the challenger, and perhaps "just the weight") of God—what she in an early poem calls her "rival Claim" over against God. What God has given her makes her a rival of God: rebelliousness is faith encouraged by Puritan self-reliance. There is a kind of exemplary voluptuousness in her speaking out thus. In the light of Puritan covenants it is to her not an arrogant stance, but organic, even likely. "Unless we become as Rogues," she wrote gleefully in a letter in 1881, "we cannot enter the Kingdom of Heaven."[26] If a person may expect God's great expectations of mankind (the hope *and* the doubt are always present), then to talk to him as she does (with her arch tone, her preposterous poses, the daring itself of writing her poems) is her duty, her fulfillment. Her security of faith has made it possible to be assertive. A divine errantry is the resulting individuality. It is not heresy but accomplishment. She is not witch but Woman.

---

less honestly, less completely in her letters than in her poems, the stimulus of her home should be noticed as a central motif in her letters. The theme punctuates whatever else she finds to write about. In 1851, "Home is bright and shining, 'and the spirit and the bride say come.'" In 1852, "I'm afraid I'm growing *Selfish* in my dear home, but I do love it so." In 1853, "Home is faithful, none other is so true." In 1870, "Could you tell me what home is. . . . Home is the definition of God." In 1879, "You spoke of 'Hope' surpassing 'Home' – I thought that Hope *was* Home." In 1883, "[The] Infinite Power of Home." In 1885, "Home is a holy thing – nothing of doubt or distrust can enter its blessed portals." (*Letters*, pp. 146, 197, 249, 475, 483, 638, 782). The statements are conventional, often even written to order. Yet they show her consistent concern for home as ground for self-fulfillment. She consistently has a positive view of the work of woman at home: "The good I myself derive, the winning of the spirit of patience[,] the genial housekeeping influence stealing over my mind and soul" (*Letters*, p. 97). Yet she also loathes it on occasion and wants to escape it somehow:

> I have been at work, providing the "food that perisheth," scaring the timorous dust, and being obedient, and kind. *I* call it kind obedience [but] in the books the Shadows write in, it may have another name. I am yet the Queen of the Court, if regalia be dust and dirt, have three loyal subjects, whom I'd rather relieve from service. Mother is still an invalid tho' a partially restored one – Father and Austin still clamor for food, and I, like a martyr am feeding them. Wouldn't you love to see me at these bonds of great despair, looking around my kitchen, and praying for kind deliverance, and declaring by "Omar's beard" I never was in such plight. *My* kitchen I think I called it, God forbid that it was, or shall be my own – God keep me from what they call *households*, except that bright one of "faith"! [*Letters*, p. 99]

She herself described her domesticizing process in terms of keeping a hold on that which is "haunted": "The larger Haunted House it seems, of maturer Childhood – distant, an alarm – entered intimate at last as a neighbor's Cottage" (*Letters*, p. 481). In the cottage she could contemplate mystery. At home she could be what she called "mentally permanent" while at the same time taking the man's risk of adventure. See Jean McClure Mudge, *Emily Dickinson and the Image of Home* (Amherst, 1975).

26. *Letters*, p. 703.

She knows very well how to play God's game and get a claim for herself out of it. The signals of the elfin/gamin (a role she calls in one poem "Half Child – Half Heroine") stand out in her poems like a woman standing *up*. She knows how to call God's bluff when pressed: "Burglar – Banker – Father!" She plays a child as a way of gaining acceptance into a kingdom that promises not to reject children, which is a woman's way of playing dumb-innocent to trick the judge so that his compassion will include her: "Oh Last Communion in the Haze – / Permit a child to join." She knows how to berate God, a slack husband, into his duty:

> And "Jesus"! Where is *Jesus* gone?
> They said that Jesus – always came –
> Perhaps he does'nt know the House –
> This way, Jesus, Let him pass!
>
> [#158]

She uses a nagging scrappiness as a way of competing with authority: "I'd *harass God* / Until he let [you] in!" She has protest as her best defense against what is done to her as a woman: "Enamored – of the Conjuror – / That spurned us – Yesterday!" She has the insolence to presume to remind God of his duty to act like a Christian: "Were Himself – such a Dunce – / What would we – do?" She exploits coyness to get what she wants: "I meant to have but modest needs – / Such as Content – and Heaven." She pretends to be helpless so God will care for her, and her mock humility justifies the Atonement: "Papa above! / Regard a Mouse / O'erpowered by the Cat!" She plays a naughty girl to justify the existence of her faith:

> I hope the Father in the skies
> Will lift his little girl –
> Old fashioned – naughty – everything –
> Over the stile of "Pearl".
>
> [#70]

She uses the role of woman to evoke pity and sympathy from God, not believing in the role but knowing it is required and will get her somewhere:

> He was weak, and I was strong – then –
> So He let me lead him in –
> I was weak, and He was strong then –
> So I let him lead me – Home.
>
> [#190]

This elfin/gamin role ("My little Gypsey being," she calls it) is not quite the reclusive childishness some have wanted in an Emily Dickin-

son but also not quite the mock-freak Victorian caricature others
want. It is, instead, the recognition of the relation of herself to world
and universe as a person in the form of a deviant streak.

> Elder, Today, a session wiser
> And fainter, too, as Wiseness is –
> I find myself still softly searching
> For my Delinquent Palaces –
>
> And a Suspicion, like a Finger
> Touches my Forehead now and then
> That I am looking oppositely
> For the site of the Kingdom of Heaven –

[#959]

She searches for delinquency, desires it, works at it, for it gives her a
maturity, a delight. "Blessed are they that play," she wrote playfully
but earnestly in a letter in 1881, "for theirs is the kingdom of
Heaven."[27] It is a devotional pursuit, as well, but one that takes the
form of a small, shrewd manner, an attitude of teasing and taunting, a
puritanical vigor without intimacy. She is the urchin with spleen.
"God was penurious with me," she wrote in a letter in 1859, "which
makes me shrewd with Him."[28] It is a role that both meets society's
demeaning expectations of a woman and transcends them: the deviant streak is delinquency in a holy place, a woman liberated within
bonds. In the role of her unacceptable self, she is herself: Puritan
inwardness *is* a place. Her best characterization of the role is the
drunken woman welcomed with surprise and leaning triumphantly
against the lamppost-sun in heaven (#214).

All the fulfilled Puritan women of stamina in Emily Dickinson's
poems, to be sure, stretch the conventional Puritan shape of womanhood, though without ever really violating the conventions of the
covenant. She will not sit still long for her self-portrait as woman-
fulfilled-coldly-in-her-faith-and-loud-about-it, but she does it up in
warm colors, for it is herself—poet, woman, Puritan. In one poem
(#275) she complains against the oppressive relationship between
God and woman (read *man* and woman): she taunts God for thinking
her less than she is, for assigning her a secondary role, for keeping
her low. In her, "God, would be content / With but a fraction of the
life – / Poured thee, without a stint." She admits that, like a wife, her
spirit does not give her any superiority, for that is already owned, nor
does her destiny, for that is already determined, but possibly only the
ability to delight someone:

27. *Letters*, p. 691.
28. *Letters*, p. 353.

What more the Woman can,
Say quick, that I may dower thee
With last Delight I own!

[#275]

She will not tolerate the requirement that she "Dwell timidly" with anyone, but must have opportunity for "her finest fondness." She will lose herself for love alone. Only in that way can she serve a mate and save herself whole as a woman—both.

Forever at His side to walk –
The smaller of the two!
Brain of His Brain –
Blood of His Blood –
Two lives – One Being – now –

Forever of His fate to taste –
If grief – the largest part –
If joy – to put my piece away
For that beloved Heart –

[#246]

She is aware of the ambiguities of being this woman of submission/salvation ("Born – Bridalled – Shrouded – / In a Day") but feels it is worth attempting for all the awful compromising of self in it: it is "the way" to a "Title divine":

Title divine – is mine!
The Wife – without the Sign!
Acute Degree – conferred on me –
Empress of Calvary!
Royal all but the Crown!
Betrothed – without the swoon
God sends us Women –
When you – hold – Garnet to Garnet –
Gold – to Gold –
Born – Bridalled – Shrouded –
In a Day –
"My Husband" – women say
Stroking the Melody –
Is *this* – the way?

[#1072][29]

29. It is necessary to remember that this remarkable poem, honoring yet also satirizing the position of woman in a conventional marriage, was actually a letter written to Samuel Bowles in early 1862. She adds a line following the poem asking Bowles not to reveal her interest in being his wife while unable to do so. The poem is less significant, therefore, as a general statement about the ambiguities of being a wife, since she is playing the game of excusing herself from marriage to him under the pretext of

Though it is enough for her to claim that "The Housewife in thy low attendance / Contenteth Me.... For Life – be Love" (#961), she is aware of its horrors:

> Trust entrenched in narrow pain –
> Constancy thro' fire – awarded –
> Anguish – bare of anodyne!
>
> [#1737]

She knows, too, that the Puritan requirement for women puts them in the loathsome position of beggars for love:

> You said that I "was Great" – one Day
> Then "Great" it be – if that please Thee –
> Or Small – or any size at all –
> Nay – I'm the size suit Thee –
>
> [#738]

And she knows that over against the life of men, it often means her degradation:

> A Bee his burnished Carriage
> Drove boldly to a Rose –
> Combinedly alighting –
> Himself – his Carriage was –
> The Rose received his visit
> With frank tranquility
> Witholding not a Crescent
> To his Cupidity –
> Their Moment consummated –
> Remained for him – to flee –
> Remained for her – of rapture
> But the humility.
>
> [#1339][30]

Yet for all the humiliation it may mean, puritanized womanhood is superior in its rewards:

---

reservations about the effect of the institution on women, "Born – Bridalled – Shrouded – / In a Day."

30. That Emily Dickinson saw the compensation of "rapture" amid the awful humility of the puritanized woman is seen in a comment on sex she made to the unmarried Norcross sisters in 1873: "It is not recorded of any rose that it failed of its bee, though obtained in specific instances through scarlet experiment" (*Letters,* pp. 388–89). Poem #1339 on "rapture" was originally sent in a letter in 1875 with this note: "Sweet is it as Life, with its enhancing Shadow of Death" (*Letters,* p. 545). This suggests her willingness to accept woman's "humility" as long as there is also the moment of "rapture."

I'm "wife" – I've finished that –
That other state –
I'm Czar – I'm "Woman" now –
It's safer so –

How odd the Girl's life looks
Behind this soft Eclipse –
I think that Earth feels so
To folks in Heaven – now –

This being comfort – then
That other kind – was pain –
But why compare?
I'm "Wife"! Stop there!

[#199]

As it was for Anne Bradstreet, Woman as Puritan Wife is unquestionably her ideal, the ideal she inherited and the one in which she discovers a liberatable power. She considers it a "Sufficient Royalty" to be "one that bore her Master's name." In the role of "Bride" Emily Dickinson finds a "new Grace":

I am ashamed – I hide –
What right have I – to be a Bride –
So late a Dowerless Girl –
Nowhere to hide my dazzled Face –
No one to teach me that new Grace –
Nor introduce – my Soul –
. . . .

Fashion My Spirit quaint – white –
Quick – like a Liquor –
Gay – like Light –
Bring Me my best Pride –
No more ashamed –
No more to hide –
Meek – let it be – too proud – for Pride –
Baptized – this Day – A Bride –

[#473]

She has high praise for marriage, though not without reservations. The idea of wedlock delights and exalts her, the commoner becomes a queen, and yet there are sacrifices and difficulties as well. Marriage is a heavenly state to her, but more in the anticipation than in the realization. She has almost no sense of sex as experience. In such matters she is incapable of the haptic.

Even as Emily Dickinson submits herself to the Puritan definition of holy womanhood and finds in it a source for her assertion of poetry, she is, with few exceptions, an easy light-year beyond the Puritan women of nineteenth-century fiction who, as Elizabeth Hardwick points out, have their main strength in "the overwhelming beauty of endurance, the capacity for high or lowly suffering, finally tranquilized, for the radiance of humility, for silence, secrecy, impressive acceptance." Weakness in them is made heroic.[31] But these are mainly men's portraits of Puritan womanhood as it had come down to the nineteenth century. Emily Dickinson knew better. She saw in the woman of Puritan mold fanatical stamina and independence of mind and action, having little or nothing to do with the oppressions or opportunities of society but spurred by a covenant of inner grace. The issue of woman, for Emily Dickinson, was not biology, and seldom that of relationships, but a factor even more fundamental: the issue of intrinsic, autonomous worth. Even as she struggled to violate her Puritan faith, she wrote a poetry that emerged from the Puritan issue.

Her penchant for cunning, subterfuge, ruse, and protest—the elfin/gamin in her, strengthened by her security, hyperbolized by her language, and turned into a playful and deliberate obscurity on her part—is on a spiritual level: she individualizes herself as a woman expected to be a woman expecting womanhood exceptionalized. Her piety is not distinct from her energy and vigor, her expression not separate from necessity. Tempted by heresy, she is never sterile in religious imagination: the woman in her is the presumed and the presuming. Refractory, rampant, playful, excessive, vital, tough, she animates faith, not yielding easily to masculine authority, innovating when she prays, inventing on her knees, emerging when called by the covenant. Threatening faith, she rehabilitates it. And so Emily Dickinson's discovery that a woman has a valuable world within gave her her poetry.

I do not believe it is sexist to assert that Emily Dickinson wrote the way she did because she was a woman or that Whitman wrote the way he did because he was a man or that Emerson wrote the way he did because he was neither. Her being a woman is an issue to us precisely because it was an issue to her.

There is much in the life of Emily Dickinson that shows the covenant realized in a mundane way—the devotion to a household; the willing submission to father, preceptors, "Master," and male friends; the narcissism of her interests, her experiences, her poetry; the neurotic sensitivity to the twitchings of her soul—and at the same time (and here is the wonder) the feeling of authentic fulfillment of

31. Elizabeth Hardwick, *Seduction and Betrayal: Women and Literature* (New York, 1974), pp. 200–201.

herself as a woman. It was not that she fulfilled herself in spite of it all, but that this Puritan pattern was, as it was with her literary forebear Anne Bradstreet, the cultivated condition of her fulfillment.[32] But all this must be kept in the subjunctive, for though these facts from her life tie together to make a pattern of sorts that reproduces the Puritan expectations of a woman, there is a danger that these are really unconnected pieces of a life. No use piecing out a life for her that meets this thesis. We have it better in the poetry itself: there, she is looking at herself and seeing her Self herself in a space carved out for her by Puritan demands for inwardness. My metaphors are mixed: that hole made her high.

> But this time – Adequate – Erect,
> With Will to choose, or to reject,
> And I choose, just a Crown –
>
> [#508]

The effect on her all her life (she seems almost always to have held to and seldom doubted the worth of the depth and spaciousness of herself) was like what we find in the work of Henry Moore. Like Moore (and like Erik Erikson with his "inner space of womanhood"), Emily Dickinson consistently considers woman in terms of a space

---

32. Note the ambiguity about marriage that Emily Dickinson expresses in a letter to Sue in 1852:

> Those unions, my dear Susie, by which two lives are one, this sweet and strange adoption wherein we can but look, and are not yet admitted, how it can fill the heart, and make it gang wildly beating, how it will take *us* one day, and make us all it's own, and we shall not run away from it, but lie still and be happy!
>
> You and I have been strangely silent upon this subject, Susie, we have often touched upon it, and as quickly fled away, as children shut their eyes when the sun is too bright for them. I have always hoped to know if you had no dear fancy, illumining all your life, no one of whom you murmured in the faithful ear of night – and at whose side in fancy, you walked the livelong day; and when you come home, Susie, we must speak of these things. How dull our lives must seem to the bride, and the plighted maiden, whose days are fed with gold, and who gathers pearls every evening; but to the *wife*, Susie, sometimes the *wife forgotten*, our lives perhaps seem dearer than all others in the world; you have seen flowers at noon with their heads bowed in anguish before the mighty sun; think you these thirsty blossoms will *now* need naught but – *dew*? No, they will cry for sunlight, and pine for the burning noon, tho' it scorches them, scathes them; they have got through with peace – they know that the man of noon, is *mightier* than the morning and their life is henceforth to him. Oh, Susie, it is dangerous, and it is all too dear, these simple trusting spirits, and the spirits mightier, which we cannot resist! It does so rend me, Susie, the thought of it when it comes, that I tremble lest at sometime I, too, am yielded up. Susie, you will forgive me my amatory strain. [*Letters*, pp. 209–10]

At this point in her life—that is, before she had given up the hope of marrying—she sees marriage as both sweet and dangerous. Though consistently passive in her attitude, she is both attracted to marriage and sex and scared by it.

within, marvelous hollows made by the Puritan emphasis on internality, a space that made it spectacularly possible to think of herself in heroic, worthy, and grace-filled ways. As in Moore, it is the inward space that makes the epic size possible, that pushes the rest of the form outward and upward. The mystery and energy of the woman-within is spiritual. It blew her self up to "just the weight of God." "Within," let me quote from her once again, "is so wild a place."

But the nineteenth century, like Anne Bradstreet's time under the powers of figures like Winthrop and Increase Mather, had great difficulty discriminating between a wildly inward woman of this sort and a mentally disturbed one. So Emily Dickinson, for all the ways that she fits into the darker, more conservative and solid side of the New England temperament, became to many, paradoxically, "the myth of Amherst"—to Eugene Field, "a strange, if not a weird creature," and to T. W. Higginson, "wayward," "insane," and "my partially cracked poetess."[33] Her particular use of the covenant of womanhood made her—now as then—suspect: her thinking would be taken for individual and wild expression even as it represented, to her, an authentic fulfillment of God's will and her own nature. As with Anne Bradstreet, we cannot know that she knew her source. We only know that, given her source, she knew herself.

33. Leyda, *Years and Hours*, 2:114, 213. One Harriet Montague of Amherst, a religious defector of 1845, was considered insane by the community (ibid., 1:94).

MY PURITAN SPIRIT

EMILY DICKINSON AND EDWARD TAYLOR

When to his Covenant Needle
The sailor doubting turns ...

[#851]

If everybody in the history of American literature had read
everybody else, one of the great shocks of recognition, I believe,
would have been Emily Dickinson's reading of Edward Taylor. In the
long string of unrealized but constructible literary relationships—
Emerson with Edwards, for instance, or Whitman with Poe, Stevens
with Emerson, Gandhi with Thoreau, Hemingway with Twain—this
might also be one valuable to an understanding of American culture.[1]

1. Surprisingly, the only extended commentaries on the Taylor-Dickinson relationship are Jared R. Curtis, "Edward Taylor and Emily Dickinson: Voices and
Visions," *Susquehanna University Studies* 7 (1964): 159-67; John S. Wheatcroft, "Emily
Dickinson and the Orthodox Tradition" (Ph.D. diss., Rutgers, 1959), pp. 39-49; and
Joan Phelan, "Puritan Tradition and ED's Poetic Practice" (Ph.D. diss., Bryn Mawr,
1972), pp. 61-76. Among all the differences between the two poets ("deep contrasts in
theological perspective, personal experience, and poetic technique"), Curtis finds a
biographical similarity in their seclusion and privacy and a stylistic similarity in their
interest in metaphysical wit. Wheatcroft finds Taylor looking forward to Emily Dickinson in his use of domestic figures, his roughness of form, and his sensuousness ("a
common tradition of rhetoric and a common habit of mind stand behind both"), but the
parallels are tenuous and exaggerated. The same is true in Whelan, where even the

Just as Emily Dickinson "knew" Anne Bradstreet, so there are ways in which she probably "knew" other writers out of her Puritan background.

Plainly a multitude of factors separate Emily Dickinson and Edward Taylor. They are set in sharp relief against each other. The religious writings of seventeenth-century America were no significant part of Emily Dickinson's reading, and there is little in Taylor that is of value to an understanding of the Age of Emerson and beyond. Except possibly for George Herbert, John Bunyan, the New England Primer, and the Bible, they knew no common literature.[2] Taylor gave his life in defense of the faith whereas Emily Dickinson resisted and

---

common background is not proved substantially. The poems of one cannot yield the esthetics of the other so easily.

    That the urge to compare the two has been a latent but potent one is seen in Austin Warren's comment, "Taylor is nearer to being an ancestor of another uneven village poet, Emily Dickinson" ("Edward Taylor's Poetry: Colonial Baroque," *Kenyon Review* 3 [1941]: 371). "The 'Meditations,'" he wrote, "were—like Emily Dickinson's poems, which in their defects and virtues, they most resemble—the fruits of his aloneness." Perry Miller was similarly convinced that "Out of [the] social pattern of the Connecticut Valley came Stoddard, Edward Taylor, Jonathan Edwards, and ... Emily Dickinson" (*Errand into the Wilderness* [Cambridge, Mass., 1956], p. 17). Louis L. Martz discovered that a "Meditative style ... may also be found in Robert Southwell, Edward Taylor, Blake, Wordsworth, Hopkins, Emily Dickinson, the later Yeats, and the later Eliot" (*The Poetry of Meditation* [New Haven, 1960], p. 324). And H. H. Waggoner observes that "[Taylor] suggests traits we find more fully exhibited later in Emerson, Whitman, Dickinson, William Carlos Williams, and Cummings, traits of American Transcendental poetry, in short" (*American Poets: From the Puritans to the Present* [Boston, 1968], p. 16). Albert J. Gelpi comments: "There is [in Emily Dickinson] a complexity of sensibility that brings us back to Bradford, Taylor, and Edwards. ... The deliberate and formalistic quality of Dickinson's verse associates her rather with the diverse yet Apollonian tradition which proceeds from Edward Taylor through her to Eliot, Stevens, Frost, and Marianne Moore, and thence to Robert Lowell and Elizabeth Bishop" (*Emily Dickinson: The Mind of the Poet* [Cambridge, Mass., 1965], pp. 91, 146). And Richard Sewall, in his *Life of Emily Dickinson* (New York, 1974), pp. 709–10, argues: "There is a century and a half of waning conviction between the two poets and (with Dickinson) the love of this world that 'holds – so.'" In passing, therefore, a relationship between the two has been seen as significant for American literature.

    2. "There is no evidence of her having been exposed to the writings of such authors as Nathaniel Ward, Cotton Mather, or Jonathan Edwards" (Jack L. Capps, *Emily Dickinson's Reading* [Cambridge, Mass., 1966], p. 102). Yet it might be worth noting that Taylor is mentioned by a friend of Emily Dickinson's, Josiah Holland, in his *History of Western Massachusetts* (Springfield, 1855), and because she read quite a number of Holland's writings, she might have read about him there. "A church [in Westfield] was not organized until 1679," Holland writes, "when Mr. Edward Taylor, the grandfather of the later President Stiles of Yale College, was ordained as pastor. ... Rev. Edward Taylor was the first pastor. He commenced his labors in 1671, but his settlement and the organization of the church were delayed for several years, in consequence of the disturbances connected with King Philip's war" (1:66; 2:142). Holland does not mention that Taylor was a poet.

took liberties with everything he and her other forebears in the Connecticut Valley tradition had stood for.[3] The focus of Taylor's mind was small, even if it encompassed heaven and hell; Emily Dickinson could easily include him and other worlds besides. The writing of Taylor is pitifully narrow over against Emily Dickinson's complex diversity of ecstasy and despair, humility and defiance, devotion and deep suspicion. In temperament and style his is the face of a defender and hers that of a seeker. Though they often spoke the same Puritan language and had similar artistic ends, they make an extremely uncomfortable poetic couple.

Still, the similarities are many, if merely obvious ones. The lives of both were in large measure private, obscure, isolated. The sensibilities of both were introspective, meditative, interior. They both wrote poetry in search of grace and through writing both felt they had found some measure of that grace. They wrestled with the same angel for some sign of their worth, were both examples of the *furor poeticus*. Their verse is deliberately rough, witty, self-conscious, sacramental. Both knew the Connecticut Valley spirit, its theology, its discipline, its decorum; their lives are connected more with its traditions than with those of Boston or elsewhere. Both wrote in private, resisted publication, and died without literary fame. The affinity is sure only upon generalization.

Thomas H. Johnson, who became the "discoverer" and editor of the manuscripts of both Taylor and Emily Dickinson, found it necessary—as we may find it—to talk about each in transitive, connecting terms. At the one end of the traditions of the Connecticut Valley, Johnson argues, there was Taylor living a life of quiet usefulness and faith-promoting influence, and at the other end was Emily Dickinson, whose life and thought "is inseparably a part of the Valley tradition" that Taylor helped to start. "Had [Taylor] not lived in the Valley three hundred years ago," Johnson concludes of the two, "there would have been a different drama. . . . Emily Dickinson . . . owes far more than she suspected to Valley traditions."[4]

It is primarily in that Connecticut Valley intellectual tradition, of which he was an active pioneer and defender, that Taylor has a signif-

3. See Joseph Haroutunian, *Piety versus Moralism: The Passing of the New England Theology* (New York, 1932).
4. *The Poetical Works of Edward Taylor* (Princeton, 1939), p. 14; *Emily Dickinson: An Interpretive Biography* (Cambridge, Mass., 1955), pp. vii, 20. Years of work on the manuscripts and life of both Taylor and Emily Dickinson led Johnson to see how each is fully, though not exclusively, Puritan; that is, how each struggled to understand himself/herself in his/her relation to God; how each was a constant analyst of the emotions; and how a concentrated, angular, homely style was natural to each.

icant reach beyond his own life and time, and that Emily Dickinson had a hold on what she considered—for better or for worse, in desire and in despair—real. For the biographical critic it is the substance of the life and work of both. To the life of the one it gave a definition, a foundation, fiber, bone, and blood, and to that of the other an identity, a security, a structure. By both, as we shall see, its dimensions were assumed to be reality itself; by both it was imaginatively imposed on the universe *as reality*. Connecticut Valley Puritanism was a mold in which the conceptions of both could be formed.

In the case of Taylor, all his work is informed, even defined, by the Puritanism for which he gave the testimony of his life. He cannot be seen without it or outside it or beyond it or beneath it. It defines him, he defines it. Whatever form his speech may take, it derives from the language of that system. Whatever his delights and fears, they have their source in the Calvinist system of his belief. When seen as part of the myth that it itself participated in making, Taylor's work has an importance to a tradition in American culture up to and including Emily Dickinson, not by virtue of its own power but by virtue of the myth in which it played a decisive part.

Because it has been taken for granted that Emily Dickinson's sensibility was dictated largely by the Connecticut Valley ideology, it may be forgotten as a way of seeing her whole. The facts of her life and language, even in their remarkable individuality, have forced acceptance of her poetry as an emanation of the orthodox Protestant tradition of which Taylor and Edwards are her most notable literary forebears, and taking such facts for granted has often caused the disappearance of that acceptance in our approach to her that gives her thought and art, for all its immense variety, the coherence we sense it to have.[5] Richard Chase has expressed this assumption best:

5. Allen Tate is the source of the position that the basic tenets of Puritan thought were mere scaffolding for the life and thought of Emily Dickinson (*The Outlook* 148 [1928]: 621–23). It has taken the work of Whicher, Chase, Anderson, Gelpi, Sherwood, and Sewall to correct that contention and make Puritanism *central* to her work.

The Connecticut Valley construct of reality in her has become firm in the minds of her best readers; so firm, in fact, that it is now taken for granted. William Dean Howells was the first to claim that an Emily Dickinson would have been impossible outside the Valley and its beliefs: "There is no hint of what turned her life in upon itself, and probably this was its natural evolution, or involution, from the tendencies inherent in the New England, or the Puritan, spirit" (*Harper's* 82 [1891]: 318. Similarly, Sam G. Ward, a late, minor Transcendentalist, found it necessary to refer to her as "the quintessence of that element we all have who are of Puritan descent *pur sang*" (quoted in Millicent Todd Bingham, *Ancestor's Brocades* [New York, 1945], pp. 169–70). In his biography of her, George Whicher is insistent that she is "an emanation of the region, . . . nurtured in Puritan orthodoxy": "She made it her business to embody in her poems the quintessence of New England ways of thinking and feeling. In her the region became articulate." Yet Whicher feels that Puritanism did "little more than give her a

The poetry of Emily Dickinson has its obvious relations to the American environment out of which, in spite of her seclusion, it grew. In its bluntness, its factuality, its candid roughness of form, its wit, its terseness, its peculiar combination of pragmatic practicality and supernaturalism, its lyric intimacy with power, melancholy, love, death, and infinite futurity—in all these we discern the lineaments of the culture from which it stemmed. . . . Her poems are the subtlest and most profoundly rooted flower of provincial American life in its most coherent and successful form. . . . Emily Dickinson's poetry [is] the last fine utterance of New England Puritanism.[6]

What was mythic in her supported, sustained, and organized her creative energy and gave it its durable consistency. Through it she was reconciled to her past, made free to become herself, and stirred to her forms of delight. By virtue of her commitment to Puritanism, Emily Dickinson teaches one how to read Edward Taylor; and Edward Taylor is, in a way, a creator of that tradition in American literature that includes Emily Dickinson. They become part of each other's worlds, unwittingly and irrevocably.

Use of the mythic in discussing such writers as Taylor and Emily Dickinson implies that one sees how they imposed on reality the structure they felt it had to have in order to be meaningful, a structure that

---

theological vocabulary" (*This Was a Poet* [New York, 1938], pp. 20–21, 162). Charles Anderson, on the other hand, argues that Emily Dickinson found Puritan dogma "an empty shell" and searched for new symbols of belief. Anderson does not consider the ways, however, in which the terms and goals of this search were determined by her Puritan assumptions (*Emily Dickinson's Poetry* [New York, 1960]). Similarly, Albert Gelpi understands Emily Dickinson in terms of rebellion against the received, yet finds that in spite of her flirtation with the New Liberalism of her time, "Her unshakable conception of reality and awareness of the human condition were derived not so much from Emerson as from the 'old fashioned Puritans.'" But painting her as schizophrenic undercuts the power of the mythic in her (Gelpi, *Emily Dickinson*, pp. 90–91). William Sherwood posits a conversion to Puritanism, an "inextricable commitment to [Puritan religion], a commitment she acknowledged at some time in 1862, not because she consciously adopted the ideology, but because, in the best Puritan tradition, she had the experience of being adopted by it, the experience of grace itself." Though only shakily supported and though applied too widely to all aspects of her life and work, Sherwood's discussion of her Puritanism is the most important (*Circumference and Circumstance* [New York, 1968], p. 141).

Other comments about her Puritanism remain weak. "The Puritan heritage affected her," writes Sirkka Heiskanen-Mäkelä, "not as an ideology to be accepted or rejected at will but as a *mental discipline*, a kind of psychic reality to the conditions of which her thinking and reading had been, and always remained, adapted" ("The Puritan Way," in *In Quest of Truth: Observations on the Development of Emily Dickinson's Poetic Dialectic* [Jyväskylä, Finland, 1970], pp. 13–34).

For the most part the Dickinson criticism presumes the Puritanism in her, but it ignores how it functions as myth. The way the Puritanism of her spiritual forebears (Taylor among them) acts as myth-structure helps alleviate the schizophrenia of this criticism.

6. Chase, *Emily Dickinson*, pp. 17, 23.

corresponded in general with the organization of their own lives, a structure that made an artist out of each. From the vantage point of these structuralist assumptions, their position in tradition and the contribution of each to a tradition become much clearer, as do the more controversial features of their writing—the privacy, the roughness of form, the coupling of the meditative and the revivalistic, the freedom within terribly restrictive forms.

The myth-structure that informed the life and work of both Taylor and Emily Dickinson is the Puritanism of the Connecticut Valley. That Edward Taylor's poetry represents this construct well should be fairly obvious. Without much strain, many of the fundamentals of Puritanism can be deduced in simplified form from the poetry he wrote in defense of it. With only slight variations he is its thoroughgoing representative. Of all the literature written within the confines of New England, the Puritanism of the Connecticut Valley is, I feel, most easily reconstructed and understood from his sacramental verse.

Taylor found a kind of security in that dimension of the myth-structure that puts man down to lift God up. "This world doth eye thy brightness most / When most in distance from thyselfe" (2.21).[7] To a mind like Taylor's everything else follows from this spatial juxtaposition. It was a source of both security and anxiety, the cause of both the Puritan's feeling of aristocracy and his humility, the justification for believing that as things are, they are all right.

A second dimension in the structure of Puritan thought also appears strongly in Taylor. Without the schematization of time and eternity and without the possibility of movement from the horizontal plane of things to a vertical plane, existence to a Puritan like Taylor had no plot, no adventure, no human purpose. Existence for him is a linear history and a process of time: "Life! Life! What's That? . . . It from the Worlds Birth runs unto its End. . . . But oh! Sin fould this Glory: Man hath lost it" (2.88). This is the basic drama that defines time and life to Taylor. His knowledge of the necessity of this plane consoles him ("I who once lodgd at Heavens Palace Gate / With full Fledgd Angells, now possess this fate" [2.77]), and his faith helps him accept fallen existence ("I'le kiss the Rod, and shun / To quarrell at the Stroake. Thy Will be done" [2.40]).

His writing poetry is itself a constant reenactment of the process of moving from the trap of time, the horizontal human plane, to the vertical where the divine exists. He is meditating repeatedly (however

---

7. All quotations from Taylor are from the Donald E. Stanford edition, *The Poems of Edward Taylor* (New Haven, 1960). The poems without titles are from the first and second series of Taylor's Preparatory Meditations.

illusorily) on the justifications of this one best hope and imagining rescue from the static plane to a dynamic one (as with the "Wasp Chil[le]d with cold" that Taylor identifies himself with; until "enravisht [he cannot] Climb into / The Godhead"). He tries to move in a poem from self-deprecation to thoughts of glory, from roughness of form to smoothness, from anxiety of tone to patience and peace. His whole reason for writing is to project himself in motion imaginatively from one plane to the other: "Inspire this Crumb of Dust till it display / Thy Glory through't: and then thy dust shall live" ("Prologue").

The Puritan construct in Taylor's mind is not coldly static and timebound, nor rigidly and remotely cosmological. Nor is it merely a matter of existential process and transcendental progress; it is also a matter of what fills up time and eternity, world and infinity, self and other—that is, the Puritan concern with a dimension of depth. The quality of the self that aspires, the quality of aspiration, and the quality of that state aspired to—these are a dimension in his teleology as well. He showers the Divine with his most magnanimous and amplifying terms, not always merely in praise but in justification of his goals. He rationalizes his insufficiencies lest he have to live with them and change them himself. He dramatizes his pursuits to fix them meaningfully in his own mind. He invests his praise with the greatest obsequiousness, the descriptions of his life with the most self-justifying meiosis, and his desires with anxiety-removing dramatics—all to give depth to what he wants to do and believe and be. Holiness, beauty, delight, and happiness are the ways his theology has taught him to suffuse the structure with substance. Taylor calls this an "Ebb and Flow" of warmth among Creator, Creation, and creature; it is a matter of sparks, a "mighty Tide" overwhelming all things (2.1).

This myth-structure, of which Taylor is one of the more interesting representative voices, became a tradition that stretched to the time of Emily Dickinson. The Connecticut Valley was from the outset a defensively orthodox stronghold of the faith and at the same time a unique theological unit. There was, as Perry Miller has written, "an emerging difference of temper between the east and the west." By 1700, western Massachusetts was, in anthropological terms, "a distinct cultural entity, with more ties down the river to Hartford and New Haven than to Boston or Salem."[8]

New England was effectually divided into two realms. There were still, of course, basic habits maintained from Maine to New Haven, and in

8. *Jonathan Edwards* (New York, 1949), pp. 4, 10–11.

EMILY DICKINSON AND EDWARD TAYLOR

that large sense the cultural pattern remained a unity; yet within that frame, the ecclesiastical order was definitely split, east opposed to west. When one remembers how central in the life of that society was the church, and how about it were organized concepts that have immense implications for American social history, this division becomes truly momentous, not to say prophetic.[9]

To spite the rational theology of John Cotton and others in Boston, for example, Thomas Hooker betook himself and his followers to the Connecticut River to exemplify a more sensationalized piety than they had known in the east. To the chagrin of the Boston brethren, Hooker's communities of believers, in the course of about three decades, became more and more anti-intellectual, emotionally introspective, and aggressively evangelical. When Edward Taylor went to the Valley in 1671 he was a friend of Boston's Mathers and to some extent remained under their intellectual influence all his days; but his work shows a difference as well. He appears not to have been long in the Valley when he became extremely defensive of covenant theology, he developed an obsession with emotional preparationism, and he turned from an interest in publishable prose to the writing of private, emotional verse. To a large measure his meditative poetry is a product of the Valley itself. In a number of ways, in fact, it is a description of a man's religious life in the Valley.[10]

The difference of the Valley from Boston and Cambridge is seen primarily in Hookeresque preparationism; in the ways that Yale and Dartmouth (and later Amherst College) acted as antidotes to the liberalism of Boston and Harvard; in the ease with which Solomon Stoddard moved the churches in the face of the Establishment to accept open communion; in Jonathan Edwards's insistence in opposition to Charles Chauncy and other Boston rationalists that religious experience must engage all a person's faculties, not merely the intellect; and in the ways the various awakenings battled the intellectualism and Arminianism, the "Unitarian Departure" and the growing Transcendentalism.

Taylor's poetry also represents this difference. Though he would not go so far toward pragmatism as Stoddard and could not go as far into esthetics as Edwards was to do, and though he would have been horrified at the recurring mass hysteria over sin and salvation in the area, still he is part of an antirationalistic movement within Puritanism identified primarily with the Valley.

9. *The New England Mind: From Colony to Province* (New York, 1953), p. 230.
10. See my *The Example of Edward Taylor* (Amherst, 1975).

45

He has Hooker's emphasis on an introspective piety and Edwards's emphasis on total involvement in religious experience. Where his Boston friend Increase Mather would argue a man's "effectual calling" coldly in such a work as his *Awakening Soul-saving Truths* (1720), Taylor could become ecstatic: "A Crown, Lord, yea, a Crown of Righteousness. / Oh! what a Gift is this?" (1.44). Where his Boston friend Samuel Sewall had reconciled his piety to his political and mercantile interests and ended up a moralist, Taylor centered his thought and poetry on the moved affections and thus developed another kind of power. Compared with his colleagues to the east, Taylor was much more emotional, evangelical, sensational. It is necessary to see him in the light of the more emotionally developed western orthodoxy rather than in the context of Puritanism as a whole. His life's work was in a way a defense of that difference—the Connecticut Valley way.

In time that way came to give a dark cast to Puritanism. We can look back and see that there developed a Hooker-Taylor-Edwards tradition of the long, deep journey into the self that contained an energy that inevitably produced art in each—and later in others: Emily Dickinson, Hawthorne, Melville. Taylor is important to that emerging tradition for the exemplary way he used language to move deeper into himself. We can also look back and see the development of a concept of tragedy in the Valley, a concept always latent in Puritan thought but seldom admitted to or explored. The Connecticut Valley writers seem much less able to ignore the realities of human experience than their less introspective brethren and much readier to face the possible inhumanity of the cosmos. The weight of empirical evidence of his and his world's worthlessness easily moved a writer like Taylor to anxiety about his state and anxiety about being rescued from it. In addition, in a short time a tradition of conversion emerged in the Valley that emphasized emotions as the primary directors of the will, sanctioned visionary perception, and tended to dramatize religious experience. All of these came to a head, of course, in Edwards's thought.

It is not so much that Taylor fell into this tradition and found himself responsive to it, though, as that he assisted in its creation. He helped to bear the myth-structure into the area and found ways of giving it further life by means of a new sensationalism. Because his poems show that he knew how the senses can serve the spirit, his poems have the purpose of drama in trying to stir the affections. In these ways they can be seen as counterparts to the theology of argument, definition, explication, and right reason that generally prevailed in Puritan thinking elsewhere. Though they were meant for his excitement alone, Taylor's poems can easily be compared with the revivalist sermons of Edwards and others. They are small awakenings in a tradition that in time would easily absorb the Great Awakening and in the process would lose many of its ritual and intellectual qualities. This is not to say that the skeletal structure of the Puritan myth was changed by Connecticut Valley emotions, only that it was fleshed out by feelings that would give it the means of sure survival well into the nineteenth century. Without the many Taylors of the area, Calvinism would have died sooner.

There are a number of factors that transported to Emily Dickinson both the fundamental Puritanism that descended from Calvin to Taylor and the Connecticut Valley tone as it developed from Hooker and Taylor on to Edwards and his followers. One could name, as George Whicher and others have, such factors as the geographical isolation, the emotional intellectual loyalties to local area and tradition, the proximity and itinerancy of ideas and their champions, and the infecting characteristics of Valley fear and zeal. Or one could cite the power of the defensively fundamentalist institutions in the Valley: the type of God and man at Yale, the piety of Williams and Dartmouth, and the founding of Amherst College "to check the progress of errors which are propagated from Cambridge," along with the scores of seminaries and academies (like Mount Holyoke, a "Puritan Convent," where Emily Dickinson went to school) that repressed spiritedness and yet sensationalized the spirit. Or one could simply name the name of Jonathan Edwards, who gave New England Christianity a new and powerful impulse that continued to be felt for almost a century; and, after showing his power in the area, one could list the names of all the lesser minds that for over a century bore the burden of Edwards's proofs, all working in the Connecticut Valley to keep the religious tense. The "harvests" that their Great Awakening followers let rage in frenzy spread even to the civilized East. Or, to cite further factors of the myth's course, one could find the still smaller incarnations of Edwards in the preachers and teachers that kept a town like Amherst an emotionally burnt-over district up to and during Emily Dickinson's youth—semievangelists like ministers Aaron Colton and Edward Dwight; Amherst College professor of intellectual and moral philosophy Nathan W. Fiske, father of Emily Dickinson's acquaintance Helen Hunt Jackson; and Mary Lyon, the headmistress and preacher-teacher at Mount Holyoke, who exploited the poor girls' souls (eleven successful revival campaigns in her twelve years there!) to achieve the spiritual spasms its founders desired. All are factors in the endurance of a system of belief from Taylor to the time of Emily Dickinson.

To be sure, the Valley religion declined in visibility from Taylor's day to Emily Dickinson's. Joseph Haroutunian and Perry Miller have documented the power of the Age of Edwards and the compromises that reduced the piety to a Victorian moralism by the middle of the nineteenth century. The scheme of salvation gave way to conformist programs of moral improvement. "Sublime beliefs" in the dignity of man and God's paternalism became the first principles of a new Christianity. Commonsense concern with social virtues and human happiness became a morality and eventually even a theology. The incipient legalism of Calvinism and the many humanitarian interests combined to shape a new religion. In many ways the Puritan toughness was all but lost. Haroutunian writes:

> The vision of Calvinism was being darkened by the common sense of the new age. It was losing its reality as human experience and, therefore, its appeal to the hearts and the minds of man. The logic of Calvinistic piety was being transformed into a vast, complicated and colorless theological structure, bewildering to its friends and ridiculous to enemies. It was like a proud and beggared king, hiding his shame with scarlet rags and yellow trinkets![11]

As is shown by literary history from Jonathan Edwards to Harriet Beecher Stowe, the language of the faith was kept but the piety was gone. As early as Edward Taylor's time, the fragments of the old structure were being reassembled. In Emily Dickinson's time, the reconstruction from the old fragments was much more frantic and more radical.

But myth is not history. Where history is a selected reconstruction, hoping to be representative but necessarily didactic and discontinuous, myth approximates statistical survey, indifferent to the prime movers and the high points of change but mindful of the assumptions and motives of most men's minds and the resulting racial or communal coherence. Our history kills off Puritanism early, for example, even though it lived on as the structure of men's minds for many generations. Where history is a projection out of the present onto the desirable past, myth is a description of the security of people's lives in the past regardless of modern readings of the past. The best evidence of the security that the Puritan myth-structure gave people long after its "historical death" may be seen in the continued coherence of New England culture and in the rebellious nature of those new structures that moved against the old one. The Puritan myth-structure had been seen in enough generations to make it a lasting matter, even though it appears less and less in the pulpit, in politics, in the press, and in belles

---

11. Haroutunian, *Piety versus Moralism*, p. 71.

lettres; and though by the nineteenth century it had come into weakened conflict with constructs like Lockean sensationalism, Rousseauvian naturalism, Emersonian orientalism, and the new geology and biology, it was still very much there, as is shown by the didactic subliterature of the period, the private journals and private poetry, the reports of conversations around board and hearth—really everywhere that shared assumptions are revealed. The Puritan race was very durable. History has often failed to report that fact.

History must deal with the substance of time; myth, however, is a matter not of substance but of coherent structure and relationships, a system of balanced oppositions throughout the variations. Though different forms of language actualized the myth in different ways at different points in time, the structure remained essentially the same. Though the history one writes might deny it, whatever a writer like Emily Dickinson was thinking in the middle of the nineteenth century, there was a metastructure that was thinking her. When Edward Taylor wrote, "All the Springs of Divine influence in the head, shall be carried by the hand of Love down thro' all the secret wayes and Chanells of Convayances to every member of the body for its Spiritual increase, and fulness," by virtue of the power of myth he was thinking *her*.[12]

Horror stories can be told about the revivalist life of the Valley when Emily Dickinson was growing up; the antirational and introspective frenzy resulting from the sensational ideology descending from Hooker, Taylor, Stoddard, and principally Edwards reached its peak in her place and time. She was subjected continually to the evangelical harassment of preachers and family, the neurotic personal inquiry of teachers and friends into her fears of heaven and hell, the danger of being branded with a few other students at school as being "without hope," with the simple guilt maturing over the years into acute anxiety. Though the need to convert possessed her and though in essentials she kept the faith, she rebelled against the pressure and refused to capitulate to the enthusiasm.

Rather than modifying the myth in her, however, the horrifying

---

12. *Edward Taylor's Christographia,* ed. Norman S. Grabo (New Haven, 1962), p. 325. I find only one very close parallel between Emily Dickinson and Taylor, but it is one that illustrates their common biblical/Puritan roots. In his "Preface" to *Gods Determinations,* Taylor writes:

Infinity, when all things it beheld
In Nothing, and of Nothing all did build,
Upon what Base was fixt the Lath, wherein
He turn'd this Globe, and riggalld it so trim?
Who blew the Bellows of his Furnace vast?

religious experiences drove her to it experimentally. Her poetry becomes for us a record of that lifelong experiment. Here, for example, is a description of a conversion experience, imagined or real:

> The Thrill came slowly like a book for
> Centuries delayed
> It's fitness growing like the Flood
> In sumptuous solitude –
> The desolation only missed
> While Rapture changed it's Dress
> And stood amazed before the Change
> In ravished Holiness –

[#1495]

She tried hard to practice a kind of Hookeresque preparationism, whether genuine or not:

> Safe Despair it is that raves –
> Agony is frugal.
> Puts itself severe away
> For it's own perusal.

[#1243]

Though her religious disclaimers and her skepticism must be taken seriously, in her letters and poems she keeps coming back, obsessed, to the structure of beliefs outside which she could apparently find no happiness. Of the many factors that made her a poet and made her the poet she was, the conversion tactics of hope, heat, and guilt appear to have exerted the greatest influence. Through such, the Puritan was engraved on her mind as something she would have to deal with as reality. John S. Wheatcroft writes:

> Emily Dickinson acquired more essential Puritanism from the schoolbench and the pew and from her position in the family circle than most men could from a lifetime study of Edwards. Something in the nature

---

Or held the Mould wherein the world was Cast?
Who laid its Corner Stone? Or whose Command?
Where stand the Pillars upon which it stands?
Who Lac'de and Fillitted the earth so fine,
With Rivers like green Ribbons Smaragdine?

Emily Dickinson echoes this in #128:

Also, who laid the Rainbow's piers,
Also, who leads the docile spheres
By withes of supple blue?
Whose fingers string the stalactite –
Who counts the wampum of the night
To see that none is due?

of the poet, which manifests itself in her unquestioning acceptance of a life-long family relationship that was ready-made for her, and which shows itself in the poetry in the form of a lack of analytical intelligence, a naivete in matters of thought, made the poet particularly susceptible to the effect of a tradition. Puritanism, I feel certain, was not hers to accept or reject. The collective, continuous mind of western Massachusetts had been steeped in the Puritan way too long for a single mind of the kind Emily Dickinson had to throw it off.[13]

Perhaps because the Puritan zeal ran so high, she came to certain a priori conclusions that made her yearn for orthodoxy yet resist its restricting pressures. She was never to extricate herself from her spiritual-literary forebears. Cotton Mather would *not* have indicted her for a witch, despite rumors started by Allen Tate; for a harpy maybe, but not for a witch.

The Five Points of Calvin's Synod of Dort of 1618–19 are represented often—and often reverently—in Emily Dickinson's poetry.[14] To represent her absorption of the principle of Innate Depravity (point one), she speaks of the "doubtful Dividend / Patented by Adam." To show her interest in Unconditional Election (point two), she imagines that

> Some with new - stately feet -
> Pass royal thro' the gate -
>
> [#10]

In addition, she was consistently worried about the fact of Limited Atonement (point three):

> Redemption is the one
> Of whom the explanation
> Is hitherto unknown
>
> [#1502]

Irresistible Grace (point four) fascinated her, but it baffled her as well:

> I knew that I had gained
> And yet I knew not how
>
> [#1022]

And finally, the Perseverance of the Saints (point five) became a constant theme. "Bind me," she wrote, "I still can sing - " (# 1005). It must

---

13. Wheatcroft, "Emily Dickinson," p. 13.
14. This is the argument of Ronald Lanyi, "'My Faith That Dark Adores - ': Calvinist Theology in the Poetry of Emily Dickinson," *Arizona Quarterly* 32 (autumn 1976): 264–78.

be said, however, that these Five Points were seldom matters of abstract theology to her; they were worries and hopes that she allowed to concern her personally.

Yet my purpose here is not to determine Emily Dickinson's orthodoxy, either in her own conviction or in the ways she might come into proximity with the orthodoxy of a religious literary forebear like Edward Taylor. Her religious position could be debated endlessly and futilely, for there is a wide variety of gods and devils in her mind. It may be more important to determine *where* the Puritan fundamentals are in her and *how* they sit in her mind. There is a system in her, as I would like to show, within which she moved fairly freely and experimentally. This may be one of her greatest feats as a poet. A comparison with Edward Taylor shows how.

"My Puritan Spirit," Emily Dickinson wrote in an 1883 letter, " 'gangs' sometimes 'aglay.' "[15] There are a number of factors of biography and style that justify a structural approach to the "Puritan spirit" of both Edward Taylor and Emily Dickinson. The factors that defined the Puritan spirit in each—whether as predisposition or as points of departure—are as interesting as the ways each "gangs . . . aglay" to make an individuality for himself. The structure, as Emerson was to argue in his essay "Fate," determines even the individuality.

> We are sure that, though we know not how, necessity does comport with liberty, the individual with the world, my polarity with the spirit of the times. . . . We cannot trifle with this reality, this cropping-out in our planted gardens of the core of the world. No picture of life can have any veracity that does not admit the odious facts. A man's power is hooped in by a necessity which, by many experiments, he touches on every side until he learns its arc. . . . To see how fate slides into freedom and freedom into fate, observe how far the roots of every creature run, or find if you can a point where there is no thread of connection. Our life is consentaneous and far-related. This knot of nature is so well tied that nobody was ever cunning enough to find the two ends. Nature is intricate, overlapped, interweaved and endless.[16]

The possibility that there are both the "roots," the "necessity," the "knot of nature" and also "experiments" and "liberty" in the lives and thought of both writers justifies the emphasis on myth.

15. *Letters*, pp. 797–98. She uses the expression again in a letter of 1853: "This [is] a vexing world, and things 'oft gang aglay' " (*Letters*, pp. 244–45). On only two other occasions did she use the word "Puritan": in a letter of 1881 she speaks of "my Puritan Garden" and in another letter of the same year she speaks of Nature as " 'old-fashioned,' perhaps a Puritan" (*Letters*, pp. 687, 699).
16. *Complete Works* (Boston, 1893), 6:9, 24, 40.

To identify what is mythic in Taylor it is necessary to note how in any thorough consideration of Taylor the Puritan system of thought is juxtaposed against the man himself, or rather the man against the system, the man against the myth, even as he is a part of it. In the Taylor of the *Preparatory Meditations,* for instance, we have a man arguing his guilt of sin *within* a sense of grace (so that one may feel he is merely playing at being a fallen individual yet all the while fairly sure of heavenly approval); the security of the structure is there even as he imagines his freedom from it. There is also for him in his theology always the possibility of sanctification *and* justification; that is, a feeling of freedom allowed by the structure itself, a liberating knowledge that his actions, conduct, and thought are possibly independent of his fundamental worth. The very practice of poetry itself *alongside* the practice of piety is a structural juxtaposition; on the one hand, there is the theology that demanded the preparationist verse and on the other his use of that demand as an excuse to practice a life of his own, the primary world of reality leading to despair and the secondary world of imagination encouraging hope. Even in his style the juxtaposition of man and system is revealed. The stanza form is conventional and rigid in Taylor, and yet a personality moves and breathes *within* it; quatrain and couplet, like the faith, dominate completely, and yet he pushes and pulls against their restrictions. Too, the iambic meter is the discipline for his lines (often maintained at great cost to the quality of his verse); yet with caesuras and compound stresses he tries to bend it to his will. His resorting to off-rhyme is also evidence of working within a system but allowing one's individuality its expression as well. In the form of Taylor's verse, therefore, the choice of a rigid system of belief is always present, and he becomes a poet both by virtue of the rigid system *and* as he violates it enough to make room in it for himself.

Such a structuralizing of Taylor's Puritanism clarifies where his individuality lies. As it does with Emily Dickinson. In her life, consider, for example, the phenomenon of a woman living as a spiritual renegade under her father's roof, and also the dexterity with which she moves intellectually and emotionally within her quiet conformity to New England decorum. She appears to have lived the coherent structure, though it had, as *we* know, a discontinuous surface. (This may be what she meant by one of her lines, "the mind against itself.") Consider too how she was a seeker of new forms, all the while yearning for the faith of her fathers—what she called in one poem the "pretty ways of Covenant." She had the temperament of self-assertion and constant fears of damnation: "I – the undivine abode / Of His Elect Content." She had Puritan self-consciousness (her "Columnar Self" is "not far off / From furthest – Spirit – God") and at the same time a consciousness of worthlessness:

> No Other can reduce
> Our mortal Consequence
> Like the remembering it be nought.

[#982]

She was the Jobean rebel who lived by faith. As such, her life is given meaning not by the struggle but by the structure against which she struggled. Or consider factors of her style like sprung rhythm within hymn meter (the iambic discipline jarringly antiphonal to the spoken rhythm), the persistent off-rhymes within a demanding rhyme pattern (one or another sound maintaining the pattern, the others free), the irony, paradox, and oxymorons (with surface and hidden factors both maintaining the coherence of a poem and giving opportunity for aberrant expression). The predictable form is consistently roughened, as if she would break out of the very system that gives her artistic security and that she nonetheless works to sustain. These all bear witness to the existence of the myth in her. As with Taylor, there is a syntactical juxtaposition of the *received* and the *desired* in Emily Dickinson that reveals independence amid an inextricable commitment.

It is in the disparity between mythic *language* and individual *speech,* better than anywhere else, that one may discover the nature of the Puritan spirit of Emily Dickinson. The distance between the two describes the poetic sensibility of each writer. As a theologian Taylor thinks and writes much more in the language of the structure than does Emily Dickinson, for it is much more the necessary condition of his speaking. Taylor's poetry is in a number of ways Puritanism versified. The provocative power in Taylor's poetry, as I have said, is not so much in the speech he actually uses as in the myth-structure, the theology, behind it. Yet the theology in it does not qualify his writing as literature (something Taylor knew but that Michael Wigglesworth, for one, did not). The forms that the language of the myth takes do that. It is the system of belief in his poems that ultimately gives them their significance, not the personality of the author or the significance of the speech he uses in the individual poems. The bald appearance of the theology in even his best work is evidence that Taylor recognized that though *his* is the thought and *his* the speech in his work, it is the theology which allows, indeed encourages, him to do it, and by virtue of which he can deliver his meanings. For the most part he expropriates his speech from a theological context. Yet there is in most of his verse almost always something added, something of the man himself. Sometimes it is no more than the sound of his own voice. At other times it is the imposition of himself between the subject and the reader: "I am here. I live and breathe. I long for God's love," he says over and over again in his Meditations. And then, for the most part, his better poems become his better poems when the individuality of his speech has taken us away from the doctrine he espouses and has focused our attention on himself instead. The fresher, more individual, even more eccentric his speech becomes, the better poetry he writes, for he has freed himself within the system of his beliefs.

His words have values of their own, of course, but they do not so much thereby escape the structure as bring to it the richness of these new values—values determined by the semantic associations of the imagery. The nontheological associations then add to the theology a range that includes his own personality and experience. The tendency of his words to expand cumulatively is of course limited by the system; they will not take on meanings outside or beyond that system. But by writing poetry as he does, with wit and sensuousness and allusions and ingenuity of sound and syntax, he expands the system into something large enough to include even himself, fallen and yearning for acceptance.

A comparison with Emily Dickinson should show how hard Taylor is trying to find an individual speech within the language of the myth. To make an individuality for himself within the rigidities of his thought and form, Taylor often had to resort to devices like hackneyed conceits, puns, rapid shifts in dominant metaphors, mixed metaphors, extremely far-fetched analogies, eccentricities of sound and syntax, and a whole bag of Elizabethan rhetorical devices—all of which became means for varying the divine scheme of things with something of his own personality. His meditative poems inevitably move from the quotation of (or allusion to) Scripture to the search for an individual imagery and end with an emphasis on his own needs, his own existence. Oddly enough, this represents, as it does with Emily Dickinson, his struggle to be himself within the system. In fact, without the fresh and free speech he uses, the theology would for him be nearly dead. The extent to which he creates an individual speech is the extent to which he is keeping the theology alive in his life. His freedom of speech is therefore in no way destructive of the faith but revives it constantly. In its way, his little bit of "wildness" defends and promotes the faith.

Poetry as a *liberating* art in Puritan culture may be an important idea, one that would have been instructive to another Puritan poet, Emily Dickinson. The Puritan theology was of course primary in

Taylor's thinking—and therefore latent in him. As he wrote his poetry, however—stretching metaphors to include himself, using his own person and voice as the substance of his poems, manipulating the rhythms of his lines to represent his own feelings—his art (merely a secondary system of action) developed a new myth, the myth of the Puritan Liberated by Art. By his writing as he did, reality became not what the theology called reality but what his art made it: freedom within form.

For Emily Dickinson, poetry was also the means of freedom within the forms of her belief. It is here that there is a significant parallel with Taylor, a parallel created by New England Puritanism. In Emily Dickinson we have an attachment to the Puritan myth-structure that parallels Taylor's. She is less patient with it, and it gives her considerably more agony; yet the Puritanism in her is not an onus but an assumption.

This is seen most easily in the way the language of the theology occasionally crops up in her individual speech. This gives her away. Beyond the peculiarly Puritan uses of Scripture ("'They have not chosen me,' he said, / 'But I have chosen them!' / Brave - Broken hearted statement") and beyond the pious Victorian moralism typical of her age ("I shall know why - when Time is over ... Christ will explain each separate anguish")—beyond this, Puritan language pokes out in quite a number of poems. For instance, we find such technical terms as "decree," "degree," "election," "covenant," "confirmed," "condemned," "espoused," and "saints" (in the Puritan rather than the Catholic sense). We have a number of lines right out of the theology: "Mine - by the Right of the White Election"; "men, must slake in Wilderness ... An instinct for ... necessity"; "The worthlessness of Earthly things"; "The Discipline of Man - / Compel[s] Him to Choose Himself / His Preappointed Pain"; "This dirty - little - Heart"; the "Human Soul - / That indestructible estate." We also find such standard Taylorly representations of salvation as coronation ("The Grace that I - was chosen -/ To me - surpassed the Crown / That was the Witness for the Grace - "); white robes ("this Sufferer polite -/ Dressed to meet You - / See - in White!"); marriage ("God is a distant - stately Lover -/ Woos, as He states us - by His Son"); and bread and wine ("I trembling drew the Table near -/ And touched the Curious Wine - "). And we have such juxtapositions from Puritan language as the description of the election of the just in business terms (#234), the characterization of grace in the imagery of torture (#264, 384, 414), the dramatization of her "glee" with stories of barrenness (#364), the outline of the paradoxes of man's attempts to know the unknowable

(#313, 815), and the disparate terminology for man and for nature (#9, 229, 790). These all show a dependence on the ideology for her poetry and reveal her commitment to it.

More significant, though, are the attitudes in her poetry that could have come only from New England Puritanism, though her interest in the ideology had more to do with its structure, to be sure, than its substance. As in Taylor, there is the vertical dimension in her belief in the sovereignty of God ("Ah, what a royal sake / To my nescessity – stooped down!") and the alienation of man ("Why – do they shut Me out of Heaven? / Did I sing – too loud?"). The horizontal dimension of the Puritan cosmology is seen in her acceptance of this plane of existence ("the Trap of Time," she calls it, "this brief Tragedy of Flesh") and the need for grace within this plane ("A Tooth upon Our Peace . . . To vitalize the Grace"). The Puritan's emphasis on progress from one plane to the other is seen in her hunt for signs of election ("A Light exists in Spring . . . It almost speaks to you . . . It passes and we stay") and the satisfactions of the process of regeneration and conversion ("that Campaign inscrutable / Of the Interior").

Whatever else divinity and humanity meant to her, God is always beyond man and man always beneath God: "Papa above! / Regard a Mouse / O'erpowered by the Cat!" Whatever else life was to her, it was the same static, desperate condition the Puritans experienced: "I reason, Earth is short – / And Anguish – absolute." And whatever else man's progress from "the Trap of Time" to Glory ("Spell slower – Glory") meant to her, it was, as with her Puritan forebears, a process of struggling to discover, hoping for rescue, and desperately depending on divinity:

> The Battle fought between the Soul
> And No Man - is the One
> Of all the Battles prevalent -
> By far the Greater One -
>
> No News of it is had abroad -
> It's Bodiless Campaign
> Establishes, and terminates -
> Invisible - Unknown -
>
> Nor History - record it -
> As Legions of a Night
> The Sunrise scatters - These endure -
> Enact - and terminate -
>
> [#594]

All of these are fair assumptions one can make about her Puritan outlook. The differences in substance do not matter much, however,

57

for it is the coherence of the structure that gave her Puritanism its power in her thinking. Her life had little meaning to her outside this construct.

One finds in her, as well, the stereotypic Puritan psychology—the prideful self-satisfaction of renunciation ("Success is counted sweetest / By those who ne'er succeed"); the obsessive suspicion of happiness ("Is Bliss then, such Abyss, / I must not put my foot amiss / For fear I spoil my shoe?"); the stoic self-consciousness of one's experimental temporality ("This Consciousness . . . is . . . [the] most profound experiment / Appointed unto Men"); the tragic curiosity with the unknowable, the ideal, and the impossible ("Impossibility, like Wine / Exhilirates the Man / Who tastes it")—but this often varied with her moods and warmed with her spirits and was simply the result of the structure she assumed reality had. Because of its pervasiveness in her bearing toward the world and her concept of herself, Puritanism must have appeared to her unmovable (though not immobilizing), an assertion of necessity (which one must nonetheless always question), and an equation that is reality (but allowing many interpretations, including her own).

Additional features of her poetry show that her language and attitudes derive uniquely from the Connecticut Valley brand of the myth. Throughout her poetry, for instance, she conceives of regeneration in Hookeresque terms of a long journey into herself, a journey comprised of

> larger – Darknesses –
> Those Evenings of the Brain –
> When not a Moon disclose a sign –
> Or Star – come out – within –

[#419]

This introspectiveness gives to her poetry, as it gives to Taylor's, an energy: the fascination with one's spiritual innards as a way of divining cosmic will, the obsessive curiosity with the indications of one's spiritual worth, the determination to discover the grounds of being:

> Growth of Man – like Growth of Nature –
> Gravitates within –
> Atmosphere, and Sun endorse it –
> But it stir – alone –
>
> Each – it's difficult Ideal
> Must achieve – Itself –
> Through the solitary prowess
> Of a Silent Life –

Effort - is the sole condition -
Patience of Itself -
Patience of opposing forces -
And intact Belief -

Looking on - is the Department
Of it's Audience -
But Transaction - is assisted
By no Countenance -

[#750]

As the Valley tradition taught her, the "difficult Ideal" of "Gravitat[ing] within" is a slow, dark, and lonely process, one in which "intact Belief" and "opposing forces" can be kept in balance only with immense "Effort."

Introspection, given the Puritan assumptions of man's inability to know and the dangers of knowing, leads to the tragic sense native to the Connecticut Valley writers. And of this in Emily Dickinson there is a full measure:

Doom is the House without the Door -
'Tis entered from the Sun -
And then the Ladder's thrown away,
Because Escape - is done -

[#475]

This tragic sense, unique to the Valley and absolutely missing as the thought to the east of Amherst moved from covenant theology to Unitarian liberalism and Transcendentalism, led Emily Dickinson, as it had led Taylor, to face the realities of human experience and entertain the possibility of an inhumane cosmos:

To die - without the Dying
And live - without the Life
This is the hardest Miracle
Propounded to Belief.

[#1017]

Beyond the meditative and realistic features of the Valley literary tradition there is in Emily Dickinson a fascination with religious conversion. For her, as much as for Taylor, the emotions were the primary directors of the will, perception was visionary, and poetry was the means of dramatizing religious experiences. It is necessary to remember the argument that her poetry is a reiterative rehearsal of (and compensation for) the opportunities to convert missed in her youth. As a result, she was for the rest of her life an enthusiast with designs on her own soul. Through the medium of poetry she experiments with a wide variety of conversion exercises:

> Dare you see a Soul *at the White Heat?*
> Then crouch within the door –
> Red – is the Fire's common tint –
> But when the vivid Ore
> Has vanquished Flame's conditions,
> It quivers from the Forge
> Without a color, but the light
> Of unannointed Blaze.
> Least Village has it's Blacksmith
> Whose Anvil's even ring
> Stands symbol for the finer Forge
> That soundless tugs – within –
> Refining these impatient Ores
> With Hammer, and with Blaze
> Until the Designated Light
> Repudiate the Forge –
>
> [#365]

When in its "White Heat," the soul ("the finer Forge / That soundless tugs – within") undergoes, as in any self-evangelization, a refining, anointing, and, finally, what she calls "Designa[tion]," or a sense of election.

The thoroughness with which the Connecticut Valley introspectiveness, tragic sense, and inclination toward conversion pervade her poems shows that Emily Dickinson did not give up the Puritan myth-structure for others; whatever she touches or entertains is transformed by her faith. She never really left home.

There is a very elaborate system of signs in what she writes that demonstrates that the Puritan system of ideas lies behind her poetry and shows her struggling for freedom within it. Because the direction of her enthusiasm was inward and because she had no overwhelming interest in communicating her beliefs to others, she had no need to be explicit about them; they were assumptions to her anyway, and so she turned to write about her own experiences of the world. The speech of her poems represents those experiences. There is an internal coherence and at the same time a practically unlimited capacity for extension and variety. In the individuality of her speech, Emily Dickinson could have both security and freedom from history.

In her individual expression, the Puritanic assumptions take on amazing variety. By virtue of her skill with poetry she is thereby creating a freedom for herself within the form of her belief. Notice, for instance, the ways the language of man's fall from glory and alienation from grace is actualized as she, like Taylor, plays the role of naughty, insufficient, deprived, fallen creature:

> It would have starved a Gnat –
> To live so small as I –
>
> I'm Nobody! Who are you?
>
> We play at Paste –
> Till qualified, for Pearl –
>
> Before I got my eye put out
> I liked as well to see –
>
> God gave a Loaf to every Bird –
> But just a Crumb – to Me –
>
> So keep your secret – Father!
>
> I hope the Father in the skies
> Will lift his little girl –
> Old fashioned – naughty – everything –
> Over the stile of "Pearl".

There are no terms from the theology here (except the sardonic "Father" and the satirized pearly gates), no direct references to belief, only the speech of an anomalous personality with unique personal experience. The wilder and more imaginative she is in expressing (or creating) herself, the freer she is, of course, within the tragic concept of man that binds her. Through poetry, she can, paradoxically, be both bound to the doctrine of the Fall and, because of her imaginative language, free of it.

Similarly, Emily Dickinson's descriptions of man's alienation from God, as another example, have Puritan assumptions behind them but are free in expression:

> We thirst at first – 'tis Nature's Act –
>
> I'm banished – now – you know it –
>
>   Life is over there –
> Behind the Shelf
>
> "Heaven" – is what I cannot reach!
>
> A loss of something felt I –
>
> I see thee better – in the Dark –
>
> I saw no Way – The Heavens were stitched –
>
> We grow accustomed to the Dark –
> When Light is put away –

> Sparrows, unnoticed by the Father –
> Lambs for whom time had not a fold.

> A Plated Life – diversified
> With Gold and Silver Pain

> The Light His Action, and the Dark
> The Leisure of His Will –

> God's Right Hand –
> . . . is amputated now
> And God cannot be found –

By virtue of her ability with language, she is able to believe *and* live her own life. The forms of her speech are a way out of what she called "the Trap of Time" while staying in the world and enjoying herself. ("So instead of getting to Heaven, at last – / I'm going, all along.") There was thus liberty for her within the prison:

> No Prisoner be –
> Where Liberty –
> Himself – abide with Thee –

> [#720]

The icons in her poems are full of the recollection of previous usage. The Puritanism is solidly there, though well hidden, even assumed.

There are some interesting features of her individual speech that show, as they do in Taylor, the insistence on freedom within form. We have the colloquial voice, which shows that whatever reality is, it has been personalized in the poems—that, in fact, beyond one's beliefs there is one's personality. We also have the deliberately roughened exterior of the poetry (the first-draft appearance of the rhythm, rhymes, punctuation, capitalization, spelling, and even grammar) as a form of visible *un*sainthood, cultivated even as one ponders saintly matters, showing an attractive eccentricity amid perfect knowledge of forms. We also have the shock and surprise of much of the imagery, which is not merely a way of insisting on one's individuality but a way of calling attention to oneself while being perfectly relevant and acceptable. In such instances, the individual speech is liberating while at the same time attached to conventions. It gave her the chance to live the illusion of her freedom.

The Puritanism appears in unsuspected places in her poems, though it may seem difficult to determine which facets of a given poem belong to the language of the theology and which belong to her own voice. An example (a poem that is widely regarded as one of her more heretical ones yet, I believe, one that affirms her faith as well) might illustrate the value of this tension:

I know that He exists.
Somewhere - in Silence -
He has hid his rare life
From our gross eyes.

'Tis an instant's play.
'Tis a fond Ambush -
Just to make Bliss
Earn her own surprise!

But - should the play
Prove piercing earnest -
Should the glee - glaze -
In Death's - stiff - stare -

Would not the fun
Look too expensive!
Would not the jest -
Have crawled too far!

[#338]

The poem is organized along the pattern of the myth of the Puritan Liberated by Art. It moves in its structure from assertion of belief ("I know...") to questioning belief as a result of personal experience ("Would not... Would not..."); and it moves from a simple prosaic juxtaposition (the "rare life" of the *deus absconditus* versus the "gross" life of man) to the extravagant imagery of games (a children's game of hide-and-seek that is turned into adult ambush and killing). A few terms allude to the theology ("Bliss" and "Glee" possibly from medieval uses; "piercing," "Death," and "expensive" [Christ as ransom] from the crucifixion story), but they are fantastically individualized. The rest is sheer invention: the hidden God becomes a "crawl[ing]," satanic snake in reality; Christ becomes God's cheap coinage; the "gross" life of man, no doubt a mere commodity, has become "too expensive"—all has been reversed, and terribly personal. There is tension between the trite language of the poem ("Somewhere - in Silence") and the ambiguously personal language ("should the play / Prove piercing earnest"), just as there is between the phony ideology ("make Bliss / Earn her own surprise") and the cruel reality of life ("the jest [would] / Have crawled too far!"). The tone of voice moves from mouthed platitude to personal complaint.

Even the form of the poem has become almost totally individualized. In its neatly rhymed stanzas (abcb), nothing rhymes very neatly (Silence/-ss eyes, -ush/surprise, -st/stare, -ive/far). The iambic hymn meter of the first line (-/-/-/) becomes thrusting accentual verse in the rest (/--/ [/],--/-//, -///). She thereby becomes herself even as she depends on conventional form. What the poem says, then, is that there is a disparity between belief and experience. The belief is still there (belief in the sovereignty of God and the dependence of man, the depravity of existence and the attempt at the salvation of man), but it has been expanded considerably to include her personal experience of that belief. The devices of poetry made it possible for her to create that individuality.

All of this is important only if one remembers that though reality was defined for Emily Dickinson by Puritanism, as it was for Edward Taylor, her poetry was an escape from the system—or rather, an escape *within* it. "A sublimated Puritan," Rollo Brown has called her,[17] but that misses the point: through the individual voice of her poetry Emily Dickinson gained freedom within form and, like Taylor, created a new myth in the process. Her speech is expropiated from a theological context, but it is not as close to the theology as Taylor's is; the comparison with him shows not her orthodoxy or heterodoxy but simply that by virtue of a superior practice at poetry she made greater freedom for herself within the construct. Like Taylor, she accepted the system but tried to make a place within it. Her business was not the center but the circumference. Puritanism was for her a norm of language from which her individual speech diverged into literature.

It was in the style (that is, in tone, rhythm of delivery, naturalness of expression, and atmosphere of delight or despair) that she could become that individualist. Her style is her zone of freedom. It kept her from being a prisoner of her own formal myth. A Dickinson poem therefore communicates two things: the myth behind it and the struggle for freedom by means of it.

Behind this archetypal arrangement of liberating myth and controlled speech is the Emersonian theory of indirection (writing, to him, was most effective when it expressed ideality by means of mundane realities) and the Edwardsean theory of supernatural light (man comes to truth through his personal experiences, for they are ordained of God as a spiritual test). Both esthetic theories distinguish idea from experience, the ideal from the real, and sanctify personal emotion and experience. To both, individual experience has significance because its coherence and meaningfulness derive from the ideal. And, by extension, individual speech is holy because it is informed by the mythic spirit behind it. This arrangement therefore insures both security and freedom. Under the weight of such an esthetic, Emily Dickinson should have felt comfortably orthodox in

17. "A Sublimated Puritan," *Saturday Review of Literature*, 6 October 1928, pp. 186–87.

her heterodoxy. "We know that the mind of the Heart must live," she wrote in a letter of 1877, "[even] if it's clerical part do not."

The use of expressive, individualistic speech in poetry invites speculation that the thought behind it is that of a new and different ideology. This is one of the major problems of both Taylor and Dickinson criticism: Taylor's freedom of speech does not make him unorthodox and Emily Dickinson's experimentation with language does not turn her into a Transcendentalist, Naturalist, or Existentialist. Taylor and Emily Dickinson remain Puritan even as they explore the world with their own voices.

But, as with Taylor, once an individual speech has been accomplished within the system of beliefs, a *new* myth has been created by Emily Dickinson's poetry. As we have seen, not only does reality form one's art, but reality can be formed *by* one's art. In Emily Dickinson we have the myth of the Puritan Liberated by Art emerging strongly, for her struggle with reality became itself the reality she found it necessary to hold to. Reality became what her art had made it: freedom within form. The issue of the coordinates between tradition and individual talent was alive long before T. S. Eliot sanctified it.

Discussing Emily Dickinson thus in terms of myth provides relief from the quarrels over explications and biography. One may then pay attention to her relationship to her writing without having to worry over motives. It is important to realize that the subject of her poems (and the experience we ultimately have with them) is that of freedom versus fate: her individuality within the frame of things, heresy within orthodoxy, doubt within a system of belief, creativity within tradition. The form of the variety, eccentricity, flamboyance within hymn meter is her basic subject. When viewed structurally, this is mythic. But it is not mythic in a racist, collectivist sense so much as in another way: the heretic as contributor/refresher of the system. For Kafka, belief is revived when the tiger is admitted to the temple. Emily Dickinson's example is like Blake's: "He who is out of the Church," he wrote in "A Vision of the Last Judgment," "& opposes it is no less an Agent of Religion than he who is in it; to be an Error & to be Cast out is a part of God's design."

There are instructive differences, though, in the way this new myth appears in Taylor and the way it appears in Emily Dickinson. Under the structuralist approach, the differences between them are more semantic than syntactic: words have different meanings but the same ideological relationships; the two are seriously comparable only in reference to a system of values, anyway, not in reference to personal thought or expression. The ideology enabled both to read the world—though not for its meaning so much as for its operation. Where she goes well beyond Taylor is in the recognition that though the Puritan ideology commands her world, it is not commanded *by* the world. So the *tension* between one's background and one's personal experience, between belief and feeling, between the language and one's speech becomes a factor in her beliefs where it is not in his. "Experience," for her, "is the Angled Road / Preferred against... The Discipline of Man." Neither of them finds it necessary to worry about his/her experience of the structure, but Emily Dickinson is concerned with its *control* over her life. As a result, she refuses to participate consciously in the system. She is a conscientious objector against the God she loves and cannot figure out. This is a substantial difference from Taylor, who simply wants to be seduced. The myth of the Puritan Liberated by Art is in her hands a very different one.

Or perhaps it is more accurate to say, as Borges teaches one to do, that understanding this myth in Emily Dickinson teaches one how to read Taylor. That she is able to create in him a precursor is a measure of her power as a poet. Whether there is any life in Taylor's poetry may to some extent depend on how we have learned to read Emily Dickinson first.

We read both poets, I suppose, because they dramatized what gave their very different lives meaning and what they could not shake off had they wanted to. Had they given up their beliefs and taken on others, they could not have been such poets. By keeping the myth-structure intact and using poetry as a means of gaining their freedom, they show that they would not allow others to appropriate their right to make meaning for themselves.

Three

A TOUR OF THE PIT

EMILY DICKINSON AND JONATHAN EDWARDS

Abyss is its own apology.

[Letters, p. 861]

The prospective relations of Emily Dickinson with Anne
Bradstreet and Edward Taylor prove the need to see her origins in
New England religious pressures. Its esthetics are often underestimated, but Puritanism, as it filled much of the American past, must be
seen as a major source of *her* esthetics. Like Jonathan Edwards's works
more than a century earlier, her poetry is one of its major defenses
and representatives, weakened as that representation may be in the
nineteenth century. "Young New England puritan," Simone de
Beauvoir calls her, who exemplified "a solitary cult."[1]

Yet Emily Dickinson's poetry serves as no sure index to Puritan
thought, either of the past or of her own time. Instead, even as she
carries it out well, hers is one of the most remarkable bodies of protest
literature we have *against* New England religion. To the resurgence of
Puritanism in her time, her poetry is a formidable veto. "Indeed,"
writes Richard Sewall, "her whole career may be regarded as a sustained, if muted, rebellion against this very inheritance."[2] Yet she

1. Simone de Beauvoir, *The Second Sex* (New York, 1961), pp. 320–21.
2. Richard B. Sewall, *The Life of Emily Dickinson,* (New York, 1974), pp. 19–20.

could not escape it. She indeed had what she called "An Ancient fashioned Heart."

But this alternating defense and offense creates a tense ambiguity in our understanding of her Puritan origins. She stamps her foot at what she stands on. She yells at the voice she yells with. Like the Brahma, it is with Puritan wings themselves that she has the power to flee the Puritan past.

She is more realistic than Emerson and Thoreau, or even Hawthorne and Melville, in accepting Puritanism as an undercurrent in the American blood, and closer to James and Twain, I would say, in recognizing its fascination and tyranny, its inevitability in American life, though of course with the difference of having lived and needed it, then transcended it. There is more of the first two centuries of America in her than in any other nineteenth-century writer—and more prolonged complaint against it and involved displacement of it. In her American forces converge—through her aversions and reversions—the most clearly. She is at the center.

The vital dependence on Puritan torments and the concurrent devoted rejection of Puritan claims on her faculties make a major ambiguity in Emily Dickinson. Her critics have hardly dealt with the attractions of this ambiguity, for its perplexities confirm her complexity. Jonathan Edwards is her best critic in this regard. In knowing him, we learn her needs and her denials, a tense syntax that produced much of her best poetry. The Edwards that is in her she both needs and hates: he is not so much a confrère of the mind as a stage upon which she spins and turns. It is *his* pit from which she sings.

Edwards himself she never knew very well. She was awed by a visit to Edwards's church in Northampton in 1857.[3] She may have read about Edwards in local history books, such as one by her friend Josiah Holland, *History of Western Massachusetts* (1855), wherein Edwards is acclaimed "a metaphysician and theologian, second to none in America."[4] And at the end of a letter/poem to her nephew Gilbert in 1881 she wrote her only explicit reference to him:

"All Liars shall have their part" –
Jonathan Edwards –
"And let him that is athirst come" –
Jesus –

In this she attributes (facetiously, of course) the hellishness of Revelation 21:8 to Edwards—"The fearful, and unbelieving, and the abo-

---

3. Jay Leyda, *The Years and Hours of Emily Dickinson* (New Haven, 1960), 1:204-5.
4. J. G. Holland, *History of Western Massachusetts* (Springfield, 1855), 1:168-69; 2:244-46.

minable, and murderers, and whoremongers, and sorcerers, and idolaters, and all liars, shall have their part in the lake which burneth with fire and brimstone: which is the second death"—for it is her view of the thrust of her Puritan heritage. The attribution makes Edwards the archetype of the sadistic side of American religion.[5] Yet she prefers, as she says (elfin/gaminly) in the same letter/poem, "the divine Perdition / Of Idleness and Spring" to the Puritan's "Industry and Morals / And every righteous thing."[6] This is all we know she knew of Edwards—and she mocks him.[7]

Yet the Puritanism he came to represent in rural Massachusetts at midcentury is unmistakably there in her interests. With the game of parallel texts, one could construct in Edwards a reincarnatable forebear and in her an Edwards authority and transmitter, but it is unconvincing play. Pieces of her writing merely echo his tone, an image, some reasoning—inconsequential scraps. She knew, for example, how to instate herself in the role of Edwards's "sinner":

> You have not only neglected your salvation, but you have wilfully taken direct courses to undo yourself. You have gone on in those ways and practices that have directly tended to your damnation, and have been perverse and obstinate in it. You cannot plead ignorance; you had all

---

5. Emily Dickinson may not have gotten the statement from Edwards at all; she may have taken it from the Bible, then attributed it to him as something she thought he would have said. If she read it in Edwards himself, she most likely got it from his sermon "Concerning the Endless Punishment of Those Who Die Impenitent," published among his Miscellanies in *Remarks on Important Theological Controversies* (Edinburgh, 1796), pp. 71, 80; Worcester edition, 1:630, 635. The verse from the Bible, as Professor Thomas Schafer of McCormick Theological Seminary reminds me, would have come irresistibly into the mind of almost anyone in mid-nineteenth-century New England. She uses it again in another poem, #1598, but without attribution to Edwards: " 'All' Rogues 'shall have their part in' what[?] / – The Phosphorous of God."

Millicent Todd Bingham writes of Edwards in Amherst:

> The long shadow of Jonathan Edwards, distant from 1850 in years but not in influence, still lay dark over Amherst. His ministry had begun in Northampton only seven miles away, and from that town his frightening message, instilling in many a sinner the fear of an angry God, had inspired the Great Awakening of the 1730's. . . . A century later the orthodox New Englander was still weighed down by his awareness of evil. . . . In his inaugural address President Heman Humphrey of Amherst College summed it up in these words: "Without the fear of God nothing can be secure for one moment." [*Emily Dickinson's Home: Letters of Edward Dickinson and His Family* (New York, 1955), pp. 32–33].

6. *Letters*, p. 701; poem #1522. She titled the poem "The Bumble Bee's Religion"; for the moment, apparently it was her own religion.

7. Her view of Calvin was similarly austere. "Repentance according to Calvin," she wrote in a letter in 1874, "is too late to be plausible" (*Letters*, p. 520). The best study of Emily Dickinson's understanding of Calvinism is Ronald Lanyi, " 'My Faith That Dark Adores – ': Calvinist Theology in the Poetry of Emily Dickinson," *Arizona Quarterly* 32 (autumn 1976): 264–78.

the light set before you that you could desire: God told you that you was
undoing yourself; but yet you would do it; he told you that the path you
was going in led to destruction, and counselled you to avoid it; but you
would not hearken: How justly therefore may God leave you to be
undone!⁸

I am continually putting off becoming a christian. Evil voices lisp in my
ear – There is yet time enough. I feel that every day I sin more and more
in closing my heart to the offers of mercy which are presented to me
freely. . . . Somehow or other I incline to other things – and Satan covers
them up with flowers, and I reach out to pick them. The path of duty
looks very ugly indeed – and the place where *I* want to go more
amiable – a great deal – it is so much easier to do wrong than right – so
much pleasanter to be evil than good, I don't wonder that good angels
weep – and bad ones sing songs.⁹

She knew how to define her self, as Edwards had demonstrated, in
terms of necessity, inclination, a willed and willing willessness:

A man never, in any instance, wills anything contrary to his desires, or
desires anything contrary to his will. . . . His will and desire don't run
counter at all: the thing which he wills, the very same he desires; and he
don't will a thing, and desire the contrary in any particular. . . . Volitions
are contingent events, in that sense, that their being and manner of
being is not fixed or determined by any cause, or anything antece-
dent. . . . If it be supposed that good or evil dispositions are implanted
in the hearts of men by nature itself . . . yet it is not commonly supposed
that men are worthy of no praise or dispraise for such dispositions;
although what is natural is undoubtedly necessary, nature being prior
to all acts of the will whatsoever.¹⁰

Experience is the Angled Road
Preferred against the Mind
By – Paradox – the Mind itself –
Presuming it to lead

Quite Opposite – How Complicate
The Discipline of Man –
Compelling Him to Choose Himself
His Preappointed Pain –

[#910]

8. "The Justice of God in the Damnation of Sinners," *The Works of President Edwards* (New York, 1864), 4:249.
9. *Letters*, pp. 27–28.
10. *Freedom of the Will*, ed. Paul Ramsey, in *The Works of Jonathan Edwards* (New Haven, 1957), 1:139, 190, 361. I think, however, that John Wheatcroft overestimates Emily Dickinson's ability to follow Edwards on the essence of the will ("Emily Dickinson's Poetry and Jonathan Edwards on the Will," *Bucknell Review* 10 [1961]: 102–27).

Further, she knew how to hunt for her worth after an Edwardsian manner—in the inherent good of her individual inclination:

> A holy disposition and spiritual taste, where grace is strong and lively, will enable a soul to determine what actions are right and becoming Christians, not only more speedily, but far more exactly, than the greatest abilities without it. . . . He has as it were a spirit within him, that guides him: the habit of his mind is attended with a taste, by which he immediately relishes that air and mien which is benevolent, and disrelishes the contrary, and causes him to distinguish between one and the other in a moment, more precisely, than the most accurate reasonings can find out in many hours. As the nature and inward tendency of a stone, or other heavy body, that is let fall from a loft, shows the way to the center of the earth, more exactly in an instant, than the ablest mathematician, without it, could determine, by his most accurate observations, in a whole day. Thus it is that a spiritual disposition and taste teaches and guides a man in his behavior in the world.[11]

> My Worthiness is all my Doubt –
> His Merit – all my fear –
> Contrasting which, my quality
> Do lowlier – appear –
>
> Lest I should insufficient prove
> For His beloved Need –
> The Chiefest Apprehension
> Upon my thronging Mind –
>
> 'Tis true – that Diety to stoop
> Inherently incline –
> For nothing higher than Itself
> Itself can rest upon –
>
> So I – the undivine abode
> Of His Elect Content –
> Conform my Soul – as twere a Church,
> Unto Her Sacrament –

[#751]

Her estimates of the life of man, though personalized, have, in addition, Edwards's toughness and morbidity:

> That propensity which has been proved to be in the nature of all mankind, must be a very evil, depraved and pernicious propensity; making

---

11. *Religious Affections*, ed. John E. Smith, in *Works* (1959), 2:283–84. Compare this statement with Emily Dickinson's view of predestinarian inclination from a letter of 1862: "There is much that is tenderly profane in even the sacredest Human Life – that perhaps it is instinct and not design, that dissuades us from it (*Letters*, p. 547).

it manifest that the soul of man, as it is my nature, is in a corrupt, fallen and ruined state.[12]

Of God we ask one favor,
That we may be forgiven –
For what, he is presumed to know –
The Crime, from us, is hidden –

[#1601]

Parallels such as these are authentic fragments of each in each; yet they prove nothing. Perhaps she could produce on her own what Edwards had produced. Perhaps she read him, perhaps he "read" *her.* Perhaps there was just enough of him left in Amherst air for her to breathe in and then out again on a few of her pages. A comparison of words and ideas gets at nothing essential.[13]

There is, to see her historical/religious context somewhat more dramatically, an Edwards in New England that Emily Dickinson very successfully resists *and* an Edwards that she very successfully echoes, then uses as a foil. Resisting the one Edwards that was dragged out in her youth—the one that expected commitment, ecstatic evidence, fear and trembling, a consistent heart, mindless devotion—she becomes one of the nineteenth century's best critics of American life. Her biographers put it too mildly: she more than left the church (while keeping its language and some of its constructs); she stood against it, stood up *to* it.

The Edwardsian revival in Amherst in her youth did not catch her, except as it deepened her self-examination, her self-dramatization, her self-satisfaction. This demurral has become a staple of her biography, for it is possible that it stirred almost all of her poems— debating, debunking, restating, reforming, replacing that movement. Neighbors remembered her after her death as "very early a rebel," and T. W. Higginson confessed he was most interested in "her—so to speak—unregenerate condition."[14] Protest is the genre of much of her poetry.

---

12. *Original Sin,* ed. Clyde A. Holbrook, in *Works* (1970): 3:128.
13. "Not the least of the paradoxes of her life," writes Thomas H. Johnson, "is the fact that she was closer to the Edwardsian core of thought than she ever really knew, or than were many of the orthodoxies preached in the Valley" (*Emily Dickinson: An Interpretive Biography* [Boston, 1955], p. 19). As Charles Anderson cautions, this does not hold for many of his doctrines: "Puritan dogma she found an empty shell, though she exploited its dramatization of man's life and death and fashioned a new poetry by playing variations on some of its philosophical themes" (*Emily Dickinson's Poetry: Stairway of Surprise* [New York, 1960], pp. 295–96). But this is not the whole truth. She does more than simply dramatize and vary what she knows and rejects. For her poetry, as for her life, she needed the pit of Puritanism as stimulus.

For example, she dropped out at Mount Holyoke. "My heart has been growing harder & more distant from the truth." She resisted the social pressures of religiously enthusiastic young friends in her late teens. "It is hard for me to give up the world." She refused to follow her family into church membership during the eight local awakenings that swept Amherst between 1840 and 1862. "I am standing alone in rebellion and growing very careless. . . . I am one of the lingering *bad* ones." In her late twenties she looked desperately for alternatives to the church. "The charms of the Heaven in the bush are superseded, I fear, by the Heaven in the hand, occasionally."[15] She successfully resisted ministers' designs on her soul for thirty years. "He preached such an awful sermon though, that I didn't much think I should ever see you again until the Judgment Day." She insisted on inverting the received. "'Consider the Lilies' is the only Commandment I ever obeyed." And making her own decisions. "I have heeded beautiful tempters, yet do not think I am wrong." She refused to grapple with theological issues reheated in her later years. "We . . . thought how hateful Jesus must be to get us into trouble when we had done nothing but Crucify him and that before we were born." She would not accept the local terms for defining religion. "I believe the love of God may be taught not to seem like bears." She consistently questioned Bible promises. "I seek and don't find, and knock and it is not opened. Wonder if God is just – presume he is, however, and t'was only a blunder of Matthew's." She ran from ritual. "When . . . all who loved the Lord Jesus Christ – were asked to remain . . . My flight kept time to the Words." She became more and more realistic about religious matters. "Should I . . . say all the facts as I saw them, it would send consternation." And she refused to her death to rescind the possibilities of her doubts. "'Tis a dangerous moment for anyone when the meaning goes out of things and Life stands straight – and punctual – and yet no signal comes. Yet such moments are." And yet at the same time she could cling tenaciously to her fundamentals. "You speak of 'disillusion.' That is one of the few subjects on which I am an infidel. Life is so strong a vision not any of it shall fail. Not what the stars have done, but what they are to do, is what detains the sky."[16]

But more than in this explicit rebelliousness of the letters in which she describes her stand, in her poetry—in fact, the fact of the poetry itself—we have a much stronger opposition. "Let Emily sing for you because she cannot pray," she wrote in a letter in 1863, "to

14. Leyda, *Years and Hours*, 2:65, 477.
15. In Bingham, *Emily Dickinson's Home*, p. 96.
16. *Letters*, pp. 30, 66, 82–83, 97–98, 263–64, 309, 372, 524–25, 774, 794, 919; Leyda, *Years and Hours*, 2:477.

keep the Dark away." Her "singing" ranges from questionings of dogmatic assertion ("We apologize to thee / For thine own Duplicity") to efforts at "looking oppositely / For the site of the Kingdom of Heaven"; that is, from thunderous no's to successful escapes into alternatives.[17]

She questions the local assumptions about salvation.

> Heaven is so far of the Mind
> ....
> No further 'tis, than Here –

[#369]

She doubts true-believing in favor of inherent ambiguity.

> For each extatic instant
> We must an anguish pay.

[#125]

She doubts the value of Christianity's easy system of rewards.

> I reason, that in Heaven –
> Somehow, it will be even –
> Some new Equation, given –
> But, what of that?

[#301]

She scoffs at the miraculous, the rational, the convincing. "What I see not, I better see." And then she scoffs at the opposite, personal faith. "This faith that watched for star in vain." And even scoffs at what is left her, her own desires. "Wonder . . . [is] a beautiful but bleak condition." She questions her own faith in faith. "The Dust like the Mosquito, buzzes round my faith." She debunks the notion of the liberal reform of religion.

> Belief, it does not fit so well
> When altered frequently –

[#1258]

She becomes bitter over easy religious answers. "O God! the Other one!" She fears the power of the abstract. "I know the Whole – obscures the Part." She defies the promise of Scripture.

---

17. *Letters*, pp. 561, 420–21. Compare her description of herself in 1850: "The path of duty looks very ugly indeed – and the place where *I* want to go more amiable – a great deal – it is so much easier to do wrong than right – so much pleasanter to be evil than good, I dont wonder that good angels weep – and bad ones sing songs" (*Letters*, p. 82).

> Sparrows, unnoticed by the father –
> Lambs for whom time had not a fold.
>
> [#141]

But at the same time she is afraid of her doubt. "Be sure you don't doubt about the sparrow." She questions ultimate justice.

> Why – do they shut Me out of Heaven?
> Did I sing – too loud?
>
> [#243]

She laughs at Christian hopes. "Bliss is unnatural." She doubts whether religious assertions about life and death make any sense.

> And through a Riddle, at the last –
> Sagacity, must go –
>
> [#501]

She qualifies her otherworldliness—

> When I believe the garden
> Mortal shall not see – . . .
> I can spare this summer, unreluctantly.
>
> [#40]

—with a far more convincing worldliness. "I often wonder how the love of Christ, is done – when that – below – holds so." She gives up on the Bible. "The Fiction of 'Santa Claus' always reminds me of the reply to my early question of 'who made the Bible' – 'Holy Men moved by the Holy Ghost,' and though I have now ceased my investigations, the Solution is insufficient." And yet she believes what she wants from it. "Guess I and the Bible will move to some old fashioned spot where we'll feel at Home." She parades her doubt of Christian personal assurances.

> "his Father,"
> I dont know him.
>
> [#127]

She demythologizes God—

> Himself – such a Dunce
>
> [#267]

—and godliness, too.

> As if a Kingdom – cared!
>
> [#260]

She even questions God's worth. "Is God Love's Adversary?" She finds ironic religion's claims of superiority. "Heaven hunts round for those that find itself below, and then it snatches." She mocks the push for joylessness.

> We reprimand the Happiness
> That too competes with heaven.

[#1601]

She finds discouragement in being religious—"Sermons on unbelief never did attract me"—and despair in not so being. "It is a Suffering, to have a sea – no care how Blue – between your Soul, and you." Finally, she turns on religion with a vengeance. "'We thank thee oh Father' for these strange minds that enamor us against Thee."[18]

What I am suggesting by this run-through of her spiritual biography is that perhaps Emily Dickinson is best seen (with Hawthorne and Melville) as an objector to the extremes to which American religion could be taken. "Grant me, Oh Lord, a sunny mind," she writes defiantly, hopefully, "Thy windy will to bear!" Though she was stimulated by Edwardsian Puritanism as part of the Amherst awakenings (which Samuel Bowles scoffed at by saying, "All Amherst was praying, & scarifying the body & torturing the soul into affected humility"),[19] she turned against (and when she came to the writing of her poetry, turned *on*) its idealism, its sentimentalized moralism, its cosmic sadism, its vacuity of glee.

> When much in the Woods as a little Girl, I was told that the Snake would bite me, that I might pick a poisonous flower, or Goblins kidnap me, but I went along and met no one but Angels, who were far shyer of me than I could be of them, so I hav'nt that confidence in fraud which many exercise.[20]

Her dissatisfaction with the tradition, her questions of its theology, her discarding of ideas and manners expected of her—these are the moral adjustment of a rebel. This "child of evangelical Amherst," as Richard Wilbur calls her, had not only a "Sweet Skepticism of the Heart" (her own name for it) but also a streak of stubborn resistance, what she called her "abdication of Belief." Desiring on the one hand a more catholic Christianity and esthetic liberation ("that Religion / That doubts – as fervently as it believes") and needing on the other the tough individualism of Calvinism ("eat[ing] of hell-fire," she called it), she mocked the evangelism going on around her as having neither. Not exactly defiant and outraged and not really reformist, she nonetheless saw the threat of American religion.

18. Leyda, *Years and Hours*, 2:58.
19. Sewall, *Life*, pp. 24–25.
20. *Letters*, p. 415.

Emily Dickinson found American religion out. She found out its exclusiveness—that what was organic and necessary to her life was unacceptable, that in fact *she* was unacceptable. It had her without having any place for her.[21] Furthermore, it created a world within, without putting much of anything within that world; it was barren beyond belief, without the abundance that she found the Bible and her own senses expected of religion. It was, above all, an artifice, a structure, an invention, a *made* world—which gave her leave to construct a faith (really an *un*constructed mode) of her own. And so she tended to reject creeds, ministers, and church in favor of simple introspection and a more pleasant existence. "The mind of the heart must live," she wrote in a letter in 1877, "if its clerical part do not."

> I rise, because the sun shines, and sleep has done with me, and I brush my hair, and dress me, and wonder what I am and who has made me so, and then I wash the dishes, and anon wash them again, and then 'tis afternoon, and Ladies call, and evening, and some members of another sex come in to spend the hour, and then that day is done. And prithee, what is Life?[22]

Her rebellion discovered to her (after a unique manner) her religious needs—needs that would at times turn to a nostalgia for what she called "God's old fashioned vows," not knowing very precisely what they were; needs that would stir her minister in Amherst in 1866 to confidently declare her "rather less in need of spiritual light than any person he knew" and a friend of her middle years to say she was "deeply imbued with the essential spirit of the New Testament and of our Lord and Savior Jesus Christ";[23] needs that she had to find her own means to satisfy. The local obituary said of her faith (it was written by her sister-in-law Sue, who knew her beliefs well): "With no creed, no formulated faith, hardly knowing the names of dogmas, she walked this life with the gentleness and reverence of old saints, with the firm step of martyrs who sing while they suffer."[24] Her rebelliousness can be overstated, for it was also a religious search: "Whether Deity's guiltless - / My business is, to find!" But the most important

---

21. There is an attractive argument about the relationship of Emily Dickinson's loss of close friends to her rejection of Christianity in Francis J. Molson, "Emily Dickinson's Rejection of the Heavenly Father," *New England Quarterly* 47 (September 1974): 404–26. "The evidence of Dickinson's correspondence does suggest that one major reason for her rejection of the Heavenly Father was her conviction that He reneged in His promise to give her heaven, her 'golden dream' and her 'dear fancy,' all of which represented for Emily Dickinson her expectations of success in friendship and love."

22. *Letters,* p. 304.

23. MacGregor Jenkins, *Emily Dickinson, Friend and Neighbor* (Boston, 1930), pp. 80–82; Richard B. Sewall, ed., *The Lyman Letters: New Light on Emily Dickinson and Her Family* (Amherst, 1965), p. 67.

24. *Springfield Daily Republican,* 15 May 1886.

fact is that her religious search was coterminous with her writing of poetry. Before that time, she could fear a sermon on "the disappointment of Jesus in Judas" and love a hymn telling "how blest the righteous when he dies." Early, a religious feeling occurred in her periodically even when she did not want it to and did not know how to account for it:

> I've heard an Organ talk, sometimes –
> In a Cathedral Aisle,
> And understood no word it said –
> Yet held my breath, the while –
>
> And risen up – and gone away,
> A more Bernardine Girl –
> Yet – know not what was done to me
> In that old Chapel Aisle.
>
> [#183]

But by the time she began writing poetry in earnest—1858 and 1859—her religious interests were more troubled and her life became thereafter a coherent confusion of doubts and hopes. "I pray for the tenants of that holy chamber, the wrestler, and the wrestled for."[25]

> I, grown shrewder – scan the Skies
> With a suspicious Air –
> As Children – swindled for the first
>
> [#476]

Emily Dickinson's religious state—and we find it to have been fairly consistent after the New England revival of 1859, a happening coinciding with her first poetry—was that of liminality. She got caught between institutions and free form. She found herself outside limits—and enjoyed the trouble it caused within her. It was for her, she discovered, not a state of weakness, as she had perhaps feared, but a condition of being deliberately lost because honestly unknowing. As liminalist, she then had the roles of a person lost in the forest, a bisexual, a mind in transition, someone obsessed with her own subjectivity, an ambiguist. She therefore often elevated the lack of structural roles to a virtue, even when the break with structure made her more captive of history, captive of the Edwards in her. The condition was of advantage to her because it gave her the opportunity to fantasize without incurring the obligations of community. Her efforts to achieve this liminality suggest, too, that however subjective she became, she did not become radical and could therefore move out of religion without moving away from it.

25. *Letters*, p. 356.

The major irony of being this sort of seeker is that she found in the faith she rejected a means of hope. She was sure her rejection/ search gave her sure religious ground to stand on. "I have lived by this, . . ." she wrote to Sue Dickinson in 1854, "though in that last day, the Jesus Christ you love, remark he does not know me—there is a darker spirit [that] will not disown it's child."[26]

Here is the important point: though she laughs at the Protestant evangelism of her time, whether in the form of the renewal of Puritan tortures or the intellectual revivalism of Transcendentalism, she finds she needs the individualistic Calvinism inherent in it as provided by the Edwardsian cosmology.

Awful to need what one rejects; but the ambivalence defines her religious position well. Her Christian optimism made it possible for her to locate her Puritan hope in Puritan tragedy. That harmony is one of the most remarkable features of her poetry. It made it possible for her to sustain her remarkably strong Christian faith ("I believe we shall in some manner be cherished by our Maker – that the one who gave us this remarkable earth has the power still further to surprise that which he has caused. Beyond, all is silence") and then turn on herself with the disclaimer, "I am but a Pagan." Puritanism provided not only the instinct for writing in her covenanted womanhood and the linguistic means for moving within faith, as we saw in her connections with Anne Bradstreet and Edward Taylor, but also a tragedy that stimulated her writing. "To be willing [that] the Kingdom of Heaven should invade our own requires years of sorrow."[27]

Puritanism did more than provide Emily Dickinson with drama. It stimulated a search. She plays the game of Lost Soul so well and so often that one is tempted to believe she really wanted to be one, or at least that she cultivated the role in order to make herself productive:

> I'm banished - now - you know it -
> How foreign that can be -
> You'll know - Sir - when the Savior's face
> Turns so - away from you -
>
> [#256]

For a letter of 1881 to Mrs. Holland, she found a good symbol of herself in this regard: the possibility of roses in the hard soil of a Puritan garden. "Vails of Kamtchatka dim the Rose - in my Puritan garden, and as a farther stimulus, I had an Eclipse of the sun a few Mornings ago, but every Crape is charmed. I knew a Bird that would

26. *Letters,* p. 306.
27. *Letters,* p. 914.

sing as firm in the centre of Dissolution, as in it's Father's nest."[28] When tragedy is thus "charmed" in New England, hell can give forth poets and their songs, even in "the centre of Dissolution." Her concurrent Puritan attraction and repulsion yielded her a world of her own. This Puritan struggle she called "The Battle fought between the Soul / And No Man."

The real Edwards in Emily Dickinson, therefore, is the one who digs a pit so that humanity might have firm footing for their lives, the one who keeps turning out the lights of the world to force one inward to the basis of one's condition, the one who paints the religious life dangerous and fascinating, the one who is obsessed with the dark sources of one's strength. He is a security and stimulus for her. Her Edwards is a distortion, a decapitation, a disheartening, a necrolepsy, but nonetheless the push she needed.

However else Edwards might be offered up in the intellectual history of the nineteenth century—the animator of the divine in nature to Emerson or the designer of the demonic in the divine to Melville—the Edwards that came down to Emily Dickinson was tough, definite, sure of sin and damnation, beloved of a satanic God, representative of a smothering cosmic gloom. Like Hawthorne, she needed to make Puritan things look demonic/daemonical. With him she *dug* the Puritan pit we have come to believe was part of the Puritan landscape.

It is not so much that she thought they believed it existed as that she needed that pit to symbolize the dark side of herself and to use as launching pad for her own poetic/spiritual soarings. Her fascination with the hellishness she found (or created) is all the more remarkable in view of her basic natural optimism and hopefulness. It is a deliberate device. It is not surprising that one of the stories about her handed down in the family is that she liked to ask prominent friends of her father, "Oh, sir, may one eat of hell-fire with impunity here?" For her poetry she needed to try doing so.[29]

One might feel that the Edwards in Emily Dickinson could be her impulse to worry about her inclination, her nature, as the Edwards of *Freedom of the Will* recommends. She appears unable to locate it as she fishes around inside herself, finds that it is awfully ambiguous, yet is sure that some inclination somewhere in her goes in a damnable direction, not up. One finds her convinced that she is fixed forever, incapable of any new nature or sense, unable to change

28. *Letters,* p. 687.
29. Leyda, *Years and Hours,* 1:328.

except to increase her intensity and depth. One may think she accepts her nature as a given. She is "the natural man," and she accepts her human base in an insufficient nature.

Or one might feel that she could please the Edwards of *Religious Affections,* peeling off the sweet petals of her happiness to get at the real source of her worth. She might be seen as willing to live with her illusions, but not for long. The misery of the search is a superior security. Such softer indicators of piety as excitement of the senses, articulation, epiphanies, abundance, comfort and joy, devotion— Edwards's catalog of human delusions—offer little or no security to her. Edwards might have admired the self-conscious sophistication.

Or it might be felt that the Edwards in her could be her struggle to preserve the unity and integrity of the self, her lifelong effort. Though with Emily Dickinson it was no longer a matter of piety, she thought herself acceptable, like the Edwards of *Original Sin,* only with the *whole* heart engaged and the self *as a whole* inclined toward glory in a love that is unmixed. Primary was the integrity of the self in all actions and affections. She could thus have some basis for judging the state of her own soul. Perhaps Edwards's fideism became her imperial independence.

> Adventure most unto itself
> The Soul condemned to be –
> Attended by a single Hound
> It's own identity.
>
> [#822]

But while these large issues of the Edwards Connecticut Valley post-Puritanism were also large issues for her, they form the subject of her poems without building the structures that underlie her behavior and thinking. They describe her arbitrary interests without proscribing the assumptions out of which her subjects grew. They tell what she thought without telling us how her mind worked. What she gives to her poems is not their conclusions but the way she arrives at her conclusions. From the structures of reality stored in her mind she drew forth the one that looks like an Edwards we can know.

There is a particular Puritanism, I am suggesting, that fascinated and repulsed Emily Dickinson. When she attributes to Edwards the statement "All liars shall have their part in the lake that burneth with fire and brimstone," she makes him symbolize a particular fanaticism. In her poems she makes a world that is, to be sure, one of the worlds one can find in Edwards *after* reading her poems.

She read Edwards—or his tradition—*for the terror.* It is a world under judgment, under pressure, a world subsumed, even co-opted, certainly exhausted, by a God who has changed his role of lover and redeemer for that of avenger and murderer. "It is part of the majesty and glory of God, that he is a terrible God." It is a world defined in terms of predicament, and predicament in terms of tragedy, fallenness, desolation, burial, impotence, wasteland. "How just is it that God should make [all men] useful in their sufferings!" This particular world, as Edwards imagined it, is "a loathsome prison, the receptacle of the filth and rubbish of the universe," where mankind is "in universal and desperate wickedness," under condemnation, and "tormented with the most racking pain and anguish." It is, as in Kierkegaardian existentialism, hell transferred to the present moment. "The creation is made subject to vanity, and brought into the bondage of corruption; . . . the whole creation groans, and travails in pain under this bondage." Man in his condition of totalitarian dependence—"the pit," as Edwards often called it—becomes xenophobic, because of the climate of fear, and dupe, because matters of creation and judgment, good and evil are kept a mystery. The condition, inherent in being and the being and a being, is both fixed and fortunate, suspending man in an ambiguity of hope and hopelessness. In this apocalyptic thinking, hell becomes an independent reality, a surrogate absolute. The supernumerary becomes an antagonist.[30]

Emily Dickinson's poems are a veritable tour of Edwards's hell.

A Pit – but Heaven over it –
And Heaven beside, and Heaven abroad;
And yet a Pit –
With Heaven over it.

To stir would be to slip –
To look would be to drop –
To dream – to sap the Prop
That holds my chances up.
Ah! Pit! With Heaven over it!

The depth is all my thought –
I dare not ask my feet –
'Twould start us where we sit
So straight you'd scarce suspect
It was a Pit – with fathoms under it
Its Circuit just the same
Seed – summer – tomb –
Whose Doom to whom

[#1712]

30. Edwards, *Works* (1864), 4:215, 306, 307, 310.

This is an Edwardsian pit full of "Doom," with heaven above and all around it. But Emily Dickinson's interest is not in heaven; instead, "The depth is all my thought." The pit dominates her life, through "Seed - summer - tomb," and so all that is left is illusions, dreams, hopes, and all undependable. She spits out her words in this poem because she is repulsed by the hell of the human condition, and her heartrending rhythms express the pathos she feels at this fact ("Ah! Pit! With Heaven over it!"). The awfulness of her vision energizes her speech. The "fathoms" both attract her and move her to a spiteful action. Rebellion and attraction are one act. Repelled, she is propelled to writing.

What it all comes to is that Emily Dickinson had needed, in an existential manner, to transfer hell to the present moment. She wanted hell *now* and spent much of her poetic energy in deliberately constructing it. "Emerging from an Abyss, and reentering it," she wrote in a letter to Sue in 1885, "that is Life, is it not?"

The remarkable thing about her approach is that she learned to turn the hell she was taught to believe in (and live in) into a full life.

> Impossibility, like Wine
> Exhilirates the Man
> Who tastes it; Possibility
> Is flavorless . . .
>
> [#838]

Acceptance of the pit would have been merely stoical, merely existential. Hers is an *American* stoicism, turning the pit into something productive, turning tragedy into hope, turning the dark into an opportunity.

> My loss, by sickness - Was it Loss?
> Or that Etherial Gain
> One learns by measuring the Grave -
> Then - measuring the Sun -
>
> [#574]

She boasts that the qualities of life in the pit—anguish, pain, death, despair, disappointment, anxiety—are productive. She has a world in which she can stoically accept life as a burden—but with hope:

> Our share of night to bear -
> Our share of morning -
> Our blank in bliss to fill
> Our blank in scorning -
>
> [#113]

Power comes from pain, her self from struggle, her poems from the pit. It is a trite argument, given the centuries that defended the pious rationalization that it is good if it hurts ("An actual suffering strengthens / As Sinews do, with age")—except that Emily Dickinson *doesn't* believe in the pit yet uses it to stimulate herself to power. It is hell that holds up her heaven. The "fathoms" give her world a depth, a height.

This is not mere renunciation, one of her more attractive attributes in current criticism, but esthetic use of what she morally and intellectually rejects. Renunciation is passive, but her uses of Edwards's pit are creative, aggressive. Her discovery was that she could use one set of things (the dark Puritanism she learned and left) as spur for another set (freedom, excitement, a sensed life, fulfillment). Life, she announces with conviction in one poem, is "Hopeless – / And therefore Good." And recoiling from the hopelessness, she finds, because of her obsession with contrariety, the opportunity for hope. "How sweet I shall not lack in Vain – / But gain – thro' loss – Through Grief – obtain – " [#968]. Misery is "As hopeless – as divine." As a stimulus for herself, she therefore constructs an Edwardsian hell to point herself the opposite way:

> By homely gift and hindered Words
> The human heart is told
> Of Nothing –
> "Nothing" is the force
> That renovates the World –
>
> [#1563]

The renovation of nothing into something is a description of her imagination working out the presumption of the pit and then filling it with the abundant assumption of herself. The light is already animated, but the dark—" 'Nothing' "—requires an act of imagination, and therefore something dredged out of oneself.

This can be taken for a tragic view of life—or rather, for a tragic life. Life in the pit is obsessive. But she did not succumb to the "whirl and mutability" of the darker events of her life[31] and had the stamina to find in loss a stimulus, an impetus:

> Winter under cultivation
> Is as arable as Spring
>
> [#1707]

31. This is a position of Clark Griffith, *The Long Shadow: Emily Dickinson's Tragic Poetry* (Princeton, 1964), who gives Emily Dickinson so many crises, pains and disasters, anxieties and disappointments that it is a wonder she survived to fifty-five. He has her

"Soil of Flint," as she asserts in another poem, "if steady tilled - / Will refund the Hand."

What she calls her "City of the Dead," her "box of Phantoms," her "chained steps"—a world characterized by loss of friends and opportunities—stirs her to writing and living fully. We have the fact that the "coffin / In the heart" gave her much of her poetry right from the outset: the death of individuals is so dominantly the subject of her first two years' poems that we may suspect it was the initial impetus for her caring to write at all.[32] We have the fact, too, that the long string of severed relationships and interrupted contracts about which she allowed herself an indulgent empathy made a "Cavalry of Wo... within the bosom."[33] And we have the fact that for Emily Dickinson, after she came to the enjoyment of life, nature, and growth, hell became quite simply the awareness that things fade, and that, after she came to her optimism about the possibilities for her work and mind, hell consisted most insistently in the fact that alternatives exclude and exhaust. "Beware," she wrote to herself, "lest this little brook of life, / Some burning noon go dry!"

In other words, tragedy is the mother of her beauty. That was because she discovered, within the Puritanism she hated but was

---

constantly in "a metaphysical quandary." He fails to see that she had the ability to turn these difficulties to her creative advantage.

32. To Dr. Holland and his family she wrote this remarkable note in late 1858, at about the same time she wrote her first poems: "I cant stay any longer in a world of death. Austin is ill of fever. I buried my garden last week - Our man, Dick, lost a little girl through the scarlet fever. I thought perhaps that *you* were dead, and not knowing the sexton's address, interrogate the daisies. Ah! dainty - dainty Death! Ah, democratic Death! Grasping the proudest zinnia from my purple garden - then deep to his bosom calling the serf's child! Say, is he everywhere? Where shall I hide my things? Who is alive? The woods are dead." And this note to Samuel Bowles in 1859: "I have two acquaintance[s], the 'Quick and the Dead' - and would like more." And this note to Mrs. Holland in 1883: "The Crisis of the sorrow of so many years is all that tires me" (*Letters*, pp. 341, 352, 802).

33. To Sue Gilbert she wrote this extraordinary confession about death and friends in 1854: "You need not fear to leave me lest I should be alone, for I often part with things I fancy I have loved - sometimes to the grave and sometimes to an oblivion rather bitterer than death - thus my heart bleeds so frequently that I shant mind the hemorrhage, and I only add an agony to several previous areas and at the end of day remark - a bubble burst! Such incidents would grieve me when I was but a child and perhaps I could have wept when little feet hard as mine, stood still in the coffin, but eyes grow dry sometimes and hearts get crisp and cinder, and had as lief burn." To Mrs. Holland she wrote this pathetic note in 1859: "Pardon my sanity, Mrs. Holland, in a world *insane*, and love me if you will, for I had rather *be* loved than to be called a king in earth, or a lord in Heaven." And to Samuel Bowles in 1862 she wrote how disappointing human relations were to her: "How extraordinary that Life's large population contain so few of power to us - and those - a vivid species - who leave no mode - like Tyrian Dye" (*Letters*, pp. 305–6, 418).

haunted by, the stimulating effect of opposites. "When I am most happy," she wrote in a letter to Abiah Root in 1846, "there is a sting in every enjoyment. I find no rose without a thorn."[34] "Pain for peace prepares," she wrote in one poem soon after that, "springs from winters rise, . . . night stands first – *then* noon / To gird us for the sun." In hell one is beguiled of heaven:

> As Watchers hang upon the East,
> As beggars revel at a feast
> By savory Fancy spread –
> As brooks in deserts babble sweet
> On ear too far for the delight,
> Heaven beguiles the tired.
>
> As that same watcher, when the East
> Opens the lid of Amethyst
> And lets the morning go –
> That Beggar, when an honored Guest,
> Those thirsty lips to flagons pressed,
> Heaven to us, if true.

[#121]

According to a ratio built into necessity, in her mind, anguish yields to, even makes possible, ecstasy:

> For each extatic instant
> We must an anguish pay
> In keen and quivering ratio
> To the extasy.

[#125]

> Delight – becomes pictorial –
> When viewed through Pain –

[#572]

> Transporting must the moment be –
> Brewed from decades of Agony!

[#207]

> Best Gains – must have the Losses' Test –
> To constitute them – Gains –

[#684]

> A Bomb upon the Ceiling
> Is an improving thing –

34. *Letters,* pp. 27–28.

It keeps the nerves progressive
Conjecture flourishing –

[#1128]

When she asserts that "Success is counted sweetest – / By those who
ne'er succeed," she is careful that we understand how *first* must come
the "sorest need" and "agony" and defeat—and *then* victory and comprehension. Or, as she has it in another place, in order to experience
exultation, one must *first* be "an inland soul" and *then* go to the sea—
that is, withdrawal and deprivation come before excitement and fulfillment. "Fitter to see Him, I may be," she rationalizes, "For the long
Hindrance."

How easy it becomes for her to speak of

The Stimulus there is
In Danger – Other impetus
Is numb – and Vitalless –
As 'twere a Spur – upon the Soul –

[#770]

This spur to the soul ("Danger – deepens Sum – ") would naturally lead
to the cultivation of opposites—that is, self-conscious concentration
on her despair, morbid watching of the dead, analytical gossip about
her pains, her personal watch upon the shadows—all for the sake of
stimulating herself oppositely. She needs the dark in which to light
her own way.

But she was not so simple-minded as to hold the theorem that
any action of the heart or mind must trigger an equal and opposite
reaction, only that hell has its purposes—esthetic purposes, perhaps,
more than spiritual/geographical purposes. It motivates. We might
suspect that she knew how such an esthetic was antitheological: religion cannot survive in a world of action and reaction but only in a
world in decline and decay.

Emily Dickinson's Edwardsian apocalytic—there is up only after
being downed, drama only from doom, damnation and *then* the
dreams—is not the same as Emersonian compensationism, a more
sentimental eschatology. In compensation everything is righted in
one's hopes. In Emily Dickinson's carefully selected and foiled
Puritanism, happiness is not solid ("the least push of Joy / Breaks up
my feet"); but anguish and death *can* be depended on ("How far is it
to Heavcen? / As far as Death this way – "). For her there is, instead, a
security in despair:

The Mind is smooth – no Motion –
Contented as the Eye

> Upon the Forehead of a Bust –
> That knows – it cannot see –
>
> [#305]

The pit has footing; hell is an absolute. Perhaps this is a terrifying security, but it is without destructive fear and anxiety. "I like a look of Agony, / Because I know it's true." Knowing she is in hell does not change the awfulness for her, but it does remove anxiety. "He deposes Doom," she writes, "who hath suffered him." At those moments when metamorphosis seems impossible to her, she clings to predestination, which works a transcendentalizing magic on her imagination: the self is secure, beyond perplexities, eternal.

Therefore, hell is, if force-fed with the productive energy Puritan hopes encouraged (really daemonic), an impetus to her:

> A *Wounded* Deer – leaps highest –
> I've heard the Hunter tell –
> 'Tis but the Extasy of *death* –
> And then the Brake is still!
>
> The *Smitten* Rock that gushes!
> The *trampled* Steel that springs!
> A Cheek is always redder
> Just where the Hectic stings!
>
> [#165]

Fill the horror with one's own personal daemonic and there is hope. The dark side is therefore the necessary precursor to fulfillment.

> Water, is taught by thirst.
> Land – by the Oceans passed.
> Transport – by throe –
> Peace – by it's battles told –
> Love, by Memorial Mold –
> Birds, by the Snow.
>
> [#135]

One does not learn the superior until he has experienced the inferior. Thus, a world in which suffering makes for intensity, sickness arouses consciousness, disorder raises the level of feeling, pain projects substance into existence, ordeal gives one something solid to hold onto, involuntary evil gives one's ego a unity—countering the world's flagrant unreality with sensations. Hell teaches.

> The Zeroes – taught us – Phosphorus –
> We learned to like the Fire
> By playing Glaciers – when a Boy –
> And Tinder – guessed – by power

Of Opposite - to balance Odd -
If White - a Red - must be!
Paralysis - our Primer - dumb -
Unto Vitality![35]

[#689]

By virtue of the "power / Of Opposite," she achieves the "Vitality" she desires. The genre of her method is therefore not tragedy but Christian apocalyptic—Emily Dickinson making Edwards's fears esthetic.

The position is inventive if, in Emily Dickinson at least, near-pathological. She is sure that "A chastened Grace is Twice a Grace - / Nay 'tis a Holiness." She finds it of value to her to "learn the Transport by the Pain - / As Blind Men learn the sun!" This is a Puritan existentialism: justification of life in the hell of this world because it is necessary to (in fact, encourages the concerted *creation* of) what's better. This condition she calls "the Sovereign Anguish" and "the signal wo." The destitution is not so sumptuous most of the time as has been presumed of her—merely necessary.[36] It is instead a condition of productive opposites: pain in order to know transport, blindness in order to know the sun, thirst in order to know the brooks, homesickness on a foreign shore in order to know "the blue-beloved air." The structure of opposites is an earthly one; yet she makes out of it a cosmology: our "voices [are] trained - below" and then can "Ascend in ceaseless Carol." As a cosmology her structures of productive opposites ("Defeat whets Victory. . . . 'Tis Thirsting - vitalizes Wine") is most like Melville's system of horologicals and chronometricals ("the drop of Anguish / That scalds me now" enlightens her "when Time is over"), but as an obsessive teleology her resignation to the condition of the world is a kind of pride: because she has trudged through the pit, she finds it possible, even necessary, to dream elaborately. "Our poverty entitle us . . . to supersede the Earth." Her system of opposites is a Puritan justification of hell:

'Tis Opposites - entice -
Deformed Men - ponder Grace -
. . . .

To lack - enamor Thee -

[#355]

35. Emily Dickinson wrote this poem after Samuel Bowles had referred to her in a letter to her brother in 1863 as "the Queen Recluse" who "has 'overcome the world.'" He describes her as "indulging in a sort of disgust at every thing & every body" (Leyda, *Years and Hours*, 2:76–77).

36. Richard Wilbur, "Sumptuous Destitution," in *Emily Dickinson: Three Views* (Amherst, 1960), is best on this theme but fails to identify the theology behind it or to recognize how the idea serves as stimulus.

The emphasis breeds faith in the better. First deformity, then grace. First lack and then desire. "To be assisted of Reverse," she insists, "One must Reverse have bore." Life for her is "An Ablative estate"; "This," she says, "instigates an appetite / Precisely opposite." In her hunger for what she calls "Glee," a sensed grace, she cultivates—in her life as in her imagination—that which is "precisely opposite," anticipating "reverse." She could thus participate in a mystery: beauty requires contrast, and contrast is fundamental to the creation of intense feeling.

As if she had read Kierkegaard, though still in the revived Edwardsian affections of her puritanized life, she finds (or rather makes *sure* she finds) hope and faith possible only in hell: after "decades of Agony" then "Better will be the Extasy." A chronometrical world, to extend Melville's Manichaean metaphor, teaches one to prefer the horological one:

> Two Seasons, it is said, exist –
> The Summer of the Just,
> And this of Our's, diversified
> With Prospect, and with Frost –
>
> May not our Second with it's First
> So infinite compare
> That We but recollect the one
> The other to prefer?
>
> [#930]

This smacks of Emersonian compensationism, as I said, but more than that, of cultivation of deprivation to heighten the hope. It smacks, too, of the moralistic: difficulty strengthens; there are rewards to one's hell. We gain power from the discipline that pain makes possible:

> Power is only Pain –
> Stranded, thro' Discipline,
> Till Weights – will hang –
>
> [#252]

Yet the sentimentality ("Trite," she admits, "is that Affliction which is sanctified") takes on some of the toughness of Taylor and Edwards when one realizes that what she has accepted (for her creative purposes) is the idea that affliction is a form of grace. Despair, for example, she calls "An imperial affliction / Sent us of the Air"; it gives a "Heavenly Hurt" that makes an "internal difference, / Where the Meanings, are."

Further, in a perfect Edwardsian poem, the hellish is creative, the pit full of glee, the chthonic full of sensation and life:

'Tis so appalling - it exhilirates -
So over Horror, it half Captivates -
The Soul stares after it, secure -
To know the worst, leaves no dread more -

[#281]

The awful stimulates—if, that is, "The Soul . . . [is] secure." It forces
one to grapple and conquer. The "Ghastly" makes possible a "Gay . . .
Holiday" (#281). She convinces herself of the dark to force faith in
(and enjoyment of) the light. The Edwardsian pit is in this way an
intensifier of life. This Kierkegaardian faith ("I see thee better - in the
Dark - / I do not need a Light - ") is, again, not a principle of sumptuous destitution or compensation, but of opposition: the dark makes
imagination possible, even necessary. But there *must* be the dark, the
pit.

For Emily Dickinson there is always the question, as there was
for Edwards, of being qualified, of worth, acceptable. She believes hell
qualifies one. She finds there are two kinds of "Ripenings"—one that
is easy, the other

A homelier maturing -
A process in the Bur -
That teeth of Frosts alone disclose
In far October Air.

[#332]

The harder way is not preferable, because painful, but gives greater
awareness.

Through the Dark Sod - as Education -
The Lily passes sure -

[#392]

This is hell intellectualized.

No Man can understand
But He that hath endured
The Dissolution - in Himself -
That Man - be qualified

To qualify Despair. . . .

[#539]

Her need for Edwards's pit is a greed for fulfillment, for life. Hellish
consequences she often accepts with spiritual snobbery. She can intellectually reconcile herself to what she knows to be the human condition only as long as she can infuse it with her overweening hopefulness. It exists, cruelly, painfully—*that* she accepts. But she goes beyond such stoicism and gives hell a Yankee/Puritan productivity. In

her poem beginning "A Tooth upon Our Peace / The Peace cannot deface," she asks the question, "Then Wherefore be the Tooth?" and her answer is, "To vitalize the Grace." For her, "The Heaven hath a Hell – / Itself to signalize." She asks herself what the reason is for the human condition, and since she believes in grace and heaven she concludes that it is to their service: vitalizing and signalizing the superior.

She has still another poem on the point:

> Far from Love the Heavenly Father
> Leads the Chosen Child,
> Oftener through Realm of Briar
> Than the Meadow mild.
>
> Oftener by the Claw of Dragon
> Than the Hand of Friend
> Guides the Little One predestined
> To the Native Land.

[#1021]

She does not necessarily like the dragon's-claw system; yet she accepts its validity, for it is productive of the grace/glee she wants. For her, "The Misery [is] a Compact – / As hopeless – as divine." There is, as there was for Edwards, a grace built into the hopelessness, the hellishness—almost a covenant of grace, making one productive in the pit after an American fashion.

Yet Emily Dickinson's is not quite what Denis Donaghue calls "the American style of failure."[37] It romanticizes her too much to say that, like James and Adams, she made her works out of despair, that her style comes from an apparent failure, and that she had the ability to make something out of virtually nothing. Her tone is not that of success in the face of the awful, but of gratitude for the devil. Poetry is not so much her way of coping as her way of getting some feeling into things. She is, after all, a sensationalist. If this is redemption-through-breakdown, it is a consciously cultivated agony that begets the circumference she desires:

> Must be a Wo –
> A loss or so –
> To bend the eye
> Best Beauty's way –

[#571]

---

37. Denis Donaghue, "The American Style of Failure," *Sewanee Review* 82 (summer 1974): 407–32.

First woe and then beauty, since, in her Edwardsian apocalyptic, hell "bend[s] the eye" in the opposite direction. The hopeless is good, the impossible delightful, the dark light, the damned fulfilling.

> Delight – becomes pictorial –
> When viewed through Pain –
> More fair – because impossible
> That any gain –

[#572]

"Trials are of further benefit to true religion," Edwards writes in his less-anxious tone.

> They make its genuine beauty and amiableness remarkably to appear. True virtue never appears so lovely, as when it is most oppressed: and the divine excellency of real Christianity is never exhibited with such advantage, as when under the greatest trials: then it is that true faith appears much more precious than gold; and upon this account, is found to praise, and honor, and glory.... They tend to cause the amiableness of true religion to appear to the best advantage, as was before observed; and not only so, but they tend to increase its beauty, by establishing and confirming it, and making it more lively and vigorous and purifying it from those things that obscured its luster and glory.[38]

Her life is turned "Beauty's way" by such trial, by what she calls "A loss or so"—as with Edwards, an estheticizing of the pit. Her life, her mind, and her poetry are, as she has it in another poem, "the gift of Screws":

> Essential Oils – are wrung –
> The Attar from the Rose
> Be not expressed by Suns – alone –
> It is the gift of Screws –

[#675]

Her theory of opposition in all things—the pit producing her poetry—is apparently motive enough for putting herself imaginatively into hell. She lowers herself deeper into Edwards's pit than any other major writer in that Edwards-bestirred time, the better to stir her own desires and hopes and visions. "Art," she writes, "[is] Acquired by Reverse."

It would be a temptation to allow Emily Dickinson her Edwards as a psychosis—to "eat," as she put it, "of hell-fire with impunity here." But we cannot know her needs or motives thoroughly, how the stimulus worked in her, or why it assumed such erratic, agonizing

---

38. *Religious Affections*, p. 93.

shapes in her poems. Certainly her objective was not to make her pain public. We do not even know if the hell was genuine, for her subjects are others' deaths (or playing the role of the dead), pains hyperbolized to the point of theater, conflicts nurtured for the sake of the poems themselves—that is, hell *imagined*. Biography cannot give us the fact of her needs.

We can only know that in her poetry her fight against both hard-core and nineteenth-century-sentimentalized Puritanism and her coterminous use of them as a spur is a productive syntax. It itself is a system of opposites like the one she constructed in Puritanism itself ("by power / Of Opposite") and one in which she felt her productivity and her religious sustenance "assisted of Reverse." This juxtaposition catches the role of contradition, opposition, and paradox in her experience and points up her remarkable ability to make artful her synthesis of two apparently contradictory directions in the culture—a rejection of the past plus a need for the past, resulting in a creative energy.

That she chose certain combinations from the Puritan repertoire of ideas which she found possible to reconstitute should now be apparent: she is the representative of important underlying opposites of culture. Opposition is one way her mind is structured. Her attitudes are diffuse and her language protean, but her mind operated (to her great advantage, as it turned out) according to an underlying structure, which she perhaps invented or which she inherited from some infrastructure in the culture. However it was, it was one of her major properties to move herself to writing by needing what she hated. By her example, emergence through opposition becomes an esthetic principle.

For a poetic theory, Edwardsian apocalyptic is, in Emily Dickinson's hands at least, an inventive position. If indeed "Art / [is] Acquired by Reverse," then her "discovery" that a consciously constructed "Reverse" might give her her art is unique, and was also no doubt agonizing for her. Her esthetic is one that reproduces a Christian eschatology: peace must be sought through ordeal upon ordeal, the self through selflessness, power through pain, the highest through the lowest, heaven through humility. The lame—and also the despairing, troubled, hurt, lost, deprived—enter first; the poet-in-the-pit is inspired best. Hers is a different esthetic, however, from that which comes from the Protestant teleology of Good Grief: she cannot hold with Hawthorne that art is the study of *only* the Fall. Instead, she reconstructs the Fall in her own way so as to have a security to hold to, a base to rise from, a foil for her loftier desires. It appears from this that for the most part Emily Dickinson saw Christianity in terms of struggle rather than belief. To have inner discord is to be Christian. Thus the difficulty of knowing what to label herself in her letters— believer or pagan. Emily Dickinson knew what seventeenth-century theologians knew, that hell does not include only tragedy; it has wider limits, and includes dancing.

A probabilist calculating the possibilities, she was stultified by doctrine, and so her faith was a matter of persuasion but not conviction. The distinction is important. Duplicity became the fundamental principle of her personal Christianity, entertaining opposition constantly, orthodox and heretic. This made it possible for her to have a certain transcendental pessimism that is the begetter of a temporal and terrestrial optimism. Edwards got her to Emerson by a more hellish route.

Therefore, if her method is Christian, it is one taught her by the Edwardsians of the Connecticut Valley tradition. In her poems, Emily Dickinson clearly simulates the process of awakening: going down into the pit, finding security there, balancing her fears and hopes, preparing herself for glee, and then emerging through language to her little epiphanies. She could thus have her heaven *now*. But these are heavens of her own poetic making. The legalisms gone, she can be evangelical to her own ends, moving on her own from loathing and indignation to desire and delight.

What invites Emily Dickinson to believe she is free is her consciousness of necessity in general and her own shackles in particular. This she gets in her pit. The consciousness provokes in her a feeling of autonomy and superiority—a subjective elevation. She is attached to the possible only insofar as it seems *im*possible. Her negation of the possible is one of the sources and the basis of her religion, her writing. The pit takes her eyes off eternity and focuses them on the temporal universe, a second paradise. Dispossessed, she gets more intense appetites and illusions, she becomes more aggressive in her disappointments. For her this is a poetic state: original anxieties in a simulated hell where the imagination leads to excess, to song. "Going into hell so many times tears it," wrote Jack Spicer, "which explains poetry."

Such a life may have been a Christian life, but her soul was pagan. She was resigned to the pit without being *sincere* in it. Hell is where she placed herself in order to look *up*. What is remarkable about such a life is that Emily Dickinson did not *fear* Christianity, as I think Melville did; the pit was an opportunity, a beginning, an expectation. And the anxiety was reassuring. The anomaly made a future. She was therefore an enthusiast without being an antinomian—really a transcendentalist of her own making.

The appearance of this much Edwards in Emily Dickinson's imagination shows that American culture (or rather, for our present story, New England culture) has a unity that transcends historiography. From the fund of ideas that comprised the imaginative resources of her age and its spiritual capital, she drew her poetic currency. Emily Dickinson found a common imagery, perhaps remembered from childhood and perhaps built into the images of the culture, which she rather easily deritualized and made boldly esthetic. The ability to make over a discountenanced theology into a creative source of her poetry is itself an image of her. "The subterranean," she wrote about her religious views in a letter of 1862, "stays."

That Emily Dickinson created Edwards—and not the other way around—should now be evident. His pit is not the cause but the result of hers. This is a mythic possibility that Edwards himself understood well:

> Let us suppose the appearances and images of things in a glass; for instance, a reflecting telescope, to be the real effects of heavenly bodies (at a distance, and out of sight) which they resemble: if it be so, then, as these images in the telescope have had a past actual existence, and it is become utterly impossible now that it should be otherwise than that they have existed; so they being the true effects of the heavenly bodies they resemble, this proves the existing of those heavenly bodies to be as real, infallible, firm and necessary, as the existing of these effects; the one being connected with, and wholly depending on the other. Now let us suppose future existences some way or other to have influence back, to produce effects beforehand, and cause exact and perfect images of themselves in a glass, a thousand years before they exist, yea, in all preceding ages; but yet that these images are real effects of these future existences, perfectly dependent on, and connected with their cause; these effects and images, having already had actual existence, rendering that matter of their existing perfectly firm and stable, and utterly impossible to be otherwise; this proves in like manner as in the other instance, that the existence of the things which are their causes, is also equally sure, firm and necessary; and that it is alike impossible but that they should be, as if they had been already, as their effects have.[39]

Emily Dickinson's ability to create in Edwards a forebear—a telescope to his star, a cause of his effects, an effect because of him—again illustrates her uncanny ability to set herself squarely at the center of American culture.

39. *Freedom of the Will*, pp. 265–66.

Four

MORNING HAS NOT OCCURRED

Emily Dickinson and Harriet Beecher Stowe

I've known her – from an ample nation –
Choose One –

[#303]

I would like to suggest still one more way in which Emily Dickinson accepts, challenges, and transforms Puritan tradition, one more way in which she is related to early American life and thought. Like Anne Bradstreet, as we have seen, she stood up in (but also in flamboyant exploitation of) the expectations of Puritan womanhood. Like Edward Taylor, in addition, she made a place for herself in the closed Puritan universe by means of the range of an American language. And like Jonathan Edwards she got her thrills out of a dark Puritan sensationalism, rationalizing depravity as deprivation and deprivation as opportunity and opportunity as reversal, rehabilitation, even regeneration, thus saving her unsavable self.

These arguments create for Emily Dickinson a Puritanism that had proceeded into the nineteenth century and that she used (quite naturally, I feel) to resist and exploit some of the pressures of her own times. But there was also a Puritanism that she missed out on—or rather that in its course missed her. Two different women's voices of the middle of the nineteenth century, hers and Harriet Beecher Stowe's, both of them speaking for Puritan culture, show the transformations of a New England hermeneutic tradition, with very different results. Mrs. Stowe, despite her limitations, comprehended New England rather better than any other writer and so helps to place Emily Dickinson.

She perhaps spoke for a great many of her contemporaries in the nineteenth century when she wrote:

> But there was one of my father's books that provided a mine of wealth to me. It was a happy hour when he brought home and set up in his bookcase Cotton Mather's "Magnalia," in a new edition of two volumes. What wonderful stories those! Stories too about my own country. Stories that made me feel the very ground I trod on to be consecrated by some special dealing of God's Providence.... The heroic element was strong in me, having come down by ordinary generation from a long line of Puritan ancestry, and just now it made me long to do something, I knew not what: to fight for my country, or to make some declaration on my own account ... to realize the Kingdom of Heaven on earth. I see God's mercies to New England as a foreshadowing of the glorious future of the United States of America ... commissioned to bear the light of liberty and religion through all the earth and to bring in the great millennial day, when wars should cease and the whole world, released from the thralldom of evil, should rejoice in the light of the Lord. The millennium was ever the star of hope in the eyes of the New England clergy, their faces were set eastward, towards the dawn of that day, and the cheerfulness of those anticipations illuminated the hard tenets of their theology with a rosy glow. They were the children of the morning.

This is Harriet Beecher Stowe's commemoration of her Puritan forebears.[1] It could never have been Emily Dickinson's. How they (and Mrs. Stowe) planned the future of America did not interest her in the least. She reneged. For Mrs. Stowe's "children of the morning" she only felt, in ever so many ways throughout her life on issues involving hopes, that (as she said in one poem) "Morning has not occurred!"[2]

The nineteenth-century Puritan that Emily Dickinson was *not*

1. Charles Edward Stowe, *Life of Harriet Beecher Stowe, Compiled from Her Letters and Journals* (Boston, 1889), pp. 10–11. "I was in the habit of applying to my grandmother for explanations [about New England history]," Mrs. Stowe wrote in 1834, "and she would relate to me, while I listened with breathless attention, long stories from Mather's *Magnalia* (or Magnilly, as she used to call it), a work which I earnestly longed to read, but of which I never got sight till after my twentieth year." (Introduction to 1896 edition of *Oldtown Folks*, p. xx.) Mrs. Stowe uses part of this statement about the *Magnalia* again in *Poganuc People* (Boston, 1896), pp. 122–23.

2. This line occurs in a poem suggesting that Emily Dickinson believed (in 1858, at least) that one's highest hopes can only be realized hereafter:

imbued with was the kind of sensibility that came down from Cotton Mather ("that delightful old New England grandmother," Mrs. Stowe called him): the tradition of identifying the self with America. She had little or no sense of the *imitatio Christi Americani* that Mather celebrated; no sense of one's life as "the shore of America" that Thoreau attempted; no sense of the Puritan as armed, local saint that Hawthorne saw; no sense of one's lovingly aggrandized self as embodiment of the American democratic ideal that Whitman had; no sense of the involved New England lady of millennial morals that was Harriet Beecher Stowe's example. Emily Dickinson could not find *that* America.

"We should render devout thanks to Almighty God, for our ancestry," Edward Dickinson wrote in a commemorative pamphlet he penned in 1859; "that the kingdoms of the Old World were sifted to procure the seed to plant this continent; that the purest of that seed was sown in this beautiful valley; that the blood of the Puritans flows in our veins."[3] "I love New England and New England customs and New England institutions," her brother Austin wrote in a letter in 1851, "for I remember our fathers loved them and that it was they who founded and gave them to us."[4] The loyalty was not the same in Emily Dickinson, though she nevertheless fully sensed that she saw (as she put it, a little grandly) "New Englandly." American society was for her a figment of the imagination, over against which her personal life and private poetry—her "singing"—were a separate reality. She wrote to the Hollands in 1862:

> Perhaps you laugh at me! Perhaps the whole United States are laughing at me too! *I* can't stop for that! *My* business is to love. I found a bird, this morning, down - down - on a little bush at the foot of the garden, and wherefore sing, I said, since nobody *hears?*

Morn is supposed to be
By people of degree
The breaking of the Day.

Morning has not occurred!

That shall Aurora be -
East of Eternity -
One with the banner gay -
One in the red array-
That is the break of Day!

[#13]

3. Edward Dickinson, *Celebration of the Two Hundredth Anniversary of the Settlement of Hadley, Massachusetts* (Northampton, 1859), p. 77.
4. Leyda, *Years and Hours*, 1:226.

> One sob in the throat, one flutter of the bosom – "My business is
> to *sing*" – and away she rose![5]

Her syntax of place and of time is, instead, collapsed, ambiguous,
careless, often even wrong. Mather, in his worst jeremiacal fears, had
foreseen her, one might imagine, as an enemy of The American.

As Sacvan Bercovitch has taught us to see, the American, in the
epistemes that Mather contributed to American sociology, is the
saint-in-service-of-national-destiny. His/her call to redeem the soul is
a social vocation for the common good. The inwardness/goodness/
wholeness is a public role. The self is social because microcosmic,
exemplary, vocational, purposeful. The norms of identity are collective, and spiritual biography is national history. Autonomy is au-
tochthonous, anomalous, nomist. The private, because teleological,
becomes representative; and the personal, because eschatalogical, becomes a historic enterprise. Vocation thus makes the self civic. Solipsism is a form of service. This is the American identity that Mather
bequeathed to the mid-nineteenth century.[6]

Only facetiously, however, could Emily Dickinson write, as she
did in an early poem, "My country calleth me," or address her potential readers as "Sweet – countrymen" later. America in her poems is
merely "an Apparition," a "Figment" of one's imagination.

> Flags, are a brave sight –
> But no true Eye
> Ever went by One –
> Steadily –
>
> [#582]

Her "Native Land" is within or beyond—not present, not local, not
imminent. "This World, and it's Nations" are for her "A too concluded show," that is, already determined and already dull. She ad-
vises one to "Trust in the Unexpected" rather than in the historical or
millennial. Superior are those

> Who win, and nations do not see –
> Who fall – and none observe –
> Whose dying eyes, no Country
> Regards with patriot love –
>
> [#126]

---

5. *Letters*, p. 213.
6. For a much fuller discussion of the same see Sacvan Bercovitch, *The Puritan
Origins of the American Self* (New Haven, 1975), especially the section "The Myth of
America."

In her only explicitly patriotic poem, one she perhaps wrote for some patriotic occasion in 1881, she celebrates the American past very conservatively but refuses to idealize it for the uses of a future:

My country need not change her gown,
Her triple suit as sweet
As when 'twas cut at Lexington,
And first pronounced "a fit."

[#1511]

Instead of identifying the self with America as millenarian, she postulates a self *in place of* the nation, as in the early Emerson. The imperial self, because anti-imperialistic, *replaces* the nation.

The Heart is the Capital of the Mind –
The Mind is a single State –
The Heart and the Mind together make
A single Continent –

One – is the Population –
Numerous enough –
This ecstatic Nation
Seek – it is Yourself.

[#1354]

To her, the externally utopian does not evolve, as it did in the plans of the millennialists from Puritan times down to her own, but instead dissolves:

I've known a Heaven, like a Tent –
To wrap it's shining Yards –
Pluck up it's stakes, and disappear –

[#243]

Nor does she believe that the utopian, in any form, edenic or millenarian, can last:

Paradise is that old mansion
Many owned before –
Occupied by each an instant
Then reversed the Door –
Bliss is frugal of her Leases
Adam taught her Thrift
Bankrupt once through his excesses –

[#1119]

The inexorable past she cannot force down political sidestreets, though it may be of cosmic importance:

Over and over, like a Tune –
The Recollection plays –
Drums off the Phantom Battlements
Cornets of Paradise –

Snatches, from Baptized Generations –
Cadences too grand
But for the Justified Processions
At the Lord's Right Hand.

[#367]

American history she by and large rejects for present sensations:

Witchcraft was hung, in History,
But History and I
Find all the Witchcraft that we need
Around us, every Day –

[#1583]

To her, the only purpose for the utopian lies in the compensation value of such an illusion: "Conjecturing a Climate / Of unsuspended Suns – / Adds poignancy to Winter," for "The Shivering Fancy turns / To a fictitious Country / To palliate a Cold." "I've known her – from an ample nation," she writes of herself in relation to the State, "Choose One"—that is, only *herself*. Except for an embarrassingly few instances, we cannot tell from her references that she wrote in America!

Harriet Beecher Stowe, on the other hand, was obsessed with America as Christian metaphor.[7] It was Perry Miller's opinion that, brought up in Edwards's tradition, she "understood many of its implications better than the theologians who endeavored to follow him and could evaluate his achievements in terms that are fundamental for understanding American culture."[8] She is one of the strongest nineteenth-century examples of the Puritan typologizer of American hopes. She shared the millennial politics of her father, Lyman Beecher: "It is clear that everything comes to a focus on this republic," he wrote. "It was the opinion of Edwards, that the millennium would commence in America. When I first encountered this opinion, I

---

7. In his *Atlantic Essays* (1871), Higginson wrote of Mrs. Stowe:

The greatest transatlantic successes which American novelists have yet attained—those won by Cooper and Mrs. Stowe—have come through a daring Americanism of subject, which introduced in each case a new figure to the European world—first the Indian, then the negro. Whatever the merit of the work, it was plainly the theme which conquered. [P. 66]

8. Introduction to Edwards, *Images or Shadows of Divine Things* (New Haven, 1948), p. 44.

thought it chimerical; but all providential developments since, and all the existing signs of the times lend corroboration to it."[9]

Harriet Beecher Stowe was cast in the Mather-Edwards mold. Through typology, like a host of writers over the two hundred years before her, she juxtaposed seventeenth-century eschatology over against the millennial language of the revivalists of her own time. She was nourished from childhood on the *Magnalia,* as she said, and so the American past flowed inexorably in her imagination into a covenanted American future. Her New England novels, negative as they at times are about the country's future and ideals, provide documentation of her hope in a Puritan-projected millennial America.

But for Emily Dickinson, perhaps because her faith included a strong measure of doubt regarding any such programmed hope, it was a "Sovereign Anguish" to be thus "Haunted by native lands."

> The Lands we thought that we should seek
> When large enough to run
> By Speculation [have been] ceded
> To Speculation's Son –
>
> [#1293]

Her speculative polyvalence prevented utopia from occurring in her mind in quite the same way it did in Mrs. Stowe's.

Neither would she have believed the federal philosophy of Orestes Brownson that interested Mrs. Stowe:

> Few things are less dependent on mere will or arbitrariness than litera-ture. It is the expression and embodiment of the national life. Its character is not determined by this man or that, but by the national spirit. . . . So he who would move the people, influence them for good or for evil, must have like passions with them; feel as they feel; crave what they crave; and resolve what they resolve. He must be their repre-sentative, their impersonation.[10]

For Emily Dickinson the self could not be made so political, so doctri-nal, so sure, and most certainly neither could one's writings. Personal religion was for her democratic, not republican.

"Doubtless Harriet recognized a congenial disposition in Emer-son and Thoreau," writes Charles H. Foster, "but she stood nearer to a contemporary of whom she may never have heard, . . . Emily Dick-

9. Lyman Beecher, *A Plea for the West* (Cincinnati, 1835), p. 8.
10. Brownson, *The American Republic: Its Constitution, Tendencies, and Destiny* (New York, 1866), p. 200.

inson."[11] Emily Dickinson might actually have met Mrs. Stowe (though we have no convincing proof of it) when her husband preached in Amherst in 1851 and 1853. Her comment in an 1851 letter, "Zion lifts her head – I overhear remarks signifying Jerusalem," appears to refer to his preaching in Amherst. Or the two women might have met when Mrs. Stowe spent the summer of 1872 in Amherst visiting her daughter Georgiana, wife of the Rev. Henry F. Allen, the local Episcopal rector. They could have talked with each other, if appositely. Emily Dickinson read *Uncle Tom's Cabin* at the height of its popularity in 1853 (though her father berated her for the frivolity), and she might even have seen the stage version when in played in Amherst in 1854, but they would not have moved her much.[12] She had, following Emerson, another slave to free—herself.

There are a few other connections between the Dickinsons and the Beechers that are possibly of some interest. Emily Dickinson's grandfather, Samuel Fowler Dickinson, for example, was associated with Lyman Beecher on Amherst College matters while Beecher lived at Litchfield and New Haven. And when Beecher went west to become the first president of Lane Theological Seminary in Cincinnati in 1831, Dickinson followed him to become one of the directors there for three years. He no doubt knew the young Harriet during that time and wrote to his family in Amherst about her and her family.[13] Dickinson followed Beecher in large part because he preached that "the religious and political destiny of our nation is to be decided in the West."[14] In addition, Mrs. Stowe's brother, Henry Ward Beecher, attended Amherst College between 1830 and 1834 and knew the Dickinson family. He returned to Amherst in 1862 to deliver the commencement address, a phrase from which ("the earthquake in the South") Emily Dickinson appears to have taken for a poem she wrote that year, giving her what appears to be one of her few poetic references to the Civil War:

> Thou settest Earthquake in the South –
> And Maelstrom, in the Sea –
> Say, Jesus Christ of Nazareth –
> Hast thou no Arm for Me?
>
> [#502][15]

11. Charles H. Foster, *The Rungless Ladder: Harriet Beecher Stowe and New England Puritanism* (Durham, N.C., 1954), p. 11.
12. Leyda, *Years and Hours*, 1:205–6, 268, 281, 320; 2:184. Mrs. Stowe's visit to Amherst was connected with her daughter's illness.
13. Sewall, *Life*, pp. 37–39.
14. Beecher, *Plea for the West*, p. 11.
15. Sewall, *Life*, pp. 646–47.

Further, one of Emily Dickinson's ministers in Amherst, Dr. Edwards A. Park, was also Harriet Beecher Stowe's minister and friend (and Elizabeth Stuart Phelps's as well) in Andover. Of him, Emily Dickinson wrote to her brother in 1853:

> We had such a splendid sermon from that Prof Park – I never heard anything like it, and dont expect to again, till we stand at the great white throne, and he reads from the book, the Lamb's book. The students and chapel people all came, to our church, and it was very full, and still – so still, the buzzing of a fly would have boomed like a cannon. And when it was all over, and that wonderful man sat down, people stared at each other, and looked as wan and wild, as if they had seen a spirit, and wondered they had not died.[16]

Much later, in 1872, she called this "The loveliest sermon I ever heard."[17] From Dr. Park's writings (particularly his *Memoir of the Life and Character of Samuel Hopkins, D.D.,* 1852) and from conversations with him in 1858 and 1859, Mrs. Stowe had help for her novel *The Minister's Wooing,* along with some severe criticisms. Emily Dickinson early listened to Dr. Park's theology, apparently, but Mrs. Stowe would not. Park was one of the last defenders of New England theology, especially of predestination, original sin, and infant baptism: "We are Calvinists . . . in all the essentials of our faith," he wrote, "and the man who . . . is not a Calvinist, is not a respectable man."[18] Mrs. Stowe's novels are perhaps best read as a complaint against this theology, whereas Emily Dickinson was absorbing some features of it. These reactions to Park reveal a fundamental difference between the two women, as it does about some others of the Beechers and the Dickinsons: Mrs. Stowe kept up appearances in public and generally gave the impression of steadfast loyalty to the old catechism while believing barely a word of it; Emily Dickinson was hidden from the public eye but was openly honest about her doubts.

More important than the personal convergences/divergences between them, however, are the literary ones. Though both Mrs. Stowe and Emily Dickinson rejected much of Puritan theology, they kept many of the habits of mind and some of the literary tradition. The connections with Puritan esthetics are instructive.

Emily Dickinson, for example, has many of the religious moods of Mrs. Stowe's wide variety of characters in those novels where she best outlines the flow of New England Puritanism into the nineteenth

16. *Letters,* p. 272.
17. *Letters,* pp. 502–3.
18. *Debates and Proceedings of the National Council of Congregational Churches* (Boston, 1866), p. 357.

century—*The Minister's Wooing* (1859), *Oldtown Folks* (1869), and *Poganuc People* (1878). All except one: the typological. For her, America is not the *American* issue it was for Harriet Beecher Stowe. In fact, Mrs. Stowe's New England novels repeat and emphasize the traditional analogy between the Bible and America and between early America and the America to be.[19] It is one of the more conspicuous aspects of her literary Puritanism—like Mather, heroizing the Puritan past (the early fathers, remember, are her "children of the morning") in an effort to move nineteenth-century America toward a millennial future. Emily Dickinson apparently missed the whole point. For her, experience was never historical. Though she might often have wished it otherwise, Now preempted almost everything else.

Those three historically self-conscious novels by Mrs. Stowe, only one of which—*The Minister's Wooing* as serialized in the *Atlantic*—Emily Dickinson could have had the opportunity to read, are staged in the late eighteenth century midway between Cotton Mather and these two women, in an attempt, as she said in her preface to the novel, to "paint a style of life and manners which existed in New England in the earlier days of her national existence, . . . with a reverential tenderness for those great religious minds who laid in New England the foundations of many generations, and for those institutions and habits of life from which, as from a fruitful germ, sprang all the present prosperity of America."[20]

The women (and two men) in *The Minister's Wooing* document the range of New England Puritanism along Mrs. Stowe's scale. The minister himself represents an American going right, and Aaron Burr, his antagonist, an American gone wrong. In between are various women formed by American purposes. Mary Scudder is the Puritan saint, the final flower of American faith and hope, the finest fulfillment of Edwards's requirement that one have "light in the understanding, as well as an affected fervent heart." Whereas the minister who woos her is a millennialist, Mary is a person (along with her final lover, James) *living* millennially, according to Mrs. Stowe's utopian standards for a person.

> It was only in prayer, or in deeds of love and charity, or in rapt contemplation of that beautiful millennial day, which her [Mary's] spiritual guide most delighted to speak of, that the tone of her feelings ever rose to the height of joy.

19. For a discussion of Harriet Beecher Stowe's New England novels, see Alice C. Crozier, "New England Then and Now: Children of the Morning," in *The Novels of Harriet Beecher Stowe* (New York, 1959), pp. 85–150.

20. Preface to London edition, *The Minister's Wooing*, p. 15.

Other women in the novel, Mrs. Marvyn and Mrs. Scudder, debate the theological model for American life:

> New England presents probably the only example of a successful commonwealth founded on a theory, as a distinct experiment in the problem of society. It was for this reason that the minds of its great thinkers dwelt so much on the final solution of that problem in this world, . . . a future Millennium. . . . All the careful Marthas in those days will have no excuse for not sitting at the feet of Jesus; there will be no cumbering with much serving; the Church will have only Maries in those days.[21]

With the minister of the novel, Mrs. Stowe believed in "the last golden age of Time, the Marriage Supper of the Lamb, when the purified Earth, like a repentant Psyche, shall be restored to the long-lost favor of a celestial Bridegroom, and glorified saints and angels shall walk familiarly as wedding guests among men."[22] In the eighteenth century, she wrote in *Poganuc People*, "That kingdom was coming even then."[23]

Likewise, to the women of her next New England novel, *Oldtown Folks*, where Mrs. Stowe's millennial hopes are pushed harder, America is thought of as "the Lord's garden" of the past and in the future; in fact, an Israel with a destiny. For them (and Harriet Beecher Stowe is here representing her own philosophy well) the New England past is, for anyone in the nineteenth century, inexorable and personal; America, even when unbecoming, becomes oneself. Personal and national interests, via millennial logic, converge.

> No human being grows up who does not so intertwist in his growth the whole idea and spirit of his day, that rightly to dissect out his history would require one to cut to pieces and analyze society, law, religion, the metaphysics and the morals of his times; and, as all these things run back to those of past days, the problem is still further complicated. The humblest human being is the sum total of a column of figures which go back through centuries before he was born.[24]

For Mrs. Stowe, and especially for her women characters in the novel, the hebraized New England past has already made, through typological hermeneutics, the christianized American future:

21. *The Minister's Wooing* (Boston, 1859), p. 20. "*The Minister's Wooing, . . .*" writes George F. Whicher, "is not a great novel, but it is a masterly revelation of the springs of Puritan character. The light it throws on the inner life of an intensely native New England poet like Emily Dickinson can never be too insistently brought to the attention of readers who have not cultivated a historical imagination" (*Literary History of the United States*, ed. Robert E. Spiller et al. [New York, 1948], p. 584).
22. *The Minister's Wooing*, p. 148.
23. *Poganuc People*, p. 73.
24. *Oldtown Folks* (Boston, 1869), p. 261.

> Never again shall we see that union of perfect repose in regard to
> outward surroundings and outward life with that intense activity of the
> inward and intellectual world, that made New England, at this time, the
> vigorous, germinating seed-bed for all that has since been developed of
> politics, laws, letters, and theology, through New England to America,
> and through America to the world. . . . This millennium was the favorite
> recreation ground, solace, and pasture land, where the New England
> ministry fed their hopes and courage. Men of large hearts and warm
> benevolence, their theology would have filled them with gloom, were it
> not for this overplus of joy and peace to which human society was in
> their view tending. Thousands of years, when the poor old earth should
> produce only a saintly race of perfected human beings, were to them
> some compensation for the darkness and losses of the great struggle.[25]

This millennial optimism caught from the past was one of the main
inspirations of Mrs. Stowe's reform work. Her optimism, like that of
many in the nineteenth century, derives to a large extent from the
anticipation of a Christian revolution.[26]

Also, like her Dr. Cushing in *Poganuc People,* she was rhapsodic
about America's future in Christ as planned by early New England
minds:

> After the singing came Dr. Cushing's prayer—which was a recounting
> of God's mercies to New England from the beginning, and of his de-
> liverances from her enemies, and of petitions for the glorious future of
> the United States of America—that they might be chosen vessels, com-
> missioned to bear the light of liberty and religion through all the earth
> and to bring in the great millennial day, when wars would cease and
> the whole world, released from the thralldom of evil, should rejoice in
> the light of the Lord.[27]

She was obviously raised on the Boston political apocalyptics of the
Mathers ("Boston, to all New England," she wrote, "was the
Jerusalem") as well as the more internalized eschatology of Connecticut Valley writers like Hooker, Stoddard, Taylor, and Edwards. "The
millennium," she firmly believed, "was ever the star of hope in the
eyes of the New England clergy; their faces were set eastward, towards
the dawn of that day, and the cheerfulness of those anticipations illu-
minated the hard tenets of their theology with a rosy glow. They were
children of the morning."[28]

25. Ibid., pp. 421, 444.
26. See H. Richard Niebuhr, "The Coming Kingdom," in *The Kingdom of God in
America* (Hamden, Conn., 1956), pp. 127–63, and Ernest Lee Tuveson, *Redeemer Nation*
(Chicago, 1966).
27. *Poganuc People,* p. 139.
28. Ibid.

The opinions of such millennial commentators could hardly have failed to filter down in some form, through sermons and church magazines, to Emily Dickinson. Some of the preachers she had to listen to were avowed millennialists—Charles Wadsworth, Edward Dwight, Aaron Colton, and J. L. Jenkins. And Mary Lyon, Emily Dickinson's teacher and headmistress at Mount Holyoke, was a student and follower of the Congregational millennialist Joseph Emerson. Yet this is hardly as much exposure, of course, as Mrs. Stowe had at the hands of Mather, Edwards, Samuel Hopkins, Horace Bushnell, and Mark Hopkins.

"So you think New Englanders are the best people on the Earth?" asks Margaret in Sylvester Judd's Transcendentalist novel of 1845. "I think they might become such," is the answer she gets.

> Or rather I think they might lead the August Procession of the race to Human Perfectibility; that here might be revealed the Coming of the Day of the Lord, wherein the old Heavens of sin and error should be dissolved, and a New Heavens and New Earth be established, wherein dwelleth righteousness. I see nothing to prevent them reassuming the old Hyperionic type, rising head and shoulders to the clouds, crowding out Jupiter and Mars, Diana and Venus, being filled, as the Apostle says, with all the fulness of God, reaching the stature of perfect men in Christ Jesus, and reimpressing upon the world the lost image of its Maker.

"New England! my birth place, my chosen pilgrimage," Judd concludes, "I love it."[29]

During that hysterical span of religious years from Mather to the 1850s in which Judd's and Mrs. Stowe's New England novels sit and from which Mrs. Stowe drew spiritual-imperialist assurances—really almost two whole centuries of myth-structuring—many writers worked to form the image of America as a millennial paradise and the fulfillment of scriptural promises in order to assure Americans that they were about to inherit the earth, meekly or otherwise. The New England habit of mind came to associate certain exegetical principals with visions of Christ's future kingdom *here*. This esthetic (really a borrowed hermeneutics) separated these two most articulate nineteenth-century Puritan women, who otherwise often spoke a similar language: one was of the land, the other lost; one had hope for humanity, the other had hope mixed tenuously with hopelessness. Matheresque dispensationalism, with nineteenth-century America coming (beautifully) at the end of time, got worked up into a mythology, as Sacvan Berco-

29. Sylvester Judd, *Margaret* (Boston, 1845), p. 268.

vitch has shown, and American literature became inventively prophetic through the historical analogies of typology, which was a respectable intellectual technique affecting almost everyone in one way or another up to Whitman and beyond. Only a few knew how to fight it very successfully—Hawthorne, Melville, and Twain, perhaps, and Emily Dickinson: the darker Puritans of the period. Emily Dickinson is the most exciting nineteenth-century example of denying America—not with the voice of the well-stereotyped recluse but with the voice of indifferentism, of the American-dissenter-as-sprite. She did not need bunting to decorate her world.

Those writers like Mather, like Mrs. Stowe, and like Emerson and Whitman, who saw in America the fulfillment of scriptural promises and a conclusion to God's plan for the building of the New Jerusalem ("God's mercies to New England," Mrs. Stowe called it, "as a foreshadowing of the glorious future of the United States of America") make one long tradition. Emily Dickinson lived on another kind of time-line, with a fissured and scattered eschatology that had none of those mythopoeic and archetypal symbols used successfully by early writers to produce a systematic vision of the future of New England as based on the patterns discernible in its biblical and historical past.[30] "The two Mathers," Perry Miller wrote, "were . . . possessed by the rule of the true apocalyptic spirit; they marched into the Age of Reason loudly crying that the end of the world was at hand." And "Cotton Mather firmly believed," Emory Elliott adds, "that he had been sent on a special mission by God to lead his own and his father's generations out of their years of confusion and doubt into a new time which would see the coming of Christ and the establishment of the New Jerusalem in America."[31] Rehearsing Mather for an age of ego-optimism, Harriet Beecher Stowe felt she saw that what would go "through New England to America, and through America to the world" was "the final solution, . . . a future Millennium," formed imaginatively out of a typologized world-view.[32] Emily Dickinson did not

---

30. See Sacvan Bercovitch, ed., *Typology in American Literature* (Amherst, 1972), and Earl Miner, ed., *Literary Uses of Religious Typology: From the Late Middle Ages to the Present* (Princeton, 1977). I extend my argument about typology in an essay in this first collection, "'The World Slickt up in Types': Edward Taylor as a Version of Emerson," and in an essay in the second collection, "Alephs, Zahirs, and the Triumph of Ambiguity: Typology in Nineteenth Century American Literature."

31. Perry Miller, *The New England Mind: From Colony to Province* (Cambridge, 1953), pp. 185–88; Emory Elliott, "From Father to Son: The Evolution of Typology in Puritan New England," in Miner, *Literary Uses of Religious Typology*, pp. 225–26.

32. Perhaps she is even closer to Edwards than to Mather in this regard:

It is not unlikely that this work of God's spirit . . . is the dawning or at least a prelude of that glorious work of God, so often foretold in Scripture . . . and there

have so much politics. She has her existence outside/apart from action in history.

"No Jewish maiden ever grew up," wrote Charles E. Stowe and Lyman Beecher Stowe of their mother, restating her own description of the character Dolly in *Poganuc People*, "with a more earnest faith that she belonged to a consecrated race, a people especially called and chosen of God for some great work on earth. Her faith in every word of the marvels related in this book was fully as great as the dear old credulous Doctor Mather could have desired."[33] Fascinated with the typological millennialism of Mather's *Magnalia* ("Stories," she called them, "that made me feel the very ground I trod on to be consecrated by some special dealing of God's Providence"), Mrs. Stowe located divine sanction on local soil and in local history, with herself at the center. Emily Dickinson had only dark possibility— hardly millennial, hardly American, hardly advertisable. The land was Mrs. Stowe's before she was the land's: such as it was, such it would become. Emily Dickinson's earthly kingdom was, when it appeared at all, *within*—a different Christianity, a different Calvinism. With wit and whim she broke the medieval types.

Emily Dickinson appears myopic and therefore modern where Mrs. Stowe was medieval because millennial after a typological manner, substituting manifest destinarianism for Puritan predestinarianism, determination for determinism, the future for the facts of one's own life. She saw a plan that escaped Emily Dickinson. She assumed that nothing much had changed since seventeenth-century New England. She took Puritan hermeneutics seriously as politics and was therefore doomed to a certain failure of reputation, by and large, as a writer. Emily Dickinson survived by just playing.

Something happened to millennializing typology on its way to, and during the course of, the nineteenth century, as the case of Emily Dickinson proves. It became abused, diffused, and even amusing. The conceit of medieval allegory turned into camp. The will-to-metaphor mystique of Puritan piety became de-Christianized, dis-Edened, disinherited, dysfunctional. The point of it all got lost.

---

are many things which make it probable that this work will begin in America. . . . And if we may suppose that this glorious work of God shall begin in any part of America, I think if we consider the circumstances of the settlement of New England, it must needs appear the most likely of all the American colonies. [*Some Thoughts concerning the Present Revival of Religion in New England* (Boston, 1742), p. 200]

33. Charles Edward Stowe and Lyman Beecher Stowe, *Harriet Beecher Stowe: The Story of Her Life* (Boston, 1911), pp. 12–13.

We remind ourselves disinterestedly that the settlers of early America brought an allegorical system with them carrying the tag "Typology." It was biblically sanctioned and had on it the sweet exegetical glaze of the church fathers, from Philo and Origen to Calvin and William Ames. It achieved the status of exegesis in the New World as proof of the continuity of the theology from the Old. Like other structures that helped to form early American culture, it encouraged considerable innovation, because it was a splendid abstraction and so was alive in the imagination. The tradition, even at the outset, was a handful of sterile ideas but a fertile structure. It was an overwritten version of the platonic, epic in scale and utopian in tone, frivolous in method and provincial in effect, but structurally sound because appealing to something in the American imagination.

Orthodox typologizing (the classic tradition of types) got foreshadows and prophecies out of the Old Testament to satisfy the need of Christians to make Jesus (the antitype/the light/the fulfillment) divine and therefore central to human history, even "the meridian of time." In America, orthodox typologizing sent ministers of the seventeenth and eighteenth centuries, and a few others from Winthrop to Freneau, to their pens connecting actual biblical facts imaginatively to their antitype, the Christ.

Because for the American ideologues of the early centuries classic typology was a structural means rather than a dogma, innovation began just as soon as the American sense of mission took hold. The millennium of which Mrs. Stowe and Whitman became champions in the nineteenth century was only one of the possible uses. Stripped of authoritative interpretation, classic typology in New England became a device of doctrinal convenience. Perhaps no one believed it very much as a set of ideas anyway, for into the structure they consistently inserted new material, initiating typology's service to American culture. Its truth lay in the fact that it worked in many different ways.

Thus John Cotton proclaimed the Bay Colony "the antitypical fulfillment of all Biblical types" and yet also the "prefiguration of the Second Coming." He wanted the relationship between New England saints in a wilderness and the Children of Israel in a wilderness to replace Christ's relationship *to* the Children of Israel. Similarly, William Bradford saw the Separatists at Plymouth imitating Christ in reenacting Old Testament events, and they were therefore a realized antitype to the conventional biblical types. For him, through some correspondence with Christ, what is fallen gains life. Samuel Sewall also saw an excuse to impose a typal allegory on historical events, making New England the antitype to all religious history that had preceded it, selective of those events which served and foreshadowed colonization.

Such hermeneutics as this encouraged an early nationalism. Cotton Mather followed suit in defining types in terms of "the histories of all ages, coming in with punctual and surprising fulfillments of the divine prophecies, as far as they have been hitherto fulfilled." America was for him the antitype because it would "bring a blessing upon all the nations of the earth." In a similar vein, Roger Williams wrote of the Jews "as the type of the . . . [American] Kingdome of Christ Jesus." He believed that the "full and final deliverance and restoration of the Church may be applied to us." Too, Urian Oakes saw America antitypally as "a candle in the candlestick that giveth light to the whole house." Thus, millennialism was built into the American imagination in large part because of the typology.

The great success of typologizing from the seventeenth century to the time of Mrs. Stowe and Emily Dickinson can be laid almost certainly to the writing of Cotton Mather and Jonathan Edwards. Just as materialistic as the many New England typologizers before them but more articulate in their optimism, they superimposed the type-to-antitype structure on American life with imaginative effort, forcing the metaphoric relation of tenor and vehicle to assume, well into the nineteenth century, a dominantly religious aspect. It is at the heart of much nineteenth century literature, as we see in the amateur theologizing of Mrs. Stowe. Emily Dickinson's modernity is marked, to some extent, by her refusal to play the same game.

Typology was one of the features that sustained one form of American Puritanism long after it had ceased to be socially or even religiously viable.[34] American Romanticism, moreover, reflects a notable difference from the movement in Europe, to an important extent, by virtue of the innovations of typology. We cannot know for sure what caused a nineteenth-century American imagination like Mrs. Stowe's and that of others in the period to find merit and satisfaction in the obsolete technique of typologizing. We only know that it turns up in curious and significant places. Without the various uses of it, the history of American literature would be substantially different in the nineteenth century.[35]

34. See Ursula Brumm, *Religious Typology and American Literature* (New Brunswick, 1970), where, however, both Mrs. Stowe and Emily Dickinson are overlooked in the discussion.

35. Charles Feidelson, Jr., misread a select group of nineteenth-century American writers as early *symbolistes* (*Symbolism and American Literature* [Chicago, 1953]), in part because he disregarded the workings of the Puritan typological construct in them. He missed the antitypes in the writings of each and so moved them in an existential direction away from their New England bearings.

Typology is, moreover, a helpful way of distinguishing the Aggressive Party of canonized nineteenth-century writers (Emerson with his antitypal Over-Soul, Thoreau with his Imperial Self, Whitman with his ego-cosmos) from the Disaffected Party (Poe, Hawthorne, Melville, and Emily Dickinson). Of course there never was the possibility that typology could dominate any one of these writers very completely. The strongest objections to typologizing came from the Disaffected Party, for they were annoyed with the arrogant assumptions and unquestioned demands of the method. To their minds, by and large, the antitype had become the means of a literary fascism. In Hawthorne the antitype is turned into the Evil in the Heart, a principle stimulating (yet ultimately also negating) all typal actions. In Melville the antitype appears as a tragically self- and world-destructive ship's captain, a con man, a chronometrical principle separated from all earthly types. His antitype/archetype, the whale, is a whitewashed malevolence mingling beauty and horror. Finally, in Twain the antitype takes the form of a horrifying Satan, a malevolence reducing all types to an illusion.

In such hands, the Emerson-Thoreau-Whitman-Stowe frontier of types becomes mere paradoxes. The Disaffected Party of writers is less sure of the tenor, less sure of the spirit that makes the types go, less sure of an antitype giving direction and purpose. For them, to use Melville's analogy from *Pierre,* the chronometrical is not the same as the horologicals. In their hands, typology has for the most part gone sour. It is an icon to be blasted, a whipping boy, an object of anger, a comic mistake.

Hawthorne's Mr. Smooth-it-away is Emerson's antitype-turned-deceiver. Ethan Brand's antitype, the Unforgivable Sin, drives him to suicide. Young Goodman Brown's antitypal principle of Evil scars his life. The Great Carbuncle, Peter Goldthwaite's treasure, and Owen Warland's butterfly are antitypes reduced to illusory symbols. Melville's antitypal Ahab is Whitman's passer-to-more-than-India as fascist leader. His whale is the antitype as Unnamable, his messianic Captain Delany a naif, his Billy Budd a disrupter of realities and therefore criminal. In Twain, damnation is the organizing principle of an unfathomable world, an antitype gone cynical. Moral conscience, formerly the organizing agent, is the villain.

Thus, we have among nineteenth-century American writers those (Mrs. Stowe, Emerson, Thoreau, and Whitman are the present examples) who lost faith in Puritan ideology but retained the Puritan typological structure of ideas by means of innovation. And we have those (Hawthorne, Melville, Emily Dickinson, and Twain) who maintained closer ties with Puritan ideas (however much to their personal detriment at times) but only by dismantling seventeenth-century structures that came down to them, among them the millennializing typology. To some extent, both heresies are—ironically—affirmations.

Because I see in Emily Dickinson some of the most faithful remnants of Puritan esthetics found in any nineteenth-century writer, some of the strongest resistance to Puritan controls, and some of the subtlest transformations of major Puritan assumptions of her age, I suggest that in her poetry one may find the late nineteenth century's best example of what became of religious typology.

Typological terminology turns up in Emily Dickinson's poems, as it does in the work of almost all writers in the period, but the medieval/religious sense has gone out of it. It means little that she uses it.

> Further in Summer than the Birds
> Pathetic from the Grass
> A minor Nation celebrates
> It's unobtrusive Mass.
>
> No Ordinance be seen
> So gradual the Grace
> A pensive Custom it becomes
> Enlarging Loneliness.
>
> Antiquest felt at Noon
> When August burning low
> Arise this spectral Canticle
> Repose to *typify* . . .

> [#1068]

Here "typify" makes a religious allusion that fits the religious imagery of the poem, but its intent is Wordsworthian: the crickets suggest only the idea of repose.

In two other cases, Emily Dickinson uses the terms somewhat more traditionally, if the intent is still a little vague. Here we have her definition of "types":

> The Things that never can come back, are several –
> Childhood – some forms of Hope – the Dead –
> Though Joys – like Men – may sometimes make a Journey –
> And still abide –
> We do not mourn for Traveler, or Sailor,
> Their Routes are fair –
> But think enlarged of all that they will tell us
> Returning here –
> "Here!" There are *typic* "Heres" –
> Foretold Locations –

> The Spirit does not stand –
> Himself – at whatsoever Fathom
> His Native Land –

[#1515]

And here her definition of "antitype":

> The murmuring of Bees, has ceased
> But murmuring of some[thing]
> Posterior, prophetic,
> Has simultaneous [be]come.
> The lower metres of the Year
> When Nature's laugh is done[,]
> The Revelations of the Book
> Whose Genesis was June.
> Appropriate Creatures to her change
> The *Typic* Mother sends
> As Accent fades to interval
> With separating Friends[,]
> Till what we speculate, has been
> And thoughts we will not show
> More intimate with us become
> Than Persons, that we know.

[#1115]

The terms themselves do not interest her much; the method is largely lost on her.

A number of things present themselves tentatively in Emily Dickinson's poetry as antitypes, but none of them are very convincing.[36] For her Jesus does not usually have either control over historical events or the ability to order the world spatially. He is too often reduced to the sentimental role of friend ("Jesus! thy second face / Mind thee in Paradise / Of our's!"), indifferent lover ("Jesus – it's your little 'John'! / Don't you know – me?"), lost savior ("And 'Jesus'! Where is *Jesus* gone / . . . Perhaps he does'nt know the House"), and undependable redeemer ("Say, Jesus Christ of Nazareth – / Hast thou no Arm for me?"). God is reference point for her life and for the life of nature but lacks the main feature of an antitype—a clearly absolute magnanimity and inclusiveness.

---

36. The only serious attempt to discuss typology in Emily Dickinson is Robert Weisbuch, *Emily Dickinson's Poetry* (Chicago, 1975), pp. 78–132, where death and immortality are positioned as the dominant antitypes in her life. The flaw in this otherwise attractive argument is an error that is often made by twentieth-century exegetes of typology—assuming that anything binary is typological. The thesis that Emily Dickinson's was "a connective mind" finds much that is binary in form and therefore much that *appears* to be typological, but isn't necessarily so.

I think, they call it "God" –
Renowned to ease Extremity –
When Formula, had failed –

And shape my Hands –
Petition's way,
Tho' ignorant of a word
That Ordination – utters –

My Business, with the Cloud,
If any Power behind it, be,
Not subject to Despair –
It care, in some remoter way,
For so minute affair
As Misery –
Itself, too great, for interrupting – more –

[#293]

Her "If any Power behind it be" suggests her need more than her faith, which no antitype could satisfy. She could confront God mainly as the object of her skepticism. "Grant me, Oh Lord, a sunny mind– / Thy windy will to bear!" What antitype could survive such ambiguity?

In a poem above we have still another antitype—Nature, "The Typic Mother." But try as she might to transcendentalize the world, Emily Dickinson cannot keep her mind on the iron string on which all things are strung, as types to antitype, in Emerson, Thoreau, and Whitman. It is difficult for her to personify into some antitypal force-that-through-all-the-green-fuses-of-the-world-might-drive-the-flower those characteristics of nature that her experience teaches her of, simply because it includes not only an abundance of possible types ("The spreading wide my narrow Hands / To gather Paradise") but also illusion, ellipsis, elusiveness, and delusion ("Nature is what we know – / Yet have no art to say – / So impotent Our Wisdom is / To her Simplicity"). The antitype, no matter how open, cannot be a riddle: "Can I expound the skies? / How still the Riddle lies!"

Still another place in Emily Dickinson where one might attempt to find a sufficient antitype to convince one that the Puritan structure still functions in the late nineteenth century is in the role of a superior sensibility to which she elevates herself, making a self somewhat parallel to Whitman's. All the types in the world might be seen as turned into possibilities by the influence of her strong, antitypal personality—a personality that, as she claimed in her poems, is just the weight of God, that selects its own society, that "unto itself / Is an imperial friend." She always has, after Emerson, after all, her "Columnar Self." She seems never to have thought through thoroughly enough, however, the metaphysics of sentience (Edwards and Emerson, her more accessible esthetic forbears, had made the senses the criterion of the sensed) to make of her delight a center bringing both herself and her world alive. She could not/would not elevate her knowns to an Unknown that was both cause and effect of things. Puritan meiosis in her prevented such security:

> Why – do they shut Me out of Heaven?
> Did I sing – too loud?
> But – I can say a little "Minor"
> Timid as a Bird!

[#248]

Her solipsism is not strong enough to impose a will on the world to make it yield, narcissistically, a pattern of herself. The typological structure implies a relationship, and she cannot relate very well.

In Emily Dickinson one might expect orthodox typology to have had a final glorious appearance. But Puritanism could not elevate the sacred, nor Transcendentalism the secular, to an antitype in her mind, even though she tried her hand at such in a few of her poems, as if she was sometimes tempted by the old/new orthodoxies. But she seems to have sensed for the most part that both made tyrannies out of superstitions. Such is largely missing from her poetry because it is immaterial for her to *have* an antitype. Like others, Emily Dickinson found out the inaccuracy of the structure. Like Hawthorne and Melville, she preferred uncertainty. Her "Compound vision" could not focus easily.

Vico wrote of the antitypes: "Their characteristic feature is that the thing represented must always be something very important and holy for those concerned, something affecting their whole life and thinking." Many things affected Emily Dickinson in important and holy ways, of course, but not without ambivalence and not without play. Therefore nothing could sit in her mind for long as antitype; the sure is not in flux in her but most certainly often unsure: "All we know / Is the uncertain certainty." To be sure, she tried her hand at times at the typologizer's method, but only with considerable confusion:

> Escaping backward to perceive
> The Sea upon our place –
> Escaping forward, to confront
> His glittering Embrace –
>
> Retreating up, a Billow's hight
> Retreating blinded down
> Our undermining feet to meet
> Instructs to the Divine.

[#867]

Over against the argument of the persistence of Puritanism in this woman, we have the absence of orthodox typologizing as an effective argument that she was also of sufficiently different mind.

What was left of the typological for her and others in the late nineteenth century to use was something more plebeian. The structure had to be *projected* from plebeian materials and from one's own interesting and fallible experience—an easier, less innovative, yet more dangerous method of believing. In a poem of 1862, she defines plebeian typology for us after a nineteenth-century New England fashion: the type is homely and arbitrary; the antitype is remote and spiritual; the language chosen for the type makes it possible to delight in the superiority of the antitype; and the result is that the means for exploring and explaining the antitype are more fascinating than the antitype itself.

> Least Village has it's Blacksmith
> Whose Anvil's even ring
> Stands symbol for the finer Forge
> That soundless tugs - within -
>
> Refining these impatient Ores
> With Hammer, and with Blaze
> Until the Designated Light
> Repudiate the Forge -
>
> [#365]

A catalog of such plebeian types in Emily Dickinson's poetry might run to the thousands, though presenting the annoying difficulty of requiring one to distinguish between types, simple Wordsworthian platonizing, and simple vehicles of regular metaphors. The difficulty reveals that she did not think typological distinctions worth making.

Her poetry demonstrates that the descent of typology from Cotton Mather and Mrs. Stowe to Emily Dickinson and the later nineteenth century is marked by increasing distrust of the old symbolical arrangements. With the Puritan antitypes dislodged, the types become more and more private, ambiguous, eccentric, playful, autonomous. The signs do not divine anything.

Which is not to suggest that Emily Dickinson was blind to the methodology of types, only (as suggested in the following lines from a poem of 1864) that she could not see the practice without some irony, complexity, ambiguity:

> The Finite [is] furnished
> With the Infinite -
> Convex - and Concave Witness -
> Back - toward Time -

And forward –
Toward the God of Him –

[#906]

The antitype has become an invention, a projection, a mere convexity of a mere concavity. What she calls "The Admirations – and Contempts – of time" are unsure. The ease with which she moralizes upon her theme of this world versus a better one reveals her inability to work the typological method: she has substituted hope for firm faith.

The Love a Life can show Below
Is but a filament, I know,
Of that diviner thing. . . .

[#673]

It was an easy platonic game to play.

Almost any attempt at typologizing is weakened in Emily Dickinson's poetry because she tends to reason from self to society and cosmos, which changes the structure considerably. In a poem of 1862 she reverses the process, revealing her refusal to work the typological model:

A piercing Comfort it affords
In passing Calvary –

To note the fashions – of the Cross –
And how they're mostly worn –
Still fascinated to presume
That Some – are like My Own –

[#561]

All the antitypal referents are gone, even Christ; she has only herself and her own worries. History and the world are important to her only if her window happens to look out on them, to her advantage.

Because of her American-utopian interests, however, Harriet Beecher Stowe usually gets typology right, though it is often secularized and sentimentalized more than in the hands of her precursors. "This life is the shadow," she writes in *Oldtown Folks*, "and the life to come the substance."[37]

We mark, with mystic ring, the day
Of vows that are the type of heaven,
When, as the Church unto her Lord,
The bride unto the groom is given.[38]

37. *Oldtown Folks*, pp. 59–60.
38. "Christ's Birthday," in *The Collected Poems of Harriet Beecher Stowe*, ed. John Michael Moran, Jr. (Hartford, 1967), p. 54.

"How blessed it is," she writes in *The Minister's Wooing*, "to lose herself in that eternal Love and Beauty of which all earthly fairness and grandeur are but the dim type, the distant shadow."[39] In her concern with millennial evidences Mrs. Stowe could imagine a time of American abrogation of Judeo-Christian history: "Those Jews present . . . were, as it were, a type of that last ingathering, when both Jew and Gentile shall sit down lovingly together to the gospel feast."[40] And she could almost always find a relation between physical and spiritual worlds by way of the structure of types:

> And this strange and ancient city,
>   In that reign of His truth and love,
> Shall *be* what it *seems* in the twilight,
>   The type of that City above.[41]

Watching both women struggle with this Puritan hermeneutics, we see a great difference. For one thing, Emily Dickinson cannot easily fuse religious or theological matters with matters of personality. They quarrel, and then she makes a religion out of her own needs. But Mrs. Stowe sees theology and daily life as one. The common America gets theologized, is made part of a scheme, takes on *metaphorical* importance. Types gave her the means for being American and Christian. Through millennializing typology, retrospect and prospect become one, nostalgia and reform merge, the ideal past and the ideal future become continuous. The self, though emerging in a smaller voice than we hear from Mather or Whitman, is America.

The real importance of the comparison with the typologizers— and especially in realizing Emily Dickinson's inability to use the method very well—is that it points up how she identified a fundamental problem in the nature of symbolism in America. To her there was always a great difference between the multiplicity of one and the multitude made one. Only the first is free of literary fascism. The one allows the creation of a private, personal, idiosyncratic symbolism— almost at will, certainly with whim, inevitably with wit—while the other tends toward the allegorical, the anagogical, the mythic, and even—in some hands, as we have seen—the millennializingly typological. It is dictated by forms, institutions, systems of thought— especially theological and political systems. The one is juristic (the idea of corporation), the other naturalistic (a sense of self).

But Emily Dickinson's poetry largely divests itself of the allegorical/typological. Personality to her becomes mere fiction when it be-

39. *The Minister's Wooing*, p. 66.
40. Ibid., p. 166.
41. "A Day in the Pamfili Doria," in *Collected Poems*, p. 50.

comes representative. Politics is representation, whereas personality is substance. Where Mrs. Stowe, the Transcendentalists, the Mormons and Millerites, and other contemporary millennialists were basically concerned with the unity of the representor, the antitype (whether called God, Christ, Over-Soul, or superself), Emily Dickinson concerned herself for the most part with the unit the Represented. She would not act for others. She had only herself and was not sure that she represented anything else.

Therefore it is not at all possible, I believe, to refer to her writings as political in any sense, whereas those of the others almost always are in some sense or other. Her lack of an ability to invent politics is best seen in the fact that she could not imagine anyone listening to her. For that reason—and it is a matter of typology—she sees her existence as both outside of and apart from action in history. The sphere of her religious experience is not the whole world, as New England Puritanism would have convinced her, but just her individual soul. "Only one," wrote Paul, "attains the goal." She rejected American communion for the joys of personal anxiety.

With Mrs. Stowe, to have symbols that represent is to have a history. No types, no American past or future. She redefined the country as a church. The types make "America" with a history, which then works to put down the historical action of others. And from that logic we have imperialism. The kind of symbolism *is* a cause of America's bearing in the world.

The symbols represent the people, the nation, and so stand between an individual and God. Such anagogic mysticism made Mrs. Stowe a participant without action and a passive spectator of a Bible-induced destiny, social activist though she was. This group-soul individualism of Puritan tradition, which evolved into typological-millennial imperialism by the nineteenth century, did not concern Emily Dickinson, because she had a more peaceful existence, contriving her conflicts out of her own experience. For all that, she is really far more active in (her own) American life, having pain and exuberance (her own fallen senses) in place of the usual American frontier mysticism. Emily Dickinson is therefore more of a *participant* in America than Harriet Beecher Stowe, though the geography is interior.[42]

It was not easy for a woman of the nineteenth century to be "alone with America," to again use Richard Howard's phrase about

42. Perhaps also at issue in this comparison is the role of women in the progress of nineteenth-century millennialism. In 1844 Catherine Beecher issued a book, *The Duty of American Women to Their Country*, that attempted to show a vision of a nation redeemed by women through their domestic abilities. Through the influence of "elevated and dignified women," she argued, a high morality and some homogeneous national institutions would create national unity. Women would interlock family, school, and

American writers. Emily Dickinson, for one, would not have understood the American proposition: out of many, one. Having a place
already in herself, she did not need to be alone with anything else. In
Emily Dickinson what is much stronger is what Richard Howard calls
"an impulse toward an apartheid of ecstasy."[43]

Mrs. Stowe's interest in representative institutions and the ideal
(that is, utopianism made rational) contrasts sharply, of course, with
Emily Dickinson's private activity and actualities. It is the difference
between schematized ritual and the polymorphous perverse, between
abstract structure and the senses, between subjection and freedom.

It would have been inconsistent for Emily Dickinson to have had
a serious interest in typology, as I am arguing, for it assumes an
absence made present, the unconscious made conscious, the unknown
made visible, the past made important by the present moment. We
know her dependence, instead, on "the abyss," on what Inder Nath
Kher calls "the landscape of absence." Symbolism, for her, is not
hierophancy. She could not mistake the shadows for the reality as
Mrs. Stowe had done; the shadows *were* shadows, the reality *merely* a
hope. Utopia, to her mind, cannot replace the givens. The world does
not awaken very often in this world. Morning has not occurred.

But to Mrs. Stowe, the fulfillment of prophecy was the purpose
of the world, certainly the purpose of America, and probably one of
her purposes for her own life. As with the New England generations
before her, back to Mather, typology was an eschatology. History is
fulfilled by its coming to an end. Thus, Mrs. Stowe prayed for the end
of the world, where Emily Dickinson, as she tells it in one poem,
simply would "omit to pray, . . . For my will goes the other way." To
one the kingdom of God was close; for the other it was present,
fleeting, unlikely, questionable. One was impatient for the last days
and therefore was in approach a social activist; the other was autonomous and therefore perplexed, countering the sure with the
metaphor (and sometimes the fact) of her fragmented poems.

The curious factor in this comparison of these two women's

---

church to bring about a moral revolution, a Christian utopia. With Catherine, Harriet
Beecher Stowe wrote *The American Woman's Home* in 1869, assisting in the creating of
that nineteenth-century phenomenon, the family as millennial microcosm:

> Let such a truly "Christian family" be instituted in any destitute settle-
> ment. . . . The cheering example would soon spread. . . . The Blessed Word also
> cheers us with pictures of a dawning day to which we are approaching, when a
> voice shall be heard under the whole heavens, saying, "Alleluia"—"the kingdoms of
> this world are become the kingdoms of our Lord and of his Christ, and he shall
> reign forever and ever." [Pp. 459–60]

This Mrs. Stowe called "the millennial consummation."

43. Richard Howard, "Reflections on a Strange Solitude," *Prose* 1 (1970): 87.

politics is the issue of orthodoxy. Mrs. Stowe, using the Puritan structures far more easily than Emily Dickinson, was the one who fought tenets of the theology the more vehemently, though never as sincerely as Emerson, since she stayed for the most part within its sheltering limits. She rebelled against the dogmas of her upbringing and yet managed to keep a respect for the Puritan struggle. "Calvinism, in its essential features," she wrote, "will never cease from the earth, because the great fundamental facts of nature are Calvinistic, and men with strong minds and wills always discover it. . . . All this I say, while I fully sympathize with the causes which incline many fine and beautiful minds against the system."[44] Emily Dickinson, unable to manipulate the structures to her own ends since she apparently did not understand or did not need them, lived out some features of the faith more naturally, as we have seen, giving form and force to many feelings that Harriet Beecher Stowe would not deal with.

Of both it is no doubt better to speak of literary rather than theological Puritanism, however, for both *write* from within the tradition. Yet they differ greatly, for the one turns Puritan dogma into argument and the other turns it into psychoanalysis. Both moved away from dogma—one in the direction of immanence-in-history, the other in the direction of immanence-in-feeling. Both fought the idea of predestination at various times, and yet, when needed, Harriet Beecher Stowe applied it to historical salvation and Emily Dickinson to personal salvation. In this regard the former tends toward the Marxist and the latter toward the existential. It is the difference between Boston and Amherst-Northampton, between the Bay and the Connecticut Valley, between Mather and Hooker, between mind and heart.

Perhaps this is because so many Puritan ideas she got at home or at church, in her town and in her reading, were kept neutral. Mrs. Stowe was, on the other hand, an animator of the received, transforming it into the believed and projecting it as millennial events, because unable to suppress her certitudes. Emily Dickinson was not an idolator by instinct, not much interested in the unconditional. Some of the religious forms she remained subject to and others she cast off, simply because, unlike Mrs. Stowe, she was more fascinated with evidence and with the absurd than by fiction. She did not love God; she did not own a truth. She had the faculty of indifference and, above all, the ability to renege. The Fall for her was not the pursuit of a saving truth but a reminder that we are scavengers.

44. Harriet Beecher Stowe, *Sunny Memories of Foreign Lands* (Boston, 1854), p. 400.

Five

A MAGIC PRISON

Emily Dickinson and Nathaniel Hawthorne

The shore is safer ... but I love to buffet the sea.

[*Letters*, p. 104]

The honest duplicity with which Emily Dickinson faced her Puritan background (making what she called her "Compound Vision" and "Compound manner" more of a *compounded* sensibility than a mere complex one) should warn us that her life—most certainly her life as we experience it in much of her poetry—was in many respects *deliberately* strife-torn and provisional.

Perhaps a great deal like Hawthorne's Hester Prynne. In some significant ways, Emily Dickinson is like Hester more than she is like any other woman (real or fictional) of the nineteenth century. With the persona of Hester, Hawthorne dramatized a kind of woman that Emily Dickinson, several decades later, was to represent fairly flamboyantly, varying in her act, like Hester, from what Hawthorne calls "a well-spring of human tenderness" to a "dark labyrinth of mind."

The beginning of *The Scarlet Letter* makes a crucial point. Hester's original decision—parallel to Arthur Dimmesdale's—to reject the opportunity to escape the town's severe condemnation and the restrictive limits of Puritan life for Europe, a fuller life, a new identity, and freedom of mind and spirit was also Emily Dickinson's decision about Connecticut Valley religion: instead of going in the direction of either the current conservative or the liberal religious enthusiasm (thereby escaping the past and her own needs and abilities), she went radically into what Hawthorne calls "the dark, inscrutable forest" of her own self for the purpose of "emerging into another state of being." Following the Edwardsian outline, both women fulfilled themselves by painful but rewarding reversals.

"There is a fatality," Hawthorne adds, in accounting for Hester's retreat into the dark forest and the resulting productivity of her life, "a feeling so irresistible and inevitable that it has the force of doom, which almost invariably compels human beings to linger around and haunt, ghostlike, the spot where some great and marked event has given the color to their lifetime."[1] Edwards would have recognized the scenario, whether acted out in forest cottage or village cupola, that might make one use self-imposed "doom" to give "color to [one's] lifetime." The issue is important for an understanding of Emily Dickinson's American place.

Hawthorne she perhaps knew better than any other nineteenth-century American writer we read today—and most likely for much the same reason that we read him today: his re-creation of the universe as ambiguity. When T. W. Higginson asked Emily Dickinson in 1879 what American fiction she knew, she reported: "Of Poe, I know too little to think - [but] Hawthorne appalls [and] entices."[2]

1. Though Hester toyed with both evangelical sentimentality and transcendental intellectuality, like Emily Dickinson she consistently found in the darker side of her soul "the spot" that could give "color to [her] lifetime." "Her sin, her ignominy were the roots which she had struck into the soil. It was as if a new birth, with stronger assimilations than the first, had converted the forest-land, still so uncongenial to every other pilgrim and wanderer, into Hester Prynne's wild and dreary, but life-long home." The issue of the productive pit comes up again at the end of the novel when, after seven years, Hester considers escaping to Europe with Dimmesdale: "Nor were it an inconsistency too improbably to be assigned to human nature, should we suppose a feeling of regret in Hester's mind, at the moment when she was about to win her freedom from the pain which had been thus deeply incorporated with her being. Might there not be an irresistible desire to quaff a last, long, breathless draught of the cup of wormwood and aloes, with which nearly all her years of womanhood had been perpetually flavored? The wine of life, henceforth to be presented to her lips, must be indeed rich, delicious, and exhilarating, in its chased and golden beaker; or else leave an inevitable and weary languor, after the lees of bitterness wherewith she had been drugged, as with a cordial of intensest potency" (*The Scarlet Letter*, Centenary ed. [Columbus, Ohio, 1962], 1:77–80, 227).
2. *Letters*, p. 649. We can be fairly sure that Emily Dickinson read *Mosses from an Old Manse* and *The House of the Seven Gables*, but she makes no reference in her poems and letters to *The Blithedale Romance, The Marble Faun, Twice-told Tales*, or Hawthorne's sketches (*Letters*, pp. 155, 604; Leyda, *Years and Hours*, 1:209, 218; 2:296). It is significant that in her letters she almost always connects Hawthorne with issues such as suffering, death, and immortality (*Letters*, pp. 431, 604, 432, 635, 155). What Emily Dickinson read *about* Hawthorne is difficult to find out. In 1879 she made an effort to

The ambiguity with which she thus held Hawthorne in mind also appears in her notice of Hawthorne's death in a letter to Sue Dickinson in 1864: "To include, is to be touchless, for Ourself cannot cease – Hawthorne's interruption does not seem as it did – Noon is Morning's Memoir."[3] She was drawn to the moralist in Hawthorne ("It seemed almost a lesson, given us to learn," she said of his writings)[4] but drawn more to his complexity of attitude. The appalling and enticing are concurrent in her reading of him; the "option . . . within" coexists with the "touchless[ness]" of one's attempt to "include" life and immortality.

It is the oxymoron with which Emily Dickinson describes Hawthorne that sticks: "Hawthorne appalls [and] entices."[5]

Perhaps this means she saw rather well how Hawthorne creates a reality in his better fiction that is formed out of a variety of antitheses, the attraction of opposing extremities, insoluble suspension, resolute irresolutions, ambiguity as confusion *sensed*. Whether she sensed all this or not—and capsulated it in her oxymoron about him—at least this was her reaction: ambivalent feelings about his themes and style, *both* appalling and enticing to her.[6] She was, of course, describing a side of her own temperament and something about her own artistic intent.[7]

Analysis of Hawthorne, like analysis of Emily Dickinson, can only reveal our inability to clarify the ambiguist in them. It easily escapes thesis.[8] The position is deliberate enough in both of them,

get T. W. Higginson's essay on Hawthorne in the *Atlantic Monthly*, and in 1882 she tried to obtain James Russell Lowell's newly published life of Hawthorne (*Letters*, pp. 635, 726).

3. *Letters*, p. 432. In another letter in which she notes Hawthorne's death, Emily Dickinson connects it with an illness of her own (*Letters*, p. 431).

4. *Letters*, p. 155.

5. *Letters*, pp. 649–50.

6. With her phrase about Hawthorne, she might have meant that his writings are appalling *because* enticing (very Puritan) or that they are enticing *because* appalling (very Romantic). In any event, the two opposing terms, as with any oxymoron, make *one* sensation in her. She has a similar ambiguity in poem #281: "'Tis so appalling – it exhilirates"; another in #552: "a Sunset . . . [can] Exhilirate – Debase"; and still another one in #673: "'Tis this – invites – appalls – endows." Similarly, she writes of the Bible in a letter of 1885: "It stills, incites, infatuates – blesses and blames in one."

7. The fullest case for Emily Dickinson's handling of irony, paradox, ambiguity, and the oxymoron is made by Brita Lindberg-Seyersted, *The Voice of the Poet: Aspects of Style in the Poetry of Emily Dickinson* (Cambridge, 1968): "The English language itself has here provided the poet with great possibilities of emphasizing opposites, of underlying identities, or structuring sound and meaning into the composite of sameness and indifference that constitutes the essence of art, 'the mingling of contraries,' as Yeats expresses it" (p. 89). However, the thematic, philosophical, and biographical implications of these language forms go unexplored in that study.

8. Helen Hunt Jackson was someone from Emily Dickinson's own circle of literary friends who saw in her seclusion a Hawthornian reaction (Leyda, *Years and*

however, that we can assume they understood on some level the logic of the convention they helped to establish (along with Melville and James) in American literature. The ambiguities they created—implicit in their faith, their relationship to society, and their artistic consciousness—make of the literature they wrote a still life: reactions are in suspension, life's antithetic terms are irreconcilable except in tension, assertions conflict in mere stasis, conclusions are suspect, inconclusive, or incoherent, and complexity becomes homogeneity. Ambiguity, I feel, is a possible rubric for these sensations in both of them. The esthetics of humility in American literature begins here.

The seven types of ambiguity, as advertised by William Empson and others, barely touch the method and metaphysics of Hawthorne and Emily Dickinson when the form of their Puritan humility has to have a name.[9] They are not interested in the reader's multiple and divergent readings of their works so much as in *their* multiple and divergent readings of universe and world. They are not interested in deliberate blurring and muddling for the sake of abstraction, wit, or awe so much as in documenting the blur and muddle in *their* minds. For them ambiguity is less the moderns' "reserves of meaning" than the metaphysicals' "multitude of associations"; less an intricacy, deli-

---

Hours, 2:296). This was an emphasis that another prominent contemporary, James T. Field, made in a lecture on Hawthorne in Amherst in 1874, which Emily Dickinson might have heard: "Hawthorne wrote only when he was moved to it by impulse, and then he would completely shut out the world and write in perfect seclusion" (Leyda, *Years and Hours,* 2:217). Allen Tate, in 1932, initiated a comparison of the two; for him Hawthorne and Emily Dickinson brought "the puritan tragedy of the first order.... But between her and Hawthorne there exists a difference of intellectual quality. She lacks almost radically the power to seize upon and understand abstractions for their own sake.... But Hawthorne was a master of ideas, within a limited range.... She has Hawthorne's intellectual toughness, a hard, definite sense of the physical world" ("New England Culture and Emily Dickinson," *Symposium* 3 [1932]:206–226). William Sherwood is the only student of Emily Dickinson who asserts the possibility of Hawthorne's considerable influence on her: "Emily Dickinson constructed a drama of passion, transgression, defiance, punishment, damnation, and despair, assimilating, as Hawthorne may have taught her to do" (*Circumference and Circumstance* [New York, 1968], p. 82). Several readers of Emily Dickinson and Hawthorne have found parallels and borrowings in her poems to suggest a very close affinity. Sidney E. Lind finds that she took several of her images for "Further in Summer than the Birds" from Hawthorne's essay "The Old Manse" (*American Literature* 39 [1967]: 163–69), and Dan McCall locates the source of her "I felt a Funeral in my Brain" in Hawthorne's sketch "The Hollow of the Three Hills" (*New England Quarterly* 42 1969]: 432–35). In both cases Emily Dickinson chooses and retains Hawthorne's ambiguities.

9. *Seven Types of Ambiguity* (London, 1936). Of the Empson categories, Hawthorne's and Emily Dickinson's ambiguities run the gamut of Type Three through Type Seven but come closest to being examples of Seven: ambiguity as "a fundamental division in the writer's mind." Emily Dickinson is clearly beyond them all into a Cosmology of the Coherent Possible. There, Empson's textual variants and alternative readings and multiple referents are irrelevancies. In her new space, the semantics of the diverse are subordinate to the *fact* (in her mind) of the diversity.

cacy, or compression of thought, or even a moving among ideas, than a matter of connections among apparent opposites, apparent disorder. Order is *not* in the eye of the beholder. Their ambiguity is less a matter of clarity about complexity than of confusion about the clearly complex, less a flowering out of single terms, ideas, or lives, as with a pun, a paradox, a schizophrenia, than a creating of a new space by means of differing words, with the resulting illusion of distance, dimension, context. There is a personal Unknown filled with the knowables.

Ambiguity in Hawthorne and Emily Dickinson represents not a polarized imagination or conceptual antithesis but, instead, the ability to synthesize and suspend. It is not a desperately divided state of mind or tormented perspective, not mere conflict, but balance without resolution, without coherence. It does not so much show a dual perspective or simple perception of inherent paradox as it shows a tentativeness. It is the opposite of dialectic: things do not quarrel in their heads but present themselves constant and indifferent.

The ambiguity of both Hawthorne and Emily Dickinson is different from simple antithesis ("Yesterday, undistinguished! / Eminent Today"), different from simple paradox (which may lack the features of simultaneity and tentativeness), and certainly different from a moral complementarity (in which two positions, contradictory and mutually exclusive, are both acceptable).

Ambiguity, as a way the minds of Hawthorne and Emily Dickinson worked, took rhetorical form in their writings in the oxymoron: a balanced contradiction opposed to resolution, a juxtaposition of contradictory terms of equal rank and emphasis, a compound of inclinations and responses. It is their attempt to realize in their art an ineffable complexity and, in written form, represents a struggle with materials without victory.

Oxymoronists like Hawthorne and Emily Dickinson are confessed losers. Alternatives become juxtaposed without offering a choice. All is shown, nothing wins. Something is many things, *any*thing. The oxymoron leaves factors of mind intact (the philosophical realism) but holds them in harmony (the romanticism).

In this respect, the oxymoron is an organic metaphor in the Coleridgean (and Structuralist) sense, for, as Coleridge put it, it "partakes of the reality which it renders intelligible, . . . abides itself as a living part in that unity of which it is the representative." Emily Dickinson's interest in the inherent ambiguity of words themselves is a very modern aspect of her concern for her writing.

The oxymoron as a linguistic feature of ambiguity in the works of both Hawthorne and Emily Dickinson is reductive. It diverts one from its own terms to one's reaction, one's ignorance. It frustrates our customary intellectual desire for logical resolution. It uses inconclusive or conjectural terms to modify and undercut certainty. It is a paradigm of the (in)substantial, a substantive under severe modification. Then what one has left is stasis, self-consciousness, humility. A neo-Puritanism—Hawthorne's, Emily Dickinson's—is the result.

The oxymoron is a play with words, to be sure, but it perhaps indicates a conviction (a tentative conviction) that language forms reproduce universal forms. The truth to Emily Dickinson's and Hawthorne's use of the oxymoron is that *in form* it represents their philosophical realism: that is, the recognition of reversal, ambiguity, anomaly, complexity, the impossibility of naming, identifying, knowing—and therefore the acceptance of the Fall. In a condition of innocence before the possible universe (a contrived/esthetic state), inherent probability becomes attached to natural objects rather than to the fallibility of the mind. Will is not imposed on them; they give themselves. At the same time, the use of the oxymoron represents the recognition of the richness, depth, and fullness of things (albeit unknowable, untouchable)—and therefore the grace inherent in existence. The Fall is concomitant with possibility. Oxymoronic ambiguity is a language form to match what Emily Dickinson calls "The mingled side / Of his [God's] Divinity" (#576). It is the Gnostic in her.

We have it from Emily Dickinson herself that, given the world's opportunities and confusion and given man's condition of unknowing, "Opposites - entice" (#355). This motif in her poetry was never a program of convenient, self-sustaining tension for her so much as a religious-esthetic principle: *Nothing is sure, everything is possible.* Her attitude is a Puritan, esthetic version of Ivan Karamazov's "Nothing is true. Everything is permitted." Her concept of ambiguity was religious simply because, as we have already seen, religion did not have the sharp edges and distinct shadows, the fastidiousness and legality for her that it did for almost everyone else she knew. (Hawthorne would have been the distinct exception.) Faith and doubt were grasped in a single act of vision. The substance of religion was to be enjoyed on heretical grounds where hope dominated. "Faith is *Doubt*," she expostulated. Perhaps this emblematic casuistry grew out of a deep respect for equivocation as a theological discipline. By way of her syntax of *dilemma* (in the sense of its etymology, "two premises"), theology becomes esthetics, a distinctly non-Matherian, non-Edwardsian solution.

Yet the ambiguities and the doubting in her mind are to be distinguished from Christian paradox. Paradox to Jung is "the very essence of religious assertion." But Emily Dickinson could not be that kind of religious person; it lies, for the most part, outside her Puritan esthetics. For one thing, it points to a union of elements in experience that are irreconcilable to analytical reason and so pushes one beyond what is merely human to a reliance on God the resolver. Where the experience of Dickinsonian ambiguity is static (one knows and accepts the unknowability of the Unknown), the experience of Christian paradox is dynamic because it is capable of expectations, reversals, reinterpretations, reconstructions, possible surprises among the mixed dualities, even the illusion of freedom. In paradox there is hope, whereas to Emily Dickinson many things in the universe, as we have seen, are "Hopeless – / Therefore good." The Arminian gift of seeing (the ambiguities are not real, only *apparent*) is too easy a grace for her, too much subject to illusion and therefore hoax. She preferred the reductive trouble of feeling sure that she was unsure about the reasoning.

The concept of ambiguity was to her, above all, esthetic, for in a variety of rhetorical forms (in irony, paradox, and, most conveniently, the oxymoron) she could bring heaven and earth together. As with Hawthorne, as also with Blake and Yeats, the imagination was the place for the convergence of the two. In one poem, #137, Emily Dickinson refers to the ambiguity of things as "a system of aesthetics." Nature is "Half a transport – half a trouble." Herself as a writer she describes in another poem in deliberate ambiguities:

> A still – Volcano – Life – ...
> A quiet – Earthquake Style – ...
> The Solemn – Torrid – Symbol – ...
>
> [#601]

For both her religious and her esthetic well-being, she had faith in and need for such language.

Opposites entice, Emily Dickinson held, because both faith and the imagination work ambiguously, oxymoronically: *Nothing is sure, everything is possible.* Hope and hopelessness intermix: "So bubble brooks in deserts / On Ears that dying lie." The absolute diffracts: God is simultaneously "Burglar! [and] Banker." Life persists amid flux and change: "How much can come / And much can go / And yet abide the world." Emotions, a sure thing, deceive us: grief is "A piercing Comfort"; "A woe of Ecstasy"; a "perfect – paralyzing Bliss." Life may be at various times for her a "lonesome Glory," a "mute Pomp," "sordid excellence," and "Honor honorless." In sum, existence, the unknown, is—in the perfect ambiguity/oxymoron for both her faith and her art—"a magic prison."[10]

These enticing opposites throughout her writing come from de-

10. The poem in which the remarkable phrase "a magic prison" appears was written as part of a letter in which Emily Dickinson was attempting to define her "paganism" for Helen Hunt Jackson, and that was very late in her life—March 1885 (*Letters,* pp. 866–67).

fective vision, not insight. It is what she calls "see[ing] Comparatively."
Her understanding of this is that we cannot grasp "The Thing so
towering high" and so must be content with tentative things (that is,
with "This Morning's finer Verdict - "). We are thereby spared what
she calls "The Anguish" of trying for all and failing. The duplicity of
things is still a matter for *hope:* "The waking in a Gnat's embrace - /
Our Giants further on - " (#534).

This goes beyond what she calls her "Compound Vision," a form
of esthetic guessing:

> The Finite - furnished
> With the Infinite -
> Convex - and Concave Witness -
> Back - toward Time -
> And forward -
> Toward the God of Him -
>
> [#906]

Her view is not the same, either, as what she calls the "Compound
Witness" of Jesus. He saw things consecutively (life, then death, then
immortality), whereas she sees them simultaneously (a "newer - nearer
Crucifixion / Than That -").

Not always knowing the truth, both Emily Dickinson and
Hawthorne fabricated it in a form—as one should easily sense—that
included, humbly, the possibilities. Emily Dickinson's poems are the
narration of a Creation of hers. Her resulting world is a coherent
body of disparates, sustained mainly by a contrapuntal language, a
fusion of simultaneous opposites. Out of the language of separate
realities, she created a fantasy; her poems, like Joyce's language, are
play passing into earnestness—magic within the prison.

This came from her rediscovery (Hawthorne had discovered it
before her) of the uncertainty principle, a principle that put them
both closer to modern physics than to biblical exegesis. Like him, she
became a realist by *not* understanding things: the suspension is creative. The fortunate Fall in her hands, as in Hawthorne's, is a creative
misunderstanding.

For this the oxymoron served as the main language structure for
her sense of the indecipherable ambiguity of existence. Its form, like
her thinking, is that of riddle, rebus, enigma. Her poetry is a catalog
of such, the range of which, oscillating between the extremes of
George Herbert and Dylan Thomas, is clearly of greater significance
than the items of her repertoire themselves:

> Brave - Brokenhearted statement
> the divine Perdition / Of Idleness and Spring
> Ah! Necromancy Sweet!

Niggard Grace!
Heavenly Hurt . . . An Imperial affliction
the Pain of joy
a Dome of Abyss
this smart Misery
fond Ambush
a common – Glory –
To perish – of Delight
luxury of Doubt
Hopeless – / And therefore – Good
transports of Patient
stolid Bliss
the solitary prowess / Of a Silent Life
Confident Despair
too tawdry Grace
A Haggard Comfort
Awful Father of Love
Inconceivably solemn! / Things so gay
Infinites of Nought
bright Impossibility
the Quick of Wo
a Shame of Nobleness . . . Shame of Ecstasy
the Scant Salvation
a lonesome Glee
sumptuous solitude
dull Balm
deadly sweet
Centuries of room
a piercing Comfort
an arid Pleasure
Heavenly – Hopeless Distances
our Anticipation . . . [is] a Doubt
a numb significance
Taints of Majesty
Dooms of Balm
Reward of Anguish
dear iniquity
a bliss of sorrow
Detriment divine
ecstatic limit / Of unobtained Delight
Necromancer! Landlord!
How many leagues of nowhere
so sweet a Torment – / Such sumptuous – Despair
numb alarm
sordid excellence
a Discontent / Too exquisite – to tell –
that bleak exultation

Safe Despair
Wonder . . . A beautiful but bleak condition
an abstemious Ecstasy
an appalling boon
A soul admitted to itself / Finite Infinity
Captivity is . . . Liberty
For that dear – distant – dangerous – Sake –
August – Absolved – Numb –
a Discontent / Too exquisite
Bondage as Play . . . / And Sentence – Sacrament –
sweet derision
A Hoary Boy
Delight's Despair
Homeless at home
What Exultation in the Woe
a gay unknown
arid delight
Ecstasy is peril
A crash without a Sound
The uncertain certainty

This deliberate fracturing (also focusing) of her language and thought is a structure that makes possible her dominant doubled theme of *humility* (in the face of one's unknowing) and *hope* (in light of the newly created possibilities).

Hawthorne could have read her for this. "Blessed are all simple emotions, be they dark or bright!" Melville wrote of the ambiguities of a Hawthorne story. "It is the lurid intermixture of the two that produces the illuminating blaze of the infernal regions." The intermixture of affirmations or negations—an oxymoronic quality to his vision—has become a staple of Hawthorne criticism. Hardly a "lurid" device of multiple choice, though, it is the drama of humble and hope-filled opposition in Hawthorne that attracts us even as his subjects may not, with the appalling and enticing simultaneous, as Emily Dickinson put it. "A man's bewilderment," says Holgrave in *Seven Gables,* "is the measure of his wisdom." Hawthorne's provisional reality—a world of omnipresent irony, unresolved conflicts, divergent intensities, a consciousness of antinomies—encourages a wide range of speculation. Possibility is the form of his humble Puritan optimism, and an inconclusive (and therefore voluminous) criticism is the result: *we* become provisional in his hands.

What we can be sure of is that in Hawthorne the oxymoron has been expanded to a cosmology; the universe is a cosmic oxymoron in much of his fiction. His formulation of this reality begins, as does Emily Dickinson's, in the careful phrasing of oxymoronic ambiguities:

a loathful brotherhood
a sweet unwillingness
elevate their spirits to an enthusiasm of wretchedness
the celestial fire that tortured his own breast
a wild look of wonder, joy, and horror
a more intimate revenge
that dark treasure
a quality almost majestic in the despair
hideous luxuriance
a dark light
a dark transfiguration
hope and joy shone out, indeed, but with fear betwixt them, and a kind
          of horror
a solemn joy
gild the utter gloom with final glory
with earnest haste and ecstasy
at once a shadow and a splendor
so terrible and so merciful
troubled joy
as terrible as she is beautiful
the happy sadness, the lightsome shadows
the ecstasy of inaction
inscrutable spectacles
his selfish love
a sad smile gleamed
the energy of disease
rich gravity
some beautiful infirmity of character
a substantial emptiness
a material ghost
a stern enjoyment
positive despair
splendid rubbish
negatively happy
contemptuous tranquillity
ecstatic need
by the sympathy of all that was wicked
Evil must be your only happiness
one cry of despair and triumph

Strong reliance on the subjunctive and conditional is of equal ambiguous force in his style, as in these crucial descriptions in "The Birthmark":

In those days when the comparatively recent discovery of electricity and other kindred mysteries of Nature *seemed to open* paths into the region of miracle, it was not unusual for the love of science to rival the love of woman in its depth and absorbing energy. The higher intellect, the imagination, the spirit, and even the heart *might* all find their congenial aliment in pursuits which, as some of their ardent votaries believed, *would ascend* from one step of powerful intelligence to another, until the philosopher *should lay* his hand on the secret of creative force and *perhaps make* new worlds for himself. *We know not whether* Aylmer possessed this degree of faith in man's ultimate control over Nature. He had devoted himself, however, too unreservedly to scientific studies ever to be weaned from them by any second passion. His love for his young wife *might prove* the stronger of the two; but it *could* only be by intertwining itself with his love of science, and uniting the strength of the latter love to his own.

. . . .

He more than intimated that it was at his option to concoct a liquid that *should prolong* life for years, perhaps interminably; but that it would produce a discord in Nature which all the world, and chiefly the quaffer of the immortal nostrum, *would find* cause to curse.

. . . .

yet, *had Aylmer reached* a profounder wisdom, *he need not thus have* flung away the happiness which *would have woven* his mortal life of the selfsame texture with the celestial. The monetary circumstance was too strong for him; he failed to look beyond the shadowy scope of time, and, living once for all in eternity, to find the perfect future in the present. [My emphasis][11]

And it is necessary to recognize the influence of oxymoronic motifs like the strung out, unifying "Yet . . . but . . . though" or "some . . . but others" or "as if . . . Again it seemed that . . ." or "whether it had . . . or whether . . . we shall not take upon us to determine" or "Not always, however . . . It happened . . . It might also be considered . . . To choose another figure . . . Sometimes, it is true . . . And sometimes even, here on earth" or "whether impelled by the species of terror . . . or by a . . . it were not easy to decide. Both impulses might have been wrought on him at once" or "There were circumstances which led some to suppose that . . . Others denied that there were sufficient grounds for such a conjecture."

In addition, ambiguity appears where it cannot in poetry—in character and plot. Everywhere there is a sort of doubleness in Hawthorne; balance has become an esthetic principle, tentativeness a religious principle.[12] On the ambiguity of the human heart, Haw-

11. *Complete Works*, 2 (Boston, 1854): 47, 58, 69.
12. To describe himself as an *American* writer, Hawthorne needed a series of ambiguities: "Altogether, in his culture and want of culture; in his crude, wild and misty

thorne wrote: "There is more of good and more of evil in it; more redeeming points of the bad and more errors of the virtuous; higher upsoarings, and baser degradation of the soul; in short, a more perplexing amalgamation of vice and virtue than we witness in the outward world." "There were so many anomalies in his character," he writes of the bridegroom in "The Wedding Knell." In "Fancy's Show Box" success and sin mix equally in the characters ("In truth, there is no such thing in man's nature as a settled and full resolve"). In "Young Goodman Brown" a symbolic artifact is made deliberately ambiguous: "which bore the likeness of, . . . that it might almost be seen to. . . . This, of course, must have been an oracular deception." In "The Minister's Black Veil" the ambiguities of the minister's motives provide the structure of the story; his opposite effects on people make it a story of conjecture. Wakefield we come to know as a paradox of a man of "morbid vanity" who yet retains "his original share of human sympathies"; though he is an "Outcast of the Universe," he is obsessed more by, and attached more to, what he left. The hero of "A Select Party," the Man of Fancy, is "a character of superhuman capacity and virtue," and yet, "when he happens to cast his eyes upon a looking glass, he beholds Nobody reflected there!" In *Seven Gables* we have "the horror, which was proper to Phoebe's sweet and order-loving character." The life of Donatello of *The Marble Faun* Hawthorne summarizes in terms of "the joys and sorrows, the intertwining light and shadow, of human life." The portrait of Colonel Pyncheon in *The House of the Seven Gables* has "an exceedingly pleasant countenance indicative of benevolence, openness of heart, sunny good humor, and other praiseworthy qualities of that cast" and at the same time it is that of a man who is "sly, subtle, hard, imperious, and, withal, cold as ice." And yet, from another perspective, "It is almost too soft and gentle for a man's." Rappaccini and Aylmer are both gods and devils. Beatrice is " as terrible as she is beautiful." Hester Prynne has—appallingly, enticingly—"a woman's soul, so sacred even in its pollution"; Chillingsworth's personality is "so familiar, and yet so strange and cold"; Dimmesdale is a man of "violence of passion, which [is] intermixed, in more shapes than one, with his higher, purer, softer qualities"; Pearl is nature, itself fallen yet divine. The unsureness of human observation (Hawthorne is skeptical of his own) makes the admission of multiple possibilities and definite ambiguities in his characterizations.

---

philosophy, and the practical experience that counteracted some of its tendencies; in his magnanimous zeal for man's welfare, and recklessness of whatever the ages had established in man's behalf; in his faith, and in his infidelity; in what he had, and in what he lacked—the artist might fitly enough stand forth as the representative of many compeers in his native land" (*The House of the Seven Gables*, p. 181).

"Certainly, he has a pensive air," Hawthorne observes of a young man in "Sights from a Steeple." "Is he in doubt, or in debt? Is he, if the question be allowable, in love? Or, is he merely overcome by the heat?" Hawthorne's characters are often living oxymorons. His symbol of character ambiguity is the haunted mind—half awake, half asleep.

Likewise, Hawthorne's narratives themselves are dominated by deliberate ambiguity. In "The Maypole of Merry Mount," the situation pits "grizzly saints" against "gay sinners" ("[The Puritans'] darksome figures were intermixed with the wild shapes of their foes") to represent early America as an archetypal oxymoron. In "The Great Carbuncle" we see at work the ambiguity built into Christianity: to live for the prize is to live in vain; to lose it is to live more fully; loss is gain; hell is grace. The contradictions inherent in both practical and esthetic life in "The Artist of the Beautiful" go unresolved. The discrepancies in the creation of Feathertop and the results of Peter Goldthwaite's treasure hunt go unreconciled. The heroism and foolhardiness of the actions of Ethan Brand and Young Goodman Brown are left ambivalent. Hawthorne's Central Intelligence Office is ignorant of a person's place, nature, value, even "merely delusive." His new Adam and Eve live in a *fallen* world: "There must have been shadows enough, even amid the primal sunshine of their existence, to suggest the thought of the soul's incongruity with its circumstances." What is affirmed in the story of "Dr. Heidegger's Experiment" is negated by its conclusion; in seeking youth, the four figures in the experiment do those things that will bring them to ruin. The Christmas banquet is "intended to signify that death in life which had been the testator's definition of existence." Situation, especially in the stories, is thus apprehended by Hawthorne with an indifference to differences, and so eliminating the necessity of preference, refusing to play God with his own creations. The linking of alternatives in the narrative line of his stories, even when this reduces movement, is at the same time both a confession of insecurity and a confidence in abundance. With him, as with Emily Dickinson, ambiguity makes it possible to show that nothing is sure and yet everything is possible.

In *The House of the Seven Gables,* in an aside on his own realism, his literary imitation of Perplexity, Hawthorne delivers a short discourse on ambiguity:

> It is a heavy annoyance to a writer, who endeavors to represent nature, its various attitudes and circumstances, in a reasonably correct outline and true coloring, that so much of the mean and ludicrous should be hopelessly mixed up with the purest pathos which life anywhere supplies to him. . . . If we look through all the heroic fortunes of man-

kind, we shall find this same entanglement of something mean and trivial with whatever is noblest in joy or sorrow. Life is made up of marble and mud. . . . What is called poetic insight is the gift of discerning, in this sphere of strangely mingled elements, the beauty and the majesty which are compelled to assume a garb so sordid.

To my mind, *The Scarlet Letter* embodies Hawthorne's most satisfying formulation of oxymoronic ambiguities. Characterizations are deliberately complicated, duplicitous, blurred. Hester thrives on her humiliation, fails amid her epiphanal pride, experiences (in frustrating forms) depression and success simultaneously. Chillingsworth's evil is productive of good, his depravity has godly proportions. Dimmesdale's destructive masochism is a grace-filled preparationism. Pearl is truth before swine, the fall and yet the salvation of Hester, chaos and integrity, glory amid gloom, gloom amid glory.

Narrative movement in the novel is also multidirectional. The rise of Hester to her self-reliance is coterminous with her fall from grace. The fall of Dimmesdale into perversity leads to his salvation, his justification. The success of Chillingsworth doubles as his nadir, his rejection. The emergence of Pearl as a personality in her own right makes her removal from the story necessary. The story is shades of dark shedding light on nothing.

Symbols, too, assert themselves in the novel and act self-reductively. In utopia, there is cemetery and prison. Roses bloom amid weeds. The scarlet letter is simultaneously Adultery/Able/Angel, "a design of justice and retribution" and at the same time has "a purpose of mercy and beneficence," though Hawthorne admits, "another's guilt might have seen another symbol in it." The landscape blesses, baffles, enriches, alienates, condemns. Hester is both virgin and adulteress. Sin's darkness, in the end, gules; the guling darkens the world. Thus, ambiguity is one's experience with the novel.[13]

It is remarkable that Hester can progress out of her tragic condition by accepting the many-facetedness of herself, Pearl, and life in general, for she started out by assigning things one meaning, the way townspeople gave the scarlet letter one meaning.

---

13. Emily Dickinson may have a (clearly unambiguous) reference to *The Scarlet Letter* in a letter of early 1878 about her mother's health: "She reads a little – sleeps much – chats – perhaps – most of all – about nothing momentous, but things vital to her – and reminds one of Hawthorne's blameless Ship – that forgot the Port" (*Letters,* p. 604). The reference appears to be closest to the following: "In furtherance of this choice, it so happened that a ship lay in the harbor; one of those questionable cruisers, frequent at that day, which, without being absolutely outlaws of the deep, yet roamed over its surface with a remarkable irresponsibility of character." T. H. Johnson argues that this is not a reference to Hawthorne but to a Salem legend about a ship that haunted the port but never came to land (*Poems,* p. 605).

Likewise, Melville's Ahab is tragic because of his failure to realize that every event and object has a multiplicity of meanings. Assigning one meaning to the whale, he is trapped. The whale has eyes on both sides of his head, Ahab only in front. Hawthorne's seven gables point in all directions at the same time.

Hester Prynne is not given a *consciousness* of the ambiguities of her own life, however, whereas Emily Dickinson's long struggle to "face down frustration," as George Whicher tells us in his biography, "gave her a curious doubleness of vision, as though her two eyes did not make one in sight but, bird-like, were focussed in opposite directions."[14] She seems always to have sensed that human life is ambiguous at its core—and (here is her Christian optimism) that was its advantage. Those bird's eyes of hers, focused or not, often detected life to be an oxymoronic situation where contrarieties occur simultaneously, where contingency persists amid paradise, where there is nothing sure but much possible.

Here she describes, in a Hawthornian fashion, what she calls "a Life ... Below":

> 'Tis this – invites – appalls – endows –
> Flits – glimmers – proves – dissolves –
> Returns – suggests – convicts – enchants –
> Then – flings in Paradise –

[#673]

This is one of her longest oxymorons, a deliberate juxtaposition of differences. Her motive, "focussed in opposite directions," as it were, appears to be modification of the sure ("'Tis a Baffling Earth") and documentation of the possible (what she calls "the Acres of Perhaps"). Her antinomies are a woman doing battle without victory—with faith, however, in the possible. This is reconstitution of reality as ambiguity.

In another characterization of "a Life ... Below," she gets at the simultaneity of contrary experiences—

---

14. *This Was a Poet* (Ann Arbor, 1957), p. 288. The practice of ambiguity in Emily Dickinson is more than a "characteristic swing and poise between joy and despair, between faith and skepticism, and between desire and fear," as David Porter claims (*The Art of Emily Dickinson's Early Poetry* [Cambridge, 1966], p. 38). The practice is also not quite as Archibald MacLeish has it, "a coupling back and forth, not only between incongruities, but between worlds"; it is more than "counterpoint" or "disjunction" or "dimensions" or "irony" or "tension" or "conflict," terms from New Critical ideology ("The Private World of Emily Dickinson," in *Emily Dickinson: Three Views* [Amherst, 1960], p. 96). Clark Griffith accurately identifies her ambiguities as attempts to "spurn all firm expectations" with "a style of careful, quiet inconclusiveness," but he is inaccurate, I feel, in seeing this as "a stern indifference toward them all" or a "steadfast composure which declines involvements" (*The Long Shadow* [Princeton, 1964], pp. 45, 55, 63).

Defeat whets Victory – they say –
The Reefs in Old Gethsemane
Endear the Shore beyond –
'Tis Beggars – Banquets best define –
'Tis Thirsting – vitalizes Wine

—and then, unsure of what the variety means, confesses that "Faith
bleats to understand" (#313). When she attempts to know "The
Heaven below the Heaven above," she can, in another poem, get it
down only oxymoronically: "A perfect – paralyzing Bliss – / Contended
as Despair." This stymied paradise she calls the largest "Blessing," for
it yields faith and hope in her (#756). She attempts no Faustian synthesis of the paradoxes.

Her insistence that there is an intrusion of one quality/emotion/
fact on another in our perception of the world is her way of maintaining equilibrium, balance, faith. Simultaneity of reference, the oxymoron, is her representation of a rich reality she cannot define. An
eclipse is in one poem, for instance, her symbol of reality as oxymoron, rich in variety of effects yet indefinable and so inspiring awe,
faith, sadness: "Sunset on the Dawn . . . Midnight's – due – at Noon"
(#415). Frustrated desire is another of her symbols of reality as
oxymoron: she is often "Enamored – impotent – content," that is, in
love with something but unable to love and therefore stoical about it,
all as one emotion (#505). The imagination itself is still another of her
symbols. It is

A merciful Mirage
That makes the living possible
While it suspends the lives.

[#859]

Used much more is her symbol, the dead watching life going on:

To eyelids in the Sepulchre –
How dumb the Dancer lies –
While Color's Revelations break –

[#496]

In all of these, and in many others, simultaneity represents limit and
exhilaration.

As a pioneer at ambiguity, however, Emily Dickinson was a
mess-maker. The factors of her dilemmas are hardly balanced, her
forms are elliptical and collapsed, her persona is unpredictable. She
has little ability at introconversion, which is disruptive. For Emily
Dickinson, as for Flannery O'Connor a century later (both of them
understandable only in a religious context—one Puritan, the other

Catholic), free will meant many wills conflicting in one person, and in both freedom was the same as mystery.

The simultaneity of contrarieties—ambiguity as a rich condition of unknowing—is for her an apposite order, replacing simplicities. Doubt is faith. Uncertainty is a certainty, insecurity a security. A sunset exhilarates, debases. Forever is made up of nows. The real is fictitious, fiction real. The light is dark enough. Success lives within failure. She knows the disappointment of fulfillment, the satisfactions of absence/lack/loss. Defect is a virtue, virtue defective. In this, Emily Dickinson plays with coherence yielded paradoxically out of ambiguity. Out of differences she creates a fantasy. The new order is for her like magic within a prison, or, more precisely, a magic prison, a "bright impossibility."

> Anecdotes of air in Dungeons
> Have sometimes proved deadly sweet!
>
> [#119]

> Bondage as Play – be sweet
> Imprisonment – Content –
> And Sentence – Sacrament –
>
> [#725]

Dualism replaces tragedy in one's unknowing in this apposite order of things, and one can take delight in the effort toward an impossible possession of the desired.

One important difference between the contiguities of the Transcendentalist's universe and those of Hawthorne's and Emily Dickinson's world centers on the issue of unity. To the former, all things issue from a single source, participate in a unifying spirit, and in their individual ways merge, complement, compensate, commune. It is not wrong to refer to a Transcendentalist as a mystic. But for the ambiguists, all things come from and go to an unknown, remain merely themselves, and are unified only by the common dilemma and the sympathies that are made necessary by the dilemma. This is a vastly different order: humility precludes a *uni*verse. The multiplicity is made sacramental, not as it seeks unity, not as it is endured, but as it is seen multiple, perplexing, sanctioned. Emily Dickinson's game is *being* lost.

This bringing together of contraries to form a world of ambiguity is, furthermore, a *protestant* function. Ambiguity in Emily Dickinson's poetry represents a sense of the richness in the (believed) unity of things, not despair that they fly apart. Dualism wards off tragedy. It works against the consecutive (a view of time for which paradox is a sufficient form) and for "naturalness," for the settled, determined state of things, for lush, fractured, meaningless, observed reality. By ambiguity she emphasizes her contingency and emphasizes herself as individual perceiver of the contingency. Ambiguity is a statement of faith. For Emily Dickinson, conventional faith was more mechanical than doubt, which for her could move from surprise to surprise, even within her general perplexity.

Simone de Beauvoir provides a way of seeing the ambiguity in Emily Dickinson as an ethic, as a religious position transcending conventional religion.[15] The ambiguities in Emily Dickinson, whether in the form of oxymoron or as religious position, are liberating. They are at the heart of her independence as a woman, as a person. Where the definitive excludes possibilities and stops desire, ambiguity means having a particular situation in the world and yet also a freedom through balance, a transcendence of time through equalized situations, a self through possibilities. Ambiguity for Emily Dickinson is therefore a solution to the seeming conflict of being and of being free. She can be serious without being a slave to a position or cause. She can have truth, knowing it is always a subjective choice. The position of an ambiguist like her is precisely the opposite of renunciation and is in fact really closer to a consciously constructed involvement.

The uncertainty principle, which I have asserted as a discovery of Hawthorne and Emily Dickinson for American literature and which was achievable mainly with the language of ambiguity, gives us one of their ways of talking about God. The unknowable was an elevation of mind to an infinite power.[16] In this way they could be skeptics who yet talked freely about God, using religious language freely while meaning their own unknowing. They were enabled to change their religious beliefs over the years (the only major nineteenth-century American writers for whom a progressive spiritual biography is largely impossible) without finding the need to alter their expression except in minor details. In their hands God became converted into a variety of secular and, fortunately for American literature, amazingly imaginative uses. The religious revivalism going on in both Hawthorne and Emily Dickinson at various points in their lives was only a further secularization. At the same time, giving the values of religion the acceptably secular form of ambiguity was a way, in increasingly desperate times, of saving values

15. *The Ethics of Ambiguity* (New York, 1948).
16. See M. H. Abrams, *Natural Supernaturalism: Tradition and Revolution in Romantic Literature* (New York, 1973), for a discussion of the tendency among skeptics of the Romantic movement to use religious language—institutional, conventional, traditional language—to express their nonreligious positions.

that had previously been based on the relation of God and man. Through ambiguity—which gave them a new freedom in the use of meaning—they seized, destroyed, and gave life to theology. In the reformulation, ambiguity made the object (theology = things to be believed) almost totally subjective (the believer lost amid the unknowable, the possibilities). This is the magic within the prison. Self-consciousness is therefore humility. Alienation is opportunity. Ambiguity is abundance. Puritanized esthetics thus came to good service.

Doubt was for Emily Dickinson a religious state, as I have tried to emphasize, since life for her was generally incomplete and unfulfilled in this world. Her uncertainty was an admission of her imperfect perception of the infinite. Her ambiguities result from the attempt to define. If saying is an act of faith, so is awareness of one's limited consciousness. "'Tis a dangerous moment for anyone," she wrote, "when meaning goes out of things and life stands straight – and punctual – and yet no signal comes." "Those who know [nature], know her less," she wrote in a poem in 1877, "The nearer her they get." In humility she accepts what she cannot know. "*Peasants* like me, . . ." she confessed, "Gaze perplexedly!"

Ambiguity, certainly as it appears in Emily Dickinson, should, in addition, be considered one of the defenses against authority, against religious tyranny, against mechanistic thinking, against simplicity of social outlook. Whatever presents itself in defined form—as a person, as an idea, as a point of view—she knew how to escape through irony and equivocation, thereby keeping herself free.

"But I see plainly . . . that I cannot see," says Emerson's character Montaigne-the-Skeptic, a version of Emily Dickinson.

> What is the use of pretending to powers we have not? What is the use of pretending to assurances we have not, respecting the other life? Why exaggerate the power of virtue? Why be an angel before your time? These strings, wound up too high, will snap. If there is a wish for immortality, and no evidence, why not say just that? If there are conflicting evidences, why not state them? If there is not ground for a candid thinker to make up his mind, yea or nay,—why not suspend the judgment? I weary of these dogmatizers. I tire of these hacks of routine, who deny the dogmas. I neither affirm nor deny. I stand here to try the case. I am here to consider, σκοπειν, to consider how it is. I will try to keep the balance true. Of what use to take the chair and glibly rattle off theories of society, religion and nature, when I know that practical objections lie in the way, insurmountable by me and by my mates? Why so talkative in public, when each of my neighbors can pin me to my seat by arguments I cannot refute? Why pretend that life is so simple a game, when we know how subtle and elusive the Proteus is? Why think to shut up all things in your narrow coop, when we know there are not one or

two only, but ten, twenty, a thousand things, and unlike? Why fancy that you have all the truth in your keeping? There is much to say on all sides.[17]

Participating thus in the protean and the flux, he/she is self-contained, considerable, opportune, active, open, free, magic.

I want to push the point of Emily Dickinson's attractive poetic role as perplexed peasant still further. Those who, like herself, live out their perplexities in the form of ambiguity, she admits, are "the duller scholars / Of the Mysterious Bard!"—that is, the unknowing seekers of God. They must live without assurances, meekly, dumbly.

> But who am I,
> To tell the pretty secret
> Of the Butterfly!
>
> [#167, 173]

In her poetry this condition of knowing you do not know is not accepted, however, without considerable complaint on her part.

> So keep your secret - Father!
> I would not - if I could,
> Know what the Sapphire Fellows, do,
> In your new-fashioned world!
>
> [#191]

She does not at all like the limitation placed on her by the perplexities of the Fall:

> The privilege to say
> Be limited by Ignorance -
>
> [#517]

"All this and more," she wrote in an early poem, "I cannot tell" (#140). It would therefore often be easier for her to explain the condition in terms of simple human blindness. "And then I could not see," she rationalizes, "to see." But it is far more complex than that to her, and so she speaks of "our unfitted eyes" and "our unfurnished eyes" and "my Childish Eye" and of "a Superior Grace - / Not yet, our eyes can see" and "The Blindness that beheld and blest - / And could not find it's Eye." Problems are not inherent in the universe to her but in the species, and so the need for Melvillean humility:

> Some with new - stately feet -
> Pass royal thro' the gate -

17. "Montaigne; or, The Skeptic," in *Representative Men: The Works of Ralph Waldo Emerson,* 4 (Boston, 1903):156–57.

> Flinging the problem back
> At you and I!
>
> [#10]

One lives, she reminds us, "*within* the Riddle." It is a matter of the human condition itself, a matter of personal fate, a matter of the Fall:

> Human Nature dotes
> On what it cant detect.
>
> [#1417]

Or more specifically, it is a question of the human inability to focus:

> Two – were immortal twice –
> The privilege of few –
> Eternity – obtained – in Time –
> Reversed Divinity –
>
> That our ignoble Eyes
> The quality conceive
> Of Paradise superlative–
> Through their Comparative.
>
> [#800]

"'Tis a Baffling Earth," she asserts. "This timid life of Evidence / Keeps pleading – 'I don't know'"—although the honesty is not exactly Christian humility and not exactly Transcendentalist patience with things and certainly not a skeptic's indifference. It is more in the area of Puritan content-with-ignorant-awe teleology. The Fall is a matter of wonder.

> Wonder – is not precisely Knowing
> And not precisely Knowing not –
> A beautiful but bleak condition
> He has not lived who has not felt –
>
> [#1331]

Things, she then deduces, may not be understood and certainly not apprehended; they can only be (as she has it in one poem) "comprehended by the Awe"—that is, wondered at, possibly enjoyed, but not *believed*. Perhaps this shows her to have had the radical antinomianism of a Roger Williams: since we cannot know, we cannot judge, and we are therefore at liberty because lost. An important motif of her poetry is this: "I – lost – was passing by."

To Emily Dickinson's mind there were what she called "Two Armies": "[1] Love and Certainty / And [2] Love and the Reverse." Love-and-uncertainty is, for her, the more powerful force. The concern with possibilities and limitations more than with advocacy gave her a sensibility that was close to what Emerson called "double consciousness." This is not exactly what Robert Weisbuch has called her "precise imprecision" with words and symbols but is closer to what he calls her concern "with the possibilities and limitations of each choice" in her thinking.[18]

"All we know," she wrote with a comfortable irony, "Is the uncertain certainty" (#1411). "Philosophy – don't know" the answer, she asserted, and neither, to her mind, does anything else, not even Science: "Why the Thief ingredient accompanies all Sweetness," she wrote in a letter in 1871, "Darwin does not tell us."[19] What was left, as I have tried to argue, was a productive doubting: "What merit had the Goal," she asks in one poem, "Except there intervene / Faint Doubt?" (#550). "It's finer," she concludes in still another, "not to know" (#191). Dumbing-up is not exactly what Emily Dickinson does when she is ambiguous, nor is it exactly truthing, but rather truthing about dumbing-up. That is, the uncertainty principle is *a* certainty.

I am suggesting that we can understand Emily Dickinson's understanding only by knowing her ignorance. She wants to know more than she (according to her own admission in poem after poem) has any right to know. In the last analysis, of course, she is not satisfied, yet she is humble about her dissatisfaction with things: which is perhaps the ultimate oxymoron of her life. She was unaware of the (to us, post-Freudian) issue of awareness. She was not so banal as to need it, demand it, or contrive a therapy for getting it.

> In insecurity to lie
> Is Joy's insuring quality.
>
> [#1434]

The magic of her life she found *within* the prison.

18. Robert Weisbuch, *Emily Dickinson's Poetry* (Chicago, 1975), pp. 53, 32.
19. *Letters,* p. 485.

$\mathcal{S}ix$

THE UNUSED UNIVERSE

EMILY DICKINSON AND RALPH WALDO EMERSON

Had we the first intimation of the Definition of Life, the calmest
of us, would be lunatics!

[*Letters*, p. 200]

When Emerson read four of Emily Dickinson's poems in 1860,
two of them published surreptitiously in the *Springfield Republican* and
the other two sent to him in a letter from Emily Dickinson's (and
Emerson's) friend Helen Hunt Jackson, he wrote the following in a
review of a number of "female poets" in the *Dial* for the first quarter
of that year:

> A Miss Dickenson [*sic*] writes verses as if threatened with fevers. I have
> not read enough of them to have any opinion to offer, except to say,
> that they are warm with life. She would give us her work unfinished,
> however, apparently not quite certain how to be both playful & sage.
> The few pieces of hers that I have before me are, to be sure, heavy with
> religious sentiment. She reveals that the old religion of New England
> has remarkable colors left in it; whilst the heavenly is hellish in her
> spare lines, the hellish is also made heavenly. She cannot make up her
> own mind & so she is lost in the world. Her writing her verses may help
> her find her way. I note some of her ingenious and simple lines.

Then he quotes (slightly edited) the entirety of two of her early poems.[1]

None of the above is true, of course, for of the shocks of literary recognition with which we reconstruct the nineteenth century for purposes of literary history, the contact between Emerson and Emily Dickinson is the most noticeably missing, the one most unexplainable.

1. Helen Hunt Jackson should have been an avenue by which Emily Dickinson's poems could have reached Emerson. He met her only once, when she introduced herself to him on a train in Newport in 1868. "My chief acquisition," he wrote in his journal for 13 July, "was the acquaintance of Mrs. Helen Hunt, . . . and her poetry I could heartily praise. The sonnet 'Thought' and 'Ariadne's Farewell' were the best, but all had the merit of originality, elegance, and compression" (*Journals* 10 [1914]: 252). In a letter of the same year he wrote of her, "[She] writes verses now and then in the 'Nation,' short but good, & is herself interesting" (Ralph Rusk, ed., *The Letters of Ralph Waldo Emerson* 6 [1939]: 26). Shortly after that, she sent Emerson her *Verses* (1873), and he included five of her poems in his anthology *Parnassus* (1875). Mrs. Jackson had Emily Dickinson's poems first from Higginson in 1866, two years before meeting Emerson, but she did not know the adult Emily Dickinson personally until the 1870s. All along, until her death in 1885, she thought Emily Dickinson a major poet, and one could conjecture that she might have told Emerson about her at some point, except that on the occasion of their meeting in 1868 she appears to have told him only about herself. The story is probably apocryphal, via Higginson (*Short Studies of American Authors* [1888], p. 41), that Emerson called Mrs. Jackson the greatest American poet: "When some one asked Emerson a few years since whether he did not think 'H. H.' the best woman-poet on this continent, he answered in his meditative way, 'Perhaps we might as well omit the *woman*'; thus placing her, at least in that moment's impulse, at the head of all." But it is true that, in his preface to *Parnassus*, p. x, she is one of the only three American poets Emerson singles out for mention (the other two are Forsythe Willson and Sarah H. Palfrey): "The poems of a young lady who contents herself with the initials 'H. H.' in her book published in Boston (1874) have rare merit of thought and expression and will reward the reader for the careful attention which they require." It is also true that several who knew both Emerson and Mrs. Jackson exclaimed upon his high interest in her verse. See Julia C. R. Door, "Emerson's Admiration of 'H. H.,'" *Critic*, 29 August 1885, and Annie Fields, *Diary, Collections of the Massachusetts Historical Society* (and also Leyda, *Years and Hours*, 2:159, and Ruth Odell, *Helen Hunt Jackson (H. H.)* [New York, 1939], pp. 85–86.) Emerson thus spoke affectionately of Mrs. Jackson; Higginson spoke affectionately of Emily Dickinson, Emerson, and Mrs. Jackson; Mrs. Jackson spoke affectionately of Emily Dickinson, Emerson, and Higginson; and still Emerson and Emily Dickinson did not connect!

In view of a statement like the following by Emerson, in which he gives voice to his disappointment with the poetry produced in America at the time, it is unfortunate he did not have the opportunity to read Emily Dickinson's:

Why not a mind as wise & deep & subtle as your Browning, with his trained talent? Why can we not breed a lyric man as exquisite as Tennyson; or such a Burke-like longanimity as E. Browning? . . . Our wild Whitman, with real inspiration but choked by Titanic abdomen, & Delia Bacon, with genius, but mad, & clinging like a tortoise to English soil, are the sole producers that America has yielded in ten years. Is all the granite & forest & prairie & superfaetation of millions to no richer result? [*Letters* 5:87]

So she read Emerson early—when Ben Newton sought to eman-
cipate her by giving her the 1847 *Poems* in 1850,[2] and when she got his
Essays, Second Series (1844) at about the same time.[3] Everybody else was
reading them too. So she might have heard Emerson lecture locally or
might have read in the local papers about his appearances or talked
with people who heard him lecture.[4] Anybody could have done as
much. So also she might have read essays and books about him,[5] the
way practically everyone did. So, late in her life, as well, she remembered lines by Emerson.[6] But by the 1880s his aphorisms had diffused

2. In a long letter to Jane Humphrey on 23 January 1850, mainly on personal
religious matters, Emily Dickinson mentions in an aside getting Emerson's poems. She
was nineteen at the time, "I had a letter – and Ralph Emerson's Poems – a beautiful
copy – from [Ben] Newton the other day. I should love to read them both – they are very
pleasant to me." "Pleasant" is a rather mild reaction and no stronger than her interest in
Longfellow in the same letter and later; it is Newton ("The first of my own friends")
who fascinates her more (*Letters*, pp. 84–85). In 1853 she was to say pretty much the
same thing after reading the poems of the Scottish poet Alexander Smith: "They please
me very much" and "I admire the Poems very much" (*Letters*, p. 282). The poems by
Emerson that Newton recommended to Emily Dickinson are: "Each and All," "The
Problem," "Good-bye," "Woodnotes I," and "Dirge," all of which were no doubt of
interest to Emily Dickinson but none of which appears to have been of any importance
to her own poems. She appears to have taken much more interest in Emerson's more
fanciful, less serious poems, "The Humble-Bee," "The Snow-Storm," and "Fable." The
poems in the volume that she herself marked are: "The Sphinx," "Each and All," "The
Problem," "To Rhea," "The Visit," "The Rhodora," and "Woodnotes I." Emerson's
importance to her cannot be realized very fully, I believe, from what we know she knew
about Newton. There is the possibility that she wrote what she did in her letter of 1850
about Newton's gift of Emerson merely to shock Jane Humphrey a little. At Mount
Holyoke while Emily Dickinson was at school there, Emerson was well-ridiculed reading. "Leave Lowell, Motherwell, and Emerson alone," advised one friend of the Dickinson family (Whicher, *This Was a Poet*, pp. 190–91).
    3. We do not know what essays by Emerson she read, or exactly when, except for
her theft of an image from "The Poet" for her poem #214 in 1861. *Representative Men*
(1850) she liked, calling it in a letter to Mrs. Higginson in 1876 "a little Granite Book
you can lean upon" (*Letters*, pp. 569–70). The markings on the books in the Dickinson
Collection in the Houghton Library, Harvard, indicate that she read *Essays* (1861), *The
Conduct of Life* (1861), *May-Day* (1867), and *Society and Solitude* (1879). See Sewall, *Life*,
pp. 678–79.
    4. One comment in the *Springfield Republican* for 22 March 1855 is about Emer-
son's aphoristic style: "His lecture last night . . . was a chain of brilliant ideas strung as
thickly as Weathersfield onions when packed for export," as is one in the *Hampshire and
Franklin Express* for 10 August 1855: "[Mr. Emerson] was too comprehensive and
metaphysical to be at all times understood. . . . It was a series of subtle minded, comprehensive, epigrammatic, detached thoughts." Emerson's epigrammatic style appears
to have been easily recognizable by many people; the *Express*, for example, reported
facetiously of one of his lectures in 1857: "Ralph Waldo Emerson's lecture . . . was in the
English language instead of the Emersonese in which he usually clothes his thoughts."
See Leyda, *Years and Hours*, 1:155, 331, 334, 350, 351; 2:101, 102, 309, 310.
    5. Higginson's essay in the *Atlantic Monthly* in 1876, Julia Ward Howe's and F. B.
Sanborn's in 1884, and Holmes's *Life* in 1885, all of them appearing long after Emily
Dickinson's major years. See *Letters*, pp. 551, 855; Leyda, *Years and Hours*, 2:426.
    6. In 1883 she makes passing references to Emerson's "Fable" ("take care of the

themselves everywhere. The connections are by no means very unusual, or even very convincing. These are not sufficient reasons for
insisting on an affinity with him.

Remember, she never wrote him a letter or sent him any poems
to correct. She never visited him when she went to Boston in 1844,
1846, 1851, and 1863. She never talked with him when he was in
Amherst for a lecture in December of 1857 and stayed at her
brother's house next door.[7] As far as we know, she never discussed
Emerson, his ideas or works, with anyone. The few mentions of him
in her letters, especially the ones at his death in 1872, are only comments on a great monument, larger and more respectful than most of
her capsule eulogies ("immortalized" is her grandest word for him)
but much less ardent than those on notables like George Eliot, Emily
Brontë, Helen Jackson, and Mrs. Browning, with whom she could
more easily identify her various predicaments.[8] To be sure, in an

---

small Life, fervor has made great – deathless as Emerson's 'Squirrel' – ") and to "The
Humble-Bee" ("Emerson's intimacy with his 'Bee' only immortalized him – "). In 1884
she includes a phrase from "The Snow-Storm" in a letter, and in 1885 she refers once
again to "The Humble-Bee" ("The Honey you went so far to seek, I trust too you
obtain. Though was there not an 'Humbler' Bee? 'I will sail by thee alone, thou animated Torrid Zone'" (*Letters*, pp. 756, 775, 882–83, 928). These three poems, besides
the widely recited "Concord Hymn" (*Letters*, p. 539), are the only ones we can be sure
she knew, and even those none too well. They are among Emerson's most playful
poems and are not ones from which Emily Dickinson, or anyone else, could easily
derive any comprehensive understanding of Transcendentalism.

7. Emily Dickinson's reaction to Emerson might indeed have been parallel to
Sue's in a piece called "Annals of the Evergreens," which she wrote on the occasion of
his first Amherst visit:

> The same winter brought Emerson and Phillips as lecturers to Amherst, and both
> were our royal guests.... Before [Emerson] came I grew almost nervous in my
> anticipation of the vision of our New England seer. For years I had read him, in a
> measure understood him, revered him, cherished him as a hero in my girl's heart,
> till there grew into my feeling for him almost a supernatural element; so that when
> I found he was to eat and sleep beneath our roof, there was a suggestion of meeting
> a God face to face, or one of the Patriarchs of Hebrew setting, or, as Aunt Emily
> says, "As if he had come from where dreams are born." I remember very little of
> the lecture except a fine glow of enthusiasm on my part, and an almost unconscious
> contempt for anything but Emerson and his tablelands. I felt strangely elated to
> take his transcendental arm afterward and walk leisurely home. [Leyda, *Years and
> Hours*, 1:351]

Austin said of him: "I wouldn't give a volume of Emerson for all the hogs west of the
Mississippi" (in Sewall, *Life*, p. 122).

8. In a letter to Otis Lord, 30 April 1882, she wrote: "It has been an April of
meaning to me.... My Philadelphia [the Rev. Charles Wadsworth] has passed from
Earth, and the Ralph Waldo Emerson – whose name my Father's Law Student [Ben
Newton] taught me, has touched the secret Spring. Which Earth are we in?" (*Letters*, p.
727). While she links her honor for Emerson with that for Wadsworth, neither is
intimate at all. The definite article before Emerson's name here distances him. I seriously doubt she could ever have written "*my* Waldo Emerson" the way she did of

aside to Higginson in 1870 on the subject of the burden of truth ("Glory's overtakelessness") she speaks grandly of Emerson: "With the Kingdom of Heaven on his knee, would Mr. Emerson hesitate? 'Suffer little Children,'" but perhaps she did so because she knew the great indebtedness Higginson felt toward the canonized Emerson.[9] On the occasion of his visit to Amherst in 1857, she spoke loftily of him to Sue (even though she would neither go to meet him nor go to hear him lecture): "It must have been as if he had come from where dreams are born!"[10] The high respectfulness may be taken as a sign either of indebtedness or of mere awe. But hers was a fairly standard reaction to New England's literary czar.[11]

What we know about the nonrelationship is what we cannot be sure of. Why, for example, her poetry came so long after her expo-

---

George Eliot in a letter of 1881: "Now, *my* George Eliot [is dead]. The gift of belief which her greatness denied her, I trust she receives in the childhood of the kingdom of heaven. As childhood is earth's confiding time, perhaps having no childhood, she lost her way to the early trust, and no later came" (*Letters*, p. 700). She describes, of course, herself. She could not have done the same with Emerson, for she probably did not know his life very well.

Had Emily Dickinson written a poem eulogizing Emerson, it might have come off as sentimentally obsequious as Mrs. Jackson's "Tribute [to] R. W. E." (*Poems*, 1873, p. 97):

Midway in summer, face to face, a king
I met. No king so gentle and so wise.
He calls no man his subject; but his eyes,
In midst of benediction, questioning,
Each soul compel. A first-fruits offering
Each soul must owe to him whose fair land lies
Wherever God has his. No white dove flies
Too white, no wine too red and rich, to bring.
With sudden penitence for all her waste,
My soul to yield her scanty hoards made haste,
When lo! they shrank and failed me in that need,
Like wizard's gold, by worthless dust replaced.
My speechless grief, the king, with tender heed,
Thus soothed: "These ashes sow. They are true seed."
O king! in other summer may I stand
Before thee yet, the full ear in my hand!

9. *Letters*, pp. 481–82; Leyda, *Years and Hours*, 2:148: "[Col. Higginson] told us that ... to no other writer next to Mr. Emerson, did he owe so great a debt as to Margaret Fuller."
10. *Letters*, p. 913; Leyda, *Years and Hours*, 1:351.
11. Her reaction to famous people like Emerson comes out in a poem like this one:

The Stars that stated come to Town
Esteemed Me never rude
Although to their Celestial Call
I failed to make reply –

[#932]

sure to Emerson, so different from Whitman "brought to boil" suddenly by him. Why, in addition, she was not particularly honored when the poem that Helen Jackson took from her and published in 1878 was mistaken for Emerson's.[12] Why, more significantly, Sue Dickinson did not present Emerson with her sister-in-law's poetry on that night in December 1857 when he stayed next door—indeed, press it on him. And, likewise, why Helen Jackson did not show it to him, or Higginson or Josiah Holland either, all of whom associated with him and had tried to show him other verse on a variety of occasions. Why, too, if her dedication to Emerson is supposed to have been so high, she wrote no dedicatory poem to/about him the way she did for Emily Brontë and Mrs. Browning.[13] Why, even, she cannot reveal to us any more ardently or comprehensively that she *studied* Emerson. And why, above all, although she had a fantastic talent for hiding, Emerson did not seek her out and find her, but missed her on his later visits to Amherst in 1865, 1872, and 1879. Studying the explicit possibilities, I therefore draw, by and large, a blank.[14]

Implicit material pulled from Emily Dickinson's poems is only a little more helpful. Emerson was in the air, and like many others needing the change, she inhaled the fresh wind from Cambridge and Concord. One can always fall back on that one, lazily culling liberalisms and largenesses from her lines as proof of—what? Her

12. See the exchange of letters with Mrs. Jackson (*Letters,* pp. 623–27). The review of *A Masque of Poets,* where Emily Dickinson's poem appeared labeled as Emerson's, is in Leyda, *Years and Hours,* 2:303.

13. While there are parallels and borrowings, it would not be possible, it seems to me, to write a work about Emily Dickinson and Emerson like James Walsh's *The Hidden Life of Emily Dickinson* (New York, 1971), which is an elaborate but not entirely convincing argument about Emily Dickinson's dependence on the lines and images of Emily Brontë and Mrs. Browning.

14. Perhaps I underestimate the weight of the evidence. I only want to be cautious about what seems to me fairly thin biographical grounds for many of the large assumptions that have been made about Emerson's power over Emily Dickinson. The arguments of the Emerson–Emily Dickinson advocates, from Whicher (*This Was a Poet*) to H. H. Waggoner (*American Poets: Puritans to the Present*), are probably right, even though the evidence is thin. The best critical discussions of Emily Dickinson as Emersonian, besides Whicher and Waggoner, are Sherwood, *Circumference and Circumstance,* and Griffith, *The Long Shadow.* Both are apologetic about the influence, however, with Sherwood showing that Emily Dickinson got into Transcendentalism early and briefly and quickly got out again and Griffith arguing that Emily Dickinson inverted Emerson her whole life long. For them she was a naive dabbler, even a "post-Emersonian." On the contrary, it is necessary to argue that she was one of Emerson's products.

My position also differs from that of James E. Mulqueen when he answers in the negative his question "Is Emerson's Work Central to the Poetry of Emily Dickinson?" *Emily Dickinson Bulletin,* #24 (1973), pp. 211–19: "Certainly it is an error to link her too closely to Emerson." And it does not seem quite enough to claim a literary kinship for the two in their common "double consciousness," as does Frank Davidson, " 'This Consciousness': Emerson and Emily Dickinson," *Emerson Society Quarterly,* #44 (1966): 2–7.

receptivity? And then, too, we must always remind ourselves that Emerson called, in despair and hope, for a Renaissance poet, a "scholar," even (I think) a Woman Thinking; and like many others needing the push, she felt called, modeling herself accordingly. From this one, one can make, too simply, an unforgivable story of her emergence, her ego, her style, her eventual success in a world Emerson prepared for her, even her place, *wegen* Emerson, in American literary history—an imitativeness, like Thoreau's and Whitman's, that was a spur, proving nothing less than her adaptability to the marvelous spaces in the spiritualized Emersonian void. Or we have the Emerson who filled her with his diction ("circumference" is a favorite citation), his images ("Banish Air from Air - / Divide Light if you dare - / They'll meet" is close), and his dominant ideas ("Nothing is irrevocable but ourselves"; "Explain thyself! / Therein thyself shalt find / The 'Undiscovered Continent'")—creating in her, unbeknownst to her, a disciple.[15] One will have here sure fire, rewarming Emerson in the language of the next generation of writers, even in spite of our knowledge of Emily Dickinson's own enormously original mind.[16] Not much of all this convinces.

"I ... never consciously touch a paint, mixed by another person," she boasted to Higginson defensively and perhaps somewhat

---

15. Jack L. Capps asserts that "of all American authors whom she read, Emily Dickinson can be most closely associated with Ralph Waldo Emerson." Three of the examples I cite here are Capps's, and only a few others are convincing. But tracing her reading in Emerson to her writing of her Emersonlike poems involves uncomfortable conjecture on Capps's part: "she seems to have been unaware of the way in which the poetic materials that she gleaned from [Emerson] appeared in her own verse" (*Emily Dickinson's Reading* [Cambridge, Mass., 1966], pp. 113, 118-19). We cannot be as sure as *The Literary History of the United States* puts it: it is Emerson to whom "she was most in debt . . . for staccato forms and also for the bright courage of her terse speech" (Stanley Williams, "Emily Dickinson," *LHUS*, ed. Robert E. Spiller et al. [New York, 1948], 2:909-10).

Of interest in this regard is Hamlin Garland's remark: "I admire [Emily Dickinson's] singularly concise verse. Her work is related to Emerson, but must not be counted a poor relation" (*Companions on the Trail* [New York, 1931], p. 121).

16. The easiest critical exercise has been to attribute to a common background the similarities we might find between Emerson and Emily Dickinson. Thus Whicher: "It is easy to find passages that might belong to either writer. . . . The resemblance in style, like that in substance, is not due to imitation, but to the fact that both poets were sprung from the same soil and never lost their kinship with the earth" (*This Was a Poet*, p. 205). And Jorge Luis Borges: "Despite obvious differences the poetic work of Emerson and that of Emily Dickinson have an affinity [with] each other. We should not attribute that affinity to the direct influence of the first but to the fact that they shared a Puritan environment. Both were intellectual poets; both disdained or were indifferent to the sweetness of verse. Emerson's intelligence was more lucid; Emily Dickinson's sensitivity perhaps more refined" (*An Introduction to American Literature* [New York, 1973], pp. 42-43).

self-consciously.[17] Yet some few borrowings from Emerson show through.[18] His drunk-divine poet became, for one poem, hers:

The poet knows that he speaks adequately then only when he speaks somewhat wildly . . . not with the intellect alone but with the intellect inebriated by nectar. . . .

This is the reason why bards love wine, . . . or . . . other procurers of animal exhilaration. . . . These are auxiliaries to the centrifugal tendency of a man, to his passage out into free space, and they help him to escape the custody of that body in which he is pent up. . . . The sublime vision comes to the pure soul in a clean and chaste body. . . . The lyric poet may drink wine and live generously, . . . for poetry is not "Devil's wine," but God's wine. . . .

The poet's habit of living should be set on a key so low that the common influences should delight him. His cheerfulness should be the gift of the sunlight; the air should suffice for his inspiration, and he should be tipsy with water. . . .

If the imagination intoxicates the poet, it is not inactive in other men. . . . The use of symbols has a certain power of emancipation . . . We seem to be touched by a want which makes us dance and run about happily, like children.

["The Poet"]

I taste a liquor never brewed –
From Tankards scooped in Pearl –
Not all the Frankfort Berries
Yield such an Alcohol!

Inebriate of Air – am I –
And Debauchee of Dew –
Reeling – thro endless summer days –
From inns of Molten Blue –

When "Landlords" turn the drunken Bee
Out of the Foxglove's door –
When Butterflies – renounce their "drams" –
I shall but drink the more!

Till Seraphs swing their snowy Hats –
And Saints – to windows run –
To see the little Tippler
Leaning against the – Sun –

[#214]

The blessed remoteness of Nature from Emerson's grasp also became, for one poem, her remoteness:

17. *Letters*, p. 415.

18. Percy H. Boynton (*Literature and American Life* [Boston, 1936] and George F. Whicher (*This Was a Poet*, 1938) have played a trick on students of Emily Dickinson, but none too well. They quote two of Emerson's briefer, livelier poems side by side and ask us to guess which one is by Emerson and which by Emily Dickinson. The Boynton

But this beauty of Nature which is seen and felt as beauty, is the least part. The shows of day, the dewy morning, the rainbow, mountains, orchards in blossom . . . if too eagerly hunted, become shows merely, and mock us with their unreality. . . . The beauty that shimmers in the yellow afternoons of October, who ever could clutch it? Go forth to find it, and it is gone.

["Nature"]

Go not too near a House of Rose –
The depradation of a Breeze
Or inundation of a Dew
Alarm it's walls away –
Nor try to tie the Butterfly,
Nor climb the Bars of Ecstasy,
In insecurity to lie
Is Joy's insuring quality.

[#1434]

And his compensating squirrel and mountain became, for one poem, her squirrel and mountain:

The mountain and the squirrel
Had a quarrel,
And the former called the latter
   "Little Prig;"
Bun replied,
"You are doubtless very big;

Light is sufficient to itself–
If Others want to see
It can be had on Window Panes
Some Hours in the Day.

But not for Compensation –
It holds as large a Glow

---

examples from Emerson have none of Emily Dickinson's jerky eccentricities or desperate colors:

He who has no hands
Perforce must use his tongue;
Foxes are so cunning
Because they are not strong.

Ever the Rock of Ages melts
Into the mineral air,
To be the quarry whence to build
Thought and its mansions fair.

The two Whicher examples from Emerson lack the privateness and tentativeness of Emily Dickinson's lines on similar subjects:

To clothe the fiery thought
In simple words succeeds,
For still the craft of genius is
To mask a king in weeds.

The hedge is gemmed with diamonds,
The air with Cupids full.
The cobweb clues of Rosamond
Guide lovers to the pool.

Emerson's diction here is far more archaic, bookish, and flat than Emily Dickinson would allow herself: "He who," "Perforce," "whence," "fair," "weeds," "gemmed." Except for the hymn meter, she does not write this way at all.

One poem by Emerson, "Sacrifice," was found, copied out, among her manuscripts upon her death and was almost published as her own in *Bolts of Melody* in 1944:

Though love repine and reason chafe
There comes a voice without reply,
'Tis man's perdition to be safe
When for the truth we ought to die.

These sententious lines are not very much like her terse quatrains, either, though they fooled her editors for more than fifty years (Millicent Todd Bingham, *Emily Dickinson's Home* [New York, 1955], pp. 571–72).

But all sorts of things
  and weather
Must be taken in together
To make up a year
And a sphere.
And I think it no disgrace
To occupy my place.
If I'm not so large as you,
You are not so small as I,
And not half so spry.
I'll not deny you make
A very pretty squirrel track;
Talents differ; all is well and wisely
    put;
If I cannot carry forests on my back,
Neither can you crack a nut."

To Squirrel in the Himmaleh
Precisely, as to you.

                  [#862]

            ["Fable"]

In each case, however, the theft is small. The image of the poet
as drunk was standard Romantic, and in Emerson, cheerful and
grand, but in Emily Dickinson, quite a bit more humorous, personal,
extreme, specific, daring; she pushes it until it describes *her,* until, in
her reckless style, she becomes *it.* The example of remoteness from
nature was also not a very new subject; in Emerson it is a warning, but
in Emily Dickinson an apocalyptic fear which, with Edwardsian logic,
she turns into a more positively arguable position; his terms are soft
and sweet, hers determined and tough. The two squirrels are different too, for she seems to have inverted Emerson; the talents of
Emerson's squirrel balance off the qualities of the mountain, each
having its claim on worth, but Emily Dickinson's light is "sufficient to
itself" and is "*not* for Compensation"; both squirrel and "you" behold
it equally because of *its* self-sufficiency.

Some other lines could have come from some of Emerson's more
popular (and triter) epigrams. Her "Beauty – be not caused – It Is – "
(#516) may come from his "Rhodora": "Then beauty is its own excuse
for being." Phrases in her poem "The Soul selects her own Society – "
(#303) may come from his inscription to "Society and Solitude":
"That each should in his house abide, / Therefore was the world so
wide." Her use of W. E. Channing, Jr.'s, "If my Bark sink / 'Tis to
another sea – / Mortality's Ground Floor / Is Immortality – " (#1234)
is no doubt from Emerson's use of the popular Channing line at the
end of his "Montaigne": "If my bark sink, 't is to another sea." Her line
about "those old – phlegmatic mountains" (#175) could possibly have
come from Emerson's "mountain chains of phlegm." Her talk of her

"Columnar Self" being "not far off / From furthest Spirit – God" (#789) could be an adaptation of Emerson's "within man is the soul of the whole" in his "Over-Soul" essay or from some other definition of God-in-man by him.

But her kleptomania is negligible, not because she transforms well what she takes but because what she takes is generally insignificant to what she is doing, maybe for the most part even mistaken readings. She did not really need the small items she took from Emerson, who also would not have easily recognized, I believe, what she had done with them.[19] I would suggest that the two writers connected in these insignificant places more because Emerson had made room for her in his universe than because her world could contain him. Therefore, for all the adaptation, the minor effect.

"Calvinism," Emerson wrote in a letter of 1859, "was still robust & effective on life & character in all the people who surrounded my childhood, & gave a deep religious tinge to manners & conversation. I doubt the race is now extinct, & certainly no sentiment has taken its place on the new generation,—none as pervasive & controlling."[20] This appreciation of the Puritan strain of his own time would

---

19. This is even more the case with her interest in Thoreau. She read his *Cape Cod* just after its publication in 1866 and wrote of him somewhat enigmatically in a note to Sue: "Was the Sea cordial? Kiss him for Thoreau" (*Letters*, p. 455). And in a letter of 1881 (*Letters*, p. 692), she amusingly makes him the archetype of the anti-institutional rebel in a reference to *Walden*: "The fire-bells are oftener now, almost, than the church-bells. Thoreau would wonder which did the most harm." She also left markings on her copy of *Walden*, but we should not presuppose an enthusiasm from that (Sewall, *Life*, pp. 678–79). The other stories inserting Thoreau into her purview seem apocryphal; one such is a newspaper story in 1894 by Mrs. Ellen E. Dickinson:

> Thoreau was naturally one of her favorite authors from his love of nature and power of description in that direction. On one occasion when a lady recently introduced in the family by marriage quoted some sentences from Thoreau's writings, Miss Dickinson recognizing it hastened to press her visitor's hand as she said, "From this time we are acquainted"; and this was the beginning of a friendship that lasted till the death of the poetess. [Leyda, *Years and Hours*, 2:141]

"One would expect Thoreau, rather than Emerson, to be the Transcendentalist especially appealing to Emily Dickinson," writes Thomas W. Ford ("Thoreau's Cosmic Mosquito and Dickinson's Terrestrial Fly," *New England Quarterly* 48 [1975]: 487–504). "His fondness for solitude, his firsthand familiarity with plants and flowers, his single state, his renunciation of worldly goods, his awareness of being a rebel—these traits would certainly attract Emily Dickinson, who shared them." Yet she appears to have read Thoreau with only superficial interest, could not have held most of his idealism for very long, and is herself ironical about most of the things that interested him. His cosmic was to her largely comical. The suggestions that he was a stimulus to her writing have so far been unconvincing; see Ford, above, and Nathalia Wright, "Emily Dickinson's Boanerges and Thoreau's Atropos: Locomotives on the Same Line?" *Modern Language Notes* 72 (1957): 101–3.

20. Ralph Waldo Emerson, *Letters*, ed. Ralph L. Rusk (New York, 1939), 5:145.

have made him appreciative, I believe, of Emily Dickinson's concurrent attraction to and repulsion by him. Her "uses" of him make an
understandable duplicity.

The parallels with Emerson could easily be judged parodies because for the most part they diverge so far from the sources—and
critically, even mockingly. She is often similar to Emerson in such
instances yet quite distinct from him, so that to us a number of her
lines have the look of conscious parody. It was perhaps her way of
having a dialogue with "the Ralph Waldo Emerson," having him plus
getting him at the same time.

Her drunk poet, for instance, is not at all an Emerson intellectual speaking wildly but, oxymoronically and humorously, a
drunk Congregationalist, a *religious* drunk; the pure transcendental
mind and chaste transcendental body have become by worldly standards debauched and by heavenly ones heretical; Emerson's low key
has been changed into epiphanal abandon and raucous triumph; the
Emersonian child is a lush. Likewise, when she has at it with Emerson's man-versus-nature obsession, she plays a turncoat in his camp,
seeing what Emerson calls a tragic breach in the integral scheme of
nature as a fortunate situation forcing man to make his own games in
the great, new dark. And in her poem with an Emerson squirrel and
an Emerson mountain in it, she catches her mentor looking too
narrowly—at only the synecdoches—while she opens her eyes wider
than he does his and calls his attention to a light (a grace?) larger than
these vulgar considerations; she has to remind him of *his* Over-Soul.

Or as we have it in additional parallels/parodies, the Emersonian
possibilities are severely limited by Emily Dickinson's abrasive skepticism. In his poem "Each and All," for example, Emerson writes of the
necessity of an organic view of life:

> The lover watched his graceful maid,
> As 'mid the virgin train she strayed,
> Nor knew her beauty's best attire
> As women still by the snow-white choir.
> At last she came to his hermitage,
> Like the bird from the woodlands to the cage; —
> The gay enchantment was undone,
> A gentle wife, but fairy none.

Using this same image, Emily Dickinson turns Emerson's criticism of
human displacement into awful pathos of personal loss, scoffing at
the optimism and pointing out the pain:

> The smallest Housewife in the grass,
> Yet take her from the Lawn

> And somebody has lost the face
> That made Existence – Home!

[#154]

For Emerson the loss can be understood, avoided, righted, but for Emily Dickinson the loss is real and permanent; it is *somebody's* loss, maybe her own.

She has a similar, destructive parallel with Emerson's attempt to define possibility with the figure of a spiritual spiral in his essay "Circles":

> The life of man is a self-evolving circle, which, from a ring imperceptibly small, rushes on all sides outwards to new and larger circles, and that without end. The extent to which this generation of circles, wheel without wheel, will go, depends on the force or truth of the individual soul. For it is the inert effort of each thought, having formed itself into a circular wave of circumstance—as for instance an empire, rules of an art, a local usage, a religious rite—to heap itself on that ridge and to solidify and hem in the life. But if the soul is quick and strong it bursts over that boundary on all sides and expands another orbit on the great deep, which also runs up into a high wave, with attempt again to stop and to bind. But the heart refuses to be imprisoned; in its first and narrowest pulses it already tends outward with a vast force and to immense and innumerable expansions. . . . Let the claims and virtues of persons be never so great and welcome, the instinct of man presses eagerly onward to the impersonal and illimitable.

In her version of the same cosmic scene Emily Dickinson is shut out of a conventional heaven and so goes on, in Emersonian fashion, to a wider circle, her "Circumference":

> I saw no Way – The Heavens were stitched –
> I felt the Columns close –
> The Earth reversed her Hemispheres –
> I touched the Universe –
>
> And back it slid – and I alone –
> A Speck upon a Ball –
> Went out upon Circumference–
> Beyond the Dip of Bell –

[#378]

The trouble with this Emersonian trip of hers, however, is that though she "Touche[s] the universe" as she goes out, she is "alone," a mere speck in a void, a drowning swimmer out beyond the buoys. She loses touch, identity, and purpose—and is therefore tragic. The new largeness is a smallness. Given the opportunity for endless opportunity, she becomes lost in Emersonian space.

Emily Dickinson's laugh at Emerson's democratic humanism (still another skeptical parody) comes when she echoes his "Ode to Channing":

> The over-god
> Who marries Right to Might,
> Who peoples, unpeoples,—
> He who exterminates
> Races by stronger races,
> Black by white faces,—
> Knows to bring honey
> Out of the lion;
> Grafts gentlest scion
> On pirate and Turk.

In her own version, Emily Dickinson plays Melville's game of horologicals/chronometricals over against Emerson's idealism: equality is indeed a possibility, but only *after* the fact of death, which makes simple other-worldly faith more important than social activism:

> Color - Caste - Denomination -
> These - are Time's Affair -
> Death's diviner Classifying
> Does not know they are -
>
> As in sleep - All Hue forgotten -
> Tenets - put behind -
> Death's large - Democratic fingers
> Rub away the Brand-
>
> [#970]

There is an inherent unity in the cosmos in both cases, but Emily Dickinson (somewhat triter than Emerson here) is skeptical of its achievability in this life and merely (though also cheerfully) hopeful of it in death. It is as if she has to remind Emerson that life has its tragedies, that death, not some over-god, is the divine democrat; that, in fact, happiness lies beyond this world. The knowledge of "our minuter intuitions," she goes on to admit at the end of the poem, prevents Emersonian presumptuousness. With her darker eye, she goes beyond the Transcendentalist.

Her easiest—and cruelest—parody of Emerson comes whenever she attacks the ground Emerson was surest of, his reliance on the concept of the imperial self:

> Trust thyself: every heart vibrates to that iron string. Accept the place the divine Providence has found for you; the society of your contemporaries, the connexion of events. Great men have always done so and confided themselves childlike to the genius of their age, betraying their

perception that the Eternal was stirring at their heart, working through their hands, predominating in all their being. And we are now men, and must accept in the highest mind the same transcendent destiny; and not pinched in a corner, not cowards fleeing before a revolution, but redeemers and benefactors, pious aspirants to be noble clay plastic under the Almighty effort, let us advance on Chaos and the Dark.[21]

Her version of this new philosophy appears to play Emerson straight:

> On a Columnar Self –
> How ample to rely
> In Tumult – or Extremity –
> How good the Certainty

But her "ample" is sly and her "good" ironic, for the self when in a tumult or in an extremity does *not,* she implies, have "Certainty." She concludes her mocking nod to Emerson with this:

> Suffice Us – for a Crowd –
> Oneself – and Rectitude –
> And that Assembly – not far off
> From furthest Spirit – God –

> [#789]

To Emerson's sufficient self she has added a Puritan's "Rectitude" and to the independent individual she has added a conventional believer's "Companion [a variant for "Assembly"] . . . God." She has seen through Emerson's boldness and found his allegedly independent Yankee highly dependent on a prior good ("Rectitude") and a prevenient God. She has caught Emerson at making a smiling Frankenstein's monster that does not know the Fate that made it.[22]

Yet we know that the Emersonian spirit, certainly a larger consideration than the matter of such parallels and parodies as these, was without doubt the largest pressure in nineteenth-century American literature and was certainly the largest nineteenth-century pressure on Emily Dickinson.[23] But in the absence of any fully explicit response

21. *Works,* 2:53–54.

22. Two more attempts by Emily Dickinson at turning Emersonian terms or concepts on their heads are cited by Mario L. D'Aranzo in "Emily Dickinson's and Emerson's 'Presentiment,'" *Emerson Society Quarterly,* #58 (first quarter, 1970): 157–59, and in his "Emersonian Revelation in 'The Way I Read a Letter's This," *American Transcendental Quarterly,* #17 (winter 1973): 14–15.

23. Emily Dickinson is most like Blake, T. W. Higginson suggested in his introduction to the first edition of her poems. But, added William Dean Howells in his review essay in *Harper's* in 1891, "it is a Blake who had read Emerson who had read Blake. The fantasy is as often Blakean as the philosophy is Emersonian; but after feeling this again and again, one is ready to declare that the utterance of this most

to that spirit on her part, should one expect it to have meant to her what it meant to, say, Higginson?

> It was the direct result [of Emerson] to arouse what is the first great need in a new literature—self-reliance. The impulse in this direction, given during the so-called Transcendental period, was responsible for many of the excesses of that time, but it was the only way to make strong men and women.[24]

Or to Julia Ward Howe, to draw closer to her literary sisters?

> [I think it is possible to exaggerate] Emerson's solid and practical effect in the promotion of modern liberalism. The change was in the air and was to come. It was in many minds quite independently of Mr. Emerson. He was the foremost literary man of his day in America, philosopher, poet, reformer, all in one. But he did not make his age, which was an age of great men and of great things.[25]

Or to Harriet Beecher Stowe, to stay within similar Puritan bounds?

> [Jonathan Edwards] was the first man who began the disintegrating process of applying rationalistic methods to the accepted doctrines of religion. . . . He sawed the great dam and let out the whole waters of discussion over all New England, and that free discussion led to all the shades of opinion of our modern days. Little as he thought it, yet Waldo Emerson and Theodore Parker were the last results of the current set in motion by Jonathan Edwards.[26]

Or to the Hollands, her early mentors?

> [Emerson] has been an oracle always breathing the purest morality whom no consideration could swerve from utterance of the largest truths. . . . So far as Emerson is an interpreter of permanent elements in human nature, his marvelously fine workmanship is destined to be a joy forever. So far as he is merely the expounder of a system of the universe, we fear that it is fated to decay. . . . That is a noble and beautiful world into which this high soul leads us. It is a real world—but is it the whole world? . . . There is one thing in which Emerson, as a poet, is preeminent. Not even Wordsworth can excel him in his power to put a moral idea into artistic form.[27]

singular and authentic spirit would have been the same if there had never been an Emerson or a Blake in the world" ("Editor's Study," *Harper's* 82 [1891]: 318-21).

24. T. W. Higginson, *Contemporaries* (Boston, 1899), p. 12.

25. In Laura E. Richards and Maude Howe Elliott, *Julia Ward Howe* (Boston, 1916), p. 76.

26. Harriet Beecher Stowe, *Oldtown Folks* (Boston, 1869), p. 229.

27. J. G. Holland, *Scribner's* 16 (1876): 903; *Century* 23 (1882): 623; 24 (1882): 457.

We can perhaps only guess at *her* definition of this spirit. There are, of course, rather sure signs of the liberal in her—whether of the age or of Emerson, we cannot know—that made a difference in her from her other, darker interests, even as her poetry is the best living proof of the *continuity* of the new liberalism from the old conservatism, the continuity of the modern from the medieval, the Emersonian from the Edwardsian—"a kind of critical Transcendentalism," as Glauco Cambon calls it.[28] For her that Emerson spirit should have meant, we might safely if only generally conjecture, a marvelous daring with a religious bearing to it, a spur to her own spiritualizing, a license, the encouragement of whim.[29] It should have meant the opportunity for private audacity, the imaginative elaboration of will, the histrionics of being oneself, the idiosyncratic and anomalous moved to the level of myth.[30] It also should have meant an extravagant regard for language pushed to its limits as a paradigm of someone out far and in deep. Beyond these we guess, I believe, unsafely.[31]

I am suggesting that it was not Emerson's ideas, certainly not his ideology, that Emily Dickinson experienced, so much as it was Emerson as push, as stimulus, as prophet-motivator, as prime mover, as provocateur—his intended service to any devotee. Even as she answers him, she is, thanks to Emerson, standing *up* to do so. He made her even without her having to know him very well, even though, as

28. Glauco Cambon, "Emily Dickinson and the Crisis of Self-Reliance," in *Transcendentalism and Its Legacy,* ed. Myron Simon and Thornton H. Parsons (Ann Arbor, 1966), p. 132.

29. Richard Chase summarizes the possibility:

The presence of the Emersonian spirit—its delight in spiritual aggrandizement, its celebration of the sufficient self and the majesty of the individual—can easily be detected in several of her minor poems. In the years of her attachment to Benjamin Newton, Emerson probably represented intellectual adventure, the stimulation of new and radical ideas, the excitement of prophetic utterance calling the soul to regeneration, to freedom and openness of experience without the threat of dogmatic closure. [*Emily Dickinson*, pp. 70–71]

30. Henry James describes the syndrome as it proceeded from Emerson:

The doctrine of the supremacy of the individual to himself, of his originality and, as regards his own character, *unique* quality, must have had a great charm for people living in a society in which introspection, thanks to want of other entertainment, played almost the part of a social resource. ... There was ... much relish for the utterances of a writer who would help one to take a picturesque view of one's internal possibilities, and to find in the landscape of the soul all sorts of fine sunrise and moonlight effects. [Quoted by Conrad Aiken in Richard B. Sewall, ed., *Emily Dickinson* (Englewood Cliffs, N.J., 1963), pp. 12, 19]

31. Higginson thought Emily Dickinson heeded Emerson's call for a distinctive American literature because of "the peculiarly American quality of the landscape, the birds, the flowers" in her poems (*Nation* 53 [1896]: 275). He saw so little!

with Thoreau and Whitman, he would not/could not have accepted the offspring, I fear, very easily. She became his response to *her*.[32]

If it is possible to conceive of Emily Dickinson's poetry as a single, unified production from a single, unified sensibility—admittedly a dangerous assumption, given the individual biographical/psychological reasons for each poem, each scrap, and given the unlikelihood of the unity in the diversity of a personality like hers—it provides an argument *against* much of Emerson. In our literature she is one of the few who did not convert. Like Hawthorne and Melville, also shaped strongly by Emerson, she stood up to him.

Imagine Emily Dickinson reading Emerson. The essays of his early fame—"Nature," "American Scholar," "The Divinity School Address"—were bound to seem, if she knew them at all, programmatic and political, too presumptuously universal, other-directed, though also moving. From her small circle the ideas would have seemed too grand and, though justifying of her own definitions, therefore probably passed over her head. My guess is that what might have hit her instead is the authorial pose: Emerson is imperial, imperious, empirical, sure. She could follow him, I would guess, only by imagining herself also at that high pitch, "a real person." But "our age"/"each age," the dominant motif of the essays, was never her concern, nor was "the uniform effect of culture," nor "the absolute existence of nature." Such large, generous concerns would have made her feel lost in the epiphanal condition of the style. Height, not insight, is bound to have been the effect for her, sentences rather than sense, tone rather than truth. Feeding on Emerson's proffered stimuli, she would have been Woman Thinking herself high, autonomous, explosive, and therefore capable.

The same is apt to have been the case (I am guessing again) with her reading Emerson's two series of essays of 1841 and 1844, Ben

---

32. This point is in contradistinction to that of Clark Griffith, that Emily Dickinson's thinking is by and large an inversion of Emerson's:

> Miss Dickinson could not—and did not—abandon Emersonian principles. Much more complexly, she inverted them. . . . Nevertheless, her inversions have the ring of criticism. The paradoxical truth is that she used Emerson's means to pursue Emerson's ends, until she discovered that those ends could have their cruel and tragic opposites. However painful the discovery . . . this inverted "shock of recognition" is among the qualities in Miss Dickinson's work that makes her one of ours. [*The Long Shadow* (Princeton, 1964), pp. 24, 239]

I argue that she did not think Emerson through thoroughly enough to reverse his major positions, but instead responded *in her own direction* to his stimulus. There is a substantial difference.

Newton's design on her: she was bound to be moved by, more than she was infused with, Transcendentalist doctrine—though to the anarchist Emerson (as opposed to the theorist Emerson) there may not have been any difference. If these became her concerted diet— learning from "History" that autobiography is an intensified focus on all the world, from "Self-Reliance" that the latent is directable to an alternate, superior existence, from "The Poet" that genius is energized desire, and from "Experience" that whatever is, when animated, is superior—she was affected by the Emerson poetic method, that is, to *over*-be oneself. She learned the metaphysics of the method and rejected the convincing coherence of the Emerson system. She did not learn how to be an advocate, for rarely does she sell, or even convey, Emerson's ideas very well for the benefit of liberal reform, failing her forebear in this respect as medium of his intentions. She could therefore be an Emersonian product without being either a student or a disciple of his, given the metabolism of a believer without the bother of a belief.

In her case, it is as if the American Scholar were still a Puritan: the liberated poet as a drunken regenerate in a fundamentalist heaven. Which makes, I believe, an important comment on both Emily Dickinson and Emerson—that she reveals just how well rooted in American Puritanism the Transcendentalist urge was. She could be moved by Transcendentalism without being moved *into* it.

The later *Letters and Social Aims* and *Society and Solitude* essays would have given her the same lift, even an equally provocative one, but without her having a sense of the world view there. Again, the Emersonian motive is to move, to motivate, to mobilize, and so the style is audacious, canonizing the common as it attempts to elevate the unique to the status of the heroic. The style turns illusion into hope and hope into potential by means of its aggressive sententiousness. It is sure that *you*, solitary in the social, are right. It is confidential and confident. The assertive *is*ness of Emerson's comments on everything prompts a lofty security. It is a knowing style even as it merely *supposes* the truth, axiomatic even in the absence of evidence, definitive even when indefinite. It is a style that was bound to impress Emily Dickinson with its author's ability to *create* ideas. The style sounded authoritative because each of his sentences was an inflated aphorism that commanded belief regardless of the content.

Every bit of this about Emily Dickinson's reading Emerson is speculative, of course; she would no doubt have been puzzled by our worrying the issue. The point is a rather simple one: even when she did not "get" Emerson, she got self-confidence from him. Instead of being made new, she was enlarged. Instead of converting, she developed desires. Instead of being formed, she was translated. Emerson could have thus been the major stimulus to her own forms of regeneration.[33]

I am attracted even more (though I submit it as also a conjecture) to what Emily Dickinson might have felt while reading *Representative Men,* in large part because it is the only Emerson prose we know she singled out for mention. This "little Granite Book [that] you can lean upon," as she named it in a letter to Mrs. Higginson in 1876,[34] gave her some grand personalities to match against Emerson's evangelical, hyperbolic, uplifting style—something he had not invited earlier. Any attempt on her part at identifying her Emersonized self with these figures, however, was bound to be frustrated in the main. Plato is the synthesizer of too much, the inflated forebear of the divine in the modern world, the reference point of all modern power, poetic

33. Harold Bloom is helpful in understanding the nature of Emerson's influence on Emily Dickinson:

> The war of American poets against influence is part of our Emersonian heritage, manifested . . . in Thoreau, Whitman, [and] Dickinson. . . . It can be called the only poetic influence that counsels against itself, and against the idea of influence. Perhaps in consequence, it has been the most pervasive of American poetic influences, though partly unrecognized. In nineteenth-century America, it operated as much by negation (Poe, Melville, Hawthorne), as by discipleship (Thoreau, Very, Whitman) or by a dialectical blend of the two relations (Dickinson, Tuckerman, the Jameses). [*Map of Misreading* (New York, 1975), pp. 162–63]

Bloom suggests an idea coming from Emerson regarding the necessity of one's nature to shed all influences and at the same time the yearning to be influenced. This is, to Bloom, "the American burden."

> Post-Emersonian American poetry . . . is uniquely open to influencings, and uniquely resistant to all *ideas* of influence. From Whitman to our contemporaries, American poets eagerly proclaim that they reject nothing that is best in past poetry, and as desperately succumb to poetic defense mechanisms, or self-malformings, rhetorical tropes run wild, against a crippling anxiety of influence. . . . The crux of the matter is a fundamental question for American poets. It could be phrased: In becoming a poet, is one joining oneself to a company of others or truly becoming a solitary and single one? [Ibid., pp. 167–68]

Emily Dickinson is therefore an example of the involuntary Emersonian.

> Whitman was a knowing Emersonian and said so; Dickinson and Stevens read Emerson and were equivocal in their knowing response, but their profound misprision of him is essential to nearly everything they wrote. . . . Dickinson, who had her own antithetical struggle against the maleness of her central precursors, violently swerves from the model, yet its traces are strong in her. [Ibid., pp. 177–78]

34. *Letters,* pp. 569–70. Higginson, long after Emily Dickinson's death, mistakenly wrote that she said this of *Middlemarch* when she sent it to his wife: "Once she sent [my wife] one of George Eliot's books, I think 'Middlemarch,' and wrote, 'I am bringing you a little granite book for you to lean upon'" (*Carlyle's Laugh, and Other Surprises* [Boston, 1909], p. 277). The comment was in reality made by her about Emerson's *Representative Men.*

and political—and therefore beyond her grasp, really unthinkable. Likewise, his Shakespeare is the writer of an overwhelming range, the enlarged representative of "the times," the all-absorbing genius, the sieve of marvels—and therefore over against the spectacle, she would have felt herself eccentric, precious, pinched. His Goethe is the writer as philosopher—and therefore for her taste too heady, too heavy, formidably independent.

Only Emerson's Montaigne could she possibly have considered herself a match for. There are no women among Emerson's representative persons, but the Montaigne he created casts a shadow that is very much like the form Emily Dickinson, suitably Emersonized, presumed to take in much of her poetry.[35] Montaigne is superior mind wedded to daily fact, senses bringing their own philosophy, egotism made succinct and profound, "treating every thing without ceremony, yet with masculine sense." He is eloquent sentiment, unpretentious philosophizing, highly individualized questing and creating, frankness and honesty. He is wisdom in a questionable world.

> The expansive nature of truth comes to our succor, elastic, not to be surrounded. Man helps himself by larger generalizations. The lesson of life is practically to generalize; to believe what the years and centuries say, against the hours; to resist the usurpation of particulars; to penetrate to their catholic sense. . . .

> Let a man learn to look for the permanent in the mutable and fleeting.

Emerson describes Montaigne as having his own (and, to be anachronistic, *her*) style and mind: "a certain nakedness of statement," "a biblical plainness coupled with a most uncanonical levity," "superfluous frankness," "a shower of bullets." "Cut these words, and they would bleed; they are vascular and alive."[36]

---

35. Emerson's own regard for Montaigne could not have been higher. "No book before or since [Charles Cotton's Montaigne]," he wrote in his journal in 1843, "was ever so much to me as that" (*Journals*, 6:372). "I remember the delight and wonder in which I lived with [the Montaigne]," he wrote later. "It seemed to me as if I had myself written the book, in some former life, so sincerely it spoke to my thought and experience" (*Works*, 4:162).

36. Ibid., pp. 164–86. In his 1862 "Letter to a Young Contributor," the essay that brought Emily Dickinson out, Higginson appears to be paraphrasing Emerson on Montaigne—possibly a further connection among the three:

> Human language . . . may in itself become so saturated with warm life and delicious association that every sentence shall palpitate and thrill with the mere fascination of the syllables. . . . Often times a word shall speak what accumulated volumes have labored in vain to utter: there may be years of crowded passion in a word, and half a life in a sentence. . . . It is this unwearied literary patience that has enabled Emerson not merely to introduce but even to popularize, thoughts of such a quality as never reached the popular mind before. [*Atlantic Monthly* 9 (1962): 403–4]

The possible radical affinities here, in both intent and style, between Emily Dickinson and Emerson, via Montaigne, have to do with what Emerson called "flowing law": the desire for assurances without the pretense of assurances, consideration without affirmation or denial, candid thinking without either tension or austerity. What Emerson projects through his Montaigne is a practical morality colored by skepticism, a wise ignorance, and unpretentious sententiousness, a way or wording the moral sentiment so that it gives some sense of contact with ultimate reality, however finally elusive.[37]

It is this Montaignesque tendency to moralize in Emerson, and the attendant sententiousness, that I suggest was Emily Dickinson's attraction to him. How she escaped the Emerson morality while picking up the Emerson method (at least the *manner* of the moralizing) we cannot entirely account for. As she avoided ideas, the Emerson sentence ("nakedness of statement . . . vascular and alive") became for her a hold on the universe. He therefore became her stimulus and security, as I have tried to argue, more than her sense and substance.[38]

Emerson gave Emily Dickinson a *way* to believe: her sententiousness is evidence of that. In the range of forms from the gnomic and aphoristic to the epigram and maxim, she found a security, perhaps something close to the illusion of fulfillment and permanence, even as she wanders, like Montaigne, amid uncertainties, lost. The triteness and wisdom of such are irrelevant over against her need to write in aphoristic form. The Emerson sentence became for her a simulation of truth. It would not matter that we cite her for cheap profundity. In the aphoristic, she plays at creating assurances for

37. For the violence Emerson did to Montaigne in turning his character from that of stoical skeptic in the Cotton translation to that of Transcendentalized moralist in his 1850 essay, see Charles Lowell Young, *Emerson's Montaigne* (New York, 1941). "The final solution in which skepticism is lost," Emerson concluded in his essay, "is in the moral sentiment, which never forfeits its supremacy. All moods may be safely tried, and their weight allowed to all objections: the moral sentiment as easily outweighs them all, as any one" (*Works*, 4:183).

38. Others have made the point before me, regarding her aphorizing tendency, though for different purposes. "Her principal interest in Emerson seems not to have been Transcendentalism," writes Jack Capps, "but unencumbered ideas that she could detach from his essays and poetry" (*Emily Dickinson's Reading*, p. 119). There is a tendency," writes Charles Anderson, "towards the sententious in her letters from the middle 1850s, that later became a distinct mannerism, so the poems after 1865 move more and more in the direction of the epigrammatic. . . . Apparently she even came to talk, as she wrote, in aphorisms" (*Emily Dickinson's Poetry*, pp. 5–6). "She is vain enough," writes Conrad Aiken, "to indulge in [Emersonian] sententiousness. . . . Emerson's gnomic style she tunes up to the epigrammatic—the epigrammatic she often carries to the point of the cryptic; she becomes what one might call an epigrammatic symbolist" (in Blake and Wells, eds., *The Recognition of Emily Dickinson* [Ann Arbor, 1964], pp. 114–15). "Fully half her canon," writes Sewall, "could be called 'wisdom pieces,' thoughts on life and living, sometimes exhortations, sometimes warnings, sometimes pure clinical analyses" (*Life*, p. 712).

herself, determined to make her own enduring paradise. Considering her experiences to the point of generalization, like Emerson's Montaigne, she could maintain a strong ego and at the same time explore, however illusorily, what Emerson called "an unused universe."

Although she was definitely humble before the knowable and Unknowable, Emily Dickinson indeed has what she called her "philosophizing strain,"[39] that is, a well-developed metaphysical consciousness or ability to reason from her own feelings. She sought to be someone who "Distills amazing sense / From ordinary Meanings" (#448).

"My country," she wrote, "is truth." The result was what Richard Sewall called her conscious effort to achieve the "instantaneous line."[40] At times, indeed, her method of composition appears to have been one in which she would save aphoristic scraps of prose and work up letters or poems out of them. Many of her compositions are elaborations on, subversions of, frames for, and deviations from a quotable. She was sometimes even tempted to equate her poetry with philosophy: "Yesterday is Poetry - / 'Tis Philosophy."

While one cannot claim for her any impressive system of thought, she needs to be recognized as one of the finest moralists and epigrammatists in American literature—the product of her "strain."[41] "Emily Dickinson's aphorisms," writes Richard Chase, "remain one of

---

39. *Letters,* pp. 9, 576. The sententious she thought especially pleasing to her father (*Letters,* p. 344). In her letters to the Hollands, in addition, she is quite a bit more aphoristic than she is with other friends, perhaps because they encouraged her (just as much as the Emerson she probably read did) to make a religion of her own out of Christian fragments. "I do not respect 'doctrines,'" she wrote in a letter in 1859; yet in her aphorisms she tried making some of her own more comfortable to her own ways of thinking.

40. Sewall, *Life,* p. 541.

41. In his account of his first visit with Emily Dickinson, Higginson reports the aphoristic tendency of her conversation with him:

> She went on talking constantly and saying, in the midst of narrative, things quaint and aphoristic. "Is it oblivion or absorption when things pass from our minds?" "Truth is such a rare thing, it is delightful to tell it." "I find ecstasy in living; the mere sense of living is joy enough," . . . and then added, after a pause, "I feel that I have not expressed myself strongly enough," although it seemed to me that she had. . . . Interspersed with these confidences came phrases so emphasized as to seem the very wantonness of overstatement, as if she pleased herself with putting into words what the most extravagant might possibly think without saying, as thus: "How do most people live without any thoughts? There are many people in the world—you must have noticed them in the street,—how do they live? How do they get the strength to put on their clothes in the morning?" Or this crowning extravaganza: "If I read a book and it makes my whole body so cold no fire can ever warm me, I know that is poetry. If I feel physically as if the top of my head were taken off, I know that is poetry. These are the only ways I know it. Is there any other way?" [*Carlyle's Laugh, and Other Surprises* (Boston, 1909), pp. 274-75]

the striking mementoes of American inventiveness, like Whitman's free verse or Melville's combination of American folk language and traditional English forms."[42] It represents her lusting after security in what was for her at a great many points a disorienting universe and a discredited world. Here she is all ideas. Her emotions are not so much felt as thought. She gets her thrills out of abstractions. She is trying to make sense. The Emerson she took to gave her a form that she had to have as a hold: the security of *is*. Like him, she insists on meanings and tries her hand at making some after his epigrammatic manner. In those days, Emerson argued, there were truths to be stated!

> The memorable words of history and the proverbs of nations consist usually of a natural fact, selected as a picture or parable of a moral truth. . . . In their primary sense these are trivial facts, but we repeat them for the value of their analogical import. What is true of proverbs, is true of all fables, parables, and allegories.
>
> This relation between the mind and matter is not fancied by some poet, but stands in the will of God, and so is free to be known by all men . . . for the universe becomes transparent, and the light of higher laws than its own shines through it.[43]

A simple anthology of her aphorisms, collected here for the first time, shows Emily Dickinson straining in all her years' writings for gnomic generalization, for maximizing maxim, for statements of (what was for her) truth, if only tentative. She is attempting—a wide range, from the folksy to the enigmatic—to equal what Carlyle called Emerson's buckshot. They are a Poor Emily's Almanac. Collected, they make a Way to Wonder and Woe, a Way to the Overwhelming.

I wish to celebrate these aphorisms of hers (extracted from her letters and poems and from notes taken by friends of hers) in roughly chronological order, with those for which no date is known at the end. The order does not reveal changes in thought or style over the years, however, except of course the increased interest in aphorizing in her later years. I have regularized punctuation and capitalization and in a couple of instances the grammar, though in no case have I altered the syntax of a statement, for her aphorisms rarely have the roughness of the rest of her poetry and prose.

Of course, not all these axioms of hers are original. Yet, even when stolen, they become expanded and refreshed considerably by her. "A friend in need is a friend indeed," for example, becomes "A shady friend for torrid days is easier to find than one of higher tem-

42. Richard Chase, *Emily Dickinson* (New York, 1951), pp. 105–6.
43. "Nature," *Works*, 1:19.

POOR EMILY'S ALMANAC

It's so trying to be read out of the wrong book when the right one is out of sight.

There is a darker spirit [that] will not disown its child.

Confidence in daybreak modifies dusk.

Who never lost are unprepared a coronet to find.

To comprehend a nectar requires sorest need.

Insanity to the same seems so unnecessary.

Fasting gives to food marvelous aroma, but by birth a bachelor disavows cuisine.

Bliss_is unnatural.

One is a dainty sum. One bird, one cage, one flight, one song in those far woods as yet suspected by faith only.

Exultation is the going of an inland soul to sea.

Water is taught by thirst, land by the oceans passed, transport by throe.

A wounded deer leaps highest.

Mirth is the mail of anguish.

If summer were an axiom, what sorcery had snow?

To learn the transport by the pain as blind men learn the sun, this is the sovereign anguish.

That bareheaded life under the grass worries one like a wasp.

Hope is the thing with feathers that perches in the soul.

Power is only pain stranded through discipline.

The hallowing of pain makes one afraid to convalesce, because they differ wide as engines and madonnas.

The seeing pain one can't relieve makes a demon of one.

Heaven hunts around for those that find itself below, and then it snatches.

Delight is as the flight, or in the ratio of it.

A shady friend for torrid days is easier to find than one of higher temperature for frigid hour of mind.

'Tis beggars banquets best define. 'Tis thirsting vitalizes wine.

Honor is its own pawn.

Today makes yesterday mean.

The pride that stops the breath in the core of woods is not of ourself.

The true are not ashamed.

There is no gratitude like the grace of death.

Pain has an element of blank; it cannot recollect when it begun or if there were a time when it was not.

Delight becomes pictorial when viewed through pain.

Doom is the house without the door.

Prayer is the little implement through which men reach where presence is denied them.

Much madness is divinest sense to a discerning eye, much sense the starkest madness.

We grow accustomed to the dark when light is put away.

If what we could were what we would, criterion be small; it is the ultimate of talk the impotence to tell.

How many flowers fail in wood or perish from the hill without the privilege to know that they are beautiful.

Except thyself may be thine enemy, captivity is consciousness—so's liberty.

The privilege to say [is] limited by ignorance.

When winds take forest in their paws, the universe is still.

Faith [is] the experiment of our Lord.

A small weight is obnoxious upon a weary rope.

Gold may be bought and purple may be bought, but the sale of the spirit never did occur.

So few that live have life [that] it seems of quick importance not one of those escape by death.

The supernatural is only the natural disclosed.

Life is death we're lengthy at; death, the hinge to life.

Not revelation 'tis that waits, but our unfurnished eyes.

Best gains must have the loss' test to constitute them gains.

Nature is what we know yet have no art to say, so impotent our wisdom is to her simplicity.

Drama's vitalest expression is the common day.

The spirit is the conscious ear.

Remorse is memory awake, her parties all astir.

Renunciation is a piercing virtue, the letting go a presence for an expectation.

Renunciation is the choosing against itself, itself to justify unto itself.

Presentiment is that long shadow on the lawn indicative that suns go down, the notice to the startled grass that darkness is about to pass.

Want is a meager art acquired by reverse.

The hallowing of pain, like hallowing of heaven, obtains at a corporeal cost. The summit is not given to him who strives severe at middle of the hill, but he who has achieved the top. All is the price of all.

The service without hope is tenderest because 'tis unsustained by stint. Rewarded work has

impetus of gain and impetus of goal. There is no diligence like that that knows not an until.

Apprehensions are God's introductions, to be hallowed accordingly.

Despair's advantage is achieved by suffering despair. To be assisted of reverse, one must reverse have bore.

Who court obtains within himself sees every man a king. And poverty of monarchy is an interior thing.

Expectation is contentment, gain, satiety.

Danger deepens sum.

Powder exists in charcoal before it exists in fire.

Impossibility, like wine, exhilarates the man who tastes it. Possibility is flavorless.

A doubt if it be us assists the staggering mind in an extremer anguish until it footing find. An unreality is lent, a merciful mirage, that makes the living possible while it suspends the lives.

Experience is the angled road preferred against the mind, by paradox the mind itself presuming to lead quite opposite. How complicated the discipline of man, compelling him to choose himself his preappointed pain.

Faith is the pierless bridge supporting what we see unto the scene that we do not.

Presumption is vitality.

Love is anterior to life, posterior to death, initial of creation, and the exponent of earth.

Patience is the smile's exertion through the quivering.

Denial is the only fact perceived by the denied.

Faith is constancy's result.

He who in himself believes, fraud cannot presume.

Not what we did shall be the test when act and will are done, but what our Lord infers we would had we diviner been.

Those that are worthy of life are of miracle, for life is miracle and death as harmless as a bee, except to those who run.

To include is to be touchless, for our self cannot cease.

There is no first or last in forever; it is center there all the time.

Not to discover weakness is the artifice of strength.

Satisfaction is the agent of satiety, want a quiet commissary for infinity.

To die without the dying and live without the life, this is the hardest miracle propounded to belief.

Gratitude is not the mention of a tenderness but its still appreciation out of plumb of speech.

The definition of beauty is that definition is none.

Ideals are the fairy oil with which we help the wheel. But when the vital axle turns, the eye rejects the oil.

Not all die early dying young. Maturity of fate is consummated equally in ages or a night.

Sharper than dying is the death for the dying's sake.

Time is a test of trouble but not a remedy. If such it prove, it prove too there was no malady.

The supper of the heart is when the guest has gone.

To escape enchantment, one must always flee.

To undertake is to achieve, be understanding blent with fortitude of obstacle and toward encouragement.

Superiority to fate is difficult to gain. 'Tis not conferred of any but possible to earn.

Perception of an object costs precisely the object's loss.

Revolution is the pod systems rattle from when the winds of will are stirred.

Exhilaration is the breeze that lifts us from the ground and leaves us in another place whose statement is not found.

[Death] invalidates the balm of that religion that doubts as fervently as it believes.

It is difficult not to be fictitious in so fair a place, but test's severe repairs are permitted all.

Dying is a wild night and a new road.

The things of which we want the proof are those we knew before.

Gratitude is the timid wealth of those who have nothing.

The incredible never surprises us because it is the incredible.

Truth is such a rare thing, it is delightful to tell it.

Landscapes reverence the frost though its grip be past.

Women talk; men are silent.

Candor is the only wile.

The vein cannot thank the artery, but her solemn indebtedness to him even the stolidest admit.

Gratitude is the only secret that cannot reveal itself.

Best witchcraft is geometry to a magician's eye.

Experiment escorts us last; his pungent company will not allow an axiom an opportunity.

Enough is so vast a sweetness I suppose it never occurs, only pathetic counterfeits.

The risks of immortality are perhaps its charm. A secure delight suffers in enchantment.

Life is the finest secret. So long as that remains, we must all whisper.

What miracles the news is: not Bismark but ourselves.

Even the possible has its insoluble particle.

We never know how high we are till we are asked to rise, and then if we are true to plan our statures touch the skies.

Trust is better than contract, for one is still but the other moves.

Transport is not urged.

It comforts the criminal little to know that the law expires with him.

Each expiring secret leaves an heir, distracting still.

The thief ingredient accompanies all sweetness.

Truth, like ancestor's brocades, can stand alone.

The stimulus of loss makes most possession mean.

It is the meek that wear valor too mighty for the bold.

The show is not the show but they that go.

Our own possessions, though our own, 'tis well to board anew, remembering the dimensions of possibility.

Gratitude grieves best.

In adequate music there is a major and a minor. Should there not also be a private?

Only love can wound. Only love assists the wound.

The finest wish is the futile one.

Thank God the loudest place he made is licensed to be still.

Too much of proof affronts belief.

Subjects hinder talk.

A finite life is that peculiar garment that were it optional with us we might decline to wear.

The giant in the human heart was never met outside.

The imperceptible has no external face.

Remoteness is the founder of sweetness. Could we see all we hope or hear the whole we fear

told tranquilly like another tale, there would be madness near.

Life is a spell so exquisite that everything conspires to break it.

Trite is that affliction which is sanctified.

Dominion lasts until obtained.

Utmost is relative.

In this short life that only lasts an hour, how much, how little is within our power.

To lose what we never owned might seem an eccentric bereavement, but presumption has its affliction as actually as claim.

Wonder is not precisely knowing and not precisely knowing not—a beautiful but bleak condition. He has not lived who has not felt suspense.

Surprise is like a thrilling pungent upon a tasteless meat, alone too acrid but combined an edible delight.

Trial as a stimulus far exceeds wine though it would hardly be prohibited as a beverage.

To have been immortal transcends to become so.

Dreams are the subtle dower that make us rich an hour, then fling us poor out of the purple door into the precinct rawly possessed before.

The happiness without a cause is the best happiness, for glee intuitive and lasting is the gift of God.

There is so much that is tenderly profane in even the sacredest human life that perhaps it is instinct and not design that dissuades us from it.

Nature is a haunted house, but art a house that tries to be haunted.

The tie to one we do not know is slightly miraculous, but not humbled by test if we are simple and sacred.

Fear, like dying, dilates trust or enforces it.

Were the velocity of affection as perceptible as its sanctity, day and night would be more affecting.

The joy we most revere we profane in taking.

Always begins by degrees.

Who knocks not yet does not intrude is Nature.

Labor might fatigue though it is action's rest.

So truthful is transport.

Silence's oblation to the ear superceded sound.

We part with the river at the flood through a timid custom, though with the same waters we have often played.

Love is its own rescue, for we at our supremest are but its trembling emblems.

When you have strength to remember that dying dispels nothing which was firm before, you have avenged sorrow.

God seems much more friendly through a hearty lens.

The time to live is frugal, and good as is a better earth, it will not quite be this.

The mind of the heart must live if its clerical part do not.

Torture for worthless sakes is equally torture.

Hope is a strange invention, a patent of the heart in unremitting action yet never wearing out.

The most intangible thing is the most adhesive.

The moment that a plot is plumbed, prospective is extinct.

We must be less than death to be lessened by it, for nothing is irrevocable but ourselves.

To be human is more than to be divine, for when Christ was divine he was uncontented till he had been human.

The power to fly is sweet though one defer the flying, as liberty is joy though never used.

The beginning of always is more dreadful than the close, for that is sustained by flickering identity.

Adulation is inexpensive except to him who accepts it.

To the faithful absence is condensed presence.

God cannot discontinue himself. This appalling trust is at times all that remains.

Why the full heart is speechless is one of the great wherefores.

To hope with the imagination is inevitable, but to remember with it is the most consecrated ecstasy of the will.

Cherish power. Remember that stands in the Bible between the kingdom and the glory because it is wilder than either of them.

The solaces of theft are, first, theft; second, superiority to detection.

In insecurity to lie is joy's insuring quality.

Whoever disenchants a single human soul by failure of irreverence is guilty of the whole.

Consciousness is the only home of which we now know. That sunny adverb had been enough were it not foreclosed.

How destitute is he whose gold is firm.

To congratulate the redeemed is perhaps superfluous, for redemption leaves nothing for earth to add.

The only balmless wound is the departed human life we had learned to need.

Time is short and full, like an outgrown frock.

What is each instant but a gun, harmless because unloaded, but that touched goes off.

Most of our moments are moments of preface.

These sudden intimacies with immortality are expanse, not peace, as lightning at our feet instills a foreign landscape.

Grace perhaps is the only height from which falling is fatal.

Great hungers feed themselves, but little hungers ail in vain.

Unless we become as rogues we cannot enter the kingdom of heaven.

The broken heart is broadest.

Fascination is portable.

Higher is the doom of the high.

God chooses repellent settings for his best gems.

Fondness' untold load does tire rugged baskets some.

Area [is] no test of depth.

There is something in the unlawfulness that gives it a saving flavor.

An enlarged ability for missing is perhaps a part of our better growth, as the strange membranes of the tree broaden out of sight.

Banquets have no seed or beggars would sow them.

To believe the final line of the card would foreclose faith. Faith is doubt.

Death cannot plunder half so fast as fervor can re-earn.

Success is dust, but an aim forever touched with dew.

To try to speak and miss the way and ask it of the tears is gratitude's sweet poverty, the tatters that he wears.

How little of our depth we tell, though we confide our shallowness to every passing breeze.

To the bugle every color is red.

Fear makes us all martial.

There is no trumpet like the tomb.

No dreaming can compare with reality, for reality itself is a dream from which but a portion of mankind have yet waked and part of us is not a familiar peninsula.

Hope never knew horizon.

Emblem is immeasurable. That is why it is better than fulfillment, which can be drained.

Hopelessness in its firm film has not leave to last. That would close the spirit and no intercession could do that. Intimacy with mystery, after great space, will usurp its place.

The withdrawal of the fuel of rapture does not withdraw the rapture itself.

The stars are not hereditary.

Is there not a sweet wolf within us that demands its food?

How deep this lifetime is; one guess at the waters and we are plunged beneath.

Believing that we are to have no face in a farther life makes the look of a friend a boon almost too precious.

Within is so wild a place, we are soon dismayed.

Not what the stars have done but what they are to do is what detains the sky.

Nothing is the force that renovates the world.

Work might be electric rest to those that magic make.

How much can come and much can go and yet abide the world.

Anger as soon as fed is dead. 'Tis starving makes it fat.

Not to outgrow suspense is beloved indeed.

Vastness is but the shadow of the brain which casts it.

Blessed are they that play, for theirs is the kingdom of heaven.

Hope is a subtle glutton. He feeds upon the fair and yet, inspected closely, what abstinence is there.

The joy we most revere we profane in taking.

All we secure of beauty is its evanescence.

The one who gave us this remarkable earth has the power still further to surprise that which he has caused Beyond that all is silence.

To be worthy of what we lose is the supreme aim.

Mines in the same ground meet by tunneling.

The instant acquiescence was delightfully hearty; the suddenness of a tenderness making it more sweet.

Who has not found the heaven below will fail of it above.

Moving on in the dark like loaded boats at night though there is no course—there is boundlessness.

Awe is the first hand that is held to us.

No message is the utmost message, for what we tell is done.

Tasting the honey and the sting should have ceased with Eden. Pang is the past of peace.

To die before one fears to die may be a boon.

Emerging from an abyss and entering it again, that is life, is it not?

Spirit cannot be moved by flesh. It must be moved by spirit.

It is strange that the most intangible is the heaviest, but joy and gravitation have their own ways.

We do not think enough of the dead as exhilarants. They are not dissuaders but lures, keepers of that great romance still to us foreclosed. While coveting their wisdom we lament their silence. Grace is still a secret.

Were departure separation there would be neither nature nor art, for there would be no world.

Belief is unconsciously to most of us ourselves an untried experience.

Fame is fickle food upon a shifting plate whose table once a guest but not the second time is set. Men eat of it and die.

Glory is that bright tragic thing that for an instant means dominion, warms some poor name that never felt the sun.

To do a magnanimous thing and take oneself by surprise, if one is not in the habit of it, is precisely the finest of joys. Not to do a magnanimous thing, notwithstanding it never be known, notwithstanding it cost us existence, is rapture herself spurned.

To be willing [that] the kingdom of heaven should invade our own requires years of sorrow.

One noble act makes a whole neighborhood tender with the new or forgotten grace possible to each.

How invaluable to be ignorant, for by that means one has all in reserve and it is such an economical ecstasy.

A climate of escape is natural fondness.

As it takes but a moment of imagination to place us anywhere, it would not seem worth while to stay where it was stale.

Common sense is almost as omniscient as God.

Consummation is the hurry of fools, but expectation the elixir of the gods.

Death being the first form of life which we have had the power to contemplate, our entrance here being an exclusion from comprehension, it is amazing that the fascination of our predicament does not entice us more. With such sentences as these directly over our heads, we are as exempt from exultation as the stones.

Did we not find as we lost we should make but a threadbare exhibition after a few years.

Honey grows everywhere but iron on a seldom bush.

Nature is so sudden she makes us all antique.

Nothing is so old as a dilapidated charm.

Paradise is no journey because it is within, but for that very cause, though, it is the most arduous of journeys, because as the servant conscientiously says at the door, we are invariably out.

The appetite for silence is seldom an acquired taste.

The blood is more showy than the breath but cannot dance as well.

There are those who are shallow intentionally and only profound by accident.

Train up a heart in the way it should go and as quick as it can it will depart from it.

To know whether we are in heaven or on earth is one of the most impossible of the mind's decisions, but I think the balance always leans in favor of the negative—if heaven is negative.

Peril is a possession 'tis good to bear.

We must travel abreast with nature if we want to know her, but where shall be obtained the horse?

Danger disintegrates satiety.

perature for frigid hour of mind" (#278). The biblical claim that "That which is born of the flesh is flesh; and that which is born of the Spirit is spirit" (John 3:6) is made more attractive as "Spirit cannot be moved by flesh. It must be moved by spirit." Some trite (and therefore questionable) maxims she simply takes and inverts for witty effect: "Train up a heart in the way it should go and as quick as it can it will depart from it." Most of her aphorisms, however, are completely original in expression, if also often perhaps a part of the world's wisdom.

Some few features of her aphorisms are worth pointing out. They are, for instance, very seldom in the first person singular, for she is able to generalize her personal experience considerably; and almost never in the second person, for she wishes to avoid being so universal as to imply that her observations are *always* applicable to the reader. Truer to the form of the conventional aphorism, in the third person she can feel sure without feeling *absolutely* sure. The sure form of the aphorism is also checked by her wit. Because of it she can be both positive and tentative about an idea she asserts. She can be both delightful and didactic, making the moral esthetic.

This impressive sense of the art of the epigrammatic suggests that Emily Dickinson shared with Emerson (and with Edwards and Borges as well) an esthetic of ideas: the thrill of being on the brink of a revelation. She desired, she said, "the extatic limit / Of unobtained Delight." "Generalization," Emerson asserted, "is always a new influx of the divinity into the mind. Hence the thrill that attends it."[44] Ideas are a means of enjoyment. The intellect gives pleasure. Morality is an esthetic good. All of which might be thought of as the Romantic superimposed on the Puritan: ideas as sensation, idea as sensed thing. This collection of Emily Dickinson's most attractive moralizing (maxims written on a pinhead!) is an esthetic expression, for the means is more alive than the meaning made; thinking is a tease; possibility intellectualized satisfies. Whether trite or wise, her sayings are intended for pleasure because thought true: truth-trying exhilarates. This is a Puritan legacy reinforced by the strong presence of Emerson.

Yet there is a difference between Emerson and Emily Dickinson in this regard. The ideas in Emerson's epigrams, whether in his journals or his lectures or his published essays, are mosaic work. Emily Dickinson's, on the other hand, are individual rocks on an unordered landscape. She would never have allowed hers to construct a philosophy. She only *plays* with profundity.

Her playing with the epigrammatic makes it possible to call

44. "Circles," *Works*, 3:283.

Emily Dickinson a post-Puritan. She has filled the didactic with new material—dancing, sometimes wildly, sometimes sentimentally, sometimes tritely, in an old-fashioned dress. Hers is not a struggle against inherited styles but against inherited assumptions—seeing a difference.

One could proceed further along these lines, however, and hypothesize that Emily Dickinson was the first really *anti*philosophical poet in American literature. A poetry of experience categorically denies the possibility of a poetry of comment, of ratiocination; a poetry of sensation goes even further in closing off its universe to the *merely* felt, the profoundly thought. If Emily Dickinson's epigrams *seem* profound, it is their seeming so that makes us aware that their wit is, like that of her poems, viscerally wrung from the strictures of daily experience. It is the sheer unlivability of her life that strikes us so intensely, and so we dismiss her as a recluse on the grounds that the unlived life is not worth examining.

I would like to suggest in addition that the more formal syntax of this aphoristic style served Emily Dickinson as a corrective to the improvisations of her lines—that is, the erratic metaphors, the collapsed syntax, the roughened off-rhymes and off-rhythms, and the short-circuited ellipses, or what Louise Bogan argues is the style of a cat trying to speak English. Against this, Emily Dickinson is ordering the universe. Sententiousness, like the hymn meter played over against her own voice, is a location, a place, a space, a monument. In her aphoristic statements she replaces *I* with universals for the sake of balance—even though her personality never entirely disappears amid all the abstracting of possible truths. They represent her concern for what *is*, regardless of appearances. They simulate deliverance from doubt, relative values directly felt, intrinsic excellence, even perhaps Emersonian "flowing law."

A poem like "There came a Wind like a Bugle" (#1593) about chaos, destruction, and the apocalyptic she will therefore end with a balancing, correcting, resolving aphorism:

> How much can come
> And much can go,
> And yet abide the World!

And in a poem like her indictment of the confusions of churchgoing, "He fumbles at your Soul" (#315), where the chaos appears in the jerky, imitative rhythms and in the violently mixed metaphors, she will bring all to rest and resolution, though bitterly here, with a sententious couplet at the end:

> When Winds take Forests in Their Paws –
> The universe – is still –

By this point I do not mean to suggest that Emily Dickinson is normally given to wrapping things up at the end of a poem with a neat aphorism. If one has an ending, it is often in bewilderment, ambiguity, inconclusiveness. Her aphoristic talent is not used, usually, to give finality, or even certitude, to a poem.

Swinging thus between improvisation and aphorism, between her confused experience and the hopefully sure universal, between metaphor and idea, she proceeds with the illusion that the making of meaning gives life quality. Her didacticism produces the universe in miniature for her. Importance comes from the immanence of infinitude in the finite, no matter if invented. Her attractive sentences are things made, made things, things to be hoped for. Feeling words in the structure of the aphoristic gives that which passes some permanence, and so the codification of some universals for herself becomes more important than the meanings themselves, about which, for all the certainty of their tone, she is bound to have felt somewhat uncertain, simply because they are *made*. Making is an ultimate act.[45]

Emily Dickinson appears to have been forgetful, however, that poetry conceived as philosophy—the thrust of Emerson's "climb[ing] / For his rhyme"—easily becomes platitude. One of her substantive problems in writing poetry was a tragic one, to reconcile intellectual necessities of heart and will, for under the pretext of seeking truth she was seeking life in truth. Her search for disinterested truth can be seen as an escape from self, the desire to do violence to her own nature. But the beginning of her wisdom is not fear that she might not have satisfied the mind and given herself something to understand, but a saving skepticism, a saving incertitude. Intellectuality, at least when she attempted to be philosophical, is an aberration with her, whereas her skepticism is not cold but comic; she acts as if she doubted without really doubting. Her skepticism tries to make a clean sweep of all received ideas so she may construct her intellectual house anew. Playing the role of a woman of reason, however, she says less interesting things because she does not always relate her abstract thought with herself as an exciting being. She forgets that thinking and being are the same thing. As a maker of abstractions in her "philosophizing strain," she thinks in order that she may not cease to exist—or perhaps thinks in order to forget that she will have to cease to exist. It is, I believe, a weakened function. It is the illusion of strength and confidence that Emerson bequeathed her.

Yet the maxims Emily Dickinson makes, thanks to Emerson,

45. For a discussion of aphorism as rebellion, see Norman O. Brown, *Love's Body* (New York, 1970), pp. 187–88, 231, 234.

have the redeeming virtue of giving her a public voice even as she writes a private poetry. Often this voice is not as authentic as that of her privacy; yet there is a *total* presence of character in them that is missing when she improvises her individual moods. Her aphorisms no doubt provide her the illusion of contact with an audience: they are didactic, formal, communicative, and (for the most part) clear. In them she has a public face, a facade, a facile self, a facility. There is in them little emotion, certainly a minimum of verbal decoration. They were, perhaps, a way out of a private mess. They perhaps represent a manliness, a thing *men* make. They may therefore be the least interesting, the most assertive, the most finely honed—and tritest—lines she wrote.

But the most important issue is that she appears to have had some sense of truth from aphorisms; words are used aptly and stated precisely. They appear to have meant to Emily Dickinson what they did to Wallace Stevens, "a place to spring from, a refuge from the heights, an anchorage of thought." Yet the sense of truth from aphorisms was always tentative because one knows how easy they are to make and how they balance each other, even cancel each other out. Still, they may have been a momentary stability amid the multiplicity of her potential selves in a world of constant change. Emily Dickinson's aphorisms do not presume to capture permanently or didactically some absolute truth; they give her imagination a momentary hold on some aspect of experience through the power of her own expression. The aphorism appears to have been important to her because it gave (structurally) a sense of finality and stability. It was for her a device of closure. Her cryptic, riddle-making language served her illusion of self-contained thought. She aphorized for consolation and invigoration, trying to capture experience for a few minutes. Every "homily by Emily D.," Ray Bradbury wrote in a poem, "shows dust-bin Man's anomaly."[46]

This is Emerson's Poetry of the Portfolio. Emerson stimulated her sententious moralizing, I think we can be fairly sure, probably more than anyone else could have. A central irony about the most liberating of our nineteenth-century writers stimulating a post-Puritan aphorizing in someone like Emily Dickinson is understandable only in light of the durability of American Puritanism's literary forms. There is much in Emersonian thinking that could have diffused her abilities. As it turned out, however, she took to that in him which would both free her and at the same time strengthen her backbone. This is the point: the Emerson stimulus, even as it freed

46. Ray Bradbury, *San Diego Union Books*, 16 October 1977, p. 1.

her from it, also reinforced her Puritan background. After all, she is bound to have read Emerson not to escape her self but to justify it.

Emily Dickinson, I think we can be fairly sure, took to only those coinages of the new liberalism popularized by Emerson that were recast contributions from New England tradition—detecting the Yankee and missing the Oriental, attracted to the strong ironies and repulsed by the recommended life-styles, claiming for her own its solecism and unfeeling of its mellowing effect, superimposing herself on its backbone but not on its brain. In other words, it did not change her at all! She withstood it, all the while thinking she had failed to bear up under it.

That the Emersonian course was a *luxury*—Emerson providing her with somewhere to go, with "possibility"—shows itself in the fact that we feel we know Emily Dickinson best *not* when she is going to his "unused universe" with her almost-sure generalizations, but rather when she gets back from the universal and the "true" to the private troubles and exhilarations of house and heart, the more honest mess of her life. Emerson freed her to be herself in stimulating her own direction; but also, in the tendency toward moral sententiousness, he gave her a means of security fearfully close to a kind of spiritual arteriosclerosis. The Puritanism of which he was her literary medium required significance, stasis, status, surety, *knowing*. The security of the form of her maxims was a trap. She was too wild for only that.

Seven

GOD BE WITH THE CLOWN

Emily Dickinson and Her Circle of Literary Friends

What is each instant but a gun, harmless because "unloaded," but that touched "goes off"?

[*Letters*, p. 670]

Emily Dickinson's circle of literary friends could have included Emerson but for unacceptable if understandable reasons it did not. It included other, lesser lights, however, few of whom were of much value to her poetic progress and most of whom were a bad influence altogether. The circle was wide, varied, and distinguished, but the mainstream of which they were a part—her *elected* affinities—almost drowned her kangaroo.

Emily Dickinson at the center of a small literary circle is not difficult to imagine or reconstruct. Practically everyone literary in the area knew her or knew about her, and she knew and, if she wanted to, she met almost everyone literary who came around. She was (for better or worse) very much associated with, and not at all hidden from, many of the literary currents of her time—such as they were. She was, in fact, not far from the main line of American literature. It has been easier, however, to name those writers in America with whom *we* find loyalties and affinities for her from her books and reading—Emerson and Thoreau, Lowell and Whittier and Longfellow, Harriet Beecher

Stowe and Elizabeth Stuart Phelps—than those whose relationships actually did mean something to her personally during her writing years. She nonetheless made a literary circle for herself that we can watch. It is as colorful, and as deadly, as any in the country at the time and accounts for much in her poetry. Her personal literary contacts make a transition point in her relationship to America.

It is an ugly fact of Emily Dickinson's life, as Richard Sewall's biography of her now proves, that almost everybody around her who had literary opinions and skills, from some members of her own family to some of the most successful novelists, poets, and critics of the time, was out to help her—and to get her. Her literary circle was one that was sometimes helpful but was consistently closing in on her, and as a result hers is often a poetry under siege—and not always winning. The threat to her literary life cannot be underscored too heavily. She survived the trap of everybody's love by, perhaps, the Puritan devices of privacy, backbone, self-confidence, indifference to the world; or perhaps by sheer excellence, parrying neglect with bitterness, stoicism, and a judicious narcissism; or perhaps by other traits we can never know. "If I knew for a certainty that [someone] was coming to my house with the conscious design of doing me good," that other hidden Puritan of the age, Henry Thoreau, said for her, "I should run for my life." We have for literary anecdote the record of her survival.

Her family, the first circle to give her a self-consciousness about her language, tried, for example, to stimulate her mind and expression but also to dampen her wit as being indecorous, too flamboyant, indeed *masculine*. Most of them wrote and spoke a little flamboyantly themselves (with what Richard Sewall calls "the Dickinson rhetoric") and so took her trial runs with language for granted; yet they were no audience for her.

> You say you dont comprehend me, you want a simple style [she wrote in a letter to Austin in 1851]. *Gratitude* indeed for all my fine philosophy! I strove to be exalted[,] thinking I might reach *you* and while I pant and struggle and climb the nearest cloud, you walk out very leisurely in your slippers from Empyrean, and without the *slightest* notice request me to get down! As *simple* as you please, the *simplest* sort of simple—I'll be a little ninny, a little pussy catty, a little Red Riding Hood, I'll wear a Bee in my Bonnet, and a Rose bud in my hair, and what remains to do you shall be told hereafter.[1]

1. *Letters*, p. 117. With regard to Emily Dickinson's style of writing, Austin wrote to Sue Gilbert just before the above letter: "I have a sort of Canaan letter from Emily yesterday—but she was too high up to give me any of the monuments on earth." Of

In another letter to Austin that same year, she brings up the family's suppression of the wit and poetry in her:

> When I know of anything funny, I am just as apt to cry, far *more* so than to *laugh*. . . . We don't *have* many jokes tho' *now*, it is pretty much all sobriety, and we do not have much poetry, father having made up his mind that its pretty much all *real life*. Fathers real life and *mine* sometimes come in collision, but as yet, escape unhurt.[2]

Among the family, she could assert herself only facetiously:

> Austin is a Poet, Austin writes a psalm. . . . I've been in the habit *myself* of writing some few things, and it rather appears to me that you're getting away [with] my patent. . . . *Mademoiselle* has come, quite to the surprise of us all.[3]

Though these anecdotes show only early attitudes, they describe an environment in which Emily Dickinson had to prove her voice all her life. When she was thirty-two, she remembered something about their treatment of her as a writer:

> They shut me up in Prose –
> As when a little Girl
> They put me in the Closet –
> Because they liked me "still" –
>
> Still! Could themselves have peeped –
> And seen my Brain – go round –
> They might as wise have lodged a Bird
> For Treason – in the Pound –

[#613]

As a result, she appears by and large to have written her poetry in contradistinction to their lives and for the most part to have kept her poems away from them. She gave only a few to Austin to read, even though he said (after her death) that he sensed her "intellectual brilliancy" and thought her "imagination sparkled" and felt that "no one surpassed her in wit or brilliancy."[4] Also, when Emily Dickinson died, Vinnie—who loved her well, she later said, for "her inciting voice" and who after she died announced that "her power of language was

---

Emily Dickinson's letter in reply, Lavinia wrote to Austin: "Emilie has fed you on air so long, that I think a little 'sound common sense' perhaps wouldnt come amiss *Plain english* you *know* such as Father likes" (Leyda, *Years and Hours*, 1:203).

    2. *Letters*, p. 161. In another letter to Austin, she feels it necessary to apologize to him for "my essays . . . [which] were rather too much for you. . . . Father was very severe to me; he thought I'd been trifling with you, so he gave me quite a trimming . . . so I'm quite in disgrace at present" (*Letters*, p. 237).

    3. *Letters*, p. 235.

    4. Sewall, *Life*, pp. 222–23.

unlike any one who ever lived"[5]—had not really known very much that she had written. Her parents, especially, would have scoffed, of course, had they known her writings. She knew that her family thought her writing "unholy of purpose," as she put it herself, and she imagined them criticizing it as "vain fictions."[6] The causes of the deafness at home were myriad: she was a female; they lived by intransigent morals and esthetics; living precluded expression; thought had to have sharper edges and severer distinctions than hers; nature was inexorable. What could they do with a clown in the house?

Almost the same must be said of sister-in-law Sue, whose literary pretensions Emily Dickinson fell for for a long time. During the course of their relationship, she gave her 276 poems to see, out of confidence in her judgment. Originally obsequious, even desperate, with what she let Sue see ("my tiny services," she called the exchange), and later (after 1862) bemused with what Sue wanted her to do with her verse ("I could not drink it, Sue, / Till you had tasted first," she wrote facetiously in a note), Emily Dickinson found herself stimulated by Sue but struggling to transcend the limits Sue represented.

She seems to have associated Sue with a certain vague poetic process very early in their relationship:

> You know how I must write you, down, down, in the terrestrial; no sunset here, no stars; not even a bit of *twilight* which I may poetize – and send you!... Wont that make a poem such as can ne'er be written?[7]

And she sometimes allowed Sue to dictate her esthetics:

> All life looks differently, and the faces of my fellows are not the same they wear when you are with me. I think it is this, dear Susie; you sketch my pictures for me, and 'tis at their sweet colorings, rather than this dim real that I am used [to], so you see when you go away, the world looks staringly, and I find I need more vail.[8]

For anecdote, Emily Dickinson tells how she would sit in church thinking of Sue and composing new words to the old hymns—no doubt a source fixing the form of the bulk of her poems later.[9] The respect for Sue's literary views, though severely tested by family quarrels, never faded.

5. Ibid., p. 153.
6. *Letters*, pp. 82, 88.
7. *Letters*, pp. 181–82.
8. *Letters*, p. 229.
9. *Letters*, p. 201. "And Susie, when they sang – it would have made you laugh to hear one little voice, piping to the departed. I made up words and kept singing how I loved you, and you had gone, while all the rest of the choir were singing Hallelujahs. I presume nobody heard me, because I sang so *small*, but it was a kind of comfort to think I might put them out, singing of you."

Most important, however, as we look at the earliest of the literary circle that enclosed her, is the fact that Emily Dickinson wrote her first poems to/for Sue (#4–15, between 1853 and 1858), fashioned, there is reason to believe, primarily to please her in both attitude and form. For certain, Sue is the initial stimulus and critic. She writes that she has learned some "Melod[ies] new" just for Sue: "Tell I my doubting heart / They're thine."

But after she came into her own voice (in early 1858) she was no longer as dependent on Sue for friend-critic, and her verses to her thereafter are often weak ones.[10] She showed poems to her all along until she was very sick just before she died, but she found the *desire* of Sue's friendship a greater stimulus than her actual help,[11] attributing to her help, as she did with anyone who was close to her, much of the breadth and depth of her life: "With the exception of Shakespeare," she wrote hyperbolically in a note in 1882, when she had finished the bulk of her writing, "you have told me of more knowledge than any

---

10. At times Emily Dickinson pointed out to Sue the differences in their literary tastes. In a letter to her in 1851 she writes:

> You would love to know what I read – I hardly know what to tell you, my catalogue is so small.
>   I have just read three little books, not great, not thrilling, but sweet and true. . . . I know you would love them all, yet they dont *bewitch* me any; . . . yet read, if you meet them, Susie, for they will do one good. [*Letters*, p. 195]

11. An example of Emily Dickinson's rather desperate grabbing for Sue's friendship is in a letter of 1852:

> You did not come, Darling, but a bit of Heaven did, or so it *seemed* to us, as we walked side by side and wondered if that great blessedness, which may be ours sometimes, is granted now, to me. This union, my dear Susie, by which two lives are one, this sweet and strange adoption wherein we can but look, and are yet admitted, how it can fill the heart, and make it gang wildly beating, how it will take *us* one day, and make us all its own, . . . Susie, you will forgive me my amatory strain. [*Letters*, pp. 209–10]

Of which desperation, she was often painfully self-conscious:

> Why dont you write me, Darling? Did I in that quick letter say anything which grieved you, or made it hard for you to take your usual pen and trace affection for your bad, sad Emilie? [*Letters*, p. 195]

> You need not fear to leave me least I should be alone, for I often part with things I fancy I have loved – sometimes to the grave, and sometimes to an oblivion rather bitterer than death – thus my heart bleeds so frequently that I shant mind the hemorrhage, and I only add an agony to several previous ones, and at the end of day remark – a bubble burst! [*Letters*, pp. 305–6]

On Sue's part the relationship appears to have been far less intimate, certainly less physical. Emily Dickinson was for her an entertainment in a dull community, a source of ideas, an outlet for her sophomoric intellect. Given her temperament, Sue was found to feel threatened at times both by Emily Dickinson's passion and by her superior intellect.

one living – To say that sincerely is strange praise." "To be Susan is Imagination, / To have been Susan, a Dream – ," she exclaimed a year later, "What depths of Domingo in that torrid Spirit!"[12]

Two poems of 1877 to/about Sue, which are regular in rhythm and rhyme and easy of metaphor, tell the attraction and the difference between them—something that would communicate to her:

> But Susan is a Stranger yet –
> The Ones who cite her most
> Have never scaled her Haunted House
> Nor compromised her Ghost –
>
> To pity those who knew her not
> Is helped by the regret
> That those who know her know her less
> The nearer her they get –

[#1400]

> To own a Susan of my own
> Is of itself a Bliss –
> Whatever Realm I forfeit, Lord,
> Continue me in this!

[#1401]

With only a few exceptions, these occasional and personal verses, rather than her more difficult work, appear to be the poetry Sue knew her for.[13]

Sue's summation of her sister-in-law's poetic abilities (the obituary for the *Springfield Republican*) was as follows:

12. *Letters,* pp. 733, 791.
13. Though many knew Sue's interest in poetry, no one but Emily Dickinson ever attributed to her any critical abilities (Leyda, *Years and Hours,* 1:153, 192, 218, 228, 249, 323, 361, 376; 2:20, 41, 85, 132, 196). Others in town thought Sue

> a really brilliant and highly cultivated woman of great taste and refinement, perhaps a little too aggressive, a little too sharp in wit and repartee, and a little too ambitious for social prestige, but, withal, a woman of the world in the best sense, having a very keen and correct appreciation of what was fine and admirable. Her imagination was exceedingly vivid, sometimes so vivid that it got away with her and she confounded its pictures with objective things.... She was vacillating in her mental processes and not always interesting, but at times she seemed almost inspired. [John W. Burgess, *Reminiscences of an American Scholar* (New York, 1934), pp. 60–62]

Apart from the two brief pieces she wrote in 1850 and 1857 on society in Amherst (which include comments on Richard Henry Dana and on one of Emerson's visits to Amherst), neither of them published, she appears to have had no literary aspirations of her own and is not known to have tried to analyze anyone else's verse at any time. For the sake of friendship, Emily Dickinson appears to have asked for the criticism, knowing most of the time, however, that it was appreciative but inept.

Her talk and her writings were like no one's else. . . . A Damascus blade gleaming and glancing in the sun was her wit. Her swift poetic rapture was like the long glistening note of a bird one hears in the June woods at high noon, but can never see. Like a magician she caught the shadowy apparitions of her brain and tossed them in startling picturesqueness to her friends, who, charmed with their simplicity and homeliness as well as profundity, fretted that she had so easily made palpable the tantalizing fancies forever eluding their bungling, fettered grasp.[14]

This was one of the most positive literary criticisms she was to be given in the nineteenth century, but it was written (in Francis Murphy's words) by "one of the lions who devoured [her]."

Though stimulating and appreciative of the poetry, Sue was, like almost all the others who made up Emily Dickinson's growing circle of "literary" friends, messily intrusive. The case of "Safe in their Alabaster Chambers" (#216) in 1861 and 1862, the only fully documentable instance of Sue's working over an Emily Dickinson poem, shows Emily Dickinson dealing defensively with Sue's help with her poetry, even making fun of the assistance proffered.[15]

The story begins in 1859 when Emily Dickinson wrote a satire of the Christian concept of death and resurrection current around her in Amherst, playing ironically with the Protestant consolatory language of the time:

Safe in their Alabaster Chambers –
Untouched by Morning
And untouched by Noon –
Sleep the meek members of the Resurrection –
Rafter of satin,
And Roof of stone.

Light laughs the breeze
In her Castle above them –
Babbles the Bee in a stolid Ear,
Pipe the Sweet Birds in ignorant cadence –
Ah, what sagacity perished here!

[Version 1]

14. *Springfield Republican*, 18 May 1886.
15. Sue may have also had a hand in the doctoring of "A narrow Fellow in the Grass" (#986) for publication in the *Springfield Republican* in 1886, since she is the one who gave it to Samuel Bowles for publication, unbeknown to her sister-in-law. Emily Dickinson protested against the changes in punctuation and line arrangement. See the story of Sue's involvement in *Poems*, pp. 713–14. Additional comments on Sue's involvement are in Thomas A. Davis, ed., *14 by Emily Dickinson with Selected Criticism* (Chicago, 1964), pp. 19–30.

Sue saw the poem in 1861 and apparently disapproved of some of it. So Emily Dickinson rewrote it in the form of a satire (the first stanza) that turns into horror (a new second stanza). "Perhaps this verse would please you better – Sue," she wrote.[16]

> Safe in their Alabaster Chambers,
> Untouched by Morning –
> And untouched by Noon –
> Lie the meek members of the Resurrection –
> Rafter of Satin – and Roof of Stone!
>
> Grand go the Years – in the Crescent – above them –
> Worlds scoop their Arcs –
> And Firmaments – row –
> Diadems – drop – and Doges – surrender –
> Soundless as dots – on a Disc of Snow –
>
> [Version 2]

But Sue complained even more about this version, failing entirely to recognize the mock sentimentality and deliberate triteness of the first part of the poem (she thought it had a "ghostly shimmer" to it) and failing to see the difference between the oversweet tone at the beginning and the toying with nihilism at the end:

> I am not suited dear Emily with the second verse – It is remarkable as the chain lightening that blinds us hot nights in the Southern sky but it does not go with the ghostly shimmer of the first verse as well as the other one – It just occurs to me that [since] the first verse is complete in itself it needs no other, and can't be coupled – Strange things always go alone – as there is only one Gabriel and one Sun – You never made a peer for that verse, and I *guess* you[r] kingdom does'nt hold one – I always go to the fire and get warm after thinking of it, but I never can again –[17]

Attempting to please Sue at this point, she then wrote two other stanzas that were more in keeping with what Sue liked about the poem. These too sentimentalize death and are only a little less trite. In deference to Sue's eschatology, she yielded to her less-demanding esthetics. It was easy for her to please Sue, for the poem itself was a parody of Sue's position.

16. *Letters*, p. 379.
17. *Letters*, pp. 379–80. Sue should have sensed the more skeptical thinking behind Emily Dickinson's poem from a further sentence in this same letter. The letter goes on: "The flowers are sweet and bright and look as if they would kiss one – ah, they expect a humming-bird – Thanks for them of course – and not only thanks either – *Did it ever occur to you that is all there is here after all* – 'Lord that I may receive my sight' – " (my emphasis).

Springs - shake the sills -
But - the Echoes - stiffen -
Hoar - is the window -
And numb the door -
Tribes - of Eclipse - in Tents - of Marble -
Staples - of Ages - have buckled - there -

Springs - shake the Seals -
But the silence - stiffens -
Frosts unhook - in the Northern Zones -
Icicles - crawl from Polar Caverns -
Midnight in Marble - Refutes - the Suns -

[Version 3]

"Is *this frostier?*" she then asked Sue playfully, mockingly, knowing she could like the easier imagery. "Your praise is good - to me because I *know* it *knows* - and suppose - it means -." Which is to say that she wants Sue to like her poetry even when Sue does not know what she is saying. To please her she must, I believe she is saying subtly, sacrifice her intent. "Could I make you and Austin - proud - sometime - a great way off - 'twould give me taller feet -."[18] In other words, she was willing to compromise some aspects of her poetic performance to gain their approval, hoping that at some point in the future—even if "a great way off"—they would understand what she wanted to do and be. Perhaps it is unforgivable that she would thus change her lines to fit their views even while she knew they did not understand what she knew on the subject of death. How often, with her verse in hand as payment, was she in such desperate need of a friend?

When she let Samuel Bowles publish the poem in the *Republican* in March of 1862, she stuck to her guns, however, completely ignoring Sue's disapproval and printing her original version. And when she sent a version of the poem to Higginson in April of the same year, it was again a version of the poem Sue could not approve of, the second version—which he, however, in 1890, was to find "too daring." Here, side by side, are the two poems she published *in spite of Sue,* one a satire throughout and the other a juxtaposition of easy hope and hard stoicism, a usual device of hers.

THE SLEEPING

Safe in their alabaster chambers,	Safe in their Alabaster Chambers -
Untouched by morning,	Untouched by Morning -
And untouched by noon,	And untouched by Noon -

18. *Letters,* p. 380.

Sleep the meek members of
 the Resurrection,
  Rafter of satin, and roof
  of stone.

Light laughs the breeze
In her castle above them,
 Babbles the bee in a stolid ear,
Pipe the sweet birds in
 ignorant cadences:
 Ah! what sagacity perished here!
  [Version 4 from version 1]

Sleep the meek members of
 the Resurrection,
 Rafter of Satin – and Roof of Stone –

Grand go the Years,
In the Crescent above them –
Worlds scoop their Arcs –
And Firmaments – row –
Diadems – drop –
And Doges – surrender –
Soundless as Dots,
On a Disc of Snow.
  [Version 5 from version 2]

All this suggests that in Sue's presence Emily Dickinson would stoop to writing what Sue could read, even if insensitively, but when out from under her sometimes domineering eye she could rise to a taller, tougher stature—and to far better verse. The Sue versions, after all, got discarded.

We cannot know if this near-suicidal example represents Sue's effect on Emily Dickinson's verse at all times. Surely Sue was a constant stimulus, important as a concerned and appreciative audience, and a representative of the world to her. Sue sent her sister-in-law's poems out to several magazine editors, hoping that, like the verse of Celia Thaxter and Harriet Prescott, it would catch on, genuinely believing it the best. She did not succeed at this until 1890, but by then her heart was not in it and she eventually gave up, afraid the public would not care for the poems. But, like any critic, Sue was simultaneously help and hindrance. The anecdotes show only that, for a surety, Emily Dickinson sometimes gave in when she considered her verse a communication and was usually much better when she gave up communicating. It says little for Sue, and it documents Emily Dickinson's poetic vulnerability. If we knew the stories behind all her poems, would we know who and what encouraged and then weakened some of them?

Besides Sue there were very few in the town able to help her verse any, even though the local newspaper liked to refer to "the numerous authors and authoresses in town."[19] Local teachers of writing at the college like Aaron Warner and William Chauncey Fowler had no contact with her and published nothing of their own besides

19. Leyda, *Years and Hours*, 2:210.

sermons. Mable Loomis Todd, who found Emily Dickinson's poetry remarkable, arrived in Amherst too late to be an influence, as did Alice Ward Bailey, also an Amherst poet. Georgiana Allen, daughter of Harriet Beecher Stowe, lived in Amherst for a few years and wrote verse that Emily Dickinson never saw. "Beautiful piece[s] of poetry," as Emily Dickinson called them, often appeared in the local newspapers but were seldom from any local hands that might have helped her.[20] Ben Newton, her first "friend," warmly encouraged her desire to work with language ("[He] told me that he would like to live till I have been a poet"),[21] but he died before he saw any of her mature writings; the correspondence with him is almost entirely lost, and so we cannot know very much about his later effect on her writing. Henry Emmons, a boyfriend of her early twenties with whom she exchanged poems, spoke to her about the "metric chant of blessed poems."[22] The local dentist, Jacob Holt, published several verses in local newspapers,[23] and Joseph Lyman, an early intimate, wrote articles and a book about housekeeping.[24]

Then, too, several relatives and friends wrote and published, but nothing of any importance to her: Lavinia penned seventeen rather conventional verses; Asa Bullard, an uncle, edited Sunday school books and tracts; Elizabeth Dickinson, her aunt, wrote doggerel for family occasions and in 1844 published a poem about New Year; her own father wrote some pieces for the *New-England Inquirer* between

20. *Letters*, p. 34. One such verse attractive to Emily Dickinson at sixteen was a poem by one Florence Vane, "Are We Almost There?":

"Are we almost there? are we almost there?"
Said a dying girl, as she drew near home . . .
. . . .
For when the light of that eye was gone,
And the quick pulse stopped
She was almost there.

(Leyda, *Years and Hours*, 1:110.) This is the earliest verse we know Emily Dickinson to have liked.
21. *Letters*, p. 408.
22. In the *Amherst Collegiate Magazine*, 31 July 1854, Emmons published a piece that concluded:

And I arose, and looked forth upon the broad plain with a
strange earnestness thrilling in my heart.
The gold morning's open flowings,
Did sway the trees to murmurous bowings,
In metric chant of blessed poems.

(Leyda, *Years and Hours*, 1:311.) To which Emily Dickinson replied appreciatively in a letter (*Letters*, p. 303). See Sewall, *Life*, pp. 410–15, for the story of this relationship.
23. Sewall, *Life*, pp. 402–3.
24. *The Lyman Letters: New Light on Emily Dickinson and Her Family*, ed. Richard B. Sewall (Amherst, 1966).

1826 and 1828; Henry Sweetser, a cousin by marriage, was a New York publisher (he published one of her poems in *The Round Table* in 1864); Zebina Montague, the only literary cousin, contributed comic pieces to the local newspapers.

Helen Hunt Jackson, of course, is identified with Amherst, and Emily Fowler Ford was a local poet of light verse publishing in the *Atlantic Monthly* and elsewhere whom Emily Dickinson knew quite well (of her poems *My Recreations* she wrote, "The little Book will be subtly cherished – All we secure of Beauty is it's Evanescence") until she moved away from Amherst.[25] Higginson therefore said he thought "Amherst must be a *nest* of poetesses," but he overestimated the scene.[26]

On the fringes of the community were some important literary names. There was F. B. Sanborn, abolitionist, friend of Bowles and Higginson, and apologist for Transcendentalism, who in 1873 asked to see some poems of Emily Dickinson's.[27] And there was, at Greenfield, Frederick Goddard Tuckerman, poet, brother of an Amherst professor, and father of some close friends of Emily Dickinson's.[28] Both of them had opportunity to know her but did not.

Though cluttered with possibilities, the landscape was fairly bleak. For a small country town of the mid-1800s, Amherst was intellectually unique; yet Emily Dickinson wrote virtually alone.

25. Emily Dickinson acted rather obsequiously toward Mrs. Ford, but Mrs. Ford was rather scornful of how Emily Dickinson lived and what she wrote, referring to her with such phrases as "demur manner" and "adder's tongue." On one occasion in 1882 when Emily Dickinson would not receive her in her home, she wrote a poem about the incident (and then published it in the *Republican*, 11 January 1891):

> ...... Social with bird and bee
> Loving your tender flowers with ecstasy,
> You shun the eye, the voice, and shy elude
> The loving souls that dare not to intrude
> Upon your chosen silence ...
> And beauty is your song, with interlude
> Of outer life which to your soul seems crude,
> Thoughtless, unfeeling, idle, scant of grace;
> Nor will you touch a hand, or greet a face,—
> For common daily strife to you is rude,
> And, shrinking, you in shadow lonely stay
> Invisible to all, howe'er we pray.
>   [Leyda, *Years and Hours*, 2:372–73, 450, 478]

26. Leyda, *Years and Hours*, 2:193.

27. "Had I a trait you would accept," she wrote Sanborn, apparently mistrustful of his ability to deal with her poems, "I would be most proud" (*Letters*, p. 516).

28. "Intriguing as it may be to conjecture that Tuckerman knew Emily Dickinson," writes Samuel A. Golden, Tuckerman's biographer, "there is little support for such a possibility." Though Emily Dickinson knew Tuckerman's uncle and his son and daughter-in-law, and though Tuckerman lived in Greenfield just twenty miles away,

Someone from her literary circle who did make a substantial difference to Emily Dickinson—that is, someone who was a spur to her writing yet also a barrier to her emergence—was Samuel Bowles. Her relationship with him was her first hoped-for avenue to publication; but Bowles was somewhat obtuse. Mrs. Annie Fields wrote of Bowles, "He has learned to know almost everybody of literary celebrity," but we have his confession of his inabilities: "My 'weakness' is not poetry."[29] Most of his literary judgments are hard to understand now: he liked the poetry of a Collette Loomis ("compact, thoughtful, mysterious and suggestive poems") and a Mrs. Vandenhoff, both of Springfield, and he thought Helen Jackson a writer who "stands on the threshold of the greatest literary triumphs ever won by an American woman."[30] Emily Dickinson he could never focus on very well. She was, as Richard Sewall points out, "out of *his* reach."[31]

Bowles wrote one fascinating sketch of Emily Dickinson for the *Republican* at the time when he was trying to discover who had written the Saxe Holm stories. In distinguishing between the style of Helen Hunt Jackson and that of Emily Dickinson ("Suppose We Look for 'Saxe Holm' in Amherst?"), he wrote:

> [She] is always morbid, and morbid to the last degree. The morbidness . . . is, however, the ideal element of her poetry pushed to its extremity. . . . Her poems are like strains of solemn music floating at night from some wayside church. Each thought is complete and rare, solemn with the solemnity of intense conviction. . . . Her scenes are mostly in-door scenes, of domestic life in the parlor, kitchen and garden. Of busy streets and natural scenery she says almost nothing . . . [yet] she seems to feel a kinship to the natural world, is as exquisitely sensitive to the feelings produced by birds and flowers and is familiar with their ways and language as if she were, indeed, one of them. In variety of incident her resources are limited; in the growth and experiences of the inner life they never are. . . .
>
> Her expressions are often quaint and old-fashioned. . . . With all this quaintness there is an accompanying timidity and shrinking. . . . The gems of thought and felicitous expressions . . . are not so much the flashes of genius as the products of long, quiet thinking. . . .

she does not mention him in her letters, and he makes no mention of her in his. Higginson knew both poets but never mentioned the one to the other. "It is incredible that Tuckerman's poetry was never mentioned to her, and it is unlikely that his published volume [*Poems*, 1860, 1863, 1864, 1869] did not come to her attention. Yet, all this is conjecture; and it must, therefore, be that they were strangers" (*Frederick Goddard Tuckerman* [New York, 1966], p. 47).

29. Leyda, *Years and Hours*, 2:122; 1:368.
30. Ibid., 1:362; 2:17, 214–15.
31. Sewall, *Life*, p. 473.

All these lead us to the conclusion that the author may be a person long shut out from the world and living in a world of her own; that perhaps she is a recluse. . . . We may imagine her to be a member of one of those "sleepy and dignified" New England families whom she has so vividly described; of a timid nature; separated from the outside world, devoted to literature and flowers.[32]

From 1861 until his death in 1878, Emily Dickinson wanted Bowles for a lover and publisher, or what she called, noncommittally, "a guide"—perhaps as a philosophical guide ("When did the Dark happen?" she asked him) and as a moral guide ("[F]orgive the Gills that ask for Air - if it is harm - to breathe!") but especially as a literary guide ("If you doubted my [poem about] Snow - for a moment - you never will - again - I know -").[33] He was someone she loved personally who she thought understood her and her abilities and who would, she hoped, guide her into print. At his death Emily Dickinson said Bowles had been "a constant stimulus."[34]

Bowles's interest in the Dickinsons was, however, far more civic and political than literary, and so her claim to his critical attention was as presumptuous as her claims on his emotions. In her letters and poems to him (and these most certainly include the three Master letters of 1858–61) she has a passion for passion and for publication: she is a poet trying to get her lover to accept her for the whole person she is. But Bowles rejected her as lover and therefore as poet: she had, perhaps mistakenly, connected the two too closely. Bowles kept his distance, somewhat bemused, from both Emilys. It is curious that he would refer to her as late as the age of thirty-six as "that girl."[35]

What Emily Dickinson was trying to do in sending Bowles her poems was the simple business of communicating with a friend/lover—with as many as thirty-seven separate poems, more than she gave anyone else except Sue and Higginson. Like Whitman's spider, she was sending out filaments in friendship; they were indeed her letter to that part of the world she loved and longed for. "Because I could not say it," she wrote in a letter to him in 1862, "I fixed it in the Verse - for you to read - when your thought wavers, for such a foot as mine."[36] Her poems to him are not always on the subject of love, yet

32. I conjecture that this sketch is by Bowles, and it seems most likely. I have cut into the column to show how it was probably Emily Dickinson that Bowles had in mind, and so I refer the reader to the complete text in Leyda, *Years and Hours*, 2:295–97.

33. *Letters,* p. 394. By "Snow" she is probably referring to her poem beginning "Title divine - is mine!" (#1072), a satire of marriage.

34. *Letters,* p. 668.

35. *Poems,* p. 713.

36. *Letters,* p. 394.

they appear almost always to have been given out of that motive. "Would you like Summer?" she asked him in one poem. "Taste of our's – / Spices? Buy, here!" Her last letter to him (in 1877, shortly before he died) is a love letter with the lines in it: "I have no Life but this – ... Except through this extent / The love of you." Bowles was the stimulus that any lover could be, but he also turned out to be one of her stumbling blocks. "It is fully apparent," writes Sewall, "that Bowles was a powerful presence on whom for a while she focussed with extraordinary intensity both her ambition and her love."[37]

The five poems that Bowles published in the *Springfield Republican* are not ones she gave him herself and in general appear in a slightly modified form she could not approve. The first, "A Valentine" (#3), published 20 February 1852, was sent to Bowles by its recipient, William Howland, and no changes are known. But in the second, "The May-Wine" (#214), published 4 May 1861, Bowles made substantive changes. We do not know how he got this poem: there is no reference to it in the letters. Emily Dickinson originally wrote:

> I taste a liquor never brewed –
> From Tankards scooped in Pearl –
> Not all the Frankfort Berries
> Yield such an Alcohol!

Because he (or Josiah Holland) thought he knew better than she how it should go, in Bowles's hands it became:

> I taste a liquor never brewed,
> From tankards scooped in Pearl;
> Not Frankfort berries yield the sense
> Such a delirious whirl.

And her final lines:

> To see the little Tippler
> Leaning against the – Sun –

were drawn out to:

> To see the little tippler
> Come staggering toward the sun.

The "corrections" in imagery, rhythm, and rhyme amount to his mistrust of her abilities. Her roughness and her ingenuities—*herself*—could not be trusted.

The other three poems Bowles published came to him from Sue.

---

37. Sewall, *Life,* p. 493.

He (or Holland) doctored them as well. In "The Sleeping" (#216), published 1 March 1862, he made one major change, in the rhythm: "Pipe the Sweet Birds in ignorance cadence – " became "Pipe the sweet birds in ignorant cadences." In "Sunset" (#228), published 30 March 1865, he made an important change in the imagery.

> Stooping as low as the kitchen [Otter's] Window
> Touching the Roof and tinting the Barn
> Kissing her Bonnet to the Meadow
> And the Juggler of Day is gone

became in the *Springfield Republican*:

> Stooping as low as the oriel window
>   Touching the roof, and tinting the barn,
> Kissing her bonnet to the meadow –
>   And the Juggler of Day is gone!

When Bowles published "The Snake" (#986) in February 1866, she complained (in a letter to Higginson) about the changes he (or Holland) had made: "[The poem] was robbed of me – defeated too of the third line by the punctuation. The third and fourth were one."[38] Her version read:

> A narrow Fellow in the Grass
> Occasionally rides –
> You may have met Him – did you not
> His notice sudden is –

Bowles's version reads:

> You may have met him – did you not?
> His notice instant is.[39]

The important point is not the changes Bowles made, however, but the fact that he, along with almost everyone else who handled her lines, felt he should not trust her completely: the private poet is an aberrant child who needs help.

Bowles really made very little effort to publish the best poet he knew personally. Apparently Emily Dickinson failed to convince friends like Bowles about herself (and her desperate sexual-professional relationship with Bowles is the best example in her biography), and so her poems were always vulnerable. Their insistence on

38. *Letters*, p. 450.
39. Johnson's edition makes an error and puts a comma where Bowles had a question mark. Emily Dickinson accepted Bowles's change of "sudden" to "instant" for a copy she made of the poem for Sue in 1872.

helping her is, I believe, a criticism of *her*. What saved her was her ability to keep her distance—a security that made her "the myth of Amherst" even as the recluse in her was largely a myth. Though out far, with her poems she is waving, not drowning. The filaments found no summits to hold onto; her own height was a saving station.

Her friends the Hollands saw this and pretty much left her alone. Yet here too Emily Dickinson shows herself to have been vulnerable to personal contacts. The Hollands were prominent literary people in Emily Dickinson's circle of friends, and their influence on her cannot be disregarded. "Cling tight to the hearts that will not let you fall," Emily Dickinson advised herself in a letter to Mrs. Holland.[40] From 1854 on, Emily Dickinson was very worshipful of the liberally religious, conservatively literary Hollands—whom she called "the dark man with the doll-wife." She could, above all, take her religious questions to them: "I longed to come to you, and tell you about [my worries about death], and learn how to be better."[41] Her letters to them are consistently more religious than those to any other people she corresponded with. But though she appears to have trusted their literary judgments (calling, after Dr. Holland, Whitman "disgraceful" and Theodore Parker "poison"), she never discussed writing or anything literary with them. She read Dr. Holland's fiction and poetry out of duty. Her thirty-five poems to them—most of them written in the last ten years of her life—represent her reaching out (again) for friends, for the most part, and should not be read out of the context of that relationship.[42]

> For, when Frosts, their punctual fingers
> On her forehead lay,
> You and I, and Dr Holland,
> Bloom Eternally!
>
> [#163]

With them she appears to have felt a kind of security, and so she went to Elizabeth Holland with some of her heaviest loads for almost three decades and in return learned softened religion and softened esthet-

---

40. *Letters,* p. 713.

41. *Letters,* p. 308. "Holland often thought Bowles irreverent, not to say heathenish, and Bowles thought Holland something of a prig" (George S. Merriam, *The Life and Times of Samuel Bowles* [New York, 1885], 1:51). Emily Dickinson stood somewhere in between.

42. We do not have any comments on her poems from the Hollands, and she comments on Dr. Holland's writings only twice, calling one of his poems ("Things New and Old") an "exquisite hymn" and saying of a serialized novel of his, "Our sacred

ics. "I shall never forget the Doctor's prayer, my first morning with you – so simple, so believing," she wrote to her in 1881. "*That* God must be a friend – that was a different God – and I almost felt warmer myself, in the midst of a tie so sunshiny."[43]

Holland and Bowles, she reported to Higginson in 1862, asked on one occasion to publish some of her poetry, but she demurred. "Two Editors of Journals came to my Father's House, this winter – and asked me for my Mind," she reported, "and when I asked them 'Why,' they said I was penurious – and they would use it for the World –."[44] If the Hollands should be counted part of the circle of friends whose literary gestures she knew and possibly imitated, then Emily Dickinson's miserliness in keeping back her poems from "use" was wise. Mrs. Holland she loved dearly, and through her came the conservative influence of Josiah Holland, "The Apostle to the Naive." Though she was stimulated by the contact, it was detrimental to some of her poetry.

Higginson wrote on one occasion that he felt Holland had had "much formative power over the intellect of the nation," especially as editor of *Scribner's Monthly/Century Magazine* but also through his fiction and poetry.[45] "He could think the thoughts and speak the speech of the common people," wrote George S. Merriam in his biography of Bowles. "He represented that democratic quality in literature which our social conditions demand."[46] Holland, Allan Nevins has said, wrote "truisms insipid enough for a young ladies' boarding school and religious enough for the most bigoted sectarian."[47] Reviewers of his works during his lifetime took him as representative of mainstream literary taste during the 1860s and 1870s and as representative of the new religious spirit: less creed and more character.

"Art is a very thin diet for any human soul, . . ." Holland wrote in one of his columns. "For art, it should be remembered, adds nothing to morality, nothing to religion, nothing to science, nothing to knowledge except a knowledge of itself, nothing to social or political wis-

Neighbors . . . were so enamored of 'Nicholas Minturn', that they borrow our Number before it is cold" (*Letters*, pp. 324, 582, 713).

43. *Letters*, p. 612.
44. *Letters*, pp. 404–5. I do not personally believe the suggestion that it was Holland, not Bowles, who got her five poems into the *Republican*, for the reason that after he left the newspaper to work on literary journals in New York, he did not publish any of the poems she sent him, though he had ample opportunity to do so.
45. *Carlyle's Laugh, and Other Surprises* (Boston and New York, 1909), p. 378.
46. In Mrs. H. M. Plunkett, *Josiah Gilbert Holland* (New York, 1894), pp. 34–35.
47. *The Emergence of Modern America* (New York, 1927), p. 232.

dom, theoretically or practically."[48] Perhaps it was this kind of moralizing influence that came to Emily Dickinson as long as she read his Timothy Titcomb pieces in the *Springfield Republican* during the 1850s and as long as she followed his religious and literary essays later in *Scribner's/Century*. She always seems to have known what he and his wife stood for—gentle orthodoxy (perhaps what Emily Dickinson needed as she lost religion), a homiletic tone to life (perhaps encouraging the moral aphorizing in her), an aggressive conservatism in esthetics (perhaps leading to her temptation to see poetry as piety), and a reserved attitude toward the role of woman in society (perhaps adding to her ambivalence about herself).[49]

We have only one sure bit of evidence on what Dr. Holland thought about the poetry of Emily Dickinson. The condescending (and not entirely reliable) Emily Fowler Ford remembered of Holland the following:

> Once I met Dr. Holland the Editor then of Scribner's Magazine, who said, "You know Emily Dickinson. I have some poems of hers under consideration for publication—but they really are not suitable—they are too ethereal." I said "They are beautiful, so concentrated, but they remind me of orchids, air plants that have no roots in earth." He said "That is true—a perfect description, I dare not use them."[50]

The Hollands' level of poetry during the years when Emily Dickinson knew them personally in Amherst and Springfield is represented by the poems of a Springfield woman, Dolly Ellen Goodman Shepard, who died in 1853 at thirty-two, which they put together and published

48. *Every-Day Topics* (New York, 1882), pp. 78–79.
49. Because of the example of Mrs. Holland's happy acceptance of her husband's view of women, perhaps a dominant one during the 1860s and 1870s, Emily Dickinson must have been impressed. On the equality of women he wrote:

> Have women a sphere? I think they have; but we will compromise and call it a hemisphere. Her mission is to love, and it argues depravity of soul when a woman pants to enter the race and contend with man in the labor of life. Her work is to uplift the world by her refinement and love. The hard work is to be done by man; woman's apostleship is to cheer him in his struggle. [In Peckham, *Josiah Gilbert Holland in Relation to His Time* (Philadelphia, 1940), p. 55]

On women's rights he wrote further:

> I have always observed that the most truly lovable, humble, pure-hearted, God-fearing and humanity-loving women of my acquaintance, never say anything about these rights, and scorn those of their sex who do. I have never known a woman who was at once satisfied in her affections and discontented with her woman's lot and her woman's work. There is a weak place, or a wrong place, or a rotten place in the character or nature of every woman who stands and howls upon the spot where her creator placed her, and neglects her own true work and life while claiming the right to do the work and live the life of man. [Ibid., pp. 60–61]

50. Leyda, *Years and Hours*, 2:193.

as *Cut-Flowers* in 1854. If they liked these verses, they would have had little interest in the tougher poems Emily Dickinson was to begin to write and send to them five years later. And by the influence of their taste in these formative years, her work would have been sentimentalized. A sample:

> The ice is on his brow! My hand hath lain
> Upon its polished surface long, to feel
> The warm life-blood come creeping back again:
> And I have watched to see the faint flush steal
> Over the marble cheek: to mark the lid
> That droops so coldly o'er the azure eyes –
> Where such a world of noble love lies hid –
> In this full, radiant burst of glory rise!
>
> ["The Lament"]

Holland gave this advice to an emerging woman poet in 1877: "I'm a bit tired of *subjective* poems. Try going outside for topics, and get an interest in some thing beside yourself and your emotions. That is the way to grow."[51] Holland's view of poetry during Emily Dickinson's own productive years is seen in his anthology *Christ and the Twelve; or, Scenes and Events in the Life of Our Saviour and His Apostles, as Painted by the Poets* (Springfield, 1867). Piety was the criterion for inclusion. And of course there was nothing by Emily Dickinson in it, even though she had sent Mrs. Holland quite a number of her more egregiously moralistic poems.[52] But then none of the more liberal, experimental writers of the time were represented either.

Holland wrote and published widely his own moralistic verse until his death in 1881. He read it in public in Amherst in the 1850s; the Dickinsons had it in their libraries, for the father thought it safe. It gave him wide fame for over two decades.

> All alone in the world! all alone!
> With child on my knee, or a wife on my breast,
> Or, sitting beside me, the beautiful guest
> Whom my heart leaps to greet as its sweetest and best,
> Still alone in the world! all alone!
>
> ["Alone"][53]

In the verses Emily Dickinson sent the Hollands we have a great deal of similar—perhaps imitative—moralizing, especially those she ad-

---

51. Ibid., 2:272.
52. Perhaps this is evidence that the Hollands did not think of her as a poet at all. Ibid., 2:115–16.
53. J. G. Holland, *Complete Poetical Writings* (New York, 1917), p. 480.

dressed to "the Doctor." Such a representative poem as this, didactic and simple of image, was sent him in 1864:

> Truth – is as old as God
> His Twin identity
> And will endure as long as He
> A Co-Eternity –

[#836]

The poems to Mrs. Holland tended to be about surprises in nature or to generalize upon worldly interests:

> The Road to Paradise is plain,
> And holds scarce one.
> Not that it is not firm
> But we presume
> A Dimpled Road
> Is more preferred.

[#1491]

But those to Dr. Holland are much triter and closer to his religious taste:

> Not all die early, dying young –
> Maturity of Fate
> Is consummated equally
> In Ages, or a Night –

[#990]

We have one fairly sure example of Emily Dickinson's imitation of Holland's moralizing lines, and it suggests that she indeed might have fallen rather severely under his influence because of their friendship. In a poem called "Gradatim" he wrote:

> Heaven is not reached in a single bound;
>   But we build the ladder by which we rise
>   From the lowly earth to the vaulted skies,
> And we mount to its summit round by round.[54]

In a poem of 1870 Emily Dickinson parrots the sentiment:

> We never know how high we are
> Till we are asked to rise
> And then if we are true to plan
> Our statures touch the skies –

[#1176]

---

54. Ibid., p. 487.

Holland stood for a Christian art—that is, for moral earnestness, lucidity, gentleness. And the extent to which Emily Dickinson tried to be like him is perhaps the extent to which she wanted to stand for it, too. She was good at it even when *it* was not any good.

> Not what We did, shall be the test
> When Act and Will are done
> But what Our Lord infers We would
> Had We diviner been –

[#823]

The strong presence of the Hollands in her circle of literary friends suggests not so much that she temperamentally had her feet firmly on bourgeois soil[55] as that her desperation for friends made her a dupe for a morality/esthetic that weakened a number of things she wrote—to please them and to sustain the person she saw them expecting her to be. Her demurral, for her better poetry, from the soft literary principles of friends like the Hollands shows that, to their mind, she lost her sense of virtue and responsibility and lived by pleasures. Anticipating their view of her, she signed a letter to them in 1856, "From your mad . . . Emilie." Her daily life was, except for the smaller scale, very much one that was acceptable to the likes of the Hollands. But her poetry was another life—and that was its advantage for her. It is not difficult to discriminate between her bad Hollandized verse and the good poetry she wrote to escape them.

Her main difference from such literary friends lies in the fact that she saw poetry as being essentially without commitment. The others wanted what they wrote to make some ultimate claim on our belief. Her literary experience was *not* a religious experience, however, but merely a momentary mythologizing, brief, tentative, fanciful, provisional, a suspension. That is why theirs eventually failed: they tied their words to a religion that would fade. They tried to get poetry to assume the functions of religion, thus restricting its range of belief: the provisional beliefs of their writings hardened into fixed creeds. Theirs lacked her precious freedom, for it took as its task justifying a particular course of action instead of contemplating, like hers, imaginatively various courses of action. Her poetry is therefore more detached than theirs; esthetic spectacle is more important than the mighty whole. Gaiety, a tragic ploy to be sure, transfigures all the dread. Their device was mere cheer—blind and mindless cheer. Her poems last because they proceed from a Puritan esthetic endemic to

---

55. The viewpoint of Margaret Bloom, "Emily Dickinson and Dr. Holland," *University of California Chronicle* (Berkeley) 35 (1933): 96–103.

the culture—the tension between worth and worthlessness. Her earnest play escaped them; *she* escaped them by means of her play. The personal focus and the personal accent has *their* religion as her resource (they were therefore literary/religious friends), but she shapes it to fit *her* drama. Though her poetry needed some kind of religious grounding, it actually only needed (and her Puritanism, again, would have taught her this) herself, a more complex system.

"You are a great poet," Emily Dickinson's most appreciative literary friend Helen Fiske Hunt Jackson wrote to her in 1875, "and it is a wrong to the day you live in, that you will not sing aloud. When you are what men call dead, you will be sorry you were so stingy."[56] The stinginess with Bowles and Holland is perhaps understandable, but it is less so with Helen Jackson. The two grew up together in Amherst and became friends in the late 1860s when Helen Hunt reappeared in Amherst and was gaining a small reputation for her poetry and fiction. After reading her *Verses* (1870), Emily Dickinson commented, perhaps imitating Bowles's judgment: "Mrs. Hunt's Poems are stronger than any written by women since Mrs. Browning, with the exception of Mrs. Lewes."[57] Between 1868 and 1875 Emily Dickinson worked by letter to make a friend of her, and yet from the outset she never really trusted her poems in her hands. Helen Jackson was appreciative, hearty, and presumptuous. She is another member of a literary circle that was helpful but also on the attack.

The literary relationship began in 1875 when Emily Dickinson sent Helen Jackson part of a poem on the occasion of her second marriage:

> Upon a Lilac Sea
> To toss incessantly
> His Plush Alarm
> Who fleeing from the Spring
> The Spring avenging fling
> To Dooms of Balm –

[#1337][57]

But Helen Jackson could not understand the lines at all and asked for an explanation. "Thank you for not being angry with my impudent request for interpretations. I do wish I knew just what 'dooms' you meant, though!" Though baffled by much that Emily Dickinson

56. *Letters*, pp. 544–45.
57. She sent only the last three lines of this poem to her.

wrote, she was nonetheless attracted to her and became a major stimulus to her poetry during the last decade of her life: "I hope some day, somewhere I shall find you in a spot where we can know each other. I wish very much that you would write to me now and then, when it did not bore you. I have a little manuscript volume with a few of your verses in it – and I read them very often."[58] But Helen Jackson was, as Higginson pointed out on one occasion, "a dangerous correspondent," often failing to understand the full effect of what she said.[59]

These verses of Emily Dickinson's Helen Jackson tried to get into print in 1876, even over protests. She visited her twice in Amherst to persuade her to release a poem to her for publication. "I want to see some of your verses in print. Unless you forbid me, I will send some that I have," she wrote from Colorado.[60] However, Emily Dickinson did forbid her—"I told her I was unwilling [to publish], and she asked me why? – I said I was incapable and she seemed not to believe me"—and even asked Higginson to intervene on her behalf and prevent Mrs. Jackson from publishing anything of hers: "If you would be willing to give me a note saying you disapproved it, and thought me unfit, she would believe you."[61] But Helen Jackson went ahead anyway and without her permission published one of the poems she had on hand in a volume of Roberts Brothers's No Name Series, *A Masque of Poets* (1878).[62] Five changes were made in the text

58. *Letters,* p. 491.
59. Anna Mary Wells, *Dear Preceptor: The Life and Times of Thomas Wentworth Higginson* (Boston, 1963), p. 211.
60. Ibid. She had almost all of the poems from Higginson, however, not from Emily Dickinson herself.
61. *Letters,* pp. 562–66. Higginson thought Mrs. Jackson wanted some fiction from Emily Dickinson and so advised her against submitting anything. Emily Dickinson corrected him, still begging him to help her keep her poems out of Helen Jackson's hands: "Mrs Jackson has written. It was not stories she asked of me. But may I tell her just the same that you dont prefer it?" (*Letters,* p. 566).
62. Emily Dickinson simply would not give her permission to Helen Jackson for the publication of any of her poems. She wrote Emily Dickinson a second time about this matter, 29 April 1878, "Would it be of any use to ask you once more for one or two of your poems.... If you will give me permission I will copy them ... and promise never to tell any one, not even the publishers, whose the poems are." Not knowing how to say no without doing injury to the friendship, Emily Dickinson remained silent on the matter. But Mrs. Jackson persisted in a third letter, and she was a little dishonest about the matter at this point, for the letter was written when Emily Dickinson's poem was already in press: "Now—will you send me the poem? No—will you let me send the poem? No—will you let me send the 'Success'—which I know by heart—to Roberts Bros for the Masque of Poets? If you will, it will give me a great pleasure" (*Letters,* pp. 623 – 27). T. H. Johnson is incorrect to assume that Emily Dickinson eventually gave permission to publish the poem and to assume that it was Thomas Niles and not Helen Jackson who made the changes in the poem before it was published.

of the poem by either Helen Jackson or the editor of the series, Thomas Niles, all of them largely inconsequential yet still showing her friends' mistrust of her workmanship.

Success is counted sweetest
By those who ne'er succeed.
To comprehend a nectar
Requires sorest need.

Not one of all the purple Host
Who took the Flag today
Can tell the definition
So clear of Victory

As he defeated – dying –
On whose forbidden ear
The distant strains of triumph
Burst agonized and clear!

            [#67]

SUCCESS

Success is counted sweetest
By those that ne'er succeed.
To comprehend the nectar
Requires the sorest need.

Not one of all the purple Host
Who took the Flag today
Can tell the definition
So plain of Victory

As he defeated – dying –
On whose forbidden ear
The distant strains of triumph
Break, agonizing clear.

The friendship with Helen Jackson had to be a strong one on Emily Dickinson's part, for she was mildly critical of Emily's life-style ("you never see anybody!") and appearance ("[I was] accusing you of living away from the sunlight—and [telling] you that you [looke]d ill"),[63] and she was often baffled by what Emily wrote, hoping for something simpler from her:

> This morning I have read over again the last verses you sent me: I find them more clear than I thought they were. Part of the dimness must have been in me. Yet I have others which I like better. I like your simplest and [most direct] lines best.[64]

She was richly and honestly appreciative of Emily Dickinson's poems ("I know your 'Blue bird' by heart—and that is more than I do of any of my own verses.—I also want your permission to send it to Col. Higginson to read. These two things are my testimonial to its merit"),[65] just as Emily Dickinson tried to be appreciative of Helen Jackson's writings ("I have finished Ramona. Would that like Shakespeare, it were just published!").[66] Emily Dickinson wrote her a couple of poems on

63. *Letters,* pp. 565, 625. Further on Emily Dickinson's appearance, she wrote: "You look[ed] so [wh]ite and [mo]th-like[!] Your [hand] felt [l]ike such a wisp in mine that you frigh[tened] me. I felt [li]ke a [gr]eat ox [tal]king to a wh[ite] moth."
64. *Letters,* p. 565.
65. *Letters,* p. 639.
66. *Letters,* pp. 866–67.

request but virtually ignored the plea for simplicity and directness.[67] Some of these are riddles and elaborate conceits, with extreme imagery and strained logic, and therefore should perhaps be taken as satiric comments on Helen Jackson's weaker view of poetry.

Envy of Emily Dickinson's abilities was something Helen Jackson could be facetious about ("I am inclined to envy, and perhaps hate you"), but it was probably nonetheless real. In Colorado in 1877 Mrs. Jackson told her husband, "Emily Dickinson is a great poet and I would like to talk with her." She clearly envied her her abilities.[68] Just before her death in 1885, she sought to take advantage of Emily Dickinson by asking to be the inheritor of her poems:

> What portfolios of verses you must have.—
> It is a cruel wrong to your "day & generation" that you will not give them light.—If such a thing should happen as that I should outlive you, I wish you would make me your literary legatee & executor. Surely, after you are what is called "dead," you will be willing that the poor ghosts you have left behind, should be cheered and pleased by your verses, will you not?—You ought to be—I do not think we have a right to with hold from the world a word or a thought any more than a *deed,* which might help a single soul.[69]

Emily Dickinson pointedly ignored the request as presumptuous— perhaps because of the *Masque of Poets* incident, or perhaps because Helen Jackson was always correcting her and not accepting her for what she was, or perhaps because Mrs. Jackson's letters to her consistently had a tone of greed. Someone fastidiously collecting her poems in a portfolio, managing her manners, tidying up the form of her lines, asking to be her executor upon her death, and yet not doing very much to get the poems in print through such prominent editor-friends as Higginson, Holland, and Niles, was bound to seem ominous. Helen Jackson's mistrust was repaid by Emily Dickinson's mis-

---

67. In 1879, for example, she wrote three bird poems for her: "Before you thought of Spring" (#1465), "One of the ones that Midas touched" (#1466), and "A Route of Evanescence" (#1463). Knowing that Helen Jackson liked "simple and direct" bird poems, Emily Dickinson sent her the following quatrain in 1884:

And then he lifted up his Throat
And squandered such a Note
A Universe that overheard
Is stricken by it yet –

[#1600]

68. *Letters,* p. 639; Evelyn I. Banning, *Helen Hunt Jackson* (New York, 1973), pp. 139–41.
69. *Letters,* pp. 841–42.

trust. Sue wrote of the relationship, "She withstood even the fascinations of Mrs. Helen Jackson."[70]

In her later years no one succeeded in getting Emily Dickinson to think about publication quite as much as Helen Jackson did, but because of Helen Jackson's lack of manners, she could not face the issue very seriously with her. At several points Emily Dickinson was mistaken by local newspapers as the creator or collaborator of Helen Jackson's Saxe Holm sketches and as the heroine of her No Name novel *Mercy Philbrick's Choice* (1876).[71] Mrs. Jackson did not yet know Emily Dickinson well enough, however, to do her up fully as Mercy for her novel; but the portrait, though pathetic and colorless, comes dangerously close at a few points to the stereotype of Emily Dickinson that Mrs. Jackson's few visits and one brief stay in Amherst and the news about "the myth" from correspondents like Higginson had given her:

> Mercy's poems were so largely subjective in tone that it was hard for her readers to believe that they were not all drawn from her own individual experience.

> A WOMAN'S BATTLE

> Dear foe, I know thou'lt win the fight;
> I know thou hast the stronger bark,
> And thou art sailing in the light,
> While I am creeping in the dark
> Thou dost not dream that I am crying,
> As I come up with colors flying.

> I clear away my wounded, slain,
> With strength like frenzy strong and swift;
> I do not feel the tug and strain,
> Though dead are heavy, hard to lift.
> If I looked on their faces dying,
> I could not keep my colors flying.

> Dear foe, it will be short,—our fight,—
> Though lazily thou train'st thy guns:
> Fate steers us,—me to deeper night.
> And thee to brighter seas and suns;

70. Leyda, *Years and Hours,* 2:473.
71. See Leyda, *Years and Hours,* 2:215–16, 257, 265, 295–97, 329, 472. This has been suggested by two biographers, Josephine Pollitt and Genevieve Taggard, but Ruth Odell proves them wrong about the intentions of the characterization of Emily Dickinson as Mercy Philbrick: "Mercy, too, is more Helen herself than she is Emily Dickinson" (*Helen Hunt Jackson* ["*H. H.*"] [New York, 1939], pp. 148–49). Another heroine of Mrs. Jackson's, Elspeth Dynar, has been suggested as an Emily Dickinson characterization (only because of the initials) but this is equally unconvincing (pp. 142–43).

But thou'lt not dream that I am dying,
As I sail by with colors flying![72]

This shows either that she did not know Emily Dickinson and her style of writing very well at all or else that she hoped Emily Dickinson might develop into someone close to the idealized Mercy.

In her relationship with Helen Jackson, Emily Dickinson was spared the condescension she had to endure from Sue and from Samuel Bowles and the pieties she had to submit to under the wings of the Hollands; yet she must have been just as disappointed that the friendship should have meant little more than a grabbing for her product.

The same thing happened in the case of Emily Dickinson's relation with Helen Jackson's publisher Thomas Niles, at one point an enthusiast of both women's poems. In 1882 and 1883 he tried to "induce" Emily Dickinson to publish a volume of her poems through him at Roberts Brothers in Boston. She sent him six of her poems but said it was an "incredible opinion" that she should publish and so warned him against attempting it. He did nothing with the poems. "It has always seemed to me that it would be unwise to perpetuate Miss Dickinson's poems," he told Higginson in 1890. "They are quite as remarkable for defects as for beauties & are generally devoid of true poetical qualities."[73]

If Emily Dickinson's poetry represented the poet herself to Helen Jackson—as we have reason to believe it did—then she experienced, even with so enlightened and warm a person as Mrs. Jackson, a mistrust that must have seemed a partial rejection. Emily Dickinson no doubt saw herself and Helen Jackson as equals: the same age, both from Amherst, both unmarried when they remet, both aspiring writers, both appreciated by important critics like Higginson and Holland, both women. Therefore Emily Dickinson identified strongly with her for a while. This equality is most evident in the fact that she could write her some of her most wildly desirous lines:

72. *Mercy Philbrick's Choice* (Boston, 1876), pp. 269–70. If Mrs. Jackson did have Emily Dickinson in mind for the portrait of Mercy, she transforms what she knew about her into a New England stereotype:

To so exceptional a nature as Mercy's, a certain amount of isolation was inevitable, all through her life, however fortunate she might be in entering into new and wider relations. The loneliness of intense individuality is the loneliest loneliness in the world,— a loneliness which crowds only aggravate, and which even the closest and happiest companionship can only in part cure. The creative faculty is the most inalienable and uncontrollable of individualities. [Pp. 87–88]

73. Leyda, *Years and Hours,* 2:364, 367, 394, 396, 397; Sewall, *Life,* p. 221.

Take all away from me, but leave me Ecstasy,
And I am richer then than all my Fellow Men –

[#1640]

and some of her most boldly "pagan" poems:

Of God we ask one favor,
That we may be forgiven –
For what, he is presumed to know –
The Crime, from us, is hidden –

[#1601]

These were the kinds of poems she could not safely entrust to her other literary friends.

The experience with Helen Jackson points up one important tension in much of Emily Dickinson's poetry: her listening to her literary friends' natural assumptions with increasing skepticism and increasing distress versus the sexually traitorous need of their friendship. The conflict between hormones and integrity was real, and she whored often enough to make one wonder which was primary with her. "Perhaps Death – gave me awe of friends – striking sharp and early," she wrote in a letter in 1863, "for I held them since – in a brittle love."

Not always sensing that she was one thing as friend/lover and something totally different as poet, she allowed her loneliness to make her a dupe of the great antagonist of her friends' lives, respectability. But sensuality is at war with her words, and the urge took its toll on much of her poetry. Though in each case she gradually moved toward the formidable position of having nothing to lose, really free of hope with each of her friends, she continued to work to escape the worst of her conditions—isolation. We can dislike her dependence on a respectable world that she wanted some warmth from but was also rebelling against. Down, she overvalued some of her rescuers, giving them a significance they did not deserve. She granted this significance to people like Sue, the Hollands, Mrs. Jackson, and Higginson, expecting gods.

As a final example of her dilemma, we see that there may have been some kind of collusion between Helen Jackson and T. W. Higginson over Emily Dickinson's poems, though they worked at crosspurposes about publishing them. The two kept each other posted for a decade on how she was progressing, exchanging letters about her as well as the poems each received from her, and assisting each other in perpetuating the stereotype of a sickly provincial—the raw genius of

Romantic tradition, "the pitifully childlike poetic genius," the "worldly coquette"—who needed help.[74]

The Higginson–Emily Dickinson relationship is one of American literature's most shocking examples of the lack of recognition. The entrepreneur could not see, for almost thirty years, the starlet. As with the rest of her circle of literary friends, she made of him a stimulus ("You were not aware that you saved my Life") which became, however, also a threat, a frown. Less a mover to her than a representative of hope of publication, he could not see that she was a woman announcing her readiness to move into a man's professional world. But he was mystified by her and eventually had a polarizing effect on others' views of her. The relationship was throughout one of duplicity and poorly aimed intentions. The result was disastrous for both.

She was duped by Higginson from the outset. She read his 1862 essay "Letter to a Young Contributor" accurately enough: he was arguing that the true writer/thinker lives apart. But by the time she read it and reacted enthusiastically to the sermon, he had renounced his renunciation—that is, he had given up his advertised pacifist abolitionism, self-satisfying Christian seclusion, disillusionment with social problems, privacy as an esthetic—and rejoined the warmongers and social reformers. It was all a matter of bad timing between them. She exposed herself to him at the wrong time.

Higginson wrote the *Atlantic* piece because he had been "temporarily disappointed" about going to war. The issue of renunciation meant much more to her than the literary advice offered. In the essay he was, like her, the unorthodox protestant. But she overrated both his backbone and his withdrawal; in six months he would be the Colonel of the Black Regiment. She was thereafter stuck with him as confidant and had to invent a face for him.[75] When Higginson published her letters to him in 1891, Austin complained; he said he knew, just as she had told Higginson she was "a supposed person" in much that she wrote, that she had been *posing* for Higginson.[76] She wrote to someone who had moved, who did not exist, who could not have responded to her needs. She put herself forward as his kind of poet

---

74. Leyda, *Years and Hours*, 2:111, 214, 349; *Nation* 53 (1896): 275. Higginson repeats a number of Mrs. Jackson's views in his letters to Emily Dickinson: "It is hard [for me] to understand how you can live s[o alo]ne" (*Letters*, p. 461).

75. Tilden G. Edelstein, *Strange Enthusiasm: A Life of Thomas Wentworth Higginson* (New Haven, 1968), pp. 250–51. *Letters*, p. 412.

76. Wells, *Dear Preceptor*, p. 290. Mable Loomis Todd reported much the same thing: "[Austin] says Emily definitely posed in those letters [to Higginson]" (Sewall, *Life*, p. 227).

when he no longer cared about that kind of poet. How was he, at his point, to understand her reason for writing?—"I sing, as the Boy does by the Burying Ground – because I am afraid. . . . The Verses just relieve."[77]

Anyway, it was wrong of her to write him as she did in April of 1862. Her request for "surgery" was surely not sincere. She asked if her verse was alive, knowing it was, and asked him "what is true," knowing she probably knew as well as he did—because, ostensibly, she had "none to ask," though she did (Sue and Bowles, for instance)— and she said she was not begging to be published, though she was.[78] These first letters to Higginson—the habitual reaching out for another friend/master—were to be one of the greatest mistakes of her life: it gave her a critic but not the friend she wanted; it made her a victim (again) of a literary standard she would have to take seriously against her nature; it gave her a blind hope that reduced the more hellish stimuli of her poems; and it almost completely conditioned (as Sewall documents in his biography of her) her withdrawal.

The relationship was not very honest on Higginson's part either. He reacted in a kindly manner to her manner and to the four poems she first sent him—better ones than she had given anyone else up to that point—and yet he confided immediately to a colleague, James T. Field, that they were "fortunately not to be forwarded for publication!" and told his mother at about the same time that they were "effusions" that "quite overwhelmed" him.[79] He asked Emily Dickinson why she did not publish and then did more than anyone else to discourage such notions. He knew very well what she was after, for he paraphrased her 1862 letter to him in his book *Common Sense about Women* twenty years later, thus: "Behind almost all these letters [from "young girl authors"] there lies a laudable desire to achieve success. 'Would you have the goodness to tell us how success can be obtained?' . . . If a young girl pines after the success of Marion Harland and Mrs. Southworth, let her seek it."[80] He wrote of the integrity of one's art in his 1862 essay but could not respect Emily Dickinson's. He

77. *Letters*, pp. 404, 408.
78. *Letters*, pp. 403–5.
79. Leyda, *Years and Hours*, 2:55.
80. Higginson, *Common Sense about Women* (Boston, 1881), pp. 260–61. Higginson's enormous hypocrisy about publishing Emily Dickinson is seen when he goes on to state:

> Instead, therefore, of offering to young writers the usual comforting assurance, that if they produce any thing of real merit, it will be sure to succeed, I should caution them first to make their own definition of success, and then act accordingly. . . . There is always an opening for careful and conscientious literary work; and, by such work, many persons obtain a modest support. . . . Make your choice;

told her she wrote in a "fiery mist" with "rare sparkles of light" and "luminous flashes," and yet he often made fun of her to his wife, leading her to believe her "foolish," perhaps even a little "insane," though perhaps that was all he could say if he thought he might have to deal with her jealousy.[81]

To her face he called her "ingenuous," "wise," "brilliant," highly intellectual ("It isolates one anywhere to think beyond a certain point"), and yet later he talked about her behind her back as an ignorant and erratic child ("Dash, cleverness, recklessness, utter impatience of revision or of patient investigation, these are the common traits [of Emily Dickinson]. To a person of experience, no stupidity is so discouraging as a brilliancy that has no roots").[82]

Furthermore, he was unforgivably duplicitous over his visits to see her; to her he wrote after the first one, "I hope you will not cease to trust me and to turn to me; and I will try to speak the truth to you, and with love," but in a letter to his sister about the visit, he made fun of her, satirizing her entrance, her gift of a flower, her opening remark: "How long are you going to stay?" Perhaps sensing the egregious disparities, Emily Dickinson did not write him for half a year after that.[83]

For another example of his games, when he read some of her poems to the Boston's Women's Club in 1876, he was surpised to find that they stirred considerable interest; but he never told Emily Dickinson about this—which might have been very encouraging to her at that particularly perplexing point in her concern over her literary worth.

Also, he never asked her, contrary to his claim at the beginning of her posthumous fame much later, for *any* poems to publish. He later lied (in the early 1890s) when he said that "the impression of a wholly new and original poetic genius was as distinct on my mind at the first reading of these four poems as it is now, after half a century of further knowledge," for his enthusiasm had been slower to develop than he was willing to admit.[84] In 1871 he wrote, "The American poet of passion is yet to come. . . . There is no baptism of fire; no heat that breeds excess."[85] After her death, he said he thought her remarkable;

---

and, when you have got precisely what you asked for, do not complain because you have missed what you would not take. [P. 262]

81. Leyda, *Years and Hours*, 2:137, 138, 150, 151.
82. Ibid., 2:138, 151, 153, 212.
83. Wells, *Dear Preceptor*, pp. 326–37.
84. *Collected Letters*, p. 252.
85. *Atlantic Essays* (Boston, 1871), p. 57.

yet he reluctantly agreed to help edit her poems only "to provide a modest memorial" to her, having misgivings, right up to the last moment, about lending his reputation to her publication and confiding privately that he was mistrustful of her instant phenomenal popularity, that in fact the best minds could not value her highly![86]

Though he was to earn considerable fame from his modest interest in her, the most damning facts in the severe indictment of him are that he was initially too ashamed of her poems to take them to Roberts Brothers himself, that he took on the work of promoting her only very reluctantly, that he quit himself of her after the Second Series, that he gave only two pages to her in his final estimates of American poets, *A Reader's History of American Literature* (1903), and that he did not mention her at all, even in passing, in his long autobiography.

We now see that during their extensive epistolary relationship (I do not feel they could have faced off with each other very productively) she was playing the little girl to his patriarchal guide, though she was at the outset all of thirty-one and he was only thirty-eight, while he was playing the minister to a pale eccentric and neither was either thing. They therefore made each other out wrong initially— she him as "master" and he her as a woman of "unregenerate condition."[87] Her game was initially that of poor thing and his that of psychoanalyst. Her terms for him are, even for her, sheer hyperbole, even egregious: "Master," "Sir," "Preceptor," "Monarch," and his terms for her are patently condescending, even deprecatory: "naive," "enigmatic," "partially cracked," "tameless," "eccentric," far more extreme terms on both sides than they had used with anyone else of their acquaintance.[88]

What is remarkable to me about the relationship is how Emily Dickinson withstood Higginson—one of the best examples in her biography of her backbone amid disappointments. Richard Chase refers to "her witty and profound evasions, her interplay towards him of subservience and domination, and her final refusal to conform to any of his images of what she ought to become."[89]

He recommended severe surgery to her right from the outset,

86. Wells, *Dear Preceptor*, pp. 351–52. "He did not think a volume advisable," Mable Loomis Todd said he told her in 1890, "they were too crude in form . . . and the public would not accept even fine ideas in such rough and mystical dress—so hard to elucidate. But I read him nearly a dozen of my favorites, and he was greatly astonished— and he had no idea there were so many in passably conventional form" (Sewall, *Life*, p. 220).

87. Leyda, *Years and Hours*, 2:65.

88. Ibid., 2:213, 214, 263.

89. See Chase, *Emily Dickinson*, pp. 282–83.

and yet she persisted in her ways: "I bring you other [poems] – as you ask," she retorted in her reply to his second letter to her, "though they might not differ." She would not let him become a major event in her life, either: "Your letter gave no Drunkenness, because I tasted Rum before." She very soon became annoyed at his paternalistic tutelage: "Your second letter surprised me," she was unafraid to tell him, "and for a moment, [I] swung – I had not supposed it." "I thank you," she continued facetiously, critically, "for your justice – but could not drop the Bells whose jingling cooled my Tramp." And then she informed him, even at the risk of challenging his *right* to judge her, that she knew what was best for her herself: "My Barefoot – Rank is better." He could be her "friend" but without any attempt on his part to "control" her.[90] On his first visit to see her, Higginson sensed at last the impregnable fortress she had made of herself and thereafter, for the most part, gave up trying to shape her life or poetry. It was the beginning of her educating *him*.

Having asked him—ostensibly—for help ("I felt it shelter to speak to you"), she turned to assisting *him* at a good criticism of her. She berated him for not helping her any: "Will you tell me my fault, frankly as to yourself." Then she satirized his small interests: "Are these more orderly? . . . I think you called me 'Wayward.'" She was even annoyed, if I sense her tone right at this point in her reaction to him, with his stupidity: "You would not jest with me; . . . you cannot mean it." She parodied his weak critical criteria as well: "I send you a Gale, and an Epitaph – and a Word to a Friend, and a Blue Bird, for Mrs. Higginson. Excuse them if they are untrue – " and "I enclose those [poems] you allow, . . . lest one of them you might think profane – . . . . Reprove them as your own." She refused to compromise with his directions: "I hav'nt that confidence in fraud which many exercise."[91] She called his attention to the right places to look for what was significant to her in what she wrote: "fracture within is more critical" and "There's a noiseless noise in the Orchard – that I let persons hear." But then she reminded him that even though she had an interest in "growth," she was secure in her eccentricity, her naiveté, her excitements, her abilities, her (to him "unregenerate") self:

> Perhaps you smile at me. I could not stop for that – My Business is Circumference – An ignorance, not of Customs, but if caught with the Dawn – or the Sunset see me – [I am] Myself the only Kangaroo among the Beauty.

90. *Letters*, pp. 408–9.
91. *Letters*, p. 681.

And so though she knew that "it [meaning her kangaroo] afflicts me," she feared even more that his "instruction would take it away." More than anything else, she was confident of what she had written: "I do not let go [of] it, because it is mine." She stood firm against him.[92]

Emily Dickinson's problem with Higginson—it was never as much of an opportunity or opening for her as early biographers maintained—was almost entirely that of publication, despite her disclaimer: " 'to publish' . . . being [as] foreign to my thought, as Firmament to Fin." This cannot be taken seriously; it was the conventional pose somewhere between reserve and pushiness. Even as he left her the impression that he was "generous" with her, he led her on interminably, delaying decisions about her appearance in print and making her feel anxious and very much a failure. She knew she bothered him but could not find out why. When she spoke in her letters of learning and growing and improving and asked him to weigh her work, the assumption for the most part has to be that they were talking mainly about publication. She begged for it and he demurred:

> Will you be my Preceptor?   (1862)
>
> Would you instruct me now?   (early 1866)
>
> If I still entreat you to teach me, are you much displeased?   (late 1866)
>
> Would [you] teach me now?   (1867)
>
> Would you but guide. . . .   (1871)
>
> Could you teach me now? Will you instrument me then no more? (1873)
>
> Since you cease to teach me, how could I improve?   (1877)
>
> You were once so kind as to say you would advise me – Could I ask it now –   (1880)

Over a long period of time she wanted the truth from him about publishing and repeatedly tried to assure him that she would not embarrass him. On one occasion she even sent him a clipping of one of her poems in print to prove her acceptability. And on another occasion she reminded him of all the poems of hers in his possession that could be published. But for twenty-four years he succeeded in discouraging her about publishing her poems.[93] It is not that he was

92. This is in contrast to Helen Jackson's attitude toward Higginson as a guide: "I shall never write a sentence, so long as I live," she wrote to him, "without studying it over from the standpoint of whether you would think it could be bettered" (Sarah K. Bolton, *Lives of Girls Who Became Famous* [New York, 1886], p. 23).
93. *Letters*, pp. 431, 449, 450, 451, 457, 460, 511, 548, 571, 588.

the strongest representative of her few contacts with the literary world of the time, as many have claimed for him; he was the most formidable barrier to her emergence within her own literary circle.[94]

Though virtually innocent of the ugly editing of her poems in the first editions (he wished her accepted, but never at the cost of dishonesty and distortion), except as he acquiesced indifferently,[95] Higginson, more than anyone else in her literary circle, is the villain/ daemon of the self-conscious security of Emily Dickinson's poetic privacy. The most eminent and knowledgeable of her circle, and a friend of Emerson, Thoreau, Alcott, and Hawthorne, he inadvertently kept her within that life that made her writing possible. His service is forgivable only because it reveals her strength to survive uncorrected.

She sent Higginson poems she thought he could appreciate, as she had done with Sue, Bowles, the Hollands, and Helen Jackson— 101 in all, representing the full range of her thinking and writing— and wrote some to fit his expectations of her: softer, more conventionally moralistic poems, poems more self-conscious of regularities and often a little cowering. The most significant factor about the poetry they shared is that much of it was sent or written as comments/retorts to him in response to his criticisms of her esthetics and practice. Perhaps she had what Richard Sewall calls a "strategy"— to test, tease, and satirize him—and these were her wiles against his power over her.

> I cannot dance upon my Toes –
> No Man instructed me –
>
> [#326]

> The Soul into itself
> Is an imperial friend –
>
> [#683]

> To undertake is to achieve
> Be Undertaking blent
> With fortitude of obstacle
> And toward encouragement
>
> [#1070]

94. By 1876 she knew that he was unalterably opposed to her publishing. She could rely on him to prevent Helen Jackson, for example, from publishing her: "give me a note saying you . . . thought me unfit" (*Letters*, pp. 562–63).

95. In fact, it is difficult to prove that he had much at all to do with her publication besides promotion, even at that point; the first edition included only five of the poems Emily Dickinson had sent him.

The Sea said "Come" to the Brook –
The Brook said "Let me grow" –
The Sea said "Then you will be a Sea –
I want a Brook – Come now"!

[#1210]

How happy is the little Stone
That rambles in the Road alone,
And does'nt care about Careers
And Exigencies never fears –

[#1510]

What is surprising about the case of Emily Dickinson versus Higginson—and this is true of the rest of her literary circle—is that though they influenced her, or tried to, she had no influence whatsoever on *their* writings. Her spirit is to be found nowhere in what or how any one of them wrote. Though they were important to *her* in a variety of ways—as friends—she was largely irrelevant to *their* literary interests. We could not have known from their writings during her lifetime that she was a presence. Perhaps she was correct: the time was not right for her.

When we compare Emily Dickinson with her literary friends— evidently more of a contrast than a likeness, in view of their being offended by her in a variety of ways and so mounting small offensives against her—we see in her the beginning, for our literary history, of the literature of the minority. No one before her (with the possible exception of Edward Taylor, who could not publish) is the example. Her successful resistance of the dominant American so early in her life—whether Bowles and Holland or Helen Jackson and Higginson—suggests a separate tradition. For all her compromised association with them, she was *not* in the mainstream, though she sometimes led them to believe she cared to be. They had access to power; she did not. They left the impression of the chosen; she became increasingly sure she was an anomaly. They gave voice to a nation; she wrote poems with the strength, surprise, emotional range, and arbitrariness of a temperament. God was with the clown.

In Emily Dickinson, in opposition to her literary circle's esthetic of ease, we have, as I have tried to stress at all points, the assertion of the self—the anomalous, the indecorous, the ugly. In her relationship with each in the circle, she violated a norm, and so she made room for herself, forced by them, inadvertently, to take *herself* as her norm.

She complicated her world more than her literary friends did; in fact, she seems to have understood by complicating. And she is therefore perplexed about the quality of things. Writing amid a fixed good meant that being one's authentic self in one's writing would always result (to them) in bad writing; so why not make a virtue of "the bad"! Her negation of the pleasant, and what appears to be her deliberate irregularity, is a reaction. The disfigurement, whether natural or contrived, is an invention, not an accident, not a foil or a countertruth, nor a form of esthetic blasphemy. The Fall is also beautiful: *only* the Fall is fascinating. The deliberate (or even organic) unpleasantness—a kangaroo that she hoped would be taken for real but that was constantly unacceptable and so under attack—was her way of showing she was above the genteel conventions: not for shock, but for violation of the weak and thin, to assert her superiority. She got stuck in her opposition of the genteel and found her stakeout more exciting, more natural. The fixed character of her canon is a metaphor.

But, curiously, her anomalous esthetic was not heretical, though her literary friends seem mostly to have thought, in little ways (Sue's) and large (Higginson's), that it was. She no doubt knew that in the ethics-dominated culture they represented and sustained there could be no novelty without risk. Her esthetic heresies could not be confused, as theirs *could,* with orthodox poetic practice. She was therefore in the position of hoping that her poems (not the fragments, not the stanzas in her letters, but her personally satisfying poems) might be seen as being too different, too astounding, for the risk to be serious. Her playing the clown would then be seen as her playing the clown. But they did not know the rules of her game, and she was not very good at communicating them to the circle, though she tried. It was therefore perhaps too much for her to expect to achieve both her own voice *and* their audience.

That Emily Dickinson wrote on topics and in ways that her literary friends were attracted to, and took them to the extreme in order to achieve the opposite, should now be evident. They knew her for a trying writer of the good more than for a good writer willing to put herself on trial (confidently) before their court. Parody, camp, flamboyance, hyperbole were her ways of both getting friends and getting *at* them, going with them and going *beyond* them.

Writing from the boundaries of eccentricity, Emily Dickinson made poetry in revolt against the central culture's monopoly on universality. She represents the humanity of the eccentric, the marginal, the other. To the center she offered what she called her "sense that smote and stirred – [Her] Instincts for Dance – a caper – / An Aptitude for Bird – " (#1046).

Eight

THE HOPELESS DITCH

EMILY DICKINSON AND THE NEW ENGLAND BLUESTOCKINGS

The Snow is so white and sudden it seems almost like a Change of
Heart – though I don't mean a "Conversion" – I mean a Revolution.
[*Letters,* p. 683]

Of all the models for a liberated woman proposed by American
writers during Emily Dickinson's lifetime, none of them, not even
those by her circle of literary friends, was written as if the authors
knew anyone quite like *her.* Though Puritan, conservative, trapped,
and desperate, as I have tried to argue, she was beyond them all.

By instinct her motive was, as she said of one of her birds, to
"Breathe in Ear more modern / God's old fashioned vows," and she
could convince herself of the need to play the role of old-fashionist:
"Since I am one of the Druid," she wrote in 1858, "I'll deck Tradition's buttonhole." "The Bees," she wrote in a poem in 1862, "will
not despise the tune / Their Forefathers – have hummed." "Could
Prospect taste of Retrospect," she said in 1872, "The Tyrannies of
Men / Were Tenderer." "It is the Past's supreme italic," she asserted in
1880, that "Makes the Present mean." She was attracted, she confessed in a poem of 1881, toward "industry and ethics / And every
founded thing." Therefore, because a poet of what she considered to
be the received, really a cracked conservative, she tended to be suspi-

222

cious of the Woman of the Nineteenth Century she might often have felt she was expected to be.[1]

> Perhaps the "Kingdom of Heaven's" changed –
> I hope the "Children" there
> Wont be "new fashioned" when I come –
> And laugh at me – and stare –
>
> I hope the Father in the skies
> Will lift his little girl –
> Old fashioned – naughty – everything –
> Over the stile of "Pearl".
>
> [#70]

Her juxtaposition here of "Old fashioned" and "naughty – everything" gives her away: while she would give new value to certain old values—such as, as I have suggested, the self-reliance of an Anne Bradstreet, the struggle for self-realization of an Edward Taylor, the productive stoicism of a Jonathan Edwards—she also would be herself, that is, magic, the clown, naughty, everything. Instead of a contemporary America, she had, she said, a "Republic of Delight . . . Where each is Citizen."

Though she herself was "changed" considerably from much that was "old fashioned," Emily Dickinson was not often able (at least not often willing) to deal with the new except perhaps by the acute rebelliousness of apathy. She became innovative, dynamic, perhaps even regenerate (at least in her own eyes) by bending old forms to meet her needs. But she had little interest in risking herself at social reforms and reformations of any sort. She was never a member of state, church, sex, or literary (activist or philosophical) movements. Though Emily Dickinson made an unusually effective contribution, I believe it

---

1. One will have to decide for oneself whether Emily Dickinson measures up (or down) to the description of "women of the New England type" that George S. Merriam makes in his biography of Samuel Bowles, perhaps having the women around Bowles in mind. "Women of the New England type," he writes, are women who

> inherit a fine intellect, an unsparing conscience, and a sensitive nervous organization; whose minds have a natural bent toward the problems of the soul and the universe; whose energies, lacking the outlet which business and public give to their brothers, are constantly turned back upon the interior life, and who are at once stimulated and limited by a social environment which is serious, virtuous, and deficient in gayety and amusement. There is naturally developed in them high mental power, and almost morbid conscientiousness, while, especially in the many cases where they remain unmarried, the fervor and charm of womanhood are refined and sublimated from personal objects and devoted to abstractions and ideals. They are platonic in their attachments, and speculative in their religion; intense rather than tender and not so much soothing as stimulating. [George S. Merriam, *The Life and Times of Samuel Bowles* (New York, 1885), 1:216–17]

is off the mark to hold with Richard Chase that "she shared with other intellectual women of her time an interest in 'the position of women.' "[2]

In fact, her suspicious attitude toward conventional involvement in liberal reform was assumed very early—long before she began writing her poetry—and never really changed any, even as she developed affinities with people in the public eye whom she needed and admired. As early as 1850, when she was only twenty, she laughed at local ladies who from their armchairs had designs on a wretched world. "The Sewing Society has commenced again – and held its first meeting last week," she wrote to her friend Jane Humphrey. "Now all the poor will be helped – the cold warmed – the warm cooled – the hungry fed – the thirsty attended to – the ragged clothed – and this suffering – tumbled down world will be helped to it's feet again – which will be quite pleasant to all. I dont attend – notwithstanding my high approbation – which must puzzle the public exceedingly. I am already set down as one of those brands most consumed – and my hardheartedness gets me many prayers."[3] She preferred, she said at the time, "turning my back to this very sinful and wicked world." As it turned out, her way of relating to "the public" did not fit the liberal expectations of the Sewing Society. She escaped them and made a way of her own.

Early and late, Emily Dickinson could be interested in reform only as a very general principle—never as one that might include activities that would involve her personally. Her liberalism is seldom libertarianism.

> Revolution is the Pod
> Systems rattle from
> When the Winds of Will are stirred[.]
> Excellent is Bloom
>
> But except it's Russet Base
> Every Summer be
> The Entomber of itself,
> So of Liberty –
>
> Left inactive on the Stalk
> All it's Purple fled
> Revolution shakes it for
> Test if it be dead.

[#1082]

2. Chase, *Emily Dickinson*, pp. 142–43.
3. *Letters*, pp. 82, 84.

Reform is valuable as stimulus, she is saying here, but otherwise it is, to her, not very productive. She lacked the temperament of the libertarian. "The Ditch," she wrote in a poem of 1885, "is dear to the Drunken man . . . Oblivion bending over him / And Honor leagues away" (#1645). "Floss," she wrote, "wont save you from an Abyss" (#1322).

In August 1973 Emily Dickinson was named, with nineteen others, to the first American Women's Hall of Fame by a convention of women's liberationists. I am not sure she could have accepted the criteria that elevated her to the honor. Closer to representing her stance vis-à-vis "the public" is Irving Molbach's poem from the *Chicago Review* in 1971, "Emily Dickinson's Nobel Prize Acceptance Speech"—showing her meeting a raging world not with outrage, but with her own kind of outrageousness:

> I would like to give at least half of this prize to John Keats. And the other half to Swinging Amherst.
>
> It's possible I am the first writer, at least female, to stand before you topless. It's said I am a recluse, a nun. Even assuming that to be true don't believe a word of it. I've spent the night on pirate-ships. The opinion that God, being so religious, couldn't have made us naked is not held by me or my sons.
>
> Yes. Thank you.[4]

As I would like to argue, the outrageousness was, for her, a response, an example, a solution. But this Liberated Emily is hardly a woman the nineteenth century could have accepted, awarded, applauded. And herein lies a story.

In 1872 Elizabeth Stuart Phelps, the popular young novelist, theosophist, and religiously motivated reformer of women's conditions, wrote Emily Dickinson asking her participation in the cause. Emily Dickinson knew some of her books—certainly the popular *The Gates Ajar* (1868) and possibly also her *Hedged In* (1870) and *Silent Partner* (1871)—and probably read notices and reviews of her books in local newspapers or knew her views as editor of *The Woman's Journal*. Higginson had recommended that she read Miss Phelps's "The Door Unlatched" and "The Gate Unlatched" in *The Woman's Journal* of 1870.
In 1872, coincidentally, her cousin Louise Norcross wrote asking Emily Dickinson what she knew about Miss Phelps and her work.[5] She

---

4. *Chicago Review* 22 (January–February 1971):153.
5. Leyda, *Years and Hours*, 2:173.

replied, giving us an important anecdote for judging her social attitudes. "Of Miss P[helps] I know but this, dear," she said in her letter. "She wrote me in October, requesting me to aid the world by my chirrup more. Perhaps she stated it as my duty, I don't distinctly remember, and always burn such letters, so I cannot obtain it now. I replied declining. She did not write to me again – she might have been offended, or perhaps is extricating humanity from some hopeless ditch."[6]

Miss Phelps knew T. W. Higginson well and probably heard about Emily Dickinson from him as someone who might "aid the world." It appears that Higginson gave an inaccurate impression of her. Miss Phelps's was but one of a number of "such letters" that she received requesting involvement in some social cause, however, and she says she declined them all equally and summarily.

In a poem of 1862 she had satirized a person of causes like Miss Phelps:

> She's happy, with a new Content –
> That feels to her – like Sacrament –
> She's busy – with an altered Care –
> As just apprenticed to the Air –
>
> She's tearful – if she weep at all –
> For blissful Causes – Most of all
> That Heaven permit so meek as her –
> To such a Fate – to Minister.

[#535]

But Emily Dickinson would not get down into the "hopeless ditch" with such a New England bluestocking. Her way was entirely different—for her, more honest and also, she had reason to hope, more shocking, more moving. In a poem of 1862 Emily Dickinson projects herself as another kind of reformer than Miss Phelps had hoped to find:

> I took my Power in my Hand –
> And went against the World –
> 'Twas not so much as David – had –
> But I – was twice as bold –

[#540]

The form taken by her boldness against the world deserves discussion.

There was a great deal in Elizabeth Stuart Phelps's thinking that Emily Dickinson should have seen as corresponding with her own

6. *Letters*, p. 500.

"old fashioned vows," especially the strong hope for a sweet, personal, New Englandized afterlife, for which Miss Phelps had mainly gained her popularity and which was satirized, in time, by Mark Twain and by Emily Dickinson herself. "I suppose," she wrote in *The Gates Ajar*, "most young women of my age have their dreams, and a future probable or possible, which makes the very incompleteness of life sweet, because of the symmetry which is waiting somewhere."[7] But Emily Dickinson perhaps felt that Miss Phelps knew more about the spiritual needs of society than she did about possible solutions to its moral and physical conditions. How could she have stomached the utopian analogues? She said she burned her letter.

Miss Phelps's main interests were heaven, homeopathy, and human rights—or, more specifically, spiritualism, temperance, suffrage, and antivivisection. In her autobiography she spoke of "the impulse of my heart to keep step with the onward movement of human life, and to perceive the battle far off, charging when and where I can."[8] "I am, as perhaps you may suppose, almost *invested* in the 'Woman Cause,'" she wrote to Whittier in 1871. "It grows upon my conscience, as well as my enthusiasm, every day. It seems to me to be the first work God has to be done just now."[9] To be sure, she idealized women in her writings, thought them far finer than men, and worked to use them as the agents of social reform by way of examples to men and children. And so the cause to her primarily meant the moral reform of women themselves, not of a chauvinist, repressive society as a whole. She had, she said, a plan for "immortalizing New England" by making a utopia through exemplary women. At various times Harriet Beecher Stowe had entertained a similar feminist-millennial program—the Protestant New England virgin as hyped-up conscience. "I believe in women; and in their right to their own best possibilities in every department of life," Miss Phelps wrote,[10] and by reform for women she was thinking of improvements in dress, jobs, vocational education, health, and voting—issues that perhaps had Emily Dickinson's "approbation," as she said, but about which she also said she was fairly "hardhearted." Into such an "ear more modern" she could only breathe an anachronistic/deviant methodology of her own. As Miss Phelps would have learned if she had ever talked with the undutiful Miss Dickinson (and there is no evidence that she ever came to Amherst or met her elsewhere), in-

7. *The Gates Ajar* (Boston, 1868), p. 9.
8. *Chapters from a Life* (Boston, 1896), p. 252.
9. Quoted in Mary Angela Bennett, *Elizabeth Stuart Phelps* (Philadelphia, 1939), pp. 56–57.
10. *Chapters from a Life*, p. 250.

stead of merely writing to her as one of Higginson's many chirrupers, she would have recognized that these issues were too small for Emily Dickinson's cosmology ("Whether Diety's guiltless – / My business is, to find!") and at the same time too large for the scale of her personal anxieties and fantasies:

> An Unconcern so sovreign
> To Universe, or me –
> Infects my simple spirit
> With Taints of Majesty –

[#290]

Miss Phelps, the women's-liberationist-via-purification, could give Emily Dickinson easy assurances of life beyond "the gates," but she gave little help in the meantime.

Two other activist-feminists of the time with whom Emily Dickinson had some acquaintance and over against whom she could play off her "old fashioned vows" were Julia Ward Howe and Lydia Maria Child. Mrs. Howe personally knew the Bowleses; she often appeared in the *Springfield Republican* and the *Atlantic Monthly;*[11] and she associated closely with T. W. Higginson. But we do not know if she ever heard of Emily Dickinson the way Elizabeth Stuart Phelps had. We do know that on one occasion Higginson wrote to Emily Dickinson recommending that she read Mrs. Howe's poem "I Stake My Life upon the Red" for an example of good verse. Bowles, in the *Republican,* remarked that she had "an active intellect" as well as "perfect womanly graces and sweetness."[12] Emily Dickinson probably never met her personally, however, even after the fame of her "Battle Hymn," though we know she was in the area in the 1850s and the 1870s speaking for the suffrage movement.

Mrs. Howe's characterization of the ideal nineteenth-century woman did not differ much from Miss Phelps's and, because it did not allow for the anomalous and flamboyant, could not have excited Emily Dickinson very much. Women are the natural guardians of social morals, in Mrs. Howe's thinking; the moral initiative belongs to them. The ideal woman is simply the intelligent homemaker and housewife. "Revere the religion of home," Mrs. Howe advised in one of her suffrage lectures. "Keep its altar flame bright in your heart.

11. In November 1861, Emily Dickinson read (and quoted from) Mrs. Howe's *Atlantic* summary of George Sand's autobiography, *Histoire de ma vie.* Leyda, *Years and Hours,* 2:37.
12. Leyda, *Years and Hours,* 2:157, 214.

The college, the platform, the press, the pulpit are now open to you. Achieve in these directions what you may, but return from your furthest flight to the dear shelter of your home. Make the place beautiful with your affection. Treasure its legends and its memories. Hang your laurels, if you win any, upon its walls."[13] For Emily Dickinson the direction would have been all wrong: going out into the world to learn and strive and then returning home fit to be the perfect homebody forever. Emily Dickinson's bent went otherwise: using the perfect home to work out of, for productive imaginings, for petty violence, for poetry. In a speech "How to Extend the Sympathies of Women," Mrs. Howe's solution was to make war "against vice and frivolity in every shape" in the life of each woman.[14] But Emily Dickinson's way would no doubt have appeared frivolous and even vice-ridden to Mrs. Howe as she attempted to stretch her life as a woman, through language, until she could be noticed, enjoyed, overwhelming, powerful. She wanted to let loose "This little Hound within the Heart." Her "Tramp," as she called it in a letter to Higginson, and her "little Gipsey being," as she called it in a poem of 1860, probably would have shocked and annoyed Mrs. Howe.

As it would have, I am sure, shocked and annoyed Lydia Maria Child, who was perhaps one of the most versatile of the writing feminists of the period. She lived in Northampton, just eight miles away, for a number of years when Emily Dickinson was young. Emily Dickinson's father probably had the girls read his copy of her *Frugal Housewife* (1831), wherein Mrs. Child recommends for women "a thorough, religious, *useful* education [as] the best security against misfortune, disgrace and poverty."[15] Austin read her *Letters from New York* (1843). Charles Sumner sent Emily Dickinson's father Mrs. Child's novel *Isaac T. Hopper* (1855), and Emily Dickinson might have read these as well, though without the respect or awe others were giving. In 1870, after Emily Dickinson told Higginson about some of the books she had read and liked, Higginson commented on how suspect some of Mrs. Child's views were, along with those of others of liberal persuasion, in the Dickinson household: "A student of [Edward Dickinson's, probably Ben Newton] was amazed they [the Dickinson girls] had never heard of Mrs. Child & used to bring them books

13. Florence Howe Hall, ed., *Julia Ward Howe and the Woman Suffrage Movement* (Boston, 1913), p. 171.
14. Ibid., p. 240.
15. *The Frugal Housewife* (Boston, 1831), p. 111.

& hide [them] in a bush by the door [sometime between 1847 and 1849]. . . . After the first book [Emily Dickinson] thought it ecstasy. 'This then is a book! And there are more of them!'"[16]

Though Mrs. Child was a genuine liberal in her own activities as in her writings ("Society makes the crime it punishes") and a sincerely religious feminist as well ("Every woman has the duty of doing whatever she can to lead her country on the right path"),[17] Emily Dickinson would have found little that was either shocking or helpful in her views, even would have found herself largely excluded from womanhood by her definitions. For Mrs. Child the ideal American women, as she told it in her *Good Wives* (1883), were those who went on Christian missions, those who helped their husbands to fame, those who educated themselves within and to the benefit of their homes, and those who publicly championed moral causes. Playful boldness, therapeutic excess, and the polymorphous perverse have no place in the good woman as they had for Emily Dickinson. "American ladies are accused of being more prudish than foreigners," Mrs. Child wrote in her *Letters from New York*. "I hope the charge will always remain a true one. . . . Whatsoever can be named as loveliest, best, and most graceful in woman, would likewise be good and graceful in man. . . . The feminine ideal approaches much nearer to the gospel standard, than the prevalent idea of manhood."[18] The objective was to fit the American woman not for American living but for heaven.[19] Emily Dickinson would go this route as little tippler leaning against the sun. She tried to cope in a very different way.

There is much in these social activists' writings to interest Emily Dickinson, but it is never the social activism. For example, there is Miss Phelps's hope-inspiring otherworldliness, Mrs. Howe's emphasis on home, and Mrs. Child's respect for introspection. "No forms can reappear in another world, which are not *within* the soul," Mrs. Child wrote. "The sublime landscape *there* belongs to him who has spiritually retired apart into high places to pray."[20] But Emily Dickinson

16. *Letters*, p. 475.
17. Quoted in Milton Meltzer, *Tongue of Flame: The Life of Lydia Maria Child* (New York, 1965), pp. 68, 200.
18. *Letters from New York* (New York, 1843), pp. 234, 267.
19. All the feminists mentioned in this discussion, along with some of the women from Emily Dickinson's circle of literary friends, are represented as poets in a collection of verse published in Boston in 1885 by Eva Munson Smith, *Women in Sacred Song*. The collection shows them all to have been, to varying degrees, champions of women as bearers of Christianity into a liberalized world. Emily Dickinson is not included among them.
20. *Letters from New York*, p. 77.

apparently could not make the leap of faith her sister reformers made—from reneging to renegading.

In addition, in her poetry Emily Dickinson appears to take sport in mocking their reform language and inverting and enlarging their concepts. She uses suffrage terms, for instance, to talk about God's determinations, undercutting their applicability to temporal reform:

Dominions dowerless - beside this Grace -
Election - Vote -
The Ballots of Eternity, will show just that.

[#343]

In another poem, "This Mortal Abolition" is her metaphor for death, exploiting the contemporary radicalism of the term. Terms of rescue from the human condition simply stir her to irony: "I should have been too saved - I see -/ Too rescued - Fear too dim to me" (#313). She speaks of "My right to walk upon the Earth" to say she feels lucky to be alive, and of "Death [as] the Common Right / Of Toads and Men" to say she feels it lucky to be dead. She speaks disparagingly of "that easy thing - An independent Man." She is at times even suspicious of the democratic masses:

The Popular Heart is a Cannon first -
Subsequent a Drum -
Bells for an Auxiliary
And an Afterward of Rum -

Not a Tomorrow to know it's name
Nor a Past to share -
Ditches from Realms and a Trip to Jail
For a Souvenir

[#1226]

Human/civil/women's rights to her mind have more to do with the natural-determined than the natural-democratic:

Mine - by the Right of White Election!
. . . .
Mine - here - in Vision - and in Veto?

[#528]

This all shows that there is far more Edwards than Jefferson in her thinking. Blue stockings were to her neither fundamental nor flashy wear.

"Females, also, have a sphere of action," Emily Dickinson's father said on one occasion, "which tho' different entirely in its kind

from that of the other sex, is no less important."[21] His thinking—
which would not have corresponded very well with his daughter's
view, even though both of them could speak (equivocating, of course)
of the importance of homeboundness, intelligence, and spirituality—
corresponded roughly with the Right side of the women's movement
of the time, which Elsa Green summarizes in terms of "the duty of
cheerfulness, the practice of purity, the instinct for a domestic life
elevated to an unearthly perfection.... An American woman was
pure, fertile, peace-loving, orderly, endowed with an intuitive sense
of the Divine and charged with a selfless mission to regenerate the
fallen."[22]

Representing this reactionary view is Maria J. McIntosh's *Woman
in America: Her Work and Her Reward* (1850), a book Lavinia borrowed
from Austin and read in 1851. Perhaps Emily Dickinson read it too,
though no doubt not without asking if this was all there was to being a
woman. "The soul of woman is as precious to the Father of Spirit as
that of man," wrote Mrs. McIntosh, who, along with Catherine
Beecher and Mrs. Stowe, considered herself one of the leading activists on this side of the issue,

> and yet the unqualified assertion of equality between the sexes, would
> be contradicted alike by sacred and profane history. There is a political
> inequality, ordained in Paradise.... Let those who would destroy this
> inequality, pause ere they attempt to abrogate a law which emanated
> from the all-perfect Mind. And let not a woman murmur at the seeming
> lowliness of her lot. There is a dignity which wears no outward badge,
> an elevation recognized by no earthly homage.... All the influences of
> that lot to which God assigned her, are calculated to nurture in her that
> meek and lowly spirit with which He delights to dwell.[23]

21. Sewall, *Life*, p. 48.

22. Elsa Green, "The Splintered Crown: A Study of Eve and Emily Dickinson"
(Ph.D. diss., University of Minnesota, 1959), pp. 21, 32. Green's conclusions about the
literature on women in the 1840s and 1850s show that Emily Dickinson was most
certainly outside the conventional definitions:

> Pre-Fuller writers about women believed that God determined woman's inherent
> nature and also prescribed for all time the role she should play in society. Within
> the general theory, though, there were varied opinions about just what sort of
> characteristics God gave Eve. A number of authors sketched woman as the unfallen
> mother of mankind, spontaneously pure, cheerful, selfless and loving. Others as-
> sumed that woman must be the eternally unpardoned weakling. But despite the
> range of opinions about female nature, all the authors agreed about the ultimate
> roles God commanded women to play. The curious consequence was that while a
> woman learned to take up one role in obedience to God's will, she might not be
> certain whether the Almighty decreed her place in the social order to punish her,
> to honor her, or to allow her free expression of her nature. [P. 2]

23. Maria J. McIntosh, *Woman in America: Her Work and Her Reward* (New York,
1850), pp. 22–23.

Like Mrs. McIntosh and the Beechers, Emily Dickinson's redress of the oppression of woman was also based on theological argument rather than psychological remedy or social reform. Her consciousness of her sex is a Puritan consciousness. Stiff Puritan hope is her answer to sexual dullness, provincial smallness and triviality, and spoiled romantic dreams. She goes well beyond the Right by not pretending to understand her frustrations, only dramatizing them as given. Her Puritanism saved her from the ache and void of boredom; she did not need to struggle to escape. Like the women on the Right, she is confined but not unsatisfied. She is, like them, on the margin of the world, locked in at home, irrelevant except in her own imagination. Her deprivation is an aspect of the helplessness of nineteenth-century dependent women, and while she aches to connect, she is not so banal as to need constant happiness. Fortunately, she is not the product of a man's imagining of the feminine, and so she is quite unlike the archetypal woman of the nineteenth-century reactionaries.[24]

At the opposite extreme, on the period's Left, was the position on women taken by the Transcendentalists. This was an equally uncomfortable fit for Emily Dickinson, for it lacked the grace of the perverse, the stimulus of anxiety, and even the spaciousness of the indecisive. Emerson, Thoreau, Alcott, Very, Channing, Brownson, and almost all the others circling Concord, except Margaret Fuller, have, curiously, no women to speak of in their writings. The Over-Soul is unisexual. And Whitman's great-breasted mothers are on an entirely different earth, "disgraceful" to Emily Dickinson, as she put it herself. For the most part Emerson's liberal gentility predominated: "For me, today, Woman is not a degraded person ... but a docile daughter of God with her face heavenward, endeavouring to hear the divine word and convey it to me."[25]

The best portrait of a thoroughly transcendentalized woman of the period is Sylvester Judd's *Margaret* (1845). Margaret is a vaporous but not a vapid girl, and Emily Dickinson could easily imagine herself in some of her own poems in the role of such a God's-nature-child-with-brain, just as she could play most of the nineteenth-century stereotypes of women, though she herself, the player, is always something stronger. In the novel Margaret is, à la Emerson, fascinated with the infinite but cannot make her way out of the finite. "I had rather go into the woods" is her byword. She is an example of Transcendentalist "variety in unity," and as she grows up she remains a child: "A world

24. Daniel Smith, "Family Limitation, Sexual Control, and Domestic Feminism in Victorian America," *Feminist Studies* 5 (1973–74): 200.
25. *The Journals of Ralph Waldo Emerson* (Boston, 1908–14), 6:369.

has been created in her eyes." Judd's woman is a personality that is in perfect harmony with the universe, the transparent eyeball with gender:

> That law by which all facts in the physical, moral and religious world gravitate toward a common centre, and coalesce in one, she has an intuitive perception of. Or rather the soul of all things, the Truth and Love, of which facts are but signs, she understands by the correspondence of her own soul therewith. . . . She is more purely in a state of nature, than any civilized person I ever encountered.[26]

Emily Dickinson could never have dissolved herself like this into utility and light. Shape and time and mind and all the other human limitations she troubled herself over and got her poetry rendered out of are missing in the free-spiritedness of the Transcendental woman—though the picture of the Transcendentalist woman, like Emily Dickinson's perplexities about her sex role, at least lacked the conventional insult of rigid definition. Transcendentalized, Emily Dickinson would not have had herself, a woman, to talk about.

Somewhere between Right and Left, T. W. Higginson's view of the new woman—one of the most influential of the period and one Emily Dickinson must have sensed from her correspondence and conversations with him and especially from reading his piece "Ought Women to Learn the Alphabet?"—has about it something of both the domestic and the prelapsarian. Higginson's contributions to the movement, especially his *Common Sense about Women* (1882), show—like Miss Phelp's, Mrs. Howe's, and Mrs. Child's, all of whose he admired and promoted—a dishonest compromise between the advocacy of servitude and the encouragement of mobility. Though he wrote his book after coming to know Emily Dickinson as fully as he would ever know her, Higginson fails to recognize the kind of woman she made possible by her example, and so it is largely irrelevant to an understanding of her, except as contrast. As a male bluestocking, Higginson held out for "intellectual Cinderellas" as an ideal, meaning the socially aware paradigm of Christian virtue, someone with a few ideas and some backbone; Margaret Fuller and Elizabeth Barrett were his examples. Though he did not believe a woman was likely to develop very far in "sacred obscurity" (perhaps he had the recluse Emily Dickinson in mind), he could not see why a woman could not "form political opinions by her baby's cradle." The headlines-reading wife/mother is a freed person. He believed in what he called "the natural

26. Sylvester Judd, *Margaret* (Boston, 1845), pp. 138, 185, 223, 434.

limitations" of women and was sure that the exclusiveness of gender strengthens the conventional roles: "Men still men, women still women," developed fully in appropriate, distinct directions.[27] To this kind of view Emily Dickinson responded in her letters to him at various times, mocking him: "I think you called me 'Wayward' . . . but [I] could not drop the Bells whose jingling cooled my Tramp. . . . My Barefoot-Rank is better, . . . Myself the only Kangaroo among the Beauty."[28] The way of Higginson's intellectual Cinderella did not allow for either hell or hell-raising. He made being a woman respectable.

Margaret Fuller's term for the same kind of compromised woman was "transfigured Cinderella." Higginson wrote appreciatively about her shortly after her shipwreck and awful death because he appears to have thought of her (except for the issue of a happy homelife) as the exemplary liberated woman. "Margaret Fuller had upon me, through her writings, a more immediate intellectual influence," he wrote in 1884, "than anyone else except Emerson, and possibly [Theodore] Parker."[29] But he made the same criticism of her that he did of Emily Dickinson: "She suffered from an exuberance of mental activity, which she had not yet learned to control." Lack of control in a woman he could not tolerate. And yet Higginson felt that "no one exceeded [Margaret Fuller in her writing] at the time and place in which she lived," including, presumably, his friend Emily Dickinson. Higginson applied a quotation to her and meant it: "She is the only woman . . . who seems to associate with intellectual men on terms of equality." Yet she lacked, for him, the Cinderella trait he found in his own wife and a number of other women he admired— that is, the ability to wait in the kitchen for one's destiny.[30] For all the respect Emily Dickinson tried to show the women writers Higginson canonized, however, she would probably have responded to his Margaret much as Charles Kingsley did, writing about her in a letter to Harriet Beecher Stowe: "Better to have written *Uncle Tom's Cabin* than to have been all seven Margaret Fuller [O]ssolis—beautiful, unguided souls, wearing themselves out with vain questionings."[31]

Had she known all of her views and activities, Emily Dickinson's

27. T. W. Higginson, *Common Sense about Women* (Boston, 1882), pp. 42, 49, 123, 203.
28. *Letters*, pp. 404, 408, 412.
29. T. W. Higginson, *Margaret Fuller Ossoli* (Boston, 1887), p. 2.
30. Ibid., pp. 281, 286, 288.
31. Letter from Charles Kingsley to Harriet Beecher Stowe, 16 August 1852 (Beecher-Stowe Collection, Schlesinger Library, Radcliffe College).

reaction to Margaret Fuller might have been close to Hawthorne's when he did her up as Zenobia in *The Blithedale Romance*: "She was made ... for a stumporatress. .... Her mind was full of weeds. ... She made no scruple of oversetting all human institutions, and scattering them as with a breeze from her fan. A female reformer, in her attacks upon society, has an instinctive sense of where the life lies, and is inclined to aim directly at that spot. Especially, the relation between the sexes is naturally among the earliest to attract her notice."[32] With reference to Zenobia/Margaret, Hawthorne gives Coverdale a fairly negative view of the feminists of the time: "[Women] are not natural reformers, but become such by the pressure of exceptional misfortune."[33] Hawthorne, furthermore, could allow equality with men for his Hester Prynne only in a millennial future: "In Heaven's own time, a new truth would be revealed, in order to establish the whole relation between man and woman on a surer ground of mutual happiness."[34]

Of Margaret Fuller's writings, Emily Dickinson appears to have known only her translation of the works of Karoline von Günderode and not any of her writings for the cause. Perhaps her reputation as gadfly and Transcendentalist kept Emily Dickinson from reading her. Perhaps she heard that she was vaguely philosophical, or irrelevant, or both. Margaret Fuller was extremely interested in the spinster-artist, however, and one comment in her essay on contemporary American writers shows her to have been capable of understanding fairly fully someone like Emily Dickinson: "No man can be absolutely true to himself, eschewing cant, compromise, servile, imitation, and compliance, without becoming original, for there is in every creature a fountain of life which, if not choked back by stones and other dead rubbish, will create a fresh atmosphere and bring to life fresh beauty."[35]

32. Nathaniel Hawthorne, *The Blithedale Romance*, Centenary edition (Columbus, Ohio, 1968), p. 44. It cannot be said, however, that Emily Dickinson's view of women's reform was ever as dim as that of Hawthorne's Sybil in *The Marble Faun*: "Woman is not capable of being helped."
33. Ibid., p. 200.
34. Nathaniel Hawthorne, *The Scarlet Letter*, Centenary edition (Columbus, Ohio, 1962), p. 200. For further attitudes of Hawthorne toward the feminists contemporary with him and Emily Dickinson, see Neal F. Doubleday, "Hawthorne's Hester and Feminism," *PMLA* 54 (1939): 825-28, and Morton Cronin, "Hawthorne and Romantic Love and the Status of Women," *PMLA* 69 (1954): 89-98.
35. Margaret Fuller, "American Literature: Its Position in the Present Time and Prospects for the Future," in *Papers on Literature and Art* (New York, 1846), p. 301. Margaret Fuller's criticisms on the poetry of Elizabeth Barrett Browning, vague as they are, suggest further, by contrast, what she could have found of interest in Emily Dickinson's writing. "She is singularly deficient in the power of compression" yet has "great originality in the thought and motive powers. ... As a poet, Miss Barrett is deficient in plastic energy, and ... she is diffuse. There is often a want of pliant and glowing life; ...

Margaret Fuller has a sentimental story called "Aglauron and Laurie" in which there is an artistic Emily who, "debarred of happiness in her affections" with men, "had turned for solace to the intellectual life" and, because "too delicate," ends up very unhappy. She blames society for fettering her "individual will" and men "who made the laws that bound [her]." Margaret Fuller condemns this as "a certain savage force in the character of this beautiful woman, quite independent of the reasoning power." She cannot allow her reclusive Emily any happiness either, for she violated a marriage vow, could not understand the workings of society, and became heretical in religious matters. Her greatest fault was, as it would have been to any of the other Transcendentalists, that she lacked harmony in her life.[36]

Margaret Fuller is important to any account of Emily Dickinson because her *Woman in the Nineteenth Century* of 1845 was considered rather strong fare for the time ("damned battlewords," Gamaliel Bradford called it; "innate grossness," exclaimed an anonymous reviewer; "one of the earliest as well as ablest among American women to demand for her sex equality," wrote Horace Greeley of her); and the book is today considered one of the most progressive statements of the nineteenth century leading women to their twentieth-century successes—and Emily Dickinson goes far beyond it in a number of ways. "Let them be sea-captains, if you will" was Margaret Fuller's ostensible point in the book, for she saw a woman's liberation in terms of the individual contesting the institutions that enslaved her, including marriage. "I solicit of women that they will lay it to heart to ascertain what is for them the liberty of law." Elizabeth Stuart Phelps, Julia Ward Howe, and Lydia Maria Child all knew Margaret Fuller well and wrote about her; for them she was a bold humanitarian, an articulate, realistic rights leader, a revolutionary. "We would have every arbitrary barrier thrown down," she wrote. "We would have every path laid open to Woman as freely as to Man. . . . What Woman needs is not as a woman to act or rule, but as a nature to grow, as an intellect to discern, as a soul to live freely and unimpeded, to unfold such powers as were given her when we left our common home." "Let us be wise and not impede the soul," she commented further. "Let her work as she will. Let us have one creative energy, one incessant revelation." All of which might have been bracing to Emily Dickinson had

and we are too much and too often reminded of other minds and other lives. Great variety of metres are used, and with force and facility. But they have not that deep music which belongs to metres which are the native growth of the poet's mind."

36. Margaret Fuller, *Woman in the Nineteenth Century and Kindred Papers* (New York, 1855), pp. 204, 210, 213.

the language of liberty been closer to that of using what one already has and is (Emily Dickinson's personal application of redemption) rather than to that of escaping what one already has and is (Margaret Fuller, like Emerson, seeing all things in process of transcendence of themselves).

Yet, though she wanted all arbitrary barriers removed, Margaret Fuller believed there are natural ones that limit a woman. "Woman is, and *shall remain,* inferior to Man and subject to his will." She did not really disagree with the conservative feminists of the time: put down your wash buckets where you are; do well what women can do. And as with the others, woman to her is still the paradigm of moral perfection. Male = energy, power, intellect; female = harmony, beauty, love. "The especial genius of Woman I believe to be electrical in movement, intuitive in function, spiritual in tendency.... I wish Woman to live, *first* for God's sake." She speaks rather of "this sublime priesthood of Nature,... a religious recognition of equality," sneaking woman into the universe through Emerson's back door by equivocating, like Emerson, on the idea that integrity makes one integral with all other integrities. This is her harmony principle: "Harmony exists in difference, no less than in likeness, if only the same key-note govern both parts. Woman the poem, Man the poet! Woman the heart, Man the head!"

> Express your views, men, of what you *seek* in women; thus best do you give them laws. Learn, women, what you should *demand* of men; thus only can they become themselves. Turn both from the contemplation of what is merely phenomenal in your existent, to your permanent life as souls.... Fellow-pilgrims and helpmeets are ye.... There is but one doctrine for ye both, and that is the doctrine of the soul.[37]

In actual practice, equality therefore meant to Margaret Fuller household partnership, intellectual companionship, friendship. All of which Emily Dickinson longed for and yet sensed would have taken off her edges, accommodated her frustrations, and assimilated her into delimiting forms.

Margaret Fuller's two main instructions to American women would probably have seemed to Emily Dickinson expansive yet cheerless: "Clear your souls from the taint of vanity" and "Do not rejoice in conquests... for the pleasure of rousing passionate feelings that gratify your love of excitement." She is opposed to what she calls "wild impulses" of any sort in a woman:

> O, women, see your danger. See how much you need a great object in all your little actions. You cannot be fair, nor can your homes be fair,

37. Ibid., pp. 37–38, 73, 79, 115, 158, 176, 336–37.

unless you are holy and noble. Will you sweep and garnish the house, only that it may be ready for a legion of evil spirits to enter in?[38]

In her liberation program (somewhat different from what we know about her private life), there is little sexual freedom, no liberation of the body, no play or passion, but discipline and control instead: "The passions, like fire, are a bad master; but confine them to the hearth and the altar, and they give life to the social economy."[39] "A harmony, an obvious order and self restraining decorum," she concludes, "is most expected from [a woman]."[40] Her best examples show that she has in mind something completely different from a Dickinsonian life for American women: Swedenborg's angel, Fourier's motherer, Goethe's redemptress, Maria Edgeworth's dignified domestic, and Mrs. Jameson's refined citizen.

Margaret Fuller prophesied that a woman poet will arrive on the scene to set the perfect example:

> And will not she soon appear? — the woman who shall vindicate their birthright for all women; who shall teach them what to claim and how to use what they obtain? Shall not her name be for her era Victoria, for her country and life Virginia? Yet predictions are rash; she herself must teach us to give her the fitting name.[41]

Whatever her name, this poetess-prophetess would be disciplined, hard-minded, and alone. "The earth wait[s] for her queen." As is the case with the other feminists of the time, however, there is hardly a place in Margaret Fuller's reformed world for a female kangaroo.

Besides these four, Emily Dickinson possibly knew something about a few of the other "beautiful, unguided souls" in the "hopeless ditches" of the reform movement. She told Higginson, for example, that she had read some of the works of Harriet Prescott Spofford. Annie T. Fields was in and out of Amherst often, probably staying at the Dickinson houses on several occasions. And the writings of others appeared in places Emily Dickinson was in the habit of reading—from such hands as Louisa May Alcott, Coline H. Dall, Edna D. Cheney, Lucy Larcom, and Catherine Maria Sedgwick.[42] But the list of literary feminists of the period with whom she was not at all acquainted and in whom it would have been difficult for her to be interested is much

38. Ibid., pp. 77, 140, 365.
39. Ibid., p. 185.
40. Ibid., p. 103.
41. Ibid., p. 177.
42. *Letters*, p. 404. Leyda, *Years and Hours*, 1:6, 9–10, 60, 118, 122, 159, 195, 213, 301, 483–84.

longer.[43] Almost to a woman, they worked with their pens to make women alert, responsible, and respectable, and thereby to bring them to the greatest social visibility and action. For that reason, Emily Dickinson, who conceived of selfhood/womanhood in far more cosmic terms (and therefore more private terms) because she retained so much of her Puritan background in her view of humanity, could not see them very well. She was neither "the perfect woman" nor "the new woman" they looked for, for both were defined too narrowly, too sociologically. She nonetheless is continually underestimated as one of the most advanced examples of a radical movement going on for women at the time, though exemplary entirely on her own terms.

While she would not add her voice to it and did little reacting to it, there are some ways Emily Dickinson participated in the movement, even benefited from it, though perhaps inadvertently. For one instance we have the fact of her term at Mount Holyoke, the oldest woman's college in America and the place where a significant step was being taken during Emily Dickinson's early years with the concept that women needed an education beyond that required to carry out the duties of housewife or teacher. For that reason it was progressive of Edward Dickinson to have sent his daughter there, even though she was forbidden to read or write thoughts "which savored of rebellious or an unsubdued will." Mary Lyon's curriculum was the first attempt in the country to give women intellectual equality with men. Vassar, Wellesley, Smith, and Bryn Mawr followed the example later. Emily Dickinson was in on the early years of this bold move, even though she did not at all hold Miss Lyon's belief that education was a panacea for all evils and boldly resisted the Christian emphasis. She most certainly would not be limited by the *Mount Holyoke Female Seminary Bulletin*'s definition of a woman's role in life: "Skill and expedition in household duties. Let a young lady despise this branch of the duties of woman and she despises the appointments of the Author of her existence."[44]

Unawares, she participated in the movement, too, in quite a different way: in seeing the institutions of society and the language of identity as having gender. Several feminists of the period hinted at

---

43. For pertinent discussions of a movement that largely passed by without Emily Dickinson's notice, see the following: Harriet H. Robinson, *Massachusetts and the Woman Suffrage Movement* (Boston, 1881); Robert E. Riegel, *American Feminists* (Lawrence, Kans., 1963); Duncan Crow, *The Victorian Woman* (New York, 1972); Martha Vicinus, ed., *Suffer and Be Still: Women in the Victorian Age* (Bloomington, Ind., 1972); Eleanor Flexner, *Century of Struggle: The Woman's Rights Movement in the United States* (Cambridge, Mass., 1959).

44. *Female Education: Tenderness of the Principles Embraced and the System Adopted in the Mount Holyoke Female Seminary* (South Hadley, Mass., 1839), p. 13.

the reform of the language to reflect greater equality, but Emily Dickinson was much more thoroughgoing and inventive at doing so. Many of the things that meant the most to her have gender. Most of the time, for example, she is able to keep the soul feminine: "The Soul achieves [exhilaration] – Herself"; "The Soul selects her own Society"; "The soul her 'Not at Home' / Inscribes upon the flesh." Truth, too, she makes feminine:

> There's Triumph of the finer Mind
> When Truth – affronted long –
> Advance unmoved – to Her Supreme –
> Her God – Her only Throng –

> [#455]

Nevertheless, perhaps because of her indifference to the attempts to make a new world for women, Emily Dickinson was considerably more confused than most of the other writers of the time on the issue of being a woman—and therefore, for her purposes, considerably freer. I do not find it valuable to moan, in the tradition of much Dickinson criticism, that "she was the victim of an age that mutilated its gifted women"[45] or that she could not have been more of a man;[46] I would rather identify her routes of survival.

At one extreme of her confusion is the liberation she obtained in her privacy. She appears to have sensed the inseparability of privacy and culture. For one thing, she had no institution—such as holy orders or prison or academia—to provide her with the detachment

---

45. Rebecca Patterson, "Emily Dickinson's 'Double' Tim: Masculine Identification," *American Imago* 28 (1971): 330–62. See also Theodora Ward, *The Capsule of the Mind* (Cambridge, Mass., 1961). Both writers find Emily Dickinson forced to play masculine roles as a defense against the world around her. To my mind it is the playing of the roles that is important, not the fact that they are sometimes (and not very often) masculine.

46. Elsa Green is effective in developing a contrast between the opportunities open to Austin Dickinson and those open to Emily Dickinson:

> She was discouraged from developing qualities that could only have value for one destined to take on a vocation. The certainty that she had no prospect of public power meant that she had no valid cultural reasons for wishing to increase her intellectual force. Besides, no personal attributes could outweigh her social smallness. . . . Grown women were supposed to switch their attention entirely away from themselves as distinct, historical identities. In fact, they were supposed to break off connections with an ongoing, private self and let their behavior be directed according to the public, class image of patience, cheerfulness, submission and saintliness. . . . As a woman, . . . Emily was supposed to give over moral control of her life to the absolute authority of God, father, brother and husband. [Pp. 109–10]

What this argument overlooks, however, is Emily Dickinson's ability to assess such a situation and rise above it, work around it, tunnel under it. She did, after all—either in spite of this condition or because of it—succeed at doing what she did best, writing her poetry!

necessary for critical perspective, revaluation, or changes of course. She had to do it on her own. In that private space she had distance to see with and play in. This privacy was a natural advantage in a community that was culturally rich enough to be able to afford it. She was smart enough, too, to take advantage of it to build a world of her own. In it, in addition, there was reciprocity between herself and others in a community of values, a relationship that did not bind or dictate.

Although perhaps Amherst allowed Emily Dickinson so much privacy that it often became quirky, isolationist, and desolate, still her privacy was not narcissistic (as Thoreau's was). She seldom felt ennobled by the separation from society (as Thoreau did), and she did not assume (as Thoreau had) that society has value only as the loner serves it: they were not to her the enemy. Instead, private, she could play many roles and therefore be versatile, no doubt a defense against being overwhelmed by the present. Private, she had plenitude and the illusion of permanence, no doubt an opportunity to have tension within contemplation. Private, she could have joy of exceptional moments, no doubt the yield of disequilibrium and derangement in her imagined depths.

Her security in herself made it unnecessary to declare war on the world, though she was not so secure as to be able to avoid warring on the universe. In herself she apparently had a plenitude of freedom inaccessible to those who kept looking for it in the future. For her, revolt had nobility only in its uselessness. Revolt could not have meaning in a nonvalid—that is, a fallen—world. Because for her nothing was in its place, including the world itself, she was not very often surprised by the spectacle of human injustice. And because she found it futile to refuse or to accept the social order, she found it better to endure its changes for better or worse with conformity.

"I am glad it is a boy [born to my wife]," Samuel Bowles wrote in a letter to Henry Dawes in 1855. "Boys are institutions. They have a future, a positive future. Girls are swallowed up,—they are an appendage,—a necessary appendage, it may be—probably they are,—but still they are appendages."[47] Emily Dickinson escaped this dilemma by a privacy that would not allow dependency. Her ostensible withdrawals were a firm stand against the ostensibility of women in such a view as Bowles's: she reduced attachments and avoided situations that would swallow her up. In her liberated space, her privacy, she could go wild. In one poem she called this her desire to "populate with awe my solitude." But the privacy, the detachment, the seeking to

47. Merriam, *Life and Times of Samuel Bowles*, 1:168.

stand firm alone and sure had to come first. Loneliness was a necessary requisite to the play, was in fact a condition that served to change
the proportions of things, an extreme encouraging further extremes.
Her privacy (as long as we are speaking of a woman's rights) she
insisted on as her first right:

> The right to perish might be tho't
> An undisputed right
> Attempt it, and the Universe
> Upon the opposite
> Will concentrate it's officers –
> You cannot even die
> But nature and mankind must pause
> To pay you scrutiny –
>
> [#1692]

At the other extreme is the poetry Emily Dickinson wrote that
was meant not to communicate accommodation to the world but to
express what she insisted on as her second basic right as a woman: the
beauty of power-through-flamboyance. That too was a form of
liberation—one that has not been recognized as a reformer's method,
a means of change and challenge, an alternate model for feminists
that was not well appreciated and was usually condemned outright in
the liberationist literature of her time.

This direction in her temperament and style makes one aware of
what was to her the issue of options. Her poetry made the issue
possible, indeed forced the issue on her. The strong-willed, omnivor-
ous woman also became a clown, a gypsy, a sweetly perverse
polymorph.

> I, for glee,
> Took Rainbows, as the common way,
> And empty Skies
> The Eccentricity –
>
> [#257]

> Forbidden Fruit a flavor has
> That lawful Orchards mocks –
>
> [#1377]

She had more to offer than the New England bluestockings thought a
woman should offer: wildness.

Elizabeth Hardwick speaks of what were for a woman of the
nineteenth century "the openings, . . . the little alleys for self-display,
the routes found that are really a way of dominating the emotional

material of daily life."[48] Though she was not often a very good theoretician of her esthetics, Emily Dickinson enjoyed trying to name the routes she discovered for herself as a woman. "The Bliss," she wrote, must be "Attempt[ed] by Strategy." "The soul has moments of Escape," she wrote in a poem of 1862, "When bursting all the doors – / She dances like a Bomb, abroad." Bombed and bombing, she would call herself—seeking a reach—"A Myriad Daisy," a "Debauchee of Dews," a "Loaded Gun," someone who "Want[s] maddest Joy," someone who is possibly "dangerous" enough to need to be "handled with a Chain"—and scores of other understandable unbelievables, all such descriptions surely shockingly hyperbolic. But hyperbole was a language form representing her power within (or her yearning for power within) a controlled life:

> My Cocoon tightens – Colors teaze –
> I'm feeling for the Air –
> A dim capacity for Wings
> Demeans the Dress I wear –
>
> A power of Butterfly must be –
> The Aptitude to fly
> Meadows of Majesty concedes
> And easy Sweeps of Sky –
>
> [#1099]

She wanted to be someone who could exclaim, "Put from my simple speech all plain word... And perch my Tongue / On Twigs of singing – rather high." She wanted, she said rather epiphanally in two poems of 1862, to be someone who could "perish – of Delight," and so she cultivated:

> stimulants – in
> Cases of Despair –
> Or Stupor – The Reserve –
> These Heavenly Moments are –
>
> A Grant of the Divine –
> That Certain as it Comes –
> Withdraws – and leaves the dazzled Soul
> In her unfurnished Rooms –
>
> [#393]

Dazzle in a bare house is a perfect hyperbole for her poetic desires. She wanted, in addition, to be someone (as she put it in another poem

---

48. Elizabeth Hardwick, *Seduction and Betrayal: Women and Literature* (New York, 1974), p. 200.

of 1862) who had been "Called to my full" with "Existence's whole Arc, filled up:"

> But this time – Adequate – Erect,
> With Will to choose, or to reject. . . .

[#508]

She is by no means apologetic of such excesses ("Something's odd – within – . . . Could it be Madness – this?"), for they bring her fulfillment and power. The epiphanal pushes one.

With this, however, Emily Dickinson is doing more than playing ego-builder. Through fantastic extremity, she is making a "route" for herself, a transport through outrageous metaphor, an alternate king/queendom of heaven on earth. Her true self—in its spiritual state—she therefore refers to as "This limitless Hyperbole." Hyperbole is a signifier of her desire for capacity, for her, what she called "the Divine / Brief struggle for capacity" is all-important. "Power is," she wrote in one poem, "When Consciousness and clay / Lean forward." "Risk is," she continued, "Persuasive as Perdition." "Give a Giant room," she asserted, perhaps referring to her own elaborated/projected capacities, "And you will lodge a Giant."

Emily Dickinson as an ostensible assertive is, however, already a staple of our criticism:

> The Soul unto itself
> Is an imperial friend –
> Or the most agonizing Spy –
> An Enemy – could send –
>
> Secure against it's own
> No treason it can fear –
> Itself – it's Sovreign – of itself
> The Soul should stand in Awe –

[#683]

But Emily Dickinson the successful freak, like Whitman the obvious homosexual, has been an embarrassment and so gets covered up. As soon as she goes past Emerson and the wildest feminist fears of a woman's wildness, we may be forced to admit just how much power she feels she has in her hotly hyperbolized language. Witness one poem, for example, in which through flamboyance she pictures herself having the power to remake the universe into a circus *contra* God:

> A transport one cannot contain
> May yet, a transport be –
> Though God forbid it lift the lid –
> Unto it's Extasy!

A diagram – of Rapture!
A sixpence at a Show –
With Holy Ghosts in Cages!
The *Universe* would go!

[#184]

What she writes, while freak, is virtually unbelievable yet is to be appreciated as an almost-schizophrenic "route" because it is a joyful alternative invented by herself for play. This she calls, in one poem, "The Escapade from God" (#894). "To be alive – and Will!" she exclaimed in a poem of 1863, "'Tis able as a God" (#677). Her ability to overstate gains her a liberated space. She writes "I felt a Cleaving in my Mind" for a headache, "After great pain, a formal feeling comes" for something like flu, "The Cavalry of Wo" for some other sickness, "Imps in eager Caucus" for a pain, "I reviled Myself, / For entertaining Plated Wares" for a rebuff, and so on. How wild to be this woman!—though God forbid the convention of making a woman wild (like making a poet mad) before admitting her to the race.

Yet the wildness is most certainly there—or made up—or, still more likely, made possible by the poetry. She enjoys describing herself as explosive:

It's Hour with itself
The Spirit never shows.
What Terror would enthrall the Street
Could Countenance disclose

The Subterranean Freight
The Cellars of the Soul –
Thank God the loudest Place he made
Is licensed to be still.

[#1225]

And she will not let the wild in her be suppressed at all:

Civilization – spurns – the Leopard!
Was the Leopard – bold?
Deserts – never rebuked her Satin –
Ethiop – her Gold –
Tawny – her Customs –
She was Conscious –
Spotted – her Dun Gown –
This was the Leopard's nature – Signor –
Need – a keeper – frown?

Pity – the Pard – that left her Asia –
Memories – of Palm –

Cannot be stifled – with Narcotic –
Nor suppressed – with Balm –

[#492]

She exclaims that she has routes of escape that are violent and cannot be stopped. She will out:

The Brain, within it's Groove
Runs evenly – and true –
But let a Splinter swerve –
'Twere easier for You –

To put a Current back –
When Floods have slit the Hills –
And scooped a Turnpike for Themselves –
And trodden out the Mills –

[#556]

Her persona is a person with push. She is full of terror to others; her wild nature cannot be stifled; she is like a flood making its own route (#556), a hurricane that demolishes (#928), a volcano that can erupt at any time (#1677). She is alive, and wills, and feels "able as a God."

As soon as one probes Emily Dickinson's flamboyance, one recognizes her determination to violate the family's and the community's strict standards of simplicity and seriousness. For that reason her milieu is virtually negligible; scrutiny shows her to have been wonderfully anomalous. She would not let fatuous rules of deportment and occupation drain her energy. One cannot imagine her as responsible—as a governess or schoolteacher, for example, or a nurse or professional. Not hard to imagine her, though, as a performer of some sort, or as a hooker. Independence needed all her energy to maintain. She apparently saw the development of her abilities flamboyantly as an honorable way of life. They have a sustained brilliance and originality that we are hard pressed to account for apart from her sheer love of excess.

Her cardinal virtue, as I am suggesting, is the Temptation to Excess. And that is very Victorian of her. Her personal expansiveness, she appears to have believed, is already built into her nature and so is not something to be sought for, certainly not after the manner of the liberators of her time. The free spirit is intrinsic or not at all. Spontaneity puts her fate to a severe test, for play is radical. For that reason, Emily Dickinson did not see being a woman as a social problem. There is something about her view of women that, for her time, is peculiar and original because tentative. She did not seem to know what a woman's rights should be. She is liberated instead by the very hysteria that all the woman-programers of her time condemned as time- and life-wasting. Her freedom rests on her unredeemed and consequently unsuppressed human nature. The Fall, again, is her good fortune.

This is a Puritan response to the issue of getting attention in a drab world that was hardly willing to give a woman any world at all. Emily Dickinson's world in her poetry is one of abundance amid the sparseness, never any poverty or thinness, really God's plenty, rich words in a spare form. "My premium [for being]," she wrote, "[is] – My Bliss." It must have been difficult for her to have played the Emily Dickinson of her poems, to travel the distance from didacticism and sentimentality to absurdity and skepticism. There is, I feel, little or no connection, except that, as we know, the range is being played by one person, and in a tone that shocks, surprises, experiments, fumbles, and (quite often) fails—but almost always with flamboyance.

Emily Dickinson is not merely wild but reckless in much that she wrote. We do not like her "safe" verse much, and I am not convinced she did either. The abundance/ease of sensation appears to have made her intolerant and impatient with the banal and therefore desirous of the extreme. Her subjects shift between anxieties and fantasies, and at either extreme she is extreme. Her poetry, like Melville's virtually uncontrolled prose in several of his early novels and in *Moby-Dick,* is a trying out. Puritanism was perhaps both a spur to and a check on such recklessness in her, as is seen in the flamboyance within hymn meter in an overwhelming number of her poems. Her forms, she told Higginson, "cooled [her] Tramp." The natural (wo)man is an enemy of God, as Paul, Augustine, Calvin, and her New England forebears held, and yet she "leaned upon the Awe"; she wanted "Delight with a Cause"; she cultivated her "Tramp"; craziness was part of the normal; she tried to make sure she was "visible" in the "mighty Crack" of the Creation.

In one of her few contributions to the feminist movement at midcentury, Louisa May Alcott wrote of what was to her "a woman's power"—deviousness. In her novelette *Behind a Mask; or, A Woman's Power,* she argues for freedom for a woman achieved through artful pretense. A woman's power lies in the ability to play many seductive roles, all the while being essentially a very moral being. She has "wit and will" (and can stay moral in her strivings) mainly through wiliness. As in Hawthorne, a woman is the equal of man only in "evil."[49] Ralph

49. Louisa May Alcott, *Behind a Mask: The Unknown Thrillers of Louisa May Alcott* (New York, 1975).

Boas's survey of women in Romantic American fiction shows Alcott's heroine to be standard: dark, resolute, self-willed, and sexually aggressive. But again Emily Dickinson does not fit the stereotype very well.[50]

Deviousness did not interest Emily Dickinson, however, as much as deviance: one a matter of politics, the other of esthetics. She is really much closer to Joyce Carol Oates's "goddess" in this regard: a woman who is free and has power in a man's house/world not because she knows how to be politic (the domestic), not because she knows how to rearrange the house (the reformer), but because she knows how to play with fire (the poet). Left for her is excess, deviance, villainy, violence.[51] Oates quotes Donne for an epigraph to her *The Goddess and Other Women*: "Things naturall to the Species are not always so for the individuall." Individuality, for both Oates and Emily Dickinson, comes from energy (even if in the form of madness, hate, or crime), excitement (even to the point of violent epiphany), and power (even when arbitrary, experimental, exploratory). These qualities make a woman something more than a reacter or resister (which are still essentially passive and unfulfilled), really something like a creator-aggressor or, better still, a maker rather than made—having what Oates calls "a need for assertion, for staking the claims of a particularity of being in a gross universe."[52] The bizarre, the absurd, the distorted, the gross—here we have a new gothic: the trite situation/idea beefed up with the extravagant and gross. This is their definition of being a woman: the suppressed life is a life of deviance.

Oates teaches one to see, when turning back to the nineteenth century and Emily Dickinson, that it is the nature of a rich mind not to shrink from deviance, from foolishness, from madness—scarecrows of the feminism available to Emily Dickinson. It had little patience with the frivolous, the disconnected, the amateur—the features that now identify Emily Dickinson for us. We know her for her persistent energy, her willingness to set down the imperfect. The refinement it asked for in a woman of parts, when compared with the primitivism Emily Dickinson admitted to and was awfully self-conscious about, was a sign of deficient vitality. Distortion through awe gave her far more versions of life than they could approve of, and in reality a life *both* pitiable and fulfilled. The hell she worked at worked a miracle for her.

It is necessary to be this outrageous about Emily Dickinson, for

50. Ralph Boas, "The Romantic Lady," in *Romanticism in America* (Baltimore, 1940), pp. 66–67.
51. Joyce Carol Oates, *The Goddess and Other Women* (New York, 1974).
52. Ibid., pp. 188–89.

of all American poetry before 1900 her work, it seems to me, is the most outrageous. It is almost entirely unfinished, it is almost entirely *unfinishable*. It is almost entirely out of control. (Ellen Moers speaks, for example, of what she calls, with irritation, "the lack of her poems, hundreds upon hundreds of them, on the page: their visual bitsiness.")[53] Almost all efforts by appreciative and disinterested holizers to synthesize a poetics for her look like mere academic exercises. Hers is an esthetic of the cracked universe where fragments and pushed surprises and flash make up a life.

It is no surprise, therefore, that Emily Dickinson could not be a Woman of the Nineteenth Century in any definition used by even the most generous and helpful liberators of her time. What could they have done with a person who insisted that her eccentricities are beneficient?

53. Ellen Moers, *Literary Women* (New York, 1976), p. 244.

THE SWEET WOLF WITHIN

EMILY DICKINSON AND WALT WHITMAN

Creation seemed a mighty Crack –
To make me visible –

[#891]

When Harriet Monroe founded her magazine *Poetry* in 1912, she called for a revival of the great poetic modes of the mid-nineteenth century, especially those of Whitman and Emily Dickinson. One, to her, created a mass audience and "released the essential humanity of man," and the other wrote for a select, private audience and "*created* the essential humanity of man." A major division in American poetry—with both sides needed—was constructed. To Harriet Monroe, Whitman showed best (using Whitman's own words) that "To have great poets there must be great audiences," and Emily Dickinson, on the other hand, showed best that "To have great audiences there must be great poets." Thus, for purposes of adjusting literary history to modernist needs, the egocentric principle in art became juxtaposed over against the poetic self as once and for all apart from the world—and, as we will see later, the hope for a new American poetry took its strength, for the moment, from a belief in the old, even if divided into two different camps.[1]

1. See Harriet Monroe's editorials in the first ten numbers of *Poetry*, 1912–13.

That Emily Dickinson never met or read very much of Whitman, her ostensible antagonist in this literary-critical drama, becomes one of the supports for this dual mainstreaming of America's poetic pre-moderns. But the division may not have much basis *in theory*. "[I] was told that he was disgraceful," she said of him, and we have been smirking at the narrow-mindedness for a good century now.

To be sure, Emily Dickinson might have had a chance to see some of Whitman's lines in the *Atlantic Monthly* during those years when she followed it fairly faithfully. For example, Emerson (who also at one point thought *Leaves of Grass* a "mass of filth" even if it had "genius")[2] persuaded James Russell Lowell to print a Whitman poem, called at the time "Bardic Symbols," in the *Atlantic* for March 1860:

As I ebbed with an ebb of the ocean of life,
As I wended the shores I know,
As I walked where the sea-ripples wash you Paumanok,
Where they rustle up, hoarse and sibilant,
Where the fierce old mother endlessly cries for her castaways,
I, musing, late in the autumn day, gazing off southward,
Alone, held by the eternal self of me, that threatens to
  get the better of me, and stifle me
Was seized by the spirit that trails in the lines underfoot.

But other poetry by Whitman was not to appear in the *Atlantic* (or in any other journals that Emily Dickinson read) until 1869, 1871, and 1874, when she was no longer much of a responsive follower of trends. She most certainly knew people who had read Whitman with some interest over this period of nine years; yet she probably never did read anything else he wrote.

It was apparently Josiah Holland who was mainly responsible for her missing him. In April 1862, when T. W. Higginson, then the editor of the *Atlantic,* was attempting to direct Emily Dickinson's reading and style, he asked her if she had read this new, audacious poet. She replied to him in a letter of 25 April, "You speak of Mr. Whitman – I never read his Book – but was told that he was disgraceful."[3] She might have said this not necessarily because she believed it but because she sensed Higginson's own objections to Whitman, which he was to express the most vehemently in an article "Literature as an Art" in the *Atlantic* in 1867. "Eccentricity, though some-

2. H. H. Furness, *Records of a Lifelong Friendship* (Boston, 1910), p. 107, and Moncure Conway, *Emerson at Home and Abroad* (Boston, 1882), p. 360.
3. *Letters*, p. 404. Walter H. Eitner, "Emily Dickinson's Awareness of Whitman: A Reappraisal," *Walt Whitman Review* 22 (September 1976): 111-15, documents the basic facts of this relationship. I do not believe, however, that Emily Dickinson was as aware of Whitman as Eitner suggests.

times promising as a mere trait of youth," he wrote, perhaps having Emily Dickinson in mind as much as Whitman, "is only a disfigurement to maturer years. It is no discredit to Walt Whitman that he wrote 'Leaves of Grass,' only that he did not burn it afterwards." "A young writer," he continued in much the same tone he had used on Emily Dickinson, "must commonly plough in his first crop, as the farmer does, to enrich the soil."[4] In disclaiming any knowledge of Whitman, she was perhaps playing up to this attitude.

It would be valuable to know what Higginson had written Emily Dickinson about Whitman—perhaps something about his indecipherable formlessness (which was his objection later) or about his outrageous poses (something Emerson and Lowell might have prejudiced him about) or even about his subject matter (the usual complaint). As she told Higginson in her April 1862 letter, however, she had already been instructed by someone in her circle of literary friends on how to dislike him.

This guidance she had obtained from Josiah Holland's comments in the *Springfield Republican* for 24 March 1860, in a crudely conceived article titled "Literary Nonsense," and for 16 June 1860, in a heavy-handed editorial titled " 'Leaves of Grass'—Smut in Them." Her flip reaction, "[I] was *told* that [Whitman] was disgraceful," suggests, however, her usual skepticism of Holland's literary judgments. But as far as we know, she had no judgment of her own about him beyond this.

What Emily Dickinson read about Whitman in the *Republican,* as perhaps elsewhere in a press generally hostile to Whitman's first three editions of poems, was pitifully narrow. In the issue of 24 March, for example, Holland wrote condemnations of everyone connected with Whitman's emergence as a poet, and this statement might have formed Emily Dickinson's initial opinion of him: "It is a very sad indication of the age we live in, that a new edition of Walt Whitman's poems would be announced by a Boston publisher; we didn't suppose anybody admired them but Emerson, and that fact was the only really bad thing we ever knew of him."[5] Holland's mentioning a connection between Whitman and Emerson could have intrigued Emily Dickinson, but as usual her closer associates intervened in determining her taste.

"We had nearly forgotten [Emerson's] 'Brahma,' " Holland said in his indictment, "and were only reminded of it by the appearance in the last number of the *Atlantic* of a string of nonsense for which one

4. *Atlantic Monthly* 30 (December 1867): 753.
5. *Springfield Republican,* 24 March 1860.

Walt. Whitman is responsible before the fact of publication." Attempting to make fun of Whitman's "music, . . . the unsophisticated character of the writer, and his desires and intentions concerning the reader," Holland managed a great guffaw at the arrogant Transcendentalist poet: "What a tremendous fix [Whitman] must have been in at the fearful moment when, held by that eternal self of him, which threatened to be too much for him, and floor him utterly, he was seized by the spirit. . . . Poor fellow!" He therefore became irate at the respectability bestowed upon Whitman by the publication of his verse. "Reader, the Atlantic Monthly, the best of American magazines, publishes two pages and a half of this stuff, and for what? For its literary merit?—it is a chaos of unmeaning words and a wilderness of bad grammar. For its thought? There is not a well-defined thought in it. For any hint of 'bardic symbols?' There is not a new one in it."

Holland would have had Whitman banned in Boston right from the outset:

> The whole performance is execrable—a mass of half-crazy, half-idiotic nonsense, and, considered as a literary production, is a disgrace to the journal which gave it birth. If this production had appeared, word for word, in some modest country paper, it would have been seized upon at once by the press as a theme for immeasurable fun. . . . Yet, because some philosopher of the accepted stamp has indorsed the writer of this, and it has appeared in a magazine presided over by an excellent mind, it becomes respectable, and is blindly supposed to have excellencies, could they only be detected and measured.

Emily Dickinson's word "disgraceful" is here already in Holland's "disgrace." From him she learned to think the worst of Whitman.

"Some weeks or months ago, we remarked upon a poem published in the Atlantic Monthly," Holland wrote later that same year in an editorial in the 16 June issue, continuing his campaign against the Brooklyn poet, "from the pen of Walt. Whitman—a nonsensical, whimsical, scraggy performance, about as much like poetry as tearing off a rag, or paring one's corns." "Recently," he continued, "the writer appeared in a large volume, (published in the puritanical and transcendental city of Boston, by Thayer & Eldridge, who we hope are willing to stand the notoriety of it,) and a more scandalous volume we never saw. We had not intended to notice it, but certain of the soft heads, on the shoulders of men and women indiscriminately, have conceived that it is a pure book."[6] Holland's references are to Whit-

6. Holland, "'Leaves of Grass'—Smut in Them," *Springfield Republican,* 16 June 1860.

man's "As I Ebb'd with the Ocean of Life" and to the 1860 edition of *Leaves of Grass,* which included his heterosexual poems, "Children of Adam," as well as his homosexual ones, "Calamus." Holland's "soft heads" may have been, besides Thayer and Eldridge, also Emerson, Lowell, and Richard J. Hinton, an influential Boston friend of Whitman's. ("We read the book with profit and pleasure," the publishers had written Whitman. "It is a true poem and writ by a *true* man. . . . We want to be known as the publishers of Walt. Whitman's books. . . . We are young men. We 'celebrate' ourselves by acts. Try us.")[7] Such poetic "soft heads" should not be tolerated, Holland informed Emily Dickinson.

Emily Dickinson's impression of Whitman also probably came from the reaction of a transcendentalizing Christian woman, Mary A. Chilton, who published her outrage at the poet in the *New York Saturday Press* in an article that Holland admired because it exposed "how far into degradation certain new lights are ready to be led." He therefore reprinted it in the *Republican*:

> In childhood there is no blush of shame at sight of a nude form, and the serene wisdom of maturity covers this innocence with a halo of glory, by recognizing the divinity of humanity, and perceiving the unity of all the functions of the human body, and the inevitable tendency to harmonic adjustments and adaptation. As all of nature's forms are evolved from the same God-origin or substance, though there may be difference of rank, there can be no difference in essence, and those functions which have been deemed the most brutal and degrading, will be found the first in rank when nature's hierarchy shall be established and observed. A true delicacy will neither emblazon the individual act of communion abroad (as, sanctioned by custom, those who lay claim to the highest refinement do daily,) nor blush to a crimson when the poet of sexual purity vindicates manhood and womanhood from the charge of infamy, degradation and vice, on account of growth and development after the order of nature. Of course those who assert the doctrine of total depravity must find some part of the person too vile to think of, and will be shocked to hear another express unqualified admiration for the human body and the human soul.[8]

Holland no doubt intended that this would show Whitman, even in the most liberal eyes, to be perverse and a perverter—and thus to Emily Dickinson (if she meant it when she said it) "disgraceful."

In his 13 June article, Holland's bitter reaction against Whitman's subject matter went even further, advocating official condem-

---

7. W. S. Kennedy, *The Fight of a Book for the World* (West Yarmouth, Mass., 1926), p. 242.

8. Quoted in Holland, "'Leaves of Grass.'"

nation and total censorship. "A professedly obscene book," he complained, "carries with it its own condemnation among decent people, and finds its own market among the vicious and unclean. Besides, there are laws against its promulgation; and appeal can be made to them if it is openly exposed for sale, or advertised, or sold more secretly. This literature is not unfrequently stuck in one's face at steam boat landings by lousy scoundrels who peddle filth for a living, but one can always cry 'police' if he will, and stop it." And then Holland warned:

> Here, however, is a book with many respectable associations—respectable publishers—the author a writer for the Atlantic Monthly—"for sale everywhere" on respectable book-shelves—in very respectable type and binding—advertised in respectable papers—and yet it has page after page that no man could read aloud to a decent assembly without being hooted out of it, and that could not be published in the columns of a daily newspaper without disgusting and outraging a virtuous community. The dangers of the book lie in its claiming to be a respectable book—in its claiming to be a pure book, and in the fact that there are lecherous fools enough in the world to allow this claim, if not to maintain it.

Holland further used Whitman as an excuse to criticize the excesses of the New England Transcendentalists and other pop movements, which were to him "infidelities" encouraging "libertinism" like Whitman's.

> We are inclined to think that the author considers the book a pure one. It costs some charity to admit this, and a large allowance for eccentricity of mind and temperament; but, making the admission, we are at liberty to comment on that phase of infidelity of which it is the outgrowth.
>
> Nothing is more notorious than the fact that when any individual claims to have some light superior to that revealed in the Bible, whether that light be the "light of nature," simply, or the light of new and direct revelation or inspiration, then that individual almost invariably develops himself toward libertinism. Perhaps this fact is more notorious when we find men in masses, as in the various sects that spring up from time to time.... Spiritualism, whenever it has cut loose from the Bible as the only authoritative revelation from heaven, has gone just as naturally into free-love as water runs down hill. The very first social institution that falls into contempt after Christianity as a revelation is discarded, is Christian marriage, and of all the "teachings" in the world, we know of none that is inevitably led to impurity as those attributed to "Nature."

Whitman, as the uncleanest product of an unclean movement, was to Holland a pariah and outright criminal.

Now Walt Whitman is *par excellence* the "poet of nature." In his pure taste there is nothing unclean, because nothing seems unclean. Nature has free course in him, and runs and is glorified in all its issues. Those passions which degrade men and lead to nine-tenths of the crime of the world, he exalts. Those appetites which only a pure, true and lifelong love can hallow, are with him appetites to be cherished and fed—no matter about the love. It ought to be enough for Walt Whitman, if he honestly thinks his book a pure one, to know that the pure in society will shun it, and that it will be sought out and laughed over by lewd women and prurient boys and hoary-headed old lechers,—to know that this notice of his volume will stir to read it only the dregs of the social and moral world into which it goes. That settles the question. When men and women are led by their higher affinities, they will be led straight away from Walt Whitman's "Leaves of Grass." Otherwise, otherwise.

Holland's final indictment of Whitman—and the last thing he was to say about him for Emily Dickinson's eyes, completely ignoring his Civil War verse or the poems of his later years—was a review of the "Children of Adam" and "Calamus" poems in August 1860 in the *Republican*. This estimate—and then probably Emily Dickinson's—was even lower. To Holland, Whitman's poetry at this point was worth remarking on, but he was still unforgivably foul-mouthed. "Those who wish to gain some idea of Walt Whitman's rank as a writer, and to meet with favorable specimens of his style, without incurring the perilous risk of failing to skip in his volume the pages that should not be read, will find what they desire in the following, from the *London Saturday Review*." And then he quoted a British indictment with which he concurred:

> We are far from saying that he has nothing of the poetical fiber. He is certainly an unredeemed New York rowdy of the lowest stamp. He has obviously no sort of acquaintance with the masters of his art and his studies have been apparently confined to Mr. Tupper [a popular poet of proverbs in London at the time], his newspaper and the semi-lyrical rhapsodies of the Boston transcendentalists. But his taste, now hopelessly perverted, seems to have been naturally delicate, and he has a very vivid imagination. When his pictures happen (as is rarely the case) to be neither befouled with filth nor defaced by vulgarity, they are for the most part strikingly presented.

"We conclude with some lines," Holland then wrote, "which are more like true poetry than anything else in the volume. They are fished out from the very midst of a sea of foul impurities."[9] Holland then expurgated Whitman's poem from the *Atlantic* version, the "Bardic Sym-

9. Ibid.

bols," by providing his readers, Emily Dickinson probably among them, with some fifty lines of verse of which he decently approved.[10]

This was the news about Whitman that came to Emily Dickinson in 1860. Thanks mainly to Holland and Higginson, after that she never cared to read him at all. She had been adequately tutored to think him disgraceful or worse.[11]

There were, in addition, probably other reasons why she did not read Whitman. Except for Emerson, of course she had only the most superficial interest in contemporary American male poets anyway; they had little to say to her. "We do not have much poetry [here at home]," she complained to her brother in 1851,[12] and what American poetry she had she did not read particularly well. "Of Poe," she said, uninterested, "I know too little to think." Of course, she had respect for the position of Bryant, Holmes, Whittier, and Lowell in American letters, and she owned and marked editions of the poems of each, but for the most part she had use for them only on consolatory occasions when friends were sick or when friends' friends died and she did not have a quatrain of her own to send. The verse of Very and Channing she never did read, apparently preferring the poems of subpoets like John Pierpont and George Parsons Lathrop or the poetic prose of Augustus Hawkins and Arthur Kavanagh (alias Longfellow). Of one of Lowell's poems she said in 1869, "One does not often meet anything so perfect," but she was really more interested in Mrs. Lowell's poems, she said, than in his.[13] She admitted on one occasion that if she imitated the public poetry of the time at all—though the reference is, to be specific, to Longfellow's—she feared that her friends would "laugh at me, and call me sentimental."[14]

For another reason, Emily Dickinson was much more impressed by and therefore diverted to these poets' other efforts—Emerson's essays, for example, and Longfellow's fiction. She seems to have been more interested in Holmes's and Lowell's biographical studies and Higginson's literary and social essays. If she read men's poetry at all, generally in the *Republican* and other local publications or in the *At-*

10. It is doubtful, however, that images from this poem were borrowed for her own poems thereafter as Ruth Miller has argued (*The Poetry of Emily Dickinson* [Middletown, Conn., 1960], pp. 65–67).
11. Similarly, Gerard Manley Hopkins thought Whitman "a very great scoundrel" and said, "This . . . makes me the more desirous to read him and the more determined that I will not" (*The Letters of Gerard Manley Hopkins to Robert Bridges,* ed. Claude Colleer Abbott [London, 1935], p. 154).
12. *Letters,* p. 161.
13. *Letters,* pp. 79, 466, 480, 551, 571, 594, 612, 649, 856, 868; Leyda, *Years and Hours,* 1:154; 2:24, 132; Sewall, *Life,* p. 678.
14. *Letters,* pp. 263–64.

lantic, she read much of the worst available. So missing Whitman was not an entirely unusual oversight in the pattern of her reading.

I think that she would not have known very well how to read him, how to take him, anyway. What she could see in other American poets would have been largely missing for her in Whitman. The frivolous conceits she was attracted to in Emerson ("thou animated torrid zone") Whitman makes believable facts ("The hairy wild-bee that murmurs and hankers up and down.")[15] The oxymorons she found in Lowell ("sweet despair") in Whitman become a means of open debate with oneself ("I am indifferent to my own songs—I will go with him I love"). The sentimental animadversions on life and literature that she read in Longfellow ("Literature is rather an image of the spiritual world, than of the physical") are in Whitman programized ("The known universe has one complete lover and that is the greatest poet").[16] The death assurances she pulled out of others (as quoted, for example, from Bryant: "wrapping the drapery of his couch about him – and lying down to pleasant dreams")[17] she would have found vaguely orientalized in Whitman ("They prepare for death... To launch off with absolute faith, to sweep through the ceaseless rings and never be quiet again"). Except from Emerson, whom she read entirely differently than he did—that is, as we have seen, far more for his aphoristic method than for his spiritualist/ anarchist ideology—except from Emerson, she had no training for noticing Whitman at all. And she knew no one else who would try to understand him for her.[18] She was prepared only for rejecting him as disgraceful, or at least as irrelevant.

In fact, for the entire New York literary scene of which Whitman was a part Emily Dickinson cared very little. Her Ik Marvel was there, as were Joaquin Miller ("I could not care about him"), Irving, and Howells. But she had outgrown most of such authors by the time she came to write her own works and by the time Whitman was available for her to read, or else she did not know enough about them to care. By and large, the other New Yorkers she read or read about were movement people (social reformers, editors and publishers, ministers) and appear to have been of very little interest to her. Her tempera-

---

15. See my discussion of the Emily Dickinson–Emerson affinities above in chapter 6.

16. The only extensive discussion of the Emily Dickinson–Longfellow affinities is Sewall, *Life,* pp. 683–88.

17. *Letters,* p. 79.

18. One might have expected both Bowles and Helen Jackson to have had some interest in Whitman, but we have no record of any comment about him from either one.

ment did not allow her to go to literary New York. Like almost everyone else she read, they too were substantially different from Whitman anyway and would not have given her any assistance at all in knowing him.

Though there is no use in making Emily Dickinson out to be "a feminine Walt Whitman," as some readers did in the 1890s, the two were nonetheless contemporaries, and one might expect to find some general similarities as a result of certain pressures and paradigms of the late nineteenth century. The time's epistemes—that is, some of the possibilities for ideas and ideologies of the time—were in both, if only in form and not generally in substance. Their poetry belongs to the same phase of culture, one in which a poetic role was therapy, in which orthodoxies were discarded, in which idealization could lift one above tragedy, in which one could be obsessed with impermanence, in which personal sensitivity could be taken as a sense of well-being, in which the continuity and integrity of the individual could be a serious idea.[19]

There is possibly a side of Emily Dickinson that, if we are speaking only in generalities, is like what we accept in Whitman. There is, for example, the assertion of autonomous personality over autonomous works. There is the inclination to present themselves (not always successful in either one) as spiritual adventurers. They both work against the distinction between the work and the person who produced it. They both hold writing not as a freestanding achievement but as some kind of medium in which a unique personality heroically exposes itself. They both appear to have held that a poem derives its credentials from its place in a special, lived experience. They both appear to have felt that the poet's effort is successful when it ruptures the collective voice; and thus we have the incompleteness, the fragmentary quality in both, the tendency in both toward antigenres. All of this, in both, leads to the celebration of the quality of one's consciousness as a final standard.

But for all the attractive general affinities, we live with the truism that George Whicher established: "Emily Dickinson revolted from the literary standards to which her age paid deference. . . . She had no doubts at all about her [own] literary method."[20] And we therefore dissociate her from the age's spokesman, Whitman, that

19. For a discussion of some of these, see Mordecai Marcus, "Walt Whitman and Emily Dickinson," *Personalist* 43 (1962):497–514.
20. Whicher, "Emily Dickinson among the Victorians," in *Poetry and Civilization* (New York, 1955), pp. 41–62.

literary history gives us. "Emily Dickinson is a baffling poet," John Lynen has added, "because she seems to bear little or no relation to the historical period within which she worked. She stands apart, as indifferent to the literary movements of her day as to its great events."[21] And we therefore find no very specific ways for relating her to someone like Whitman. But this may be the case because we have had others, not *her*, to define for us what it means to relate to a historical period or movement—for the late nineteenth century, Whitman mainly, and also Howells and Twain, Henry James and Henry Adams. Her poems transpired in an epoch largely dominated—for *us*—by them, and so when we allow them to define how literary-social affinities work in a period, Emily Dickinson often gets relegated to a stereotype outside the epistemes.[22]

Yet making the two out to be America's Archetypal Private Poet and America's Archetypal Public Poet—mother and father of two poetic traditions—does nothing for us. It is ludicrous to exploit the two as "symptomatic of the critical split in the American consciousness that had yawned wide by the end of the nineteenth century."[23] The reconstruction of American poetic history, either with land for them to fight together on or two lands with a barrier between the stake-outs, is too simple to be believed.

The usual artificial distinctions between them can be largely accepted and largely ignored: Whitman's prophet versus Emily Dickinson's recluse; his certainty versus her doubt; his homosexuality versus her physical denial; and so on. We understand little as soon as we have made the one poet New English and the other American, the one

21. John F. Lynen, "The Uses of the Present: The Historian's, the Critic's, and Emily Dickinson's," *College English* 28 (November 1966): 126–36. This essay comparing Emily Dickinson and Whitman overstates thematic and stylistic similarities. For example, Emily Dickinson does not "conceive the present as an epitome of all times: the way Whitman does." She enjoys *now* far more desperately, playfully, confusedly. She enjoys phenomena, but rarely synecdochically.

22. I differ with the position of Glauco Cambon: "From Whitman to Emily Dickinson the transition is so abrupt as to make any attempt to include them in common perspective seem hopeless." "Dickinson: Confrontation of the Self with Otherness in the Inner Space," in *The Inclusive Flame: Studies in American Poetry* (Bloomington, Ind., 1963), pp. 27–52. One only needs a *way* to discuss them together.

23. Albert Gelpi, *The Tenth Muse: The Psyche of the American Poet* (Cambridge, Mass., 1975), p. 222. Babette Deutsch argues (inaccurately, I feel) a similar division of poetic labors between the two: "In her responses to the details of her outwardly ordinary existence, [Emily Dickinson] resembled Whitman. But she differed from him in two important particulars, . . . meagerness of experience and . . . [her question about] what it is that makes a few people . . . so different from others. He delighted in the universal, she in the unique. He was the poet of the general, she of the particular, the rare. He relished variety, she valued distinction" (*This Modern Poetry* [New York, 1935], pp. 22–23).

intellectual and analytical and the other imaginative and synthetic, the one intensive and concentrating and the other expansive and liberating, the one a hothouse-plant and the other wild-luxuriant-natural, the one contemplative and passionate and the other prophetic and compassionate, or the one personal and abstract and the other universal and concrete.[24] Which is which of these is difficult to remember, for the distinctions are not fine, or sure, or even very interesting. "Walt Whitman and Emily Dickinson," writes Louis L. Martz inaccurately, "have very little in common, whether in their personal lives or in their poetical manner."[25] There is no use making Emily Dickinson's poetry the epitome of home verse and Whitman's the epitome of the fringe. We can know we have an incomplete idea if Whitman is given the circumference and Emily Dickinson the center.[26]

But why substitute the obvious for some teasable opportunities of understanding them together?[27] It is foolish to construct a contest between the two, however antagonistic we know them to have become in our history and however often their interests, differently expressed, coincide in our reconstructed metaphysics of the late nineteenth century. Each wins, but on terms unlikely for the other.

Instead, by seeing how each does his/her things, one can put to rest a popular antinomy in American literature and American culture studies in general: the closed versus the open world. It only politicizes poetry anyway, asking it to sustain that one fiction, "Society," and only spiritualizes it, asking it to sustain that other fiction, "the Self." The two directions are an invented dialectic, demanding the critic's services. We must accept that Whitman and Emily Dickinson worked on different frequencies, rather than thinking of them as differently aware of the same sorts of things.

John Burdett Payne pictures the two diverging/converging through the process of countertransference—two "naked egos" on buses to the same open poetry reading:

24. See John Nist, "Two American Poets and a Spider," *Walt Whitman Birthplace Bulletin* 4 (January 1961): 8–11.
25. Louis L. Martz, "Whitman and Dickinson: Two Aspects of the Self," in *The Poem of the Mind* (New York, 1966), p. 82.
26. As Albert Gelpi does in his *Tenth Muse,* pp. 222–24.
27. As I feel Ed Winfield Parks does in his brief study of the two ("The Public and the Private Poet," *South Atlantic Quarterly* 56 [1957]: 480–85). The most elaborate comparison is by Albert Gelpi, "Walt Whitman: The Self as Circumference" and "Emily Dickinson: The Self as Center," in *The Tenth Muse,* pp. 153–299.

EMILY AND WALT, WALT AND EMILY

Crosstown buses run each way
To and from the open poetry reading,
Bearing Emily and Walt, Walt and Emily.

Emily stands at the foot of the pier,
Contemplating the Hudson, Jersey,
A city which isn't hers.
Inward, shy,
Wary of the afternoon sun,
Bombast,
The naked ego on display,
Emily turns and hastily catches
Her crosstown bus,
Eastward bound,
Thinking of her sandalwood box,
An inward private special place for poems;
And she rides,
Happier with private lyricism,
With increasing distance,
Counting each block
Away from the open poetry reading
As liberative of community,
Others.

Crosstown buses run each way
To and from the open poetry reading,
Bearing Emily and Walt, Walt and Emily.

And westward riding Walt,
Riding into the setting Jersey sun,
Hails Emily from his crosstown bus,
Yelling:
"Why aren't you coming
To the open poetry reading?"

And Walt rides on,
Impatient,
Turned outward,
Turned on,
Loving crosstown streets,
Uptown-downtown streets,
The pulse and heart and promise of a city,
The world,
The prospect ahead,
All a delight to anticipate,
Joyously excited,

Bucked up by the contemplation of all the ego-bombast,
The shared, the real, the enlarged,
All, himself,
One's self, the blade of grass,
An empire city,
The self and city and words of others,
Strengthened, multiplied
By the multiple statement/sound.

And Emily,
Briefly secure in flight,
Thinks
How dangerous
To give your heart to public rhetoric,
How perilous
To run the risk of love,
The risk of loving or being beloved.
And then she thinks of Walt,
Outward loving verbal Walt.
A sandalwood box is not enough.
We wear too many masks of privilege and privacy
Turn too often from the sun of reality
Deny too often the heart
Without or with its Pascal reasons.
And Emily, lonely on her crosstown bus,
Continues eastward,
Thinking of Walt,
Vibrant in his courage,
In his involvement.

And Walt,
Loving Emily
Even in her flight,
Thinks
How dangerous not to love,
Fully, rapaciously,
World-embracing, world-embraced
Rhetoric-fucking, rhetoric-fucked;
And he is impatient
With the blocks
Which still intervene
As crosstown buses run their way
Closer and closer
To the open poetry reading.

Counter-transference can occur
When crosstown buses
Bearing Emily and Walt, Walt and Emily

Pass,
With Walt yelling
Out of bravado and conviction and need to Emily.

And Walt,
Nearing the end of the westward line,
Asks himself:
"When did I,
Like Emily,
Last have a glorious introspective moment?"

A weathervane,
A crosstown bus,
Any vibrant authentic poet,
Can spin and turn
At the line's end.
Walt spins and turns,
Whirling with thoughts of Emily,
And he rides back east in search of self.

And Emily,
Riding vibrantly,
Passionately,
Preciously alone,
Thinks again of Walt,
Engaged poet,
Taking his chances
With the whole fucking universe,
And stays on her bus
At the end of the line
To ride westward
Into the setting Jersey sun
To wave and yell at Walt
On his crosstown bus
Passing hers:
"Why aren't you coming
To the open poetry reading?"[28]

The two meet, as I would also like to argue, on grounds that critics have not always allowed them to share. The fact that Emily Dickinson was read immediately and appreciatively by a fairly wide public as well as noticed and advertised by established critics (many of them very genteel) long before such wholesale recognition came to Whitman may lead one to believe that she is in many ways more

28. John Burdett Payne, "Emily and Walt, Walt and Emily," *ManRoot*, nos. 6–7 (1972), pp. 64–66. This poem is reprinted here with the kind permission of the poet and the editors of *ManRoot*.

conventional, more conservative, calmer, more exemplary of expected poetics and religion—and therefore *inferior* by virtue of her
proximity to the public norm. Emily Dickinson—in company with
Frost and Sandburg—has always had a public to instruct her critics
and so has sometimes been an embarrassment to the literary history.

But the fact is that in many ways Emily Dickinson matches
Whitman. She did similar things and often as boldly, if with less certainty and less self-consciousness. She escaped the Whitman influence, as few major poets since 1855 have, and so there is no use
talking about affinity in terms of influence of any sort, but it was time
to do certain bold things in poetry. She was a sister—and (as I would
like to try to show) an outrageous one. The wildness *is* an esthetic.
What might surprise one about Emily Dickinson declaiming Whitman's disgracefulness is *her own*. Trying them out together as front-
runners in four different kinds of races, if only very briefly, one can
see this. I believe she is pretty much a match for him.

AMERICAN EROTIC

The indictment of Whitman as "disgraceful" that Emily Dickinson learned from Josiah Holland and others is mainly a response to
Whitman's daring to be explicitly sexual in his poetry. "Urge and urge
and urge," he wrote in 1855, "Always the procreant urge of the
world.... Always sex,... always a breed of life." The nasty image
stuck in practically everyone's mind right from the outset.

On the subject of sex, one of Whitman's main claims to literary
realism, Emily Dickinson is, after her own fashion, often as frank.
Whitman is the poet of as much bawdry as body, and Emily Dickinson
has her bawdry, too. *If* one looks for it. The recluse was not wholly the
prude.

Of course it would be wrong to see her outnastying Whitman in
the sexual sections of "Song of Myself"—cosmic fellatio in section 5,
masturbation-in-drag in section 11, anal rape in section 28—or in his
attempts at talking dirty in "Children of Adam" and "Calamus"
("love-flesh," "quivering jelly of love," "womb," "manroot," "love-
perturbations and risings") or his ability to divulge the private for
therapeutic reasons ("this electric self out of the pride of which I utter
poems") or his sex-program gaffes ("Plunging his seminal muscle into
[America's] merits and demerits").[29] But we can find Emily Dickinson

29. See the revisionist (and, it seems to me, largely accurate) argument regarding the overwhelmingly homosexual character of Whitman's early poetry in Robert K.
Martin, "Whitman's Song of Myself: Homosexual Dream and Vision," *Partisan Review*
42 (winter 1975): 80–86.

writing about desire and passion with an almost equivalent interest, if not as pervasively and repetitiously as Whitman. I do not refer to the general category of her maudlin love poems. She is quite often a woman having her sexual way in her poetry. As with Whitman, this is unique among nineteenth-century American writers.

Why fuss whether the sex scenes she writes up are reportage or fantasy?[30] Or whether she had adequate gender identification—woman with animus, androgynous wholeness, feminine ambivalence, womanly security?[31] Or whether the poetry was adequate vicarious sexual fulfillment for her?[32] The sex in her poems survives more plausibly than that in her biography.[33]

Emily Dickinson had no intention of bathing her songs "in sex" or of producing "types of athletic love" for liberal-libertine consumption as Whitman had, of course; for her the Fall had indeed occurred, and nakedness, however much desired and desirable, is usually covered/covert. So to her mind the poet is not so much the liberating uncoverer, the facilitator of orgies, the promiscuous stroker, the voyeur, the codifier of the revolt of the body (Whitman's rather consistent roles) as the *acceptor* of sex in the chaotic, fallen scheme of things, taking it as many things: overwhelming monster, plaything, object of perplexity, escapist high, symbol of disillusionment, spiritual tease, productive pain—any and all of these. The marvel is her explicit inconsistency. She does not know what sex *is;* it is to be used.

Where Whitman is often parasexual—that is, faithful to the idea of a prevenient sexual life-force (the Holy Spirit as orgone)—Emily Dickinson is at many points *meta*sexual—that is, faithful to the nonsense of sex. Both are *watching* sex—the one fully discernibly, the other fairly indecipherably. It was a wonder to them as it had not been to any other American poets before them. They both experimented (generally unsuccessfully) with the explicitly erotic before others would dare to—though not without knowing very well how to make language itself erotic. Mainly they just watch and report.

In one Dickinson poem full of sexual puns, "My Life had stood –

---

30. For the most thorough discussion of Emily Dickinson's possible sex life see Sewall, *Life,* pp. 444–531.

31. Possibilities argued by Gelpi, *Tenth Muse,* pp. 240–61.

32. A question best raised by Clark Griffith, *The Long Shadow: Emily Dickinson's Tragic Poetry* (Princeton, 1964), pp. 149–84. Because I am not convinced that the universe and the world were quite as consistently awful to Emily Dickinson as Griffith maintains, I find it difficult to accept his argument that her love poems are either about male marauders or are maudlin. I find Emily Dickinson, with the fact of her sexual poetry, to be the aggressive one. I do not believe she had "a warped conception" of sex that made her "confound sexual experience with the gross and revolting" (p. 183).

33. For the best discussion of Emily Dickinson's passionate love letters, the Master Letters, see Sewall, *Life,* pp. 513–21.

a Loaded Gun" (#754), she watches the object of her attraction and her attraction itself and also her reaction to the attraction. As a poet, she can have her passion and observe it too. In the story of the poem, she is fascinated with the man who has carried her away and made use of her. She is very "cordial" in her feelings toward him and finds, she says, considerable "pleasure" in servicing him. Her main interest is what happens at night: she watches him sleep, still "loaded" with desire and possessive passion. Sex is for a woman, ludicrously, a waiting for "the power to die"—that is, to have sex. Sex is a consuming companionship consummately to be desired consummated. In other words, it is a making out, a trying out.

This metasexuality is also operating in her now infamously over-read poems on a phallic snake and a phallic worm, where she manages to make Freud trite:

A narrow Fellow in the Grass
Occasionally rides –
You may have met Him – did you not
His notice sudden is –

The Grass divides as with a Comb –
A spotted shaft is seen –
And then it closes at your feet
And opens further on –

He likes a Boggy Acre
A Floor too cool for Corn –
Yet when a Boy, and Barefoot –
I more than once at Noon
Have passed, I thought, a Whip lash
Unbraiding in the Sun
When stooping to secure it
It wrinkled, and was gone –

Several of Nature's People
I know, and they know me –
I feel for them a transport
Of cordiality –

But never met this Fellow
Attended, or alone
Without a tighter breathing
And Zero at the Bone –

[#986]

In Winter in my Room
I came upon a Worm
Pink lank and warm
But as he was a worm
And worms presume
Not quite with him at home
Secured him by a string
To something neighboring
And went along.

A Trifle afterward
A thing occurred
I'd not believe it if I heard
But state with creeping blood
A snake with mottles rare
Surveyed my chamber floor
In feature as the worm before
But ringed with power
The very string with which
I tied him – too
When he was mean and new
That string was there –

I shrank – "How fair you are"!
Propitiation's claw –
"Afraid he hissed
Of me"?
"No cordiality" –
He fathomed me –
Then to a Rhythm *Slim*
Secreted in his Form
As Patterns swim

Projected him.

That time I flew
Both eyes his way
Lest he pursue
Nor ever ceased to run
Till in a distant Town
Towns on from mine
I set me down
This was a dream –

[#1670]

Sexual contact is here made comic; it makes no sense. Both phallic creatures are extremely attractive to her, even though she finds her genitals alarmed, feeling what she calls "tighter breathing / And Zero at the Bone" in one case and "creeping blood" in the other. In both cases she is shocked and attracted by the male erection ("His notice sudden is"; he is "ringed with power"; he "Projected him[self]" for her), and she is fascinated with the male sexual processes (a "spotted shaft" moving in hair, a whiplash unbraiding and then wrinkling up, rhythm and secretion). Her own sexual desires are, she says, very strongly aroused; she feels "a transport / Of Cordiality," and, finally, "He fathomed [i.e., penetrated] me." But, like Whitman, as much as she might desire it, she does not connect well, dismissing the encounter with the snake as merely a boy's brief summertime adventure and the encounter with the worm-snake as merely a housewife's daydream. There is no significance in the sex; it is fun and games. The Fall obviates obsession. Bounds prevent bondings.

Quite different from Emily Dickinson, Whitman intended sexual outrage with his erotic poetry—an exposure of prurience, an exposition of body alternatives:

Through me forbidden voices,
Voices of sexes and lusts, voices veil'd and I remove the veil,
Voices indecent by me clarified

I do not press my fingers across my mouth,
I keep as delicate around the bowels as around the head and heart,
Copulation is no more rank to me than death is.

["Song of Myself"]

But for his Victorian audience he usually provided titillation instead:

O hand in hand—O wholesome pleasure—O one more desirer
and lover!

["Starting from Paumanok"]

As the hugging and loving bed-fellow sleeps at my side through
the night, and withdraws at the peep of the day with
stealthy tread,

Leaving me baskets cover'd with white towels swelling the
    house with their plenty . . .

["Song of Myself"]

They do not know who puffs and declines with pendant and
    bending arch,
They do not know whom they souse with spray . . .

["Song of Myself"]

two simple men I saw to-day on the pier in the midst
    of the crowd, parting the parting of dear friends,
The one to remain hung on the other's neck and passionately
    kiss'd him,
While the one to depart tightly prest the one to remain
    in his arms.

["What Think You I Take My Pen in Hand?"]

Emily Dickinson is sometimes as good at such titillation—and without
intending outrage. As Louis Martz points out, Emily Dickinson would
probably not have been shocked much by Whitman's material. The
conventional minds of the time would probably have found some of
her lines just as shocking and disgraceful.[34] "The Heart asks Pleasure," she wrote in a poem in 1862, "first." The sex in her poems
forms no program but is made up of individual bold moments, flashes
of desire, mainly masturbatory. Her love poems are often sex poems,
and the verse is not therapy but brag: her explicit desires become acts.
They are fictions fulfilled.

Higginson said in 1891 he was afraid "lest the malignant read
into [one of such poems, "Wild Nights - Wild Nights!"] more than
that virgin recluse ever dreamed of putting there."[35] But her imagination was not virginal at all. It was—if one believes her poetic scenes—
fully susceptible to abandon, passion, seduction.

Wild Nights - Wild Nights!
Were I with thee
Wild Nights should be
Our luxury!

Futile - the Winds -
To a Heart in port -
Done with the Compass -
Done with the Chart!

Rowing in Eden -
Ah, the Sea!

34. Martz, "Whitman and Dickinson," p. 91.
35. *Poems,* p. 180.

Might I but moor - Tonight -
In thee!

[#249]

Hers are not the kind of sexual poems that can ever be invoked
for revolutions the way Whitman's can be and have been, and so one
may forget to gather them as a sexual statement. They are the
polemics of a woman who, for once, did not have to take sex seriously.
She could play with it on wild nights in her poems without any consequences. It is, I believe, another of her areas of freedom.

Her wilder nights (and days)—her "routes of ecstasy," to borrow
a phrase of hers from another context—are often elliptical teases:

He touched me, so I live to know
That such a day, permitted so,
I groped upon his breast -

[#506]

no Man moved Me - till the Tide
Went past my simple Shoe -
And past my Apron - and my Belt
And past my Boddice - too -

And made as He would eat me up -

[#520]

Struck, was I, nor yet by Lightning -
. . . .
All my Mansion torn -

[#925]

He strove - and I strove - too -
We did'nt do it - tho'!

[#190]

Such wilder relations with a man in her poems could take the form of
an extremely passionate love-longing ("I envy Seas, whereon He
rides - /I envy Spokes of Wheels / Of Chariots, that him convey"); or
take the form of a seduction in which she feels what she calls a "Stop-
sensation on my Soul / And Thunder - in the Room -" until her "Sinew
tore, . . . forcing, in my breath - / As Staples - driven through"; or
take the form of someone ("The *splashing Men*!") attacking her physic-
ally ("A Burdock - clawed my Gown . . . A *Bog* affronts my shoe -").
And at times there are full-blown seductions:

his eye
Where e'er I ply
Is pushing close behind
. . . .

What omnipresence lies in wait
For her to be a Bride

[#1496]

Did the Harebell loose her girdle
To the lover Bee
Would the Bee the Harebell *hallow*
Much as formerly?

[#213]

This flower-bee mating is one of her favorite covers for present-ing sex acts in her poetry, though the language is fairly explicit:

A Bee his burnished Carriage
Drove boldly to a Rose –
Combinedly alighting –
Himself – his Carriage was –
The Rose received his visit
With frank tranquility
Witholding not a Crescent
To his Cupidity –

[#1339]

This carefully advocated and carefully protested coupling sometimes proceeds to the point of trying out some forms of promiscuity:

There is a flower that Bees prefer –
And Butterflies – desire –
To gain the Purple Democrat
The Humming Bird – aspire –

And Whatsoever Insect passe –
A Honey bear away
Proportioned to his several dearth
And her – capacity –

[#380]

Compare Emily Dickinson's views here of the bee-flower relation with Whitman's view from his poem "Spontaneous Me," in which the thrills are the same but the results different, with Emily Dickinson hoping for promiscuity and Whitman willing it:

The hairy wild-bee that murmurs and hankers up and down,
    that gripes the full-grown lady-flower, curves upon
    her with amorous firm legs, takes his will of her,
    and holds himself tremulous and tight till he is
    satisfied.

The sex poems of both Emily Dickinson and Whitman, as far as we can tell, are not usually records/reports of actual encounters, how-

ever; they are seldom factual. Instead they are by and large ex-
pressions of sexual loneliness, desires recalled in the tranquility of
heat. Underneath Whitman's erotic bluster, his lyrical narcissism, and
his hope for America the Queer is a desperate hunger for bonding
(the spider on the little promontary "launch[ing] forth filament, filament, filament" until it "catch somewhere"), and underneath Emily
Dickinson's sexual prowess is absence and loss:

> Think of it Lover! I and Thee
> Permitted – face to face to be –
> After a Life – a Death. . . .
> Forgive me, if the Grave come slow –
> For Coveting to look at Thee –
> Forgive me, if to stroke thy frost
> Outvisions Paradise!
>
> [#577]

The sex poems of both are therefore often in the form of mas-
turbation fantasies ("Rehearsal to Ourselves / Of a Withdrawn Delight," Emily Dickinson called it in 1862) and must be treated according to the esthetics of the hard-core. To be sure, one can find in her
poems a fairly persistent claim to virginity, however protested beyond
believability ("Bliss, is sold just once. / The Patent lost / None buy it
any more"), and one can find a rather consistent recourse to the
Puritan convention of increasing sexual desires through continence,
also moralized unbelievably ("Fitter to see Him, I may be / For the
long Hindrance"). But how to put poetry to the service of prolonging
one's sexual thrills, one's orgasms, is of greater interest to her:

> Go slow, my soul, to feed thyself
> Upon his rare approach –
> Go rapid, lest Competing Death
> Prevail upon the Coach –
> Go timid, lest his final eye
> Determine thee amiss –
> Go boldly – for thou paid'st his price
> Redemption – for a Kiss –
>
> [#1297]

> Come slowly – Eden!
> Lips unused to Thee –
> Bashful – sip thy Jessamines –
> As the fainting Bee –

> Reaching late his flower,
> Round her chamber hums –
> Counts his nectars
> Enters – and is lost in Balms.
>
> [#211]

The bee-flower poem here about praying for a slow Eden, a longer climax, takes the point of view of the flower, the female; she asks the male bee to be gentle with her for she is virginal. The sex act is to be quick (the bee "Reaching late his flower") and it is to be real (he "Enters" her) and together they become magnificent ("lost in Balms").

Though her trying out of the tease, the playful desire, and foreplay in such poems might suggest otherwise, it is difficult for Emily Dickinson to conceive of promiscuity seriously in her sex poems the way Whitman can, for, being a woman, she is not very aggressively on the hunt, she assumes some devotion on her part, and she cannot conceive of sex as a sharing. There is a limit to the roles she will play. Whitman's Transcendentalist love affair with the world, with the universe—his parasexuality—is, as Lawrence pointed out a long time ago, an extension of his personal sexual promiscuity: he desires to "know" everything/everybody. But for Emily Dickinson it is a messy universe, and promiscuity will not set it right.

The restless movement in her poetry, which makes it far more kinetic for the reader's senses than almost any American verse before Pound and Berryman, could be taken for the polymorphous perverse, giving the reader, through the form, sensuous delights suggesting the promiscuous. Whitman laves, Emily Dickinson jerks synesthetically. But Emily Dickinson cannot really bring herself to the promiscuity that Whitman advocates, even though there may be more of it to experience in the way *she* writes than in the way he does. Like Whitman, Emily Dickinson was convinced that life was to be understood in terms of energy. But her energy, while yielded up in the way she wrote, in concentrated languge and cathartic excess, often experiencing her own poetry more in terms of light and heat than craft, does not make the reader sexually *one* with the poet. Whitman's promiscuous hope ("Who touches this [book] touches a man / (Is it night, are we here together alone?) / It is I you hold and who holds you, / I spring from the pages into your arms") was never Emily Dickinson's; she keeps us at a chaste distance with abrasive charm. Whitman is the caresser-absorber, the seduced; Emily Dickinson is the prig-tease, the seducer.[36]

36. It is difficult to be convinced that Emily Dickinson is an example of the female-sexual-power-through-poetry that Patricia Meyer Spacks describes. For a number of women writers and artists of the nineteenth century, she suggests, "The function of art was to assert power, the function of power, to demand love. . . . For a woman, the artist's power—assertive, insistent, dominating—combines uneasily with orthodox modes of attraction: . . . offering herself as artistic product, she offers herself also as sexual being, . . . risking, however, the totality of self-absorption which shuts out rather than attracts others" (*The Female Imagination* [New York, 1976], pp. 160, 166-67).
"It is hard to imagine a male Emily Dickinson in any era," Spacks continues, again unable to see how Emily Dickinson is outgoing in her own way, for because of

The orgasmic in Emily Dickinson's sexual poems, as in Whitman's, is not something one can either know very well or treat very lightly. It is a private achievement for a public end: the climax is the Everyman's/Everywoman's high, really an *any*body's heaven. Still, Whitman's organic orgastics (a poetics of the oversexed) teach one to look for Emily Dickinson's. The "Awe," "Exultation," "Delight," "Exstasy," "Glory," "Glee," "Rapture," and other easy expletives throughout her poems are often mere vicarious excitement, mere surrogate climaxes, mere compensatory hyperbole, but also in identifiable sexual contexts they give her away as almost as much of a poetic voyeur as Whitman, though one can be sure that she expects more thrills and less meaning from an "experience." To Whitman, to be "hankering, gross, mystical, nude" is one and the same thing, with the sexual and the spiritual promiscuously combined. And, for Emily Dickinson, to know what she calls an "extatic instant... keen and quivering" is to have the sublime in an earthly/earthy form, often the sexual. The epiphany is often a euphemism for orgasm in both.

We know that Emily Dickinson had difficulty transferring the divine to that which she enjoyed, that which had depth to her. God is always the Other. Things are surrogates of the divine, and that makes a substantial difference from Whitman, who could make divine everything he saw and touched. Subtracting her God, as she often had to do herself in order to get along with the world, we see her epiphanies to be very much like Whitman's—a Wordsworthian mysticism with a tinge of the metasexual added, a little naughtiness, a little nastiness, a little playfulness, a little freakishness, a spectacle.

The Puritan requirement for American sex is that it be genital. But prudery (society's, Whitman's, and Emily Dickinson's own) prevented them from having any genitals very often in their poems. Such appear mainly in the euphemisms of sensation. Yet the aroused senses *are* arousals. American sexuality works it up and keeps it down at the same time.

AMERICAN HIGH

Orgasms are orgasms in both Whitman ("We must have a turn together") and Emily Dickinson ("lost in Balms") and everything else is everything else, but they also represent in both an appetite for epiphanies. "The eternal self of me... threatens to get the better of

---

their obsession with their uniqueness, women writers like Emily Dickinson were encouraged "simply to wallow in their inner lives" (pp. 176–77).

me, and stifle me," Whitman wrote in that poem that Emily Dickinson may have read in the *Atlantic* in 1860, "I . . . was seized by the spirit that trails in the lines underfoot." In both, what we have in their epiphanal language is authentic eighteenth-century Sublime americanized into Frontier-Divine, into Yankee-Exotic, into Puritan/Quaker-Excess.

For example, just at that point when he achieves climax in section 5 of "Song of Myself," Whitman flips out into the transcending Known:

> Swiftly arose and spread around me the peace and knowledge
>   that pass all the argument of the earth,
> And I know that the hand of God is the promise of my own,
> And I know that the spirit of God is the brother of my own,
> And that all the men ever born are also my brothers, and
>   the women my sisters and lovers,
> And that a kelson of the creation is love.

Likewise, when Emily Dickinson achieves a heightened sensuousness in one of her poems, though she generally knows (comically) that it will not work out, she wants it prolonged and intensified to the point of epiphany:

> Oh Sumptuous moment
> Slower go
> That I may gloat on thee –
>
> > [#1125]

"The Thrill came slowly," she wrote of one imagined epiphanal affair, "Rapture changed it's Dress" until it became "ravished Holiness" (#1495). Like Whitman, she takes the pushed senses over into something spiritual.

Thus, like Whitman, Emily Dickinson was after thrills. "I leaned upon the Awe," she confesses. In Whitman, Josiah Holland saw this need for heights as a second shameful disservice he was doing to American literature—"seized by the spirit . . . Poor fellow!" In Emily Dickinson he would have seen an almost equivalent "disgrace."

For Whitman the universe is simultaneous: one may experience it all, all of the time, even if only as Each in All. That is a mystic. "To me the converging objects of the universe perpetually flow." For Emily Dickinson the universe is largely unknowable, certainly unfathomable: one may experience it only briefly, epiphanally, if at all, and usually against God's will. That is a thief.

> A transport one cannot contain
> May yet, a transport be –

> Though God forbid it lift the lid –
> Unto it's Extasy!
>
> [#184]

Emily Dickinson can therefore only *attempt* the Whitman naiveté, the prelapsarian; her mind can be only an *amateur* of any such pure intoxication.

Perhaps that is why she has near-hallucinatory language in her epiphanal verses where Whitman's is more nearly constant-mystical. But therefore in her ephiphanal hopes and fears, there is the greater possibility of surprise and shock for her:

> Get Saints – with new – unsteady tongue –
> To say what trance below
> Most like their glory show –
>
> [#195]

Because watching the facts and features of the world multiplies her hopes, she has an exotic taste for such surprises, even a passion that they turn into journeys, but the delight is at once seductive and disheartening: she cannot live in that superior order of things that Whitman maintains his soul/self is in at all times.

That does not stop her from attempting her little ecstasies, however, if only wishfully:

> As if the Sea should part
> And show a further Sea –
> And that – a further –
>
> [#695]

To be sure, she has reservations about such reaches:

> The Glimmering Frontier that
> skirts the Acres of Perhaps –
> To Me – shows insecure –
>
> [#696]

And yet she is continually playing in her poetry with what she calls

> the limit of my Dream –
> The focus of my Prayer –
> A perfect – paralyzing Bliss –
>
> [#756]

As experimental, hyped-up, sensual antinomian, she knows she seeks (though she does not appear always to know *why*)

Delight without a Cause –
Arrestless as invisible –
A matter of the Skies.

[#774]

In addition, as an existentialist resisting her own stoicism, she is fairly sure that "Contained in this short life / Are magical extents" and fairly sure that she can (if only momentarily and illusorily) achieve what she calls "the extatic limit / Of unobtained Delight." "Take all away from me," she wrote in a late poem, "but leave me Ecstasy, / And I am richer then than all my Fellow Men." If she could, she would, she said, "populate with awe my solitude."

This does not mean that she actually went anywhere, just as the semimystical in Whitman does not mean anything actually transcendent. As Americans, they were bound to worldly forms for their thrills. The mundane catalog compounded and intensified is as far as Whitman gets, and Emily Dickinson has her church at home, hyping herself up on her birds. Both are earthbound—the "mystical" in the "gross," the "hankering" in the "nude," the "awe" within the awful.

Emily Dickinson apparently also sought spiritual epiphanies like Whitman's, even when his ecstatic motif, the "O," is replaced by her "Ah": the marvel is sadder. Perhaps the religious pretense was not of advantage to her poetry, however, as it most certainly was to Whitman's, for the "inspiration" led to exaggeration and the rapture often dilates her words almost to the point of explosion. She was most certainly a heretic to *believe* her own feelings, even when the peak experiences that her poetry often made possible were productive of good poems. The result of her flashes is often flashy, but because they are based on what was for her an impossible cosmogony, one gets the impression that the verbal equivalents of her inner dilations for the most part feed on what was for her inaccessible. When her specifics are swollen to the heavens, as Whitman's often are, she has deserted herself, which in another frame of mind she knows she cannot do. When she asks the question "Dare you see a Soul *at the White Heat?*" we know she is just conjecturing again. Verse did not permit *everything*.

She was not as good as Whitman in combining brag and hope, not as good at tricking out crusades as sublimities, not as good at generating a universe. It may have been at times what she wanted, but it was not what she could have. Though she was as much obsessed by a perpetual elsewhere as Whitman was, she knew she could only play with the possibility here. Only when she was like Whitman-the-Ecstatic did her poetry represent what she could not possess. Joy became merely a poetic sentiment, life made tolerable by endowing it with a degree of mystification. It is her one American vulgarity.

COPING IN AMERICA

Richard Chase argues that though Emily Dickinson was often as intoxicated as Whitman, she was "a good deal more firm."[37] Whitman's firmness lay in the ability to achieve peak sensations from the everyday, and Emily Dickinson's was the same. They coped by fighting off their visions. The language of the common, whenever we cite them for precursing the modern, is their major common poetic contribution.[38] But that was for both, we can believe, an easy talent, an easy accomplishment, and we may have canonized both for the wrong realism. What we know to have been more difficult as each accepted the given and wrote about it (Whitman: "objects than which none else is more lasting, . . . you dumb, beautiful ministers"; Emily Dickinson: "How much can come / And much can go, / And yet abide the World!") and as each attempted to give the given some glory (Whitman: "as the sun falling around a helpless thing"; Emily Dickinson: "A something in a summer's Day") was accepting the chaos, the inherent trouble, that went with "the World."

One might suggest—as Stephen Black has, using Freud—that their poetry was for both of them "a talking cure," that their poetry came from conflicts and was an attempt to respond to those conflicts.[39] Their poetry is not so much an escape from chaos as their sexual scenes and epiphanal points sometimes suggest, but often a series of "journeys *into* chaos"—poetry as coping. They both knew how to romanticize the Fall. In a late poem Emily Dickinson wrote:

The worthlessness of Earthly things
The Ditty is that Nature Sings –

37. Chase, *Emily Dickinson,* p. 126.
38. Babette Deutsch agrees. "Miss Dickinson's intense concern for the unique and the particular and her thrifty accuracy have nothing Whitmanesque about them. Yet her use of metaphors taken from the kitchen and the law courts, even more than her dreadless delight in the natural world, bespeaks her kinship with the disgraceful, blackguardly man. Both were forerunners of those compatriots who returned poetry to its roots in common experience and the language of daily converse. But Miss Dickinson was able to view that experience and to use that language with a fine sense of irony, a fact that places such penetrating young practitioners as Elizabeth Bishop and Jean Garrigue in direct line of descent from the witty recluse of Amherst" ("Poetry at the Mid-Century," *Virginia Quarterly Review* 26 [1950]: 69–70).
39. Stephen A. Black, *Whitman's Journeys into Chaos: A Psychoanalytic Study of the Poetic Process* (Princeton, 1975).

And then – enforces their delight
Till Synods are inordinate –

[#1373]

The cathartic experience in Whitman is an escape, an elevation, perhaps even orgasmic. In Emily Dickinson it is also a heightening of the mundane—problematic and unendurable, but closer to the egregious than to the transporting. She does not go anywhere else for long. Whitman's illusion was that his poetry would communicate transcendentally, but it seldom does. His insistence is not enough to make his highly accomplished specifics spiritual. Emily Dickinson avoided that level most of the time and, except for her occasional hopes for immortality and eternal life, she stays in the world. Whitman does succeed, however, in documenting his confusion-on the-way-to-unity, and Emily Dickinson succeeds in playing with it. In Whitman "the sweet fire within" hurts, but he knows how to smother it with transcendental ideals; Emily Dickinson doesn't know how. There is no illusion of grandeur; she will not play god. He is confident that he can survive chaos; she is unsure and so plays with it in the meantime.

Reading all of Whitman from Emily Dickinson's often-troubled vantage point, one finds their closest affinity to be a dark one. Negation is, for *both* of them, one of the sides of the "square deific." Though to be sure what we have in Whitman is dark moods and in Emily Dickinson dark generalizations, still they both had a sense of the tragic and saw their writing as a way of coping. It is often difficult to distinguish their darker sentiments, transcendentalist from existentialist. Except for the sense of absurdity on her part and the sense of solution on his, their darker texts are often surprisingly alike.

Because Whitman defined the self—*him*self—mainly in terms of relationships with others and because the hopes of relationships are seldom fulfilled, his is often a poetry of frustration and disappointment. For Whitman, as E. Fred Carlisle has already pointed out, identity "involved contradiction and ambiguity, confusion and uncertainty, as well as clarity and confidence, . . . genuine doubt and occasional despair."[40] His invention, the self, was as much an experiencer of failure as of fulfillment. It was problematic. Oneself, however celebrated, however expanded to include all possibilities, even *all* selves, is uncertain. A similar uncertainty dominates the self that Emily Dickinson fills out in her poetry, though it results not so much from frustration as from the very condition of being human. Emily Dickinson begins with the fact of the Fall; Whitman eventually runs up against it.

40. E. Fred Carlisle, *The Uncertain Self: Whitman's Drama of Identity* (Lansing, Mich., 1973), p. xiii.

For instance, both dared at times to challenge God and the benevolent order of things:

We, capricious, brought hither
   we know not whence, spread
   out before you, [God,]
You up there walking or sitting,
Whoever, you are, we too lie in
   drifts at your feet.
["As I Ebb'd with the Ocean of Life"]

Read – Sweet – how others – strove –
Till we – are stouter –
What they – renounced –
Till we – are less afraid –
How many times they – bore the
   faithful witness –
Till we – are helped –
As if a Kingdom – cared!
             [#260]

Both feared at times that existence was a botch:

O what is my destination?
O I fear it is henceforth chaos!

Have you guessed you yourself
   would not continue? ...
Have you feared the future would
   be nothing to you?
       ["To Think of Time"]

Those – dying then
Knew where they went –
They went to God's Right Hand –
That Hand is amputated now
And God cannot be found –
           [#1551]

Both were at times able to take their doubts seriously, as fundamentals:

The sense of what is real ...
   the thought if after all it
   should prove unreal,
The doubts of daytime and the
   doubts of nighttime ... the
   curious whether and how.
Whether that which appears so is
   so. ... Or is it all flashes
   and specks?
["There Was a Child Went Forth"]

I, grown shrewder – scan the Skies
With a suspicious Air –
As Children – swindled for the
   first ...
           [#476]

Both felt at times that tragedy dominates:

I have not once had the least idea
   who or what I am ... the real
   Me stands yet untouch'd, untold,
   altogether unreach'd.
["As I Ebb'd with the Ocean of Life"]

A Doubt if it be Us
Assists the staggering Mind
In an extremer Anguish
Until it footing find.
           [#859]

And both at times experienced momentary discouragement with society:

I sit and look out upon all the
   sorrows of the world, and upon
   all the oppression and shame,
....

All these—all the meanness and
   agony without end I sitting
   look out upon,
See, hear, and am silent.
     ["I Sit and Look Out"]

Had I a mighty gun
I think I'd shoot the human race
And then to glory run!
               [#118]

Though it is quite often seriously underestimated, dealing with doubt is the dominant effort throughout the Whitman canon, as it is in Emily Dickinson's. "Song of Myself" is, after all, an attempt to discover every imaginable self-doubt, from ambivalence to experiencing changing senses of order: "Agonies are one of my changes of garment. . . . I know the sea of torment, doubt, despair and unbelief." The thrust of the first and second editions of *Leaves of Grass* is the juxtaposition of limitations and possibilities: "I too knitted the old knot of contrariety, . . . Refusals, hates, postponements, meanness, laziness, none of these wanting." The liberating sexual exhilaration of "Children of Adam" and "Calamus" is almost canceled out by fears of death and by what Whitman calls "The terrible doubt of appearances, . . . the uncertainty after all, that we may be deluded."[41] In similar fashion, "Drum-Taps" balances horror off with compassion, compassion with horror. And the poems of his other clusters consistently move cheerfully over the surface of old conflicts:

Ah poverties, wincings, and sulky retreats,
Ah you foes that in conflict have overcome me,
(For what is my life or any man's life but a conflict with
   foes, the old, the incessant war?)
You degradations, you tussle with passions and appetites,
You smarts from dissatisfied friendships, (ah wounds the
   sharpest of all!)
You toil of painful and choked articulations, you meannesses,
You shallow tongue-talks at tables, (my tongue the shallowest
   of any;)
You broken resolutions, you racking angers, you smother'd
   ennuis!
     ["Ah Poverties, Wincings, and Sulky Retreats"]

41. See Clark Griffith, "Sex and Death: The Significance of Whitman's *Calamus* Themes," *Philological Quarterly* 39 (1960): 18–38.

A dark side in Whitman is almost always imminent if of course never preeminent.[42]

Likewise, Emily Dickinson's first competent poem (#10, 1858) complains, "My wheel is in the dark," and anxiety is the form her humility takes for hundreds of poems after that. The connecting link of the poems of her most productive years, 1860–64, is what she calls "that precarious Gait / Some call Experience" (#875, 1864). And "To try to speak, and miss the Way" (#1617, 1884) is a theme persisting to her latest verses. Though both poets developed what they felt were adequate defenses against these needs—fantasies, assertions, language—at the Hawthornian level of the Fall, whenever both would admit to the general fate, they produced best. In them we have success born of reproducing their failings in verse. American literary hagiography is assisted more by knowing their common interest in such earthly paradoxes than by knowing their separate platonic-transcendentalist successes, over which they themselves were sometimes troubled anyway.

The Whitman of "the great Idea," I am trying to suggest, was also a Dickinsonian neurotic, and the Emily Dickinson of "sumptuous Destitution" laid her hopes in follies heavy with celestial/millennial exoticism like Whitman's. Their ecstasies and epiphanies are almost always qualified by disappointments. The two writers are closest not so much in their ideas of their subjects as in their neurasthenia. Though Whitman was not renewed by the disorder as Emily Dickinson was, did not have as adequate a rhetoric for disappointment and despair, and did not know as well how to classify his frenzy and depravity, he appears, when we put their poetry side by side, as much a poet of disequilibrium as she was. That both tried to be lovers of an unqualified/unqualifying universe—with Whitman stretching out his arms to embrace the chaos as a *system* of disorders, a "Kosmos . . . includ[ing] divinity," and with Emily Dickinson "spreading wide [her] narrow Hands / To gather Paradise?"—did not keep them from caprice and hysteria, from fevers. Their infatuations were not unconditional. They coped with wonder by wondering if it was all wonderful.

With regard to the firmness in the world that Richard Chase mentions, on a number of darker subjects Emily Dickinson is, to be sure, a good deal more daring than Whitman. The subject of death,

---

42. It is necessary to disagree with Stephen Black that Whitman's conflicts were regressive and his frustrations unresolved and debilitating. That is irrelevant. What is more significant is Whitman's determination, like Emily Dickinson's, to use poetry as a means of coping.

for instance, obsesses them about equally. They are stoical about its possible ultimacy, troubled about its ultimate possibilities. Death for Whitman is a system of esthetics, to be experienced now.

And again death, death, death, death...
My own songs awaked from that hour,
And with them the key....

["Out of the Cradle Endlessly Rocking"]

But in Emily Dickinson's death verse she has to try death out, to get as close to it as possible in order to know what it means:

Just lost, when I was saved!
....
Therefore, as One returned, I feel,
Odd secrets of the line to tell!

[#160]

Where Whitman uses death to stir his imagination, Emily Dickinson uses her imagination to find ways of risking death without really dying. Imagination comes for Whitman after the fact of death; for Emily Dickinson imagination is needed before the fact of death so that she can face it. She risks it as much as she imaginatively dares to. For Whitman death remains by and large an *issue*.

On another dark subject, confronting the demonic, Emily Dickinson is more honest than Whitman in her daring. Whitman is willing to make the satanic "equal with any, real as any," and willing to admit duplicity in reality:

(This is curious and may not be realized immediately, but
   it must be realized,
I feel in myself that I represent falsehoods equally with
   the rest,
And that the universe does.)

["All is Truth"]

But on this score Whitman equivocates; evil is just another form that good takes, is really subsumed by the good.

the truth includes all, and is compact just as much
  as space is compact,
And that there is no flaw or vacuum in the amount of the
  truth—but that all is truth without exception;
And henceforth I will go celebrate any thing I see or am,
And sing and laugh and deny nothing.

["All is Truth"]

Emily Dickinson does not equivocate but sees a problem in the moral order of the universe and tries to confront it directly:

> Whether Deity's guiltless –
> My business is, to find!
>
> [#178]

> We apologize to thee
> For thine own Duplicity –
>
> [#1461]

> God of the Manacle
> As of the Free
> Take not my Liberty
> Away from Me –
>
> [#728]

She dares address herself to the "windy will" of God; Whitman can only talk to himself. She is capable of bitter irony over the universal arrangements ("the thoughtful grave,... The cautious grave"); Whitman has perceptibly little irony; for the most part his good has no underside, his surfaces no lies, his knowledge few equivocations. She can imagine herself at a metalevel, outside the given and the experienced, and see the assumptions, the sources, the means; Whitman takes up a position among results, accepting being as being all. She thus confronts the demonic, setting herself *there*. It is a form of suspicion. It is her faculty for disappointment.

To cope with such chaos and frustration, the troubling facts and specifics of "the World," they had *poetic method*—or what Emily Dickinson called the "bells" that "just cooled [her] Tramp." Both show the hope of containing their anxieties: Emily Dickinson with the severely institutional tool of hymn meter and Whitman with the illusion of a rhythmic form organic to his bodily functions. Both fail themselves, of course—or rather, they succeed in escaping their own arbitrary controls—for Emily Dickinson developed an extravagant diction with little or no contingency on the rhythm, and Whitman's run-on stychomythia with himself became for the most part poetry-in-process rather than produced poems. By and large their methods of ordering their lives through poetic form did not work. We can more often identify them by their mishandlings—Whitman's uncontrolled catalogs and Emily Dickinson's fragmentation. They give themselves away as lost lovers of the inverse. Form was an inadequate check on the possible. The Tramp survives.

I do not wish to suggest that a common element in the poetry of

Emily Dickinson and Whitman is a parade of lapses, or that we can best enjoy that work of theirs that disappoints their most heavily promoted hopes and well-being, but only that when their lives reflected some of the disorder they recognized in the world and when that reflection is itself reflected in what and how they wrote, then we have poetry of a very modern kind. Then they work *with* nature as they recognized it rather than against it. Coping for them meant living with the frustration of facts, about the world, about themselves, and about its hold on them. They did not prize their souls more than the universe but prized experiences more than sequences or systems, and that meant exerting their senses to discover the possible, however incoherent. "And if indeed I fail," Emily Dickinson wrote in a poem of 1860, "At least, to know the worst, is sweet!" (#172).

The meaning the two found in the *things* of their lives suggests that they found they could not *will* the world. This retrenchment is one of the major contributions of late nineteenth-century American literature; Whitman and Emily Dickinson are its brightest representatives, their poetry the key transition to modern realism. *All* things of the world are available for and necessary to programs and fantasies, for ideals and hopes. Anything goes—suggesting how they considered an individual's deficiencies as determiners of a civilization's flexibility and subtlety. Democracy in American literature begins with their fearlessness before nature, the frustrations of their own nature, and the frustrating nature of the world. Their confusion—their Inclusion Principle—made the form of their art.

CO-OPTING AMERICA

One additional way Whitman was "disgraceful" to Josiah Holland, and perhaps also then to Emily Dickinson, was his presumptuousness—one of the things I believe he meant when he referred to Whitman's "eccentricity of mind and temperament." The "Bardic Symbols" that Emily Dickinson read in the *Atlantic* and the *Republican* in 1860, like a majority of Whitman's early poems, has him in the presumptuous role of self-appointed spokesman/generator-generalist/professional typifier: "Because I have dared to open my mouth to sing at all . . . I close with you." The danger here is not his persistent presuming so much as his very inventive *sub*suming, his "closing" with everything, his successful subjective expropriation of materials for new ends.

Whitman is our early literature's most skilled co-opter. He takes the means used by others to define something—America, the self,

God—and uses them to satisfy his own personal needs. Co-optation is the process of subsuming an idea for one's own end, canceling out its conservative intent. It means taking all things into account and adjusting them to one's sense of reality, including them. It is not the process of translation or transfusion but of suborning, usurping, expropriating, dispossessing. In the process, all things become impregnated with subjectivity, as one perceives oneself behind all things. All universality is merely one's mask. Everything is an excuse for one's autobiography. One's temperament is one's sole doctrine. The self infests all things. In a broad gesture, one's personal needs become converted into criteria, into the sole reality. "Wonderful to be here!..." Whitman asserted, "To be this incredible God I am!" It is a considerable poetic skill.

It is Emily Dickinson's too—on, of course, different subjects and out of different motives. Her ability to use her poetry to co-opt a world for herself is perhaps equally "disgraceful."

When Whitman announces, as he does in "By Blue Ontario's Shore," perhaps the poem best defining his role:

> I myself make the only growth by which I can be appreciated,
> I reject none, accept all, then reproduce all in my own forms,

he is playing co-opter. His America, for instance, is not just anybody's America, not just *an* America, but Whitman incarnate, with all things reproduced in *his* own forms. "America isolated yet embodying all, what is it finally, except myself?" Whitman and the nation become one, not by his identification with what it is but by taking idealized features of himself and naming *them* "America" with "his spirit surrounding his country's spirit." That is different from typology, wherein the ego abrogates its sources, fusing autobiography and political faith, and different from Emersonian compensationism, wherein the nation is redeemed by one's superior example,[43] and also different from poetic fascism, wherein megalomania overwhelms the social facts through language.[44]

43. See Sacvan Bercovitch, *The Puritan Origins of the American Self* (New Haven, 1975), pp. 181–86, for a discussion of Whitman as maker of "the Myth of America." Bercovitch finds Whitman working the same method as Cotton Mather, fusing/confusing self and nation. But the important difference is Whitman's sexual motivation for his Christian politics: he is hungry for all American bodies to be united with his own, whereas Mather just wants to whip everybody into line and is convinced that the nation is whole when everybody follows his own perfect example. The one is a fascist working by equivocating his biblical terminology, the other a glutton for friendship.
44. See Quentin Anderson, *The Imperial Self* (New York, 1971), pp. 88–118, for this argument. Anderson's Whitman is blindly assertive and self-righteous, a True

Whitman's process of co-optation is more than a matter of identification—with the nation, with God, with the self, whatever—and it is more than a matter of consumption, that is, of transferring features of nation, God, and self to make up the mythic persona Walt Whitman. It is more a matter of Whitman conceiving of an ideal self and then giving it various interchangeable names—America, God, soul—and undercutting and eliminating others' conceptions and definitions and thereby establishing his own. This escapes the inherited; the subjectivity is revolutionary; oneself becomes a nation—*the* nation ("I will make cities and civilizations defer to me, / This is what I have learnt from America . . . O I see flashing that this America is only you and me"), *the* God ("Taking myself the exact dimensions of Jehovah"), *the* self ("I swear I will have each quality of my race in myself, . . . Surrounding the essences of real things"). He sees "One common indivisible destiny for All" simply because he reproduces all things in his own image. All is appropriate because expropriated. For Whitman things correspond, merge, corroborate (variants of these terms make a rather consistent motif in all his writings) because all get read the same. The universe becomes one soul, one person, and named for him: "Walt Whitman, a kosmos."

More, then, than an identification with things American or an inclusiveness of certain things to *make* an American identity. Whitman's art of co-optation makes a new America no different from the idealized Whitman himself. In his 1855 Preface, he defines co-optation in terms of personal incarnation: "[The poet's] spirit responds to his country's spirit, . . . he incarnates its geography and natural life. . . . To him enter the essences of the real things and past and present events—of the enormous diversity. . . . Off from him things are grotesque or eccentric or fail of their sanity. Nothing out of its place is good and nothing in its place is bad. He bestows on every object of quality its fit proportions neither more nor less. He is the arbiter of the diverse and he is the key." The poet is therefore the provider of "equivalents out of the stronger wealth of himself" that will subsume all things in himself. Whitman looks out and sees (constantly, lovingly) himself. "I tread master here and everywhere."

"As the attributes of the poets . . . emit themselves," he continues, "facts are showered over with light. . . . What answers for me an American must answer for any individual or nation that serves for a part of my materials." Such co-opting is a political act, for Whitman

---

Believer who arrogated his flabby emotions above the social contract. But Anderson does not entirely recognize Whitman's politics of selfhood: one creates space for one's own life by asserting one's needs against those of the state.

wishes to alter the nerves and marrow of a nation by substituting the large dimensions of his own nerves and marrow for what others have outlined as America around him. It is thereby transformed into his personal ideal, and self and nation become one—"the great Ideal Nationality of the future, the Nation of the Body and the Soul." Only in this way is his idea of "a great composite *Democratic Individual*" the same as his idea of "an aggregated, inseparable, unprecedented, vast, composite, electric *Democratic nationality.*"

Whitman the Co-opter shows how millennialism is largely a matter of art, a matter of making definitions artfully. One's autonomous existence must be attractively projected as a national ideal. It is a matter of proclaiming. *Leaves of Grass* is a book of visions, and Whitman's millennialism is an attempt to create an alternate vision to that of the past (embodied in the current state), but since the past is all-inclusive, really omnipresent, one must take its terms and, in order to shape the alternative, deliberately distort them to mean what they would mean *without* the past. The stolen instruments make a different music. The form remains but the content—and then of course the result—is new. Oneself is the past embodied, but since terms define the uses of the past, a distortion/expansion of the terms is necessary if one is to be oneself at all. The past thereby becomes provocation. The ideal is possible, in true prophetic manner, only by lying. Anarchy (the millennial future) is possible only in conservative guise. The millennialist is a charlatan, a poet. Such poet-liberators are those who get us some new epistemes. Co-optation is one way of getting some new ones: new wine under old labels makes a different kind of drunk. So Whitman's ostensible patriotism is ultimately disloyal, and, similarly, Emily Dickinson's apparent Christianity is heretical. Co-optation is artful deception. One is taken in.

The America around Emily Dickinson to be co-opted was not at all the same as the one around Whitman. In earlier chapters I have tried to describe it in terms of an inherited piety of considerable substance softened to a smug moralism and a repressive set of manners, against which she had some rather remarkable defenses, mainly the invention of her poetry. Her daring coped. It co-opted part of that world, too, and in a way similar to Whitman's.

What there was for her to co-opt was the ready-made Christian life. In its semidoctrinal form—"Mine - by the Right of the White Election! / Mine - by the Royal Seal!"—she took conventional, ritualized terms (here, from covenant theology) and, without resorting to irony, came up with something very personal: being alive is exhilarating, self-sufficing, pride-inducing, ego-building—surely an anti-Puritan pose. She deritualizes the terms through idiosyncratic use.

The conservative terms are used but the conservative intent is canceled out, making the assertion of herself possible.

This can also be seen in a similar poem of 1862: the theology of grace is expropriated to suggest its opposite ("'twas Otherwise"), a self-derived "Majesty." Common grace is special enough.

> The Day that I was crowned
> Was like the other Days –
> Until the Coronation came –
> And then – 'twas Otherwise –
>
> As Carbon in the Coal
> And Carbon in the Gem
> Are One – and yet the former
> Were dull for Diadem –
>
> I rose, and all was plain –
> But when the Day declined
> Myself and It, in Majesty
> Were equally – adorned –
>
> The Grace that I – was chose –
> To me – surpassed the Crown
> That was the Witness for the Grace –
> 'Twas even that 'twas Mine –

[#356]

The terms (no doubt ones of wide acceptance bearing up the church at the time) have been wrenched from their institutional contexts, not allowed their conventional connotations, and made to serve something entirely different, the heretical assertion of autonomous being ("'twas Mine").

In other poems, she expropriates phrases from the Lord's Prayer for excitement over her garden and the items in it normally excluded from religious grace ("In the name of the Bee – / And of the Butterfly – /And of the Breeze – Amen!"). She takes biblical references honoring God and turns them into private disappointment at divine intentions ("Sparrows, unnoticed by the Father – /Lambs for whom time had not a fold"). She uses the conventional terms giving heaven an elevated time and place and makes them serve the epiphanal excitements of her own present passions ("My *Kingdom's worth* of Bliss!"). She saves such a word as "grandeur" from officialdom by expropriating it to represent her personal heresy. She makes Christian humility serve her own private thrills:

> "They have not chosen me," he said,
> "But I have chosen them!"
> Brave – Broken hearted statement –

Uttered in Bethleem!

I could not have told it,
But since *Jesus dared* –
Sovreign! Know a Daisy
Thy dishonor shared!

[#85]

The result is a homemade religion to suit her: the old terms are made
to mean their opposites; the rituals are stolen and deritualized; the
sacred is desecrated; the forms are reformed. She has subsumed the
received and sustained her heretical desires by stealing terms to name
her private heresy. The allusions function as camp; the naiveté is
revolutionary. She can therefore claim inoffensively, as she does in
one poem, "Some keep the Sabbath going to Church – / I keep it,
staying at Home." Old labels stuck on new spices yield a different
delight.

Her popular (because apparently faith-promoting) poems are
often co-opting tricks.

I never saw a Moor –
I never saw the Sea –
Yet know I how the Heather looks
And what a Billow be.

I never spoke with God
Nor visited in Heaven –
Yet certain am I of the spot
As if the Checks were given –

[#1052]

The pastoral metaphors here, like those in the Psalms, lead one gently
and submissively in conventional hymn meter to an identification with
the church's projection of the abstracted Other in the usual trite
terms, God and heaven. But Emily Dickinson has her own way with
such matters, upsetting faith-promoting expectations, for she imagines speaking with a personally interested God, a presumptuous tic
forbidden by the Bible; and she imagines visiting in heaven after the
manner of rural New England neighbors, a personally fanciful projection. She even imagines salvation as simply a matter of "Checks,"
that is, tickets or communion stubs or some such. God is friend and
heaven a spot and salvation a quick ride. The metaphors bring the
hoped-for down to earth, and the present known becomes itself a
measure of that hoped for. Within the apparent orthodoxy, Emily
Dickinson achieves a personalized experience: she has her heaven
now. Through co-opting, the given thus becomes a sharing of something of her own world; Scripture thus becomes a poem; fate thus

becomes a measure of free will. She can have cake for her communion and not easily get caught; she can be something of herself while appearing to be what was expected.

Christianity is thus dispossessed for her by her poetry. She dared to try to replace it without changing its name very much. Just as Whitman created an ideal out of his own personal desires and then advertised it as "America" for popular consumption, thereby tricking the public into utopia (or hoping to), so Emily Dickinson called her little heresies by orthodox names and got away with something of a life of her own. Both were foolish, of course, to think they could bring it off for long. One only needs to open another eye to see when a revolutionary is using establishmentarian terms as a cover to gain his new ground. The poet-cheat is politic, is artful. Whitman's America is a made world overwhelming other realities with a personal ideal made attractive, and Emily Dickinson's Christianity is a made universe covering older possibilities and succeeding, for her, in their name. The co-opting thereby provides a new option, a future.

That both could thus create identities out of old materials is perhaps their confession that they recognized that identity is an illusion: it can be *created*. What remained as a lesson of the co-opting was, I believe, a gradually worked-out conviction of what *is* sure: the creator/creature creating. Identities/roles are concoctions—and in Whitman and Emily Dickinson fanciful and energetic concoctions of their two Americas—but the actor acting, the player playing, the writer writing is a dependable fundamental. America is an illusion; the poet and his/her energy are not.

On these sample subjects I do not wish to make Emily Dickinson compete with Whitman at all, but rather to appear cooperative. They share a set of interests, though articulated very differently. These are the two poets Emerson brought to a boil in the nineteenth century. I argue that perhaps they both boiled *over*. They are messy Emerson. They are Emerson (to add a metaphor of my own) in riotous color.

The affinities with Whitman reveal that within all of Emily Dickinson's sweetness, there is indeed a wolf—a characterization she made of her own needs at one point.[45] The poet is an assertive. Poetry is daring. Audacity is an esthetic. With just such a sensibility, to shift the metaphor, she worked to make herself as "visible" as possible in what she called "a mighty Crack," the Creation. There are rewards to the risk:

45. *Letters*, p. 777.

Kill your Balm - and it's Odors bless you -
Bare your Jessamine - to the storm -
And she will fling her maddest perfume -
Haply - your Summer night to Charm -

[#238]

Ten

WHEN THE SOUL IS AT PLAY

Emily Dickinson and Robert Frost

The Poets light but Lamps – ...
Disseminating their
Circumference –

[#883]

The legacy of Emily Dickinson to the poets of the twentieth century—a final set of American affinities—has been a strong one, if not always acknowledged. She could be invoked as evidence of a rich American past. She could serve as model, example, sister. She could be used as spur to experimentation, to going beyond the limits. She is the All-American Poetess as Myth.

This is not to say that in the history of twentieth-century American poetry Emily Dickinson has had a commanding presence, an aura, a large voice, the way Poe, Emerson, and Whitman assuredly have had. She has been more of a pretty assumption. "Oh, yes, and there is/was Emily Dickinson!" She comes as a surprise—but not one really to be dealt with, to be absorbed and surmounted, not one to face and face up to. She is not necessary. Only a treat. To read her now—as Frost, especially, has taught us to do, to focus in on one important instance—is to learn to play, to learn a player, to learn play. Send in the clown.

The continuity/survival of nineteenth-century American writers into a crasser, more accomplished, and critical century is a largely unwritten story. Poe made it mainly because he was lost and then exported by the French. Emerson made it because everybody became his parrot: the prophet organized a long-range following. Whitman made it because so many of his disciples for a half-century were sexual partisans, both homophobes and homophiles, who misrepresented him to get him noticed. The others—Thoreau, Hawthorne, and Melville have become the most obvious examples—are the work of academics in the role of saviors resurrecting the neglected elect. Most of the rest, deservedly, did not make it.

Emily Dickinson's poetry worked in none of these ways. By and large she entered the twentieth century on sheer audacity, hers and her champions'. The shy motives and meek look of her first appearance in print in the 1890s ought to have been enough to determine her future otherwise. Against the odds, some of the features of her wildness got her through the barriers of the beginning of a wild century.

We have an instance of her early influence when William Dean Howells used Emily Dickinson to move Stephen Crane to write his first poetry, which went into *The Black Riders*. There is a tone of the apocryphal about the story, as if ready-made for my argument: right at the outset the posthumous Emily Dickinson was stimulating to other writers.

Howells admired Emily Dickinson's poetry sufficiently to think it would move fledgling versifiers to better work. In a review essay on her in *Harper's* in 1891, he referred to her "weird witchery," her "eerie Fancy," her "almost hysterical shriek." He was surprised by the roughness and rudeness and the "harsh exterior of her poems." He called her, in conclusion, "an abrupt, exalted New England woman."[1]

Then one evening in April 1893 in New York, as the story goes, Howells invited Stephen Crane to tea—the one an impoverished young man in need of some encouragement with his writing, the other a literary broker gathering disciples—and read Crane some poems by the "new" poet Emily Dickinson. *The Black Riders* was written during the course of the next year. Apparently Crane admired the poetry enough to find it a stimulus to trying his hand at serious verse—though there was not, admittedly, any mention of her in his letters or journalism at the time.[2]

1. William Dean Howells, "Editor's Study," *Harper's Monthly* 82 (1891): 318–21.
2. Daniel Hoffman, *The Poetry of Stephen Crane* (New York, 1956), pp. 205–6;

T. W. Higginson himself was to remark, quite wrongly, I feel, that he regarded Crane as "an amplified Emily Dickinson . . . [who] thought as nakedly and simply" as she did.[3] Hamlin Garland was to write soon afterward that Crane's poems "carried the sting and compression of Emily Dickinson's verse."[4] And Carl Van Doren soon after that was to exclaim that "The poems of Emily Dickinson . . . have no heirs except Crane's ironic verse in their own century."[5]

But in spite of such vague and forced links, for Crane Emily Dickinson was merely a stimulus, as distinct from a source or affinity.[6] She may have only assisted in creating a condition in American culture in the 1890s for Crane to emerge in. Her first volumes may have helped make an audience for his.

If Crane was following Emily Dickinson in any manner, he only proved he did not know how to listen to or read her very well, for he gets the poetics, the ideology, the idiom, the roles all wrong. Except for helping to create a public for his lines, she is largely irrelevant to his history. She may have started him off (via a Howells who made her out to be a bold, odd figure), but that is all. Of his own first poems Crane said, "It is the anarchy which I particularly insist on."[7] Perhaps Emily Dickinson helped liberate him to that end. One might suspect that she was of similar service to other writers in the 1890s.

The first really serious promoter of Emily Dickinson was Amy Lowell. She came to a reading of her (and of Whitman) in Clarence Stedman's *An American Anthology* of 1900.[8] Stedman's inclusion of

---

Joseph Katz, Introduction to *The Poems of Stephen Crane: A Critical Edition* (New York, 1966), p. xx. "When Howells climaxed the evening by reading aloud some poems of Emily Dickinson," writes Kenneth S. Lynn in *William Dean Howells: An American Life* (New York, 1971), p. 312, "it was clear to Crane that his host had no idea of his own aspirations as a poet."

3. T. W. Higginson, "Recent Poetry," *Nation* 61 (24 October 1895), p. 296.

4. Hamlin Garland, *Roadside Meetings* (New York, 1930), pp. 143–44.

5. Carl Van Doren, "Stephen Crane," *American Mercury* 1 (January 1924): 11.

6. The indebtedness of Crane's line "A man adrift upon a slim spar" to Emily Dickinson's line "Two swimmers wrestled on the spar" (#201), as suggested by several, is possible, though Crane's poem was not written until 1897, four years later, and was written on the occasion of the sinking of the S.S. *Commodore* on which he had been riding. A closer parallel is the line "God is cold" and Emily Dickinson's line "Oh God! the Other One!" from the same poem. There are no other convincing parallels with Crane's verse.

7. In Katz, *Poems of Stephen Crane*, p. xxvii.

8. Virginia Terris has written a valuable account, "Emily Dickinson and the Genteel Critics" (Ph.D. diss., New York University, 1973): "Although her reviewers included the forward-looking W. D. Howells and Bliss Carman, most of her support came from those associated with the Genteel group—Noah Brooks, Louise Chandler

these two was daring. He was probably the main force behind Amy Lowell's (and a number of others') initial interest in her. Stedman's hearty approval of Emily Dickinson, as Horace Gregory reminds us, performed the service of removing official doubts of her genius.[9] The inclusion appears to have encouraged the acceptance of free verse and irregularly metered, epigrammatic verse as a new kind of poetry that could be considered American in its scenery, language, and emotions. The choice of Emily Dickinson was a first step in the broader recognition and influence of such. She was for Amy Lowell and others shortly thereafter "an original" and so laid a precedent for the writing of experimental verse that would break older conventions. Along with E. A. Robinson and Stephen Crane, she was promoted as a forerunner of a kind of poetic renaissance, a cause for originality. In a very short time, Amy Lowell, Harriet Monroe, Edna St. Vincent Millay, and others made her their precursor in daring.

Stedman's Emily Dickinson encouraged in Amy Lowell an attitude that was close to Henry Adams's in 1911: the poet as rebel.

> Poetry [in the late nineteenth century] was a suppressed instinct: and except where as in Longfellow it kept the old character of ornament, it became a reaction against society, as in Emerson and the Concord school, or, further away and more roughly, in Walt Whitman. Less and less it appeared, as in earlier ages, the natural, favorite expression of society itself. In the last half of the nineteenth century, the poet became everywhere a rebel against his surroundings.[10]

This attitude might explain how the need of Amy Lowell and others for precursors, real or imagined (made in order, perhaps, to root their minirevolution in poetic tradition), turned them in the direction of, mainly, Crane and Emily Dickinson. "Emily Dickinson and Stephen Crane had, as a trait shared in common," Amy Lowell wrote, "only audacity."[11] So she liked the story of Crane shocked by Howells's reading Emily Dickinson. "The impact of this perfectly fresh and spontaneous poetry," she wrote in her introduction to the 1922 edition of *The Black Riders,* "shook him profoundly, even to the sudden shooting up in him of a latent poetical urge. So moved, he

Moulton, Maurice Thompson, and Robert Bridges and others—whose aesthetic philosophies dominated the publishing world of the decade. Edmund Clarence Stedman, as spokesman for the American literary hierarchy, enunciated the principles of Genteel criticism in *Poets of America.* . . . The Genteel group viewed Dickinson as a good but minor poet."

9. Horace Gregory, *Amy Lowell: Portrait of the Poet in Her Time* (New York, 1950), pp. 56–58.

10. Ibid., p. 57.

11. Amy Lowell, Introduction to *The Black Riders* (New York, 1926), p. x.

wrote. . . . One can be fecundated by an art without the least desire to follow it, and Emily Dickinson may have been Crane's spark."[12] Emily Dickinson was thus used to support an experimental poetics she would not easily have recognized and an assertive circle she would not easily have joined. Amy Lowell worked up Emily Dickinson ultra-modern and sensational—perhaps her image of herself. But of course she had to radicalize her considerably to get a precursor in her.

After Stedman's canonization of Emily Dickinson and after noticing Crane's stimulation by her, Amy Lowell spoke and wrote repeatedly of her, selling her almost everywhere she went as poetic mother and sister. "One little voice, . . ." she wrote in 1916, "was the precursor of the modern day. A voice considered only as bizarre and not at all important, by its contemporaries. I refer to Emily Dickinson, who is so modern that if she were living today, I know just the group of poets [with] whom she would inevitably belong."[13] Emily Dickinson thus became, to Amy Lowell at least, the first Imagist. "[She] was published in 1890, more than twenty years before Imagism as a distinct school was heard of," Amy Lowell gloated, "but [her] reception shows that the soil was already ripe for sowing."[14]

Amy Lowell could be sure about Emily Dickinson the Modernist only after elevating her intellectual myopia and esthetic daring to primary traits of her character. "The world exists for [Emily Dickinson] solely as she sees it, and her carelessness in the matter of whether she exists for her readers or not is wholly admirable. This is maturity."[15]

Emily Dickinson's daring, to Amy Lowell, was proved best by her resistance to Puritan tradition. She was to her "a true anomaly, . . . a true pagan poet shut up in the cage of narrow provincial Puritanism."

> But the odd part of this poet was that the cage was not merely the exterior one of family and surrounds, it was the cage of her own soul. . . . She was a pagan if ever there was one, but she was also a sincerely religious woman. This led her to address poems to the Deity in so joyous and familiar a strain that her first biographer wrote many pages to explain her seeming irreverence. But really there was no explanation except the one I have given. But one cannot help feeling that sincere though her religious attitude certainly was, it was due partly to early education, and partly to atavism (her father was a minister), while

12. Ibid.
13. Amy Lowell, "The New Manner in Modern Poetry," *New Republic* 6 (4 March 1916): 124–25.
14. Amy Lowell, *Poetry and Poets* (Boston, 1930), p. 93.
15. Amy Lowell, Introduction to *The Black Riders*, p. x.

her own peculiar, personal characteristic was the pagan one. I have often wondered whether this duality of temperament was not responsible for the shyness and elusive quality which she is said to have had in a marked degree. In wider surroundings might she not have developed into a greater poet and a more tranquil woman? It is significant that those of her poems most prized by her contemporaries are the ones we care least for today.[16]

Making her "racy and forthright in her verse" and finding a whimsy balanced off by brutality, Amy Lowell considered Emily Dickinson "one of the greatest women poets who never lived" because, as she put it in a letter to Emily Dickinson's editor and apologist Millicent Todd Bingham in 1922, she could put her "half a century ahead of her time" among poets and critics hungry for a bolder, freer poetic theory.[17] She canonized Emily Dickinson as the leader of an aggressive new esthetic movement:

> She never knew that a battle was on and that she had been selected for a place in the vanguard; all she could do was to retire, to hide her wounds, to carry out her little skirmishings and advances in by-ways and side-tracks, slowly winning a territory which the enemy took no trouble to dispute. What she did seemed insignificant and individual, but thirty years after her death the flag under which she fought had become a great banner, the symbol of a militant revolt. It is an odd story, this history of Imagism, and perhaps the oddest and saddest moment in it is comprised in the struggle of this one brave, fearful, and unflinching woman. . . . The times were out of joint for Emily Dickinson. Her circle loved her, but utterly failed to comprehend. Her daring utterances shocked; her whimsicality dazed.[18]

Amy Lowell made Emily Dickinson both very feminine and very wild, and so she was sometimes out of patience with her eccentricities and narrow background.

> Frail little elf,
> The lonely brain-child of a gaunt maturity,
> She hung her womanhood upon a bough
> And played ball with the stars – too long – too long –

16. Amy Lowell, in S. Foster Damon, *Amy Lowell: A Chronicle* (Boston, 1935), pp. 331–32. See also Jean Gould, *Amy: The World of Amy Lowell and the Imagist Movement* (New York, 1975).
17. Letter to Millicent Todd Bingham, 9 August 1922, quoted in Damon, *Amy Lowell,* p. 611. In this same letter Amy Lowell wrote that it was a dream of hers "sometime to write a life of Miss Dickinson," which, however, never materialized.
18. *Poetry and Poets,* pp. 88–90.

Until at last she lost even the desire
To take it down.[19]

At times she ignored her altogether.[20] Yet she constantly recommended her boldness and inventiveness to poets on both sides of the Atlantic and to any public audience that would listen to her on the subject. In her tribute "The Sisters" ("Why are we / Already mother-creatures, double-bearing, / With matrices in body and in brain?"), she makes Emily Dickinson a woman who "would set doors ajar and slam them":

> I rather think I see myself walk up
> A flight of wooden steps and ring a bell
> And send a card in to Miss Dickinson.
> Yet that's a very silly way to do.
> I should have taken the dream twist-ends about
> And climbed over the fence and found her deep
> Engrossed in the doing of a humming-bird
> Among nasturtiums. Not having expected strangers,
> She might forget to think me one, and holding up
> A finger say quite casually: "Take care.
> Don't frighten him, he's only just begun."
> "Now this," I well believe I should have thought,
> "Is even better than Sappho. With Emily
> You're really here, or never anywhere at all
> In range of mind." Wherefore, having begun
> In the strict centre, we could slowly progress
> To various circumferences, as we pleased.
> We could, but should we? That would quite depend
> On Emily. I think she'd be exacting,
> Without intention possibly, and ask
> A thousand tight-rope tricks of understanding.
> But, bless you, I would somersault all day
> If by so doing I might stay with her.
> I hardly think that we should mention souls
> Although they might just round the corner from us
> In some half-quizzical, half-wistful metaphor.
> I'm very sure that I should never seek
> To turn her parables to stated fact.

19. *The Complete Poetical Works of Amy Lowell* (Boston, 1955), pp. 460–61. In addition, in her "Critical Fable" in 1922, Amy Lowell paid tribute to Emily Dickinson as the only American poet of the past, besides Poe and Whitman, whom she "sincerely admires."

20. "After the days of Whitman and Edgar Allan Poe," she wrote in a letter in 1919, "there was a decided slump in the quality of poetry written in this country. The main tendency seemed to be toward a diluted Tennysonism, and it was not until the year 1912 that a new vigour became visible." In Damon, *Amy Lowell,* p. 169.

Sappho would speak, I think, quite openly,
And Mrs. Browning guard a careful silence.
But Emily would set doors ajar and slam them
And love you for your speed of observation.[21]

Apart from making a model poetic rebel out of her, Amy Lowell's motives for choosing Emily Dickinson as the chief precursor of her poetic revolution are not entirely clear. She may have seen in her a fellow lesbian. Or she may have wanted to keep her own poetic roots American and New English and feminine. Or she may have indeed learned something from her, however wide of the mark. Amy Lowell intended a biography of Emily Dickinson, but she did not get around to writing it. Had it been as long and loving as her monument to Keats, it would have been a heroic creation showing Emily Dickinson's ability at tyranny over one. She forms us, awkwardly.

Emily Dickinson may actually have had something to do with some of the minor Imagists' view of images. To Amy Lowell she was "past mistress of suggestion . . . and, to a lesser degree, irony"; "form (conventional form) was utterly disregarded"; and "The exact word, the perfect image, that is what makes these short poems so telling."[22] Emily Dickinson was to Amy Lowell an Imagist because when what she wanted to say clashed with conventions of rhythm, rhyme, and image, the conventions "went to the wall." "Her genius revolted." In addition, she was for the Imagists a phenomenologist: "She, first of all in English I believe, made use of describing of a thing by its appearnace only, without regard to its entity in any other way." Only the Imagists, to Amy Lowell, were also to do this.[23] The discovery was largely self-projection.

But, as I am suggesting, Emily Dickinson was to the Imagists much more a figure of audacity, of freedom, of daring, of rebellion, than any esthetic theoretician. It was really necessary for Amy Lowell to radicalize Emily Dickinson for what she considered her radical new movement in poetry. To her the verse was "wholly original, so that it must give free rein to individualistic freedom of idea." Emily Dickinson "fit the Imagist canons."[24] "The speech of her poems," Amy Lowell concluded, "is almost without exception strong, direct, and almost masculine in its vigour."[25]

We can never know entirely if Emily Dickinson sat in Amy Low-

21. *Complete Poetical Works*, pp. 460–61.
22. Amy Lowell, Introduction to *The Black Riders*, p. x; *Poetry and Poets*, pp. 93, 102–3.
23. *Poetry and Poets*, pp. 103–8.
24. Ibid., pp. 95–96.
25. Ibid., p. 97.

ell's mind as she worked to make the New Poetry a contoversy and as she helped fashion the Imagist credo of 1915, asking for precision of metaphor, freedom of rhythm, and concentration of format. The rhythmic result, after all, was vers libre, not hymn meter; the metaphoric result was slight, tough synecdoche, not ambiguity; and the motive was programmatic, not therapeutic.

If the history of twentieth-century poetry began with Emily Dickinson, as Amy Lowell liked to claim, it did so mainly because of the date of her emergence. In the 1890s she was about the only new poet around. Nobody had heard of her and so the surprise was great. A new American poet was discovered and established. And, largely because Amy Lowell and others *failed* to understand her metrics and metaphors, they were able to establish her as a radical innovator. They failed to see that she was not merely a "pagan poet" confined within Puritanism but wrote entirely from within the New England tradition of dissent. In 1915, however, this side of Emily Dickinson was obscured by the vague but apparently useful idea that she had been something of a deliberate literary rebel.

Amy Lowell was, however, a fairly poor salesperson among her closest poetic associates. Much as she may have helped popularize the poetry of Emily Dickinson and others, she interested only a few of her Imagist friends in reading nineteenth-century American poetry. Hilda Doolittle and Richard Aldington turned to ancient Greek and modern French poetry instead, Ezra Pound to the Provençal and Chinese, and John Gould Fletcher to contemporary impressionistic verse and to Japanese.[26]

Perhaps with her assistance, however, Carl Sandburg did honor to Emily Dickinson ("that picaresque [picturesque?] Amherst wraith of a girl and woman has always fascinated and instructed me")[27] with

26. Amy Lowell's Imagist acquaintances gave only the slightest nods in the direction of Emily Dickinson. Richard Aldington included eight of her poems in his *Viking Book of Poetry of the English-Speaking World* (1941). John Gould Fletcher refers to her only once in all his critical writings: "Sara Teasdale had refined her lyricism to a simplicity of statement that was very moving and very human. . . . I admired her art, equally compounded of the quietism of Christina Rossetti and the emotional intensity of Emily Dickinson" (*Life Is My Song* [New York, 1937], p. 280). Amy Lowell herself has several poems that sound like Emily Dickinson grafted onto Whitman, and Hilda Doolittle could on occasion catch Emily Dickinson's tone. Emily Dickinson was of interest mainly to women writers in the first couple of decades of the century, perhaps because she was a woman. The image of her as a woman was in their minds at a time when her life was known only poorly. Perhaps she radicalized them to write, although it is sheer conjecture what her specific influence might have been, whether in the use of hymn meter in the early poems of Sara Teasdale or in the emotional intensity of Edna St. Vincent Millay's poems.

27. *The Letters of Carl Sandburg*, ed. Herbert Mitgang (New York, 1968), p. 465. See also his references to "the elusive quality of Emily Dickinson" (p. 255) and "The compressions of Emily Dickinson" (p. 336).

several verses, seeing in her poetry an ideal combination of sentimentality and fact.[28] And Marianne Moore, through association with Imagists, may have come to share with her what R. P. Blackmur called "an excessive sophistication of surfaces and a passionate predilection for the genuine."[29] The two most certainly shared an interest in im-

28. LETTERS TO DEAD IMAGISTS

Emily Dickinson
You gave us the bumblebee who has a soul,
The everlasting traveler among the hollyhocks,
And How God plays around a back yard garden.

ACCOMPLISHED FACTS

Every year Emily Dickinson sent one friend
the first arbutus bud in her garden

....

So it goes. There are accomplished facts.
Ride, ride, ride on in the great new blimps—
Cross unheard-of oceans, circle the planet.
When you come back we may sit by five hollyhocks.
We might listen to boys fighting for marbles.
The grasshopper will look good to us.

So it goes...

PUBLIC LETTER TO EMILY DICKINSON

Five little roses spoke
for God to be near them,
for God to be witness.

Flame and thorn were there
in and around five roses,
winding flame, speaking thorn.

Pour from the sea
one hand of salt.
Take from a star

one finger of mist
Pick from a heart
one cry of silver.

Let be, give over
to the moving blue
of the chosen shadow.

Let be, give over
to the ease of gongs,
to the might of gongs.

Share with the flame won,
choose from your thorns,
for God to be near you,
for God to be witness.

Complete Poems of Carl Sandburg (New York, 1968), pp. 73, 226–27, 670.
29. R. P. Blackmur, *The Double Agent: Essays in Craft and Elucidation* (New York, 1935), p. 171.

pertinences, leaps of wit, a propensity for hyperbole, a zest for extravagance, and taking the eccentric and fast way out—that is, in intellectual play.[30]

Someone else who promoted Emily Dickinson as an Imagist was Amy Lowell's friend Harriet Monroe, who, like her, identified what she called "the lithe nudity" of Emily Dickinson's images with a "wildly rebellious pagan imagination":

> Emily Dickinson, New England spinster of the nineteenth century, was an unconscious and uncatalogued Imagiste. She had the visual imagination, the love of economy in line and epithet, the rigorous austerity of style, and the individual subtlety of rhythm, demanded by the code of the contemporary poets who group themselves under that title. Born a Puritan her shy soul brooded upon the abstract, but her wildly rebellious pagan imagination at once transmuted the abstract into the concrete, gave it form and color.[31]

Again, Emily Dickinson is the delicate-poetess-as-rebel. "Emily Dickinson climbs much higher," she wrote shortly after this,

> than either Elizabeth [Barrett Browning] or Christina [Rossetti]; in fact, she presents a formidable claim to Sapphic honors. Her brief poems— many of them—have a swift and keen lyric intensity, a star-like beauty. They are sudden flashes into the deep well of a serene and impregnable human soul, sure of the truth in solitude. They celebrate the eternal theme—search of the mystery, the meaning of life, the relation of the human soul to the beloved of this world and of the world of vision beyond; and especially they illumine the soul's quest of the infinite, of God.[32]

To Harriet Monroe, Emily Dickinson was the most important woman poet of the past—if not a model for Imagists, at least the model for contemporary women.

Others touched by the Imagist theory though not very much by the clique—D. H. Lawrence, William Carlos Williams, and e. e. cummings—took much more easily to Whitman than to Emily Dickinson. (Whitman, Pound wrote, is "the only one of the conventionally

30. See also the connections between the two suggested by Jean Garrigue, "Emily Dickinson, Marianne Moore," in *Festschrift for Marianne Moore's Seventy Seventh Birthday*, ed. Tambimuttu (New York, 1964), pp. 52–57. George W. Nitchie comments on the "formidable intelligence, formidable wit, and formidable eccentricity" of the two. They were "poets who characteristically achieve their effects through surprise and the strategic violation of decorum" (*Marianne Moore: An Introduction to the Poetry* [New York, 1969], p. 17).

31. Harriet Monroe, Review of *The Single Hound*, *Poetry* 5 (December 1914): 138–40.

32. Harriet Monroe, *Poets and Their Art* (New York, 1926), p. 65.

recognized American Poets who is worth reading." "The free verse of Walt Whitman," Williams wrote, "opened my eyes.") One would not know from the comments about poetry and poets by most of them that the Emily Dickinson promoted by Amy Lowell and Harriet Monroe had existed.

I wish, however, that one could claim for Emily Dickinson a definite affinity with the chief twentieth-century phenomenological American poet, William Carlos Williams, however indirect or faint. His contact with Amy Lowell and the Imagist accomplishments (which, however, he branded "half-hearted"), along with his pride in nineteenth-century American poetry ("for the first time in America... literature is *serious*, not a matter of courtesy but of truth"), and his hunt for a new realism ("If I succeed in keeping myself objective enough, sensual enough, I can produce the factors, the concretions of materials by which others shall understand and so be led to see their own world"), suggest a possible interest in Emily Dickinson. Williams very likely came to the reading of Emily Dickinson at about the same time as he read Whitman, and like those around him he came to think of her as someone who wrote, as he put it, "rebelliously" and with "authenticity." Later he was to remember some of the same qualities of his own verse in hers: "a fastidious precision of thought,... a swiftness impaling beauty; ... a rapidity too swift for touch." One gets the feeling that he regarded her, though in a much more limited way, as one who, like Whitman, "broke through the deadness of copied forms." But he appears not to have been unusually fascinated with her.[33]

Perhaps there is a good reason why Imagism would not fit Emily Dickinson very well. The image to her is loaded with values, something the Imagists tried to reduce or at least to deny. Their phenomenological audacity sought facts for poetry and images as further poetic facts. But for Emily Dickinson there are only messages filtered through a changeable value system. There are no ideas *in* things, just as her Puritanism had taught her; the things do not *mean;* they are *not* values. Imagism would have seemed to her reductive, oriental, austere, passive, thin. For her, instead, the image is an episteme—a possibility, a way of seeking to know, and therefore ex-

---

33. William Carlos Williams, *Selected Essays* (New York, 1954), pp. 123, 155, 218. None of these comments are directly about Emily Dickinson. The first is made in passing in a discussion of Emerson's conventionality. The second is made to highlight features of Marianne Moore's rhythm. The last is an exclamation about Whitman. Emily Dickinson's poems appear to have been little more to Williams than an assumption. A small irony, however, about Williams: his grandmother's name was Emily Dickenson!

pansive of feeling and understanding, often to the point of becoming lost, chaotic, ambiguous, absurd. Her epistemes do not control, are not controlled, but, as she said of her poetry at one of her more playful moments, "range Possibility." Epistemological rather than phenomenological, with images she made for herself some new possibilities for thinking.[34]

In fact, it is questionable whether Emily Dickinson assisted at all in the liberation of Modernist verse, either in the new principles and judgments or in the possibilities of performance. She did not show very well that expressive rhythms were more effective than familiar meters. She did not justify erratic rhymes as appropriate only to erratic states of mind. She did not sell obscurity as an esthetic, or subtleties and complexities of form either. She did not help put the anarchic into American poetic tradition. Nor did she help define the lyric gift in the new terms of subversive ideology, esoteric learning, mysterious images, scandalous self-revelation, or devotion to literature. By contrast, her line—if there is one at all—is the poetry of ceremony: language that is different from workaday speech, hymnlike stanzas that are metered and rhymed, an often soothing morality, or what George Steiner has called "the composite picture . . . of calling, isolation, insistent gravity of the sort we associate with the Victorian manner."[35]

Pound, Williams, and other phenomenological poets, following Imagist hopes, made of images a *letting be.* But because for Emily Dickinson life was manipulative and uncontrolled, so was imagery. Poetry therefore, for her, struggles with and creates neurotic states of mind, where theirs attempts to go *with* found energy and speed. Hers encourages emotions or represses them. It is the means of entertaining and distracting us. More oriental, the phenomenologizing Moderns found most concepts transparent, things themselves the only meanings, and freedom the absence of struggle with ego, ideas, or things. Her particular way was to work with the one phenomenal given: her raw, rugged, neurotic, fascinating, unsurrendering self. For Emily Dickinson there was integrity in confusion and complication; basic simplicity would have meant little to her, nor would have objects *in sich.* Puritanism kept her from improving the situation of the watcher of phenomena. She is stuck, instead, in performance: she is to be watched. In her we have personality in place of panorama.

Her poems make a space in which she can dance. They are spaces (rather than, as with the phenomenological poets, objects in a

34. Robert Weisbuch argues otherwise: "Dickinson's poetic techniques generally put the question aside to examine things-as-they-are, a procedure which anticipates modern phenomenology" (*Emily Dickinson's Poetry,* p. 160).
35. George Steiner, "Woman's Hour," *New Yorker,* 5 January 1976, p. 71.

space) where she is dancing. *She* is the presence in the space made. A poem is less a made thing than a thing making something else—an idea, an emotion, an impression, a response, a personality.

In fact, Emily Dickinson's poetry works very much against what Kingsley Widmer calls "the profound Modernist insight that cultivated sensibility will neither redeem the self nor the society."[36] Emily Dickinson's *only* salvation is in a cultivated performance, her poetry. She can believe in no other means. The Fall for her did not make the world a wasteland.

One advantage of the near-total absence of Emily Dickinson in the reading and life of American Moderns is that we do not know her through *them,* the way we may have come to know Eliot's Dante and Milton, Pound's Orient, Williams's Whitman, Frost's Emerson, Faulkner's and O'Neill's Puritanism. "The 1920s were so powerful," Alfred Kazin writes, "in establishing the new taste that even Melville, Dickinson, Henry Adams, Whitman did not become popular until then."[37] But, if that is the case, they appear to have made her the public frog she had seen coming and protested against without having really read and discussed her very much. They actually found no real "revolution of the word" in her, no "new ways of seeing," nothing that (in Pound's phrase) "makes all things new." She was never seriously in their class.[38]

Except to one of them, who did not fit very well in their class either—Hart Crane. Crane, often seeking in the American past reasons for an American (and personal) future, found in Emily Dickinson a fellow tragedian: the intuitive poet who knew how to fail beautifully. It was his definition of America. Where Amy Lowell and others in the earlier decades of the century made her the embodiment of a latent rebel tradition in American culture, Crane invoked her as an

36. Kingsley Widmer, "*The Waste Land* and the American Breakdown," in *The Twenties,* ed. Warren French (Delano, Fla., 1975), p. 477.

37. Alfred Kazin, "On Modernism," *New Republic,* 17 January 1976, pp. 29–31.

38. It is nonetheless necessary to be appreciative of the efforts of George Whicher and Louise Bogan to link Emily Dickinson with the Moderns, if only tenuously. Whicher wrote in 1955: "[Emily Dickinson] stands as a precursor of the modern mind, whom we have not yet fully overtaken.... At a time when everything ... was tagged with an ethical message, Emily believed that a hummingbird, a snake, a mushroom, or a blade of grass was poem enough if she could only get it on her page" (*Poetry and Civilization* [New York, 1955], p. 200). Louise Bogan added: "The influence of Emily Dickinson's 'great' period on the generation of Auden, if not that of Eliot, is inestimable. She had instinctively, on her own, 'wrung the neck of rhetoric'; cleared out the trash from her versification, condensed her observation to a sharp focus.... Her influence is not yet fully absorbed; she still stands open toward the future" (*Selected Criticism* [New York, 1955], pp. 293–94).

American archetype of the endurer. I think he felt he had figured out how she had made it through, how *he* could.[39]

In the "Quaker Hill" section of *The Bridge,* Crane puts Emily Dickinson in company with Isadora Duncan as the two highest spirits acting out the American tragedy, "transmuting silence with that stilly note / Of pain that Emily, that Isadora knew!" For him, she had a

> heart of fright, [that]
> Breaks us and saves, yes, breaks the heart, yet yields
> That patience that is armour and that shields
> Love from despair—when love foresees the end—

This is Crane trying to approximate Emily Dickinson's voice as he heard it: through her he finds the patient means to endure the failure of his hopes. Emily Dickinson (along with Blake) Crane imagined as one who kept faith in the ideal even as she realized how it failed in the world, and, while to him such a life transcends fear of death, it is tragic because unsustainable.[40] Even as others had been making her a female Emersonian anarchist, Crane was making her a female Emersonian believer. She kept *a* faith.

Loving both her idealism and her failure at it, Crane wrote of her (autobiographically, of course):

To EMILY DICKINSON

> You who desired so much—in vain to ask—
> Yet fed your hunger like an endless task,
> Dared dignify the labor, bless the quest—
> Achieved that stillness ultimately best,
>
> Being, of all, least sought for: Emily, hear!
> O sweet, dead Silencer, most suddenly clear
> When singing that Eternity possessed
> And plundered momently in every breast;
>
> —Truly no flower yet withers in your hand,
> The harvest you descried and understand
> Needs more than wit to gather, love to bind.
> Some reconcilement of remotest mind—
>
> Leaves Ormus rubyless, and Ophir chill.
> Else tears heap all within one clay-cold hill.

39. Babette Deutsch writes: "Hart Crane ... derived from Rimbaud and Emily Dickinson rather than from Donne and Laforgue" (*The Modern Poetry* [New York, 1935], p. 229).

40. See Crane's comments on Emily Dickinson in his *Letters,* ed. Brom Weber (New York, 1952), p. 324.

Here Emily Dickinson is the failed overachiever, the beautifully failed seeker, the frustrated woman as mystic, the immortal botch, the American poetess as divinely called catastrophe. She "desired so much" with her "remotest mind," yet everything she (and Crane) possessed was "plundered momently" by life's defeating realities. But blessing came to her in the past, and comes to him in the present, for having tried. For him Emily Dickinson is a figure of tragedy, for she had been hurt by life, which hurt however had yielded her her art, and by writing she had risen above the hurt. The American struggler thus has salvation *in* his/her work. Emily Dickinson, for Crane, had made the Protestant ethic a Protestant esthetic.

As critical interest in Emily Dickinson in the twentieth century has waxed and waned—sometimes to great extremes—one affinity with her has remained constant: Robert Frost's. Among twentieth-century poets, his affinity has been the most substantial; his reading of her seems to me to have been the major one. Hyde Cox writes: "Frost believed she was one of the great American poets. I suspect he would have given second place to Emerson."[41] The rating should come as no surprise, though the reasons and the reservations might.

"Poetry," Frost said on one occasion when he was living in Amherst, "has never been woman's business. We don't know enough Sappho to know how good she was. We've had Christina Rossetti, Elizabeth Barrett, Alice Meynell, Edna Millay, . . . but Emily is bigger than all those. You would have to call her the greatest woman *writer* in the history of the world." In writing to his friend Robert Hillyer, Frost called Emily Dickinson "a genius, but mad," and said she was "the best of all the women poets who ever wrote, from Sappho on down." And to Louis Mertins he said on one occasion, "Emily wrote fine lines— right from the soul."[42]

41. Letter, 26 June 1977.
42. Hyde Cox, in conversation with Frost (letter, 26 June 1977). Cox cautions further: "When Robert Frost referred to Emily Dickinson as 'the greatest woman poet' and then, going further, as 'the greatest woman *writer* in the history of the world,' I am sure he was not trying to belittle her greatness by using the word 'woman.' In fact, . . . he agreed with my statement that she was one of the great American poets." G. Armour Craig recalls that Frost was "not very rational about lady poets in general, and about American poetesses in particular" (letter, 26 February 1977). "What [women poets] lacked," Frost said to friends on one occasion, "was balls" (Robert Frost and Charles H. Foster, "Miscellaneous Documents Pertaining to Their Friendship [1931–1963]," unpub. MS., p. 118). Louis Mertins remembers Frost saying that the three American poets who were the most important to him were Emily Dickinson, Thoreau, and Emerson. "Emily Dickinson was the best of all women poets who ever wrote" (*Robert Frost: Life and Times—Walking* [Norman, Okla., 1965], p. 385). Reginald Cook also remembers Frost's

It was not that Frost ever set her in a historical context in order to think of her as great—and he most certainly never associated her with anything like the making of a "New England tradition"—or that he ever thought her great because she was of poetic service as spur, muse, or co-rebel, the way Stephen Crane, Amy Lowell, and Hart Crane did. Instead, he admired her, even a little jealously (in the honorific sense), for what he considered her own phenomenal poetic achievements. "Here I come with my truth," he said he imagined her saying to us, and this made him "feel her strength."[43]

Like Stephen Crane, Frost was also called to tea-and-poetry by Howells in the 1890s, but he had come to Emily Dickinson on his own and was to do so considerably more securely than most other poets in the two decades following. While a student at Lawrence High School, in 1892, Frost read the poems when they first appeared; one of his first gifts to Elinor, his wife-to-be, when they were both in high school, was a book of Emily Dickinson's poems.[44] He later told his biographer, Lawrance Thompson, that what he liked about her at that early point was that she was "terse, homely, gnomic, cryptic," but more than that, he was "fascinated to find that this new author was also 'troubled about many things' concerning death. It seemed to him that while she developed an extraordinary capacity for running the gamut of moods in her various imaginative confrontations with death, the poems which act deepest for him were those which expressed her doubt whether any reasons fashioned by the mind concerning life in heaven could compensate for the heart's compassionate and instinctive regrets over the transience of earthly bliss."[45]

Frost read Emily Dickinson before the Imagists did, certainly before the 1915 revival, and his interest never waned; he lived with Emily Dickinson from the beginning of his writing of verse.

Frost got over the fascination with her ability to tease death and other troubles, however, and soon centered instead on the forms of her playing. He became chiefly interested in her expression—not her ideas and certainly not her life.[46] Perhaps that is because he did not

---

canonizing her in much the same way: "She's the greatest lady poet who ever lived. . . . She was, I think. That's true" (*A Living Voice* [Amherst, 1974], p. 162). See also Robert Hillyer, *A Letter to Robert Frost and Others* (New York, 1937), p. 4.

43. Cook, *The Dimensions of Robert Frost* (New York, 1958), pp. 57–58.
44. Mertins, *Robert Frost*, p. 385.
45. *Robert Frost: The Early Years, 1874–1915* (London, 1966), pp. 123–24, 509–10.
46. Frost told Reginald Cook that he was not interested in Emily Dickinson's life, even though arguments about her lovers boiled around him in Amherst for years (*A Living Voice*, p. 57). Kathleen Morrison remembers, however, Frost's being "interested in biographical details of the [Dickinson] family" (letter, 25 February 1977).

have to contend with Emily Dickinson as he did with Emerson the Social Idealist and Emerson the Egalitarian Esthete. Frost found in Emily Dickinson, almost as he did in Thoreau ("a one-man revolution"), the example of the Emersonian rebel. So he was attracted to her energy but was not uncritical of her typically Emersonian inability to submit to bounds and limits. Because suspicious of spontaneity in writing, Frost was critical of any such in Emily Dickinson. The formal control of her energy interested him the most. And for that reason, among the Emerson traditions coming into the twentieth century, Frost falls more nearly into the line of Emily Dickinson than that of Whitman.

The major affinity between Frost and Emily Dickinson—the issue of play and control, of freedom and form—is, I suggest, a New England one (perhaps one could even say it is a Connecticut River Valley issue, from Edward Taylor and Jonathan Edwards through to Emily Dickinson and Frost) and one that Frost almost always spoke of whenever he brought up Emily Dickinson's poetry.[47] He said she was in his head, in his nature; he said he knew "how to take her."[48]

47. It is necessary to respect Frost's resistance to persistent critical attempts to locate him in terms of a New England tradition or any regional attachments. He said he felt a "sympathetic detachment" from his New England poetic predecessors. Charles Foster has made a good attempt to locate Frost within a New England tradition with links to Emily Dickinson mainly because they share humor and a sense of human tragedy (Charles H. Foster, "Robert Frost and the New England Tradition," *University of Colorado Studies in the Humanities*, ser. B, 2 [October 1945]: 370–81). Others have insisted on historical connections, though almost always vaguely. See, for example, James M. Cox, "Robert Frost and the End of the New England Line," in *Frost: Centennial Essays* 1 (Jackson, Miss., 1976): 545: "There are probably many New England lines, but the one I shall pursue begins with Emerson, and ends with Frost," and includes "the incorrigible Emily Dickinson.... Certainly Emily Dickinson and Robert Lowell share much with Emerson, Thoreau, and Frost. They are rebels in the original revolutionary sense."

48. Cook, *A Living Voice*, pp. 243, 247. I think it is not possible to speak of borrowings by Frost from Emily Dickinson in the same way one could from Emerson and Thoreau. Yet the few parallels suggest some direct influence.

Emily Dickinson:

We apologize to thee
For thine own Duplicity –
[#1461]

It's such congenial times
Old Neighbors have at fences ⤴
[#529]

Frost:

Forgive, O Lord, my little tricks on Thee,
And I'll forgive Thy great big one on me.
[CP 428]

I let my neighbor know beyond the hill;
And on a day we meet to walk the line
And set the wall between us once again.
["Mending Wall"]

Frost lived in Amherst for quite a number of years—1917–20, 1923–25, 1926–38, and then intermittently in the late 1940s and throughout the 1950s when he taught regularly at Amherst College.[49] He often recited her poems from memory, and he conversed with students, friends, and townspeople about her poetry;[50] his concern was almost always over her ability to contain/limit an open-ended universe. He felt this was "what Emily Dickinson surely intends," as he put it, "when she contends: 'In insecurity to lie / Is Joy's insuring quality.'"[51]

It appears that Frost had a one-track mind about Emily Dickinson—her doggedness. For him she was an example of the poet "whose 'state,'" as he put it himself, "never gets sidetracked."

> Since she wrote without thought of publication and was not under the necessity of revamping and polishing, it was easy for her to go right to the point and say precisely what she thought and felt. Her technical irregularities give her poems strength as if she were saying, "Look out, Rhyme and Meter, here I come."

Frost apparently liked this willfulness, this unmanageability of the thought by the poetic form, and yet he thought she arrived at it a little too easily and that it was therefore sometimes indistinguishable from

---

Since then – 'tis Centuries – and yet
Feels shorter than the Day
I first surmised the Horses Heads
Were toward Eternity –
[#712]

She now felt younger by a thousand years
Than the day she was born.
["A Masque of Reason"]

This is not to suggest, however, as George Monteiro does in "Emily Dickinson and Robert Frost," *Prairie Schooner* 24 (1977): 369–86, that although Emily Dickinson's poetry was often in Frost's mind during his first decade as a poet, we have proof of substantial influence. We do not know that "her example had shown him the way to the kind of poetry he then wanted to write." See also George Monteiro, "Robert Frost's Dickinson Books," *Emily Dickinson Bulletin*, #33 (first half, 1978): 3–7.

49. Elaine Barry, in *Robert Frost on Writing* (New Brunswick, 1973), p. 50, refers to "the bibliographical evidence of his much-used copy of her poetry, which is filled with short pencil marks beside favorite poems. One wishes Frost had been more of a scribbler in margins. The full examination of his debt to her . . . has yet to be made." Frost's copy of Emily Dickinson is in the Special Collections Library at New York University; there are merely ticks beside a score of the titles and a word here and there. Other anthologies Frost used, now at the Jones Library, Amherst, also show ticks besides the titles of several of her poems.

50. Hyde Cox remembers, for instance: "I used to drive him to Amherst and stay with him in the Inn (where a suite was set aside for him) for a few days each year. At night, after we dined somewhere (and often it was late at night) he always wanted to take a walk before retiring to bed. In Amherst the usual walk took us by Emily Dickinson's front door, around her garden and up hill past the graveyard where she lies buried. Our walks were always *tout en causant*" (letter, 26 June 1977).

51. Cook, *A Living Voice*, p. 280. The poems Frost appeared to have been the most interested in were as follows:

carelessness. He felt she had given up the technical struggle too easily. For Frost, to use a general statement of his about poetic rhythm, she was a little too "easy in [her] harness."[52]

Emily Dickinson succeeded, Frost was forced to admit, by flouting poetic systems, by playing freely with the form.

> I try to make good sentences fit the meter. That is important. Good grammar. I don't like to twist the order around in order to fit a form. I try to keep to regular structure and good rhymes. Though I admit that Emily Dickinson, for one, didn't do this always. When she started a poem, it was "Here I come!" and she came plunging through. The meter and rhyme often had to take care of itself.[53]

Though envious of this carefree energy, Frost was also critical of her when she did not achieve regular forms.

> Emily Dickinson didn't study technique. But she should have been more careful. She was more interested in getting the poem down and writing a new one. I feel that she left some to be revised later, and she never revised them. And those two ladies at Amherst printed a lot of her slipshod work which she might not have liked to see printed. She has all kinds of off rhymes. Some that do not rhyme. Her meter does not always go together.[54]

She was therefore substantially different from him; her ability to be conscious of poetic conventions and yet to rise above them surprised him. He generously yielded her his highest admiration for the heresy.

> One of the great things in life is being true within the conventions. I deny in a good poem or a good life that there is compromise. When there is, it is an attempt to so flex the lines that no suspicion can be cast

---

#1173 – The Lightning skipped like (Frost: "that kind of play")
  mice
#757 – The Mountains – grow   (Frost: "reminds you that poetry is
  unnoticed   play")
#1732 – If Immortality unveil   (Frost: "the very curious use, the
  A third event to me   brilliant use")

Favorites of his, according to Cook and Cox:

#1078 – The Bustle in a House
#536 – The Heart asks Pleasure – first
#303 – The Soul selects her own Society –
#986 – A narrow Fellow in the Grass
#516 – Beauty – be not caused – It Is
#1129 – Tell all the Truth but tell it slant
#1295 – Two Lengths has every Day

52. Robert Francis, *Frost: A Time to Talk* (Amherst, 1972), pp. 53–54.
53. Daniel Smythe, *Robert Frost Speaks* (New York, 1964), p. 140.
54. Ibid.

upon what the poet does. Emily Dickinson's poems are examples of this. When the rhyme begins to bother, she says, "Here I come with my truth. Let the rhyme take care of itself." This makes me feel her strength.[55]

For him the large strain of poetry was "a little shifted from the straight-out, a little curved from the straight." Emily Dickinson's poems were, for him, the best examples of this liberty, this flawing. "Can you imagine some people taking that? Can't you imagine some people not accepting that kind of play at all?"[56]

It was this factor of play in Emily Dickinson's poetry that consistently attracted Frost. "Rime reminds you that poetry is play," he said on one occasion, after reciting a Dickinson poem ("The Mountains – grow unnoticed") and calling it "particularly fine," "and that is one of its chief importances. You shouldn't be too sincere to play or you'll be a fraud."[57] Her mischief with poetic form was an indication to him that she was serious about what she was saying and would bend conventions to get it said, and also that she was having a good time trying to say it, but more important than that, that with her poetry (and her ideas) she was *at play*. He appears to have marveled at that in her. "Poetry," Frost used to exclaim to his friends, "is fooling."[58]

The important point is that play, in Frost's own poetry, is the corrective to his subject matter. It is the Emily Dickinson in him. He called his poems "my toys" coming from "my innate mischievousness."[59] But with Frost this mischievousness is generally serious play—it is written for a purpose, to make a point, or as a symbol. It is an entirely different thing when he is concerned with the ways such formal factors as rhythm and rhyme let us know that "poetry is play."

Frost was mainly interested in how poetic form can help "make [something out] of a diminished thing," and yet, like his oven bird, "he knows in singing not to sing," that is, not to place more value on the singing than on the thing sung about. "Wildness . . . has an equal claim with sound to being a poem's better half," Frost wrote in his 1949 apologia "The Figure a Poem Makes," "[but] theme alone can steady us down. . . . The . . . mystery is how a poem can have wildness and at the same time a subject that shall be fulfilled."[60]

The double desire here for Wildness and for Fulfillment is a Puritan duplicity: be serious about the serious, knowing that the ways

55. Cook, *Dimensions*, pp. 57–58.
56. Ibid., p. 99.
57. Ibid., p. 180.
58. Ibid., p. 181.
59. *Selected Letters*, ed. Lawrance Thompson (New York, 1964), p. 344.
60. *Collected Poems* (New York, 1949), pp. v–vi.

you are serious are foolish artifices and therefore playful. Of all the poems Frost knew and commented on during the course of his life, Emily Dickinson's appear to have been the best examples of the Puritan at Play.

For Frost, "all the fun's in how you say a thing," and when "the aim was song," the central concern for him was to get things out/down "by measure."

> From form to content and back to form, . . .
> From sound to sense and back to sound.
>
> [CP 431][61]

There was one side of Frost that saw poetic form as a way of creating "a stay against confusion," and this was very much like the side of Emily Dickinson that exclaimed to T. W. Higginson in 1862, "I could not drop the Bells whose jingling cooled my Tramp." Frost concurs:

> The lowly pen is yet a hold
> Against the dark and wind and cold
> To give a prospect to a plan
> And warrant prudence in a man.
>
> [CP 364]

This reveals the deist in Frost: form to reflect a desired order, man's design to represent the Grand Design. It is the conservative in him as well: the poet as self-appointed orderer of a chaotic world. It is Frost reacting against experimentation and facile liberalism.

But there was the other side to Frost as well: the wild, the playful—or what Emily Dickinson referred to in herself as "the Kangaroo."

> The sentencing goes blithely on its way,
> And takes the playfully objected rhyme
> As surely as it keeps the stroke and time
> In having its undeniable say.
>
> [CP 491]

This is the side of Frost that James Dickey refers to as his "elephantine local New England humor," his "elephantine levity."[62] This side often finds Frost playing the roles of rascal and sly fox, but, more than that, it finds him fooling around in a disciplined fashion, varying factors within a code, inventing with the given, creating within the Creation. He too is the Puritan at Play.

61. Ibid., p. 431.
62. Donald J. Greiner, " 'That Plain-Speaking Guy': A Conversation with James Dickey on Robert Frost," in *Frost: Centennial Essays* 1 (Jackson, Miss., 1976): 46, 59.

This duplicity in Frost—that is, rhyme and meter as both checks on confusion and toys of one's humility before the confusion—is a creative tension in his poetry. Playing with artifice, he makes an order for himself. He debates the end of the world in "Fire and Ice," for instance, with a dogtrot meter and humorously repetitive rhymes to let us know he is *playing* with the apocalyptic:

> Some say the world will end in fire,
> Some say in ice.
> From what I've tasted of desire
> I hold with those who favor fire.
> But if it had to perish twice,
> I think I know enough of hate
> To say that for destruction ice
> Is also great
> And would suffice.

The effect here is an ironic limiting of his speculations and at the same time an announcement that he is toying facetiously with that over which he has absolutely no control. His little ordering of the language makes it possible to face chaos. Rhyme and meter come to the rescue when cosmic structure fails him. In his fear of designlessness, he makes a design of his own, knowing it is all human invention and therefore to be mocked—and treasured. Poetry thus makes it possible for the Puritan to survive the terror, enjoying it all. In Puritan esthetics, the fearful and the cheerful are interchangeable. Poetry is play with the world; the little toys of rhyme and meter are human toys of endurance.[63]

Emily Dickinson played away, too, but a little too fast and freely for Frost's taste, a little too "easy in [her] harness." Frost wrote in a letter, "A real artist delights in roughness for what he can do to it," that is, for how he can control it.[64] But Emily Dickinson was interested in what she could do *with* the roughness, that is, what possibilities there were for a voice of her own within the ordering. Herein lies the

---

63. Joseph J. Comprone makes some valuable suggestions concerning Frost's interest in play but sees him as someone who writes *about* playing (as in "Mending Wall": "Oh, just another kind of outdoor game, / One on a side. It comes to little more") rather than as someone who used his poetry itself as a form of play. ("Play and the 'Aesthetic State' [in Frost]," *Massachusetts Studies in English* 1 [1967]: 22–29.) Marjorie Cook has suggested (accurately it seems to me) that Frost's playful attitude in his poetry was meant to counter his own dark side. ("Acceptance in Frost's Poetry: Conflict as Play," in *Frost: Centennial Essays* 1 [Jackson, Miss., 1976]: 223–35.) In still another discussion of play in Frost's poetry, Walton Beacham argues that the playful rhythm and rhyme are almost always used ironically, thus rendering the play playful. ("Technique and the Sense of Play in the Poetry of Robert Frost," ibid., pp. 246–61.)

64. *Selected Letters*, ed. Lawrance Thompson (New York, 1964), p. 465.

major difference between the two. Frost could not handle such "compromises" himself, he said, but he granted that *she* could.

Frost was the type of *Homo ludens* that J. Huizinga describes as someone who finds *significance* in play, who uses language as a way of playing with a world parallel to nature, who defines the esthetic in terms of the creation of another order of things, who enjoys a system of play rules that fix the range of forms to be used. It is one way of defining a poet, one way of understanding Frost as a poet. "If it is with outer humor," Frost wrote, "it must be with inner seriousness. Neither one alone without the other under it will do."[65] The significance of the play is the important thing. "Play," Huizinga wrote, "is a voluntary activity of occupation executed within certain fixed limits of time and place, according to rules freely accepted but absolutely binding, having its aim in itself and accompanied by a feeling of tension, joy, and the consciousness that it is 'different' from 'ordinary life.'"[66] Emily Dickinson was this kind of player but also something more, and because of that she became the object of Frost's criticism and envy.

Puritanical thinking allowed only children to play games; the adult, because of the fully developed sense of good and evil, had to take frivolity seriously—which meant turning games into magic—and therefore could never wholeheartedly enjoy it. But in Emily Dickinson, as in Frost, there was a streak of the pagan that could not take everything seriously, though the two did not escape their consciousness of what is serious and what is not. Art for them was not magic but the toys of the fallen.

For Emily Dickinson, play was a way of transcending the rational. Play with poetic forms—or rather, in spite of them—was freedom. Play was for her a way of combating causality, the determined, even instinct itself. Play was an action outside and above the necessities of life. Play was abandon, diversion, riddle, improvisation. Emily Dickinson-the-poetic-heretic was a spoilsport, violating the rules of the game of poetry-making and then inventing her own. The refusal to fit gave her her possibilities; her "technical irregularities," Frost admitted, gave her "strength." That play could result in power was a factor inherent in Puritan esthetics surfacing well in Emily Dickinson's playfully willful jaggedness. The "flaws" are themselves a form. They are the best example in American literature of humanity as comedy: the Fall is a form of joy; to be human is to be a clown; to be fallen is to play.

65. Introduction to Edwin Arlington Robinson, *King Jasper* (New York, 1935), p. xx.

66. J. Huizinga, *Homo Ludens: A Study of the Play-Element in Culture* (Boston, 1955), p. 28.

"[Emily Dickinson's] words and phrases," T. W. Higginson commented in his introduction to her *Poems* in 1890, "are often set in a seemingly whimsical or even rugged frame."[67] The irregularities are not at all to be taken as an imitative fallacy, however, as has often been argued, with the off-rhymes and nonrhymes and collapsed syntax and idiosyncratic rhythms representing some kind of defeat, struggle, frustration, suspense, failure, disillusionment, or any number of other gross psychic maladies. That reads her poems in the wrong direction, inductively from their face to hers. Rather, such features are those of someone of immense inventiveness at play.

> Meek[ly] at [the] everlasting feet
> A Myriad Daisy play[s] –
>
> [#124]

At play, the "Myriad Daisy" is free to create and at the same time is meek before "[the] everlasting feet." That is, she is alive with human possibilities.

Charles H. Foster remembers Frost's saying on one occasion that he "could find flaws all through the Oxford Book of English Verse [but] that he preferred the kind of *natural* flawing to the modern kind. The old kind in Emily Dickinson was like the natural flaw in glass, showing that it was handmade."[68] These (to Frost, genuine) "flaws" are primitive features in her writing that she could justify as being effective for her poetic purposes:

> A Word dropped careless on a Page
> May stimulate an eye
>
> [#1261]

She thus knew the effectiveness of letting the language make its own way, have its own say, even when pushed into or emerging from given forms. "The power to contain," she wrote, "Is always as the contents" (#1286), and that led, as Frost recognized, to "technical irregularities" that made it possible for her "to go right to the point and say precisely what she thought and felt." She therefore appeared to him as someone "whose 'state' never gets sidetracked," that is, as an unregenerated woman whose unregeneracy paid off in poetic surprises.

Emily Dickinson referred to her own form/formlessness as her "spasmodic gait." But this was not so much a matter of having given up "the technical struggle," as Frost maintained, as it was a matter of flouting any such struggle. The careless word and the spasmodic meter stimulate and enliven *because* careless and spasmodic. She

---

67. Introduction to *Poems* (Boston, 1890), p. xx.
68. Foster, "Miscellaneous Documents."

therefore proceeded to write by what in one poem she called her "homely gift and hindered words" (#1563).

In another poem she said of the song of one of her birds ("a bold, inspiriting Bird") that it was

> Brittle and Brief in quality –
> [With] Warrant in every line –
>
> [#1177]

This is Emily Dickinson herself. The "Warrant" was primary in her own songs and was possible, as Frost pointed out, *because* of the brittleness, and the content was "stimulat[ing to] an eye," as she put it, *because* of the "spasmodic gait." Willfully flouting poetic forms, she could therefore have some of the characteristics of what she called "The Bird of Birds":

> Of impudent Habiliment
> Attired to defy,
> Impertinence subordinate
> At times to Majesty.
>
> Of Sentiments seditious
> Amenable to Law –
> As Heresies of Transport
> Or Puck's Apostacy.
>
> Extrinsic to Attention
> Too intimate with Joy –
> He compliments existence
> Until allured away.
>
> [#1279]

Her little defiances and heresies needed a "spasmodic gait" to succeed. The play impulse in her gave her her freedom.

There was a system of thought of sorts behind these poetics that was to be like Frost's. For Emily Dickinson, play was part of the Fall. "Earth at the best," she appears to have believed, "Is but a scanty Toy – " (#1024).

> We play at Paste –
> Till qualified, for Pearl –
> Then, drop the Paste –
> And deem ourself a fool –
>
> The Shapes – though – were similar –
> And our new Hands
> Learned *Gem*-Tactics –
> Practicing *Sands* –
>
> [#320]

Life itself was a game to be played without knowing exactly why. Any poetic scheme is a *made* scheme. It could therefore be maintained or violated as one wished to make an order or to show oneself getting free of/within order. For New Englanders like Emily Dickinson and Frost rhythm and rhyme are not natural but are human artifices. For her eagerness and ability to play with forms, Emily Dickinson was one of Frost's people who are not "a fraud." That is because rhyme and rhythm, for both of them, were a confession that they knew they were toying with the Creation. The Fall has its forms of joy.

Existence burdened her; yet she never exhausted her surprise at it. Thus the failure of most of her renunciations: one cannot always believe them. Her play with her delights—in idea and in form—is much more convincing.

But the cosmic game was, for her, only mockworthy and not something she was willing to play with any convincing seriousness.

> We dream - it is good we are dreaming -
> It would hurt us - were we awake -
> But since it is playing - kill us,
> And we are playing - shriek -
>
> [#531]

And yet Emily Dickinson's interest in play comes less from a cosmic sense of the absurd than from a belief that order, traditions, systems, institutions, and all forms are to be played with. With the one, one gives up on sense; with the other, one tries to make some sense. When, as she put it, "oftentimes, among my mind, / A Glee possesseth me" (#326), she often found that "the least push of Joy / Breaks up my feet - /And I tip - drunken - " (#252). For that reason she needed a check on what she called her "Barefoot Vision." Her play with poetry— what she called her "Shapes"—was, as it was for Frost, a means of staying the confusion, foiling the Fall, cooling the Tramp in her:

> A Frost more needle keen
> Is necessary, to reduce
> The Ethiop within.
>
> [#422]

But at the same time the given forms, both cosmic and social, are to be toyed with; one must make one's own form in order to cope. Thus the "spasmodic gait"—half a control, half a liberty.

This marvelous schizophrenia has us in awe, as it had Frost, for we are surprised by someone submitting to forms and then wrecking them. I think Emily Dickinson did not know what she had invented and was therefore shy about publishing; she did not know if she was presentable. She could apologize for shoddy workmanship and yet know at the same time that it was right, that it was justified.

> Bear with the Ballad –
> Awkward – faltering –
> Death twists the strings –
> 'Twas'nt my blame –
>
> [#1059]

The rough look and rough sound of her poems probably often surprised and annoyed her too, and yet, as Frost said of her, she went right ahead, "plunging through" to get her lines down. And the issue is not whether she did her best at it so much as whether it is good as it is. I think it is possible to judge as Frost did: her strength comes from her willful play.

Though duty often required a person to drop "The Playthings of her Life / To make the honorable Work / Of Woman, and of Wife – " (#732), she claimed that she indeed had "sung / To Keep the Dark away" (#850). She therefore constantly sought to escape what she called "shackles on the plumed feet, / And staples, in the Song" (#512). "Magic," she argued, "hath an Element / Like Deity – to keep – " (#593). That meant that she would try to play with poetry to achieve what Herbert Marcuse calls an "order of sensuousness" that is superior to the "order of reason." Play with poetic form was, for her, a free activity that was consciously outside ordinary life and clearly "a liberation of the senses," but not so much serving the ends of society as "a manifestation of freedom itself."[69] Therapy and liberty, escape and enrichment—these she could make for herself by playing. "It is easy to work," she moralized, "When the soul is at play" (#244).[70]

Emily Dickinson's playful poetics are those of the "slant," to use her own term, thus meeting Emerson's doctrine of spontaneity and individualism in writing. To tell the truth slantedly was a matter of metaphor but, as I am arguing, also of look and sound, the focus of Frost's interest in her poetry. The form toys with the world and with our senses. She therefore appears to have believed that verse is most effective when fading/failing/"off":

> that to me
> Is metre – nay – 'tis melody –

---

69. Herbert Marcuse, *Eros and Civilization* (Boston, 1955), p. 181.
70. A similar epigram of hers reads:

> But Work might be electric Rest
> To those that Magic make –
> [#1585]

And spiciest at fading - indicat[ing] -
A Habit - of a Laureate -

[#785]

To be the kind of "Laureate" she wanted to be, she therefore wrote at a "slant," playing as she wrote in order to achieve what would be "spiciest." Frost forgave her for this—though hardly anyone else he read—because it gave him one of the most remarkably animated versions of life he knew. He recognized that she achieved thereby a kind of baroque exuberance, an elegance, a luxuriance, an abundance as she played at a slant.

In Emily Dickinson the play is not for show, not for spectacle. It turns on itself and is for itself. She just plays. This is the most exotic feature of her style—in fact, her main way of achieving something exotic. And as a result, she ended up writing hymns that are absolutely unsingable; ballad quatrains that are much too "Awkward [and] faltering" to make much of a song or story; pious sermons that mock themselves, disarming what they affirm; meditations on landscapes and seascapes that gush; cold theology controverted by lush sounds. All of these are her very success as a poet. She found how to camp as she cooled her Tramp.

The issue of play in Emily Dickinson's poetry reminds one that we have in her one of the major humorists in American literature. The cheer argues best a coherence to her entire ouvres, even as her play with setting, characterization, metaphor, and the organization of a poem reveals the clown in her.

Take her macabre poem beginning "I heard a Fly buzz—when I died." The point of view is deliberately funny: a woman sitting somewhere hereafter telling other dead how *she* died. There was, she remembers with her flip tale, really nothing to it. The scene of her dying, she *now* realizes, was too grand, and by contrast the moment of death was vulgar and funny. So, she shrugs, she could not really "see to see" what death was like. It was merely a harmless incident in her long existence, but it makes a good tale to tell.

I heard a Fly buzz - when I died -
The Stillness in the Room
Was like the Stillness in the Air -
Between the Heaves of Storm -

The Eyes around - had wrung them dry -
And Breaths were gathering firm
For that last Onset - when the King
Be witnessed - in the Room -

I willed my Keepsakes – Signed away
What portion of me be
Assignable – and then it was
There interposed a Fly –

With Blue – uncertain stumbling Buzz –
Between the light – and me –
And then the Windows failed – and then
I could not see to see –

[#465]

The disciplined striving for meter and rhymes here, and the attractive
failing, represent her pushing ahead with her story/idea, toying with
hopeful approximations until they allude to poetic conventions without meeting them. The effect is not polyphonic orchestration so much
as a convincing voice, a persona, a presence—the point of the poem
anyway. Through "inadequacy" the poem achieves personality. The
play personifies.

Another form her play took—and one revealing almost a perverse streak in her remarkable humor—is in the metaphorical tease.
Metaphor as a form of play is a staple of almost all poetry, but Emily
Dickinson often played at deliberately confusing the distinction between the literal and the metaphorical. Such double takes are more
tricks than ironies and maybe even close to being literary slapstick.
She thus distinguishes herself from the Emersonian-Frostian seriousness over metaphor as being analogous to an analogy-making universe. Instead, she flaunts metaphor as another form of cheer.

In her poem beginning "I know some lonely Houses" she at first
teases us with a literal subject (the robbers) that is really, as it turns
out, merely a fanciful metaphor for her real subject (the sunrise)—all
the while claiming that that is not *her* subject, but only that of a faded,
unreliable couple. The subjunctive verbs are her tip-off to us that she
is making a joke. Her fun is in the playful connections she can think of
between thievery and dawn. As sole metaphysical poetess in the language, she baroques her way through her lexicon's puns on such
words as "stealth" and "daybreak."

I know some lonely Houses off the Road
A Robber'd like the look of –
Wooden barred,
And Windows hanging low,
Inviting to –
A Portico,
Where two could creep –
One – hand the Tools –

The other peep –
To make sure All's Asleep –
Old fashioned eyes –
Not easy to surprise!

How orderly the Kitchen'd look, by night,
With just a Clock –
But they could gag the Tick –
And Mice wont bark –
And so the Walls – dont tell –
None – will –

A pair of Spectacles ajar just stir –
An Almanac's aware –
Was it the Mat – winked,
Or a Nervous Star?
The Moon – slides down the stair,
To see who's there!

There's plunder – where –
Tankard, or Spoon –
Earring – or Stone –
A Watch – Some Ancient Brooch
To match the Grandmama –
Staid sleeping – there –

Day – rattles – too
Stealth's – slow –
The Sun has got as far
As the third Sycamore –
Screams Chanticleer
"Who's there"?

And Echoes – Trains away,
Sneer – "Where"!
While the old Couple, just astir,
Fancy the Sunrise – left the door ajar!

[#289]

But again here, the feet and the rhymes (both on- and off-), more than anything else, keep the language a plaything for her, make the lines light, make the poem fun—fun to write, fun to read. The rhymes come fast but do not match well, while the feet are a pattern of unpredictable variables. The form surprises by being near to conventions and yet having a character—a voice—of its own. The poem, a tease, is therefore *about* teasing.

Over Emily Dickinson at play with such poetic forms, Herbert Marcuse and Norman O. Brown (our best present theoreticians of play) would have quarreled productively. Marcuse would make her a liberator of her senses and therefore a liberator of civilization because she has "greatly enhanced its potentialities" through her example of playfulness. The "play impulse" in her reveals her success at being herself, reveals *our* potential success at being ourselves. The fun can be followed; the clowning is political.[71] Brown, on the other hand, would make her a child instinctively sane because of her "play activity," really subversive of society because pleasure-seeking through poetic means. Taking liberty with form is a way out of repression. This woman making her hyperbolic language, her collapsed/relaxed meters, her trite/experimental/accidental rhymes is a child again.[72]

These two views of Emily Dickinson as Redemptress and Redeemed are probably too large, too social, too libertarian and libertine. I doubt she intended to free others by looking free/freely or that she practiced regression to childlikeness as a way out of repression in adulthood. She is probably better thought of as a Primitive Winning.

It has never been the case that Emily Dickinson's playful awkwardness—again, to Frost, her nemesis/advantage—was, as her editors from Higginson to Johnson have implied, ineptitude; it can never be said that she lacked a consciousness of exact form. Also, it has never been the case that her playful awkwardness—the last example of successful near-primitivism, I feel, in American poetry—was programmatically intended; she was not, as some of her critics have argued, determined to do the forms in. Both of these misjudgments put her in the mold of Brown's child-playing-at-paste-and-attracting-us-to-the-sophisticated-naiveté or else put her in the mold of Marcuse's skilled flouter. Instead, as Frost was good to recognize, she simply invented (accidently? naturally? of necessity?) new forms. That was inevitable, of course, if she were to be Emerson's poet "climb[ing] / For his [her] rhyme," that is, someone letting ideas (for a post-Puritan, always the primary factor anyway) find some of their own forms (again, for a post-Puritan, secondary and merely worldly beauties anyway). The compromise of form with idea gave her, as Emerson had taught it would, a voice of her own, perhaps her own *real* voice, at any rate the opportunity for a recognizable, unique voice by which we can now always identify her. Her primitivism thus wins us over.

Yet Emily Dickinson never did solve—as I think none of her poetic contemporaries did, with the possible exception of Whitman—the conflict between the impulse to the sensuous and the impulse to form. Because she could not solve it, she did not publish. She solved

71. Marcuse, *Eros and Civilization*, pp. 181–96.
72. Norman O. Brown, *Life against Death: The Psycholoanalytical Meaning of History* (New York, 1959), pp. 55–67.

it *for herself* by being her awkward self; tyrannical form she submitted herself to almost passively, but then seems to have shrugged her shoulders, said "Oh, what the hell," and gone ahead, as an annoyed/ chortling Frost reminded us, with what she wanted to say, playing with the form of things as she went.

Among no doubt many other things, Emily Dickinson's willful playfulness elevated her in Frost's estimation to a high poetic status. Within her Ethics of the Fall, she had an Esthetic of Flawed Form that made it possible for her to write as joyfully as she wished to. Frost was sure this was what she meant when she wrote:

> In insecurity to lie
> Is Joy's insuring quality.
>
> [#1434]

Even when the themes run otherwise, Emily Dickinson's is, as has to be argued finally, a poetry of cheer: with poetic form she makes a world in which she would win. The Troubled Woman of much earlier criticism is, as I have tried to argue throughout, really the Joyful Gymnast. How much the fun of metering and rhyming—whether on or off—was her way of enjoying/rejoicing, we may have to learn to appreciate. It is not difficult to recognize that hers was a firm faith in language as glee. The play forms enspirited her, the fun pulled. The kangaroo obviously enjoyed being among the beauty.

A CODA

Emily Dickinson and the Rest of the World

There are other literary affinities in the life of Emily Dickinson's mind. They have either been discussed already well beyond their importance to American literary history—to us, largely forgotten figures like Ik Marvel and Longfellow the novelist[1]—or they are foreign figures against whose stature Emily Dickinson matched her own—to her, brilliant women like Elizabeth Barrett Browning, George Eliot, and the Brontë sisters.[2] I have wanted to set her in the presence mainly of key American writers in order to watch their reactions to her and to watch American literary history developing, but these others must be added in order to complete several of my points about Emily Dickinson writing in America.

Most certainly Blake, Wordsworth, and Keats are there somewhere in her poetry, I feel, as are Thoreau and Melville, maybe even Poe. By the 1850s and 1860s, however, practically everyone who read British poets at all had, to one degree or another, seen a world in a

1. See especially Sewall, *Life*, pp. 678–89.
2. See especially John Evangelist Marsh, *The Hidden Life of Emily Dickinson* (New York, 1971), pp. 90–109; George F. Whicher, "Emily Dickinson among the Victorians," in *Poetry and Civilization* (New York, 1968), pp. 55–61; and Jack Capps, "British Literature: Romantic and Victorian," in *Emily Dickinson's Reading* (Cambridge, Mass.; 1966), pp. 77–100. Also see Mary Janice Rainwater, "Emily Dickinson and Six Contemporary Writers: Her Poetry in Relation to Her Reading" (Ph.D. diss., Northwestern University, 1975).

grain of sand and had, for one purpose or another, wandered lonely as a cloud and had thought, in one form or another, that beauty was truth, truth beauty, maybe even resting together in a tomb. I suspect she read them, if she did, only vaguely, or really did not have the vaguest idea what they had done. And her connections with these additional American figures are uncertain ones too: it is trite to make out both Thoreau and Emily Dickinson as loners, and it is trite to rehearse Melville's and Emily Dickinson's common quarrel with an irresponsible and unresponsive God. She did well enough what they *said* they were doing.

Though she read other writers in English—Byron, De Quincey, Tennyson, Browning, and, above all, Dickens—the English writers she learned from and strongly identified with were hers mainly, I believe, because they were women. Because of the weakening effect of "feminization" on almost all her sister writers in America, as Ann Douglas has brilliantly shown (Harriet Beecher Stowe and Margaret Fuller were distinct exceptions),[3] Emily Dickinson came to the great enjoyment of examples she did not have at all in America: bold, affective, intellectual women achieving literary fame abroad. And although she called Elizabeth Barrett Browning's poems "divine" and George Eliot's poems "great" and her fiction "wise and tender" and the Brontës' works "cunning," her interest in their gender seems to have overshowed her interest in what they wrote. She watched—and liked—what she could of their *lives.*

It is a little sad to watch Emily Dickinson watching through these English women for a vicarious kind of life that her America could not allow her. For indictment we have the incidence of her (curious? envious?) staring out at them from Amherst.

Emily Dickinson's interest in English writers of her time is largely the story of an interest in the recognition of female accomplishment.[4] I have tried to show all along that Emily Dickinson studied with special closeness the writings of other women. Her question seems to have been whether female literary fame was transient—something she noticed about Helen Hunt Jackson and something she surely must have seen consistently brought up in the press concerning Margaret Fuller. Most women writers simply vanished. But she noticed that George Eliot, the Brontës, and Elizabeth Barrett Browning remained strong. Immortality is a motif of her concern about them.

3. Ann Douglas, *The Feminization of American Culture* (New York, 1977).
4. On the issue of women writers seeking recognition during Emily Dickinson's lifetime, see especially Elaine Showalter, *A Literature of Their Own: British Women Novelists from Brontë to Lessing* (Princeton, 1977), pp. 3–36, and Alice Anderson Hufstader, *Sisters of the Quill* (New York, 1978).

She was not so much looking for a female imagination, and certainly not any feminine movement, as trying to learn how female self-consciousness confronted the marketplace. What were their experiences as women-in-the-world? What might *hers* be?

The Victorian authoresses in which Emily Dickinson had a special interest were pioneer professionals at innovating female roles. They broke new ground and created new possibilities. For all of them, writing was a symbol of achievement, a vocation beyond womanhood itself. Elizabeth Barrett's story of Aurora Leigh was also Emily Dickinson's story of worrying herself for decades over her acceptability as a strong-minded, wild-worded woman writing; no wonder she loved reading it. "You misconceive the question like a man," Aurora tells her would-be lover Romney at a crucial point in the verse novel, "Who sees the woman as the complement / Of his sex merely."

> You forget too much
> That every creature, female as the male,
> Stands single in responsible act and thought. . . .
> I too have my vocation,—work to do,
> The heavens and earth have set me.
>
> [2.460–66]

Emily Dickinson only lacked a lover to tell her similar vocation to. How her sister writers in England escaped Victorian repression, concealment, and self-censorship interested her greatly.

Elizabeth Barrett Browning was Emily Dickinson's early favorite as a woman writing. She wrote verses about her as early as 1861:

> I think I was enchanted
> When first a sombre Girl –
> I read that Foreign Lady –
> The Dark – felt beautiful –
>
> [#593]

She was reading *Aurora Leigh* at about this time, and she marked ten lines in her copy that showed what her interest in the English poet was:

> By the way,
> The works of women are symbolical.
> We sew, sew, prick our fingers, dull our sight,
> Producing what? A pair of slippers, sir,
> To put on when you're wearv—or a stool
> To stumble over and vex you . . "curse that stool!"
> Or else at best, a cushion, where you lean
> And sleep, and dream of something we are not
> But would be for your sake. Alas, alas!

This hurts most, this .. that, after all, we are paid
The worth of our work, perhaps.

[1.455-65]

She let both Higginson and Bowles know that Mrs. Browning was an awesome example to her,[5] and she wrote three poems in her memory after she died in 1861, one of which goes:

Her - "last Poems" -
Poets - ended -
Silver - perished - with her Tongue -
Not on Record - bubbled other,
Flute - or Woman -
So divine -

[#312]

She was led to the reading of Robert Browning's poetry through Elizabeth Barrett, and he became the greater influence on her specific ideas and lines of verse,[6] but she seems not to have ceased wondering about "that Foreign lady" and her courage to show how "The works of women are symbolical" of their ability to "Stand single in responsible act and thought." Most of her comments about her concern not so much the characteristics of her poetry as they do the immortality of a poetess. Mrs. Browning had lasted.

Emily Dickinson was conscious that to some extent Elizabeth Barrett Browning leaned on the fame of a man, but she knew that Mary Ann Evans and the Brontës did not (even though they sought their vocation of writing through masculine names, George Eliot and Currer Bell, and had initially made their way because of the androgynous deception). More important, though, to her they were victims of opprobrium for the daring of their lives and language. She was hungry for word of their alleged notoriety in the press and in early biographies of them. Though surprised herself at what they said and did, she was very much attracted to them. In a poem of 1859 she wrote of Charlotte Brontë:

All overgrown by cunning moss,
All interspersed with weed,
The little cage of "Currer Bell"
In quiet "Haworth" laid.

This Bird - observing others
When frosts too sharp became

---

5. *Letters*, pp. 404, 410, 415, 491. Other references to Elizabeth Barrett Browning's poetry are in *Letters*, pp. 376, 495, 575, 607-8, 695, 759-60.
6. See Capps's account of her reading of him, *Emily Dickinson's Reading*, pp. 87-91.

Retire to other latitudes –
Quietly did the same –

But differed in returning –
Since Yorkshire hills are green –
Yet not in all the nests I meet –
Can Nightingale be seen –

Gathered from many wanderings –
Gethsemane can tell
Thro' what transporting anguish
She reached the Asphodel!

Soft fall the sounds of Eden
Upon her puzzled ear –
Oh what an afternoon for Heaven,
When "Bronte" entered there!

[#148]

The terms here honor her for her worldly abilities and for her ability to take her worldliness into the hereafter: her "cunning" *adds* to heaven.

The "gigantic Emily Bronte" was also interesting to Emily Dickinson for the ways she could talk about love in her poems and fiction;[7] several of her own love poems may actually derive from *Jane Eyre* and *Wuthering Heights*. It is a comparing of notes with the Brontës that went on.

Similarly, she was overwhelmed by George Eliot—though only late in her life—because of her erratic, boldly aggressive, and yet secluded life and because of the liveliness in the characters she created.[8] Of her she wrote:

She bore Life's empty Pack
As gallantly as if the East
Were swinging at her Back.

[#1562]

"*My* George Eliot," she called her by 1881, having come close to her. The writer in London got away with things the one in New England could not; perhaps it was a projected self. Skepticism was one thing Emily Dickinson watched her getting away with: her "greatness" denied her "The gift of belief" in anything conventionally religious; "she lost her way." Ugliness was another thing: "God chooses repellant settings, dont he, for his best Gems?" And then above all there was her ability to immortalize the mortal, to give things of the world some

---

7. *Letters*, pp. 77, 437, 543, 562, 721, 775, 802–3, 844, 848.

8. *Letters*, pp. 491, 506, 547–48, 549, 551, 685, 689, 693, 700, 769–70, 850–51, 865, 903–4.

lasting form. I think we may believe it has very much of a self-projection. To the question "What do I think of *Middlemarch*?" she answered in 1873:

> What do I think of glory – except that in a few instances this "mortal had already put on immortality."

> George Eliot is one. The mysteries of human nature surpass the "mysteries of redemption," for the infinite we only suppose, while we see the finite.

"Time," she wrote later in 1880, had "ommitted [the] Gift" of recognizing George Eliot adequately, and so Emily Dickinson hoped that her worldliness might gain some recognition "as part of the Bounty of Eternity."[9] The immortality is one the American writer wanted for herself: the wayward, eccentric woman acceptable later/hereafter.

These four, as I have tried to stress, are women writers Emily Dickinson could measure herself against. She had no one in America—blatantly no one—who was her match. (Elizabeth Barrett Browning thought that a feminist like Margaret Fuller would be better off dead in her native land; what would she have thought then of Emily Dickinson?) The problem in Ann Douglas's indictment of a Victorian America without women writers can be corrected in part by Emily Dickinson's example:

> A period which produced Nathaniel Hawthorne, Herman Melville, Walt Whitman, Henry David Thoreau, Ralph Waldo Emerson, Edwards A. Park, and Horace Bushnell, among others, produced no women, with the exceptions of Margaret Fuller and [Harriet Beecher] Stowe, who could match their claims even if the standards used were appropriately rephrased and redefined. . . . Where is . . . our George Eliot?[10]

More than any other woman writing in America in the nineteenth century, Emily Dickinson "rephrased and redefined" the standards in an attempt to show herself the match of her English sisters.

Because she hid, or because they made her hide herself, Americans of her time were thus denied a confrontation with one of the nation's real heroines. She summarily dismissed them as unworthy of her. "I now know all the people worth knowing in America, and I find no intellect comparable to my own." The words are Margaret Fuller's, but we can imagine that Emily Dickinson's sentiment was similar. The

9. *Letters,* pp. 700, 693, 506, 689.
10. Douglas, *Feminization of American Culture,* pp. 306, 309.

terms she uses on her four English writers suggest the extent to which she knew that her own country provided few of the traditional means of recognizing intellectual women that England did. Her English peers had special precedents, sanctions, and abilities that were denied her here. She emulated their opportunities; she did not have the circumstances that made them possible. That she survived the repression of the best in her is the most important part of her biography. Though she did not choose the place where she wanted to live and write, she never wavered in her determination to live her own life and not someone else's.

Her Puritan heritage reconciled her to America as much as anything could—an America that turned her into a struggler after the manner of Anne Bradstreet, Edward Taylor, and Jonathan Edwards. These kinds of Puritanism, as I have shown, were her only serious involvement in American history. And except for those who were not totally ashamed of their Puritan past—Harriet Beecher Stowe, Hawthorne, and Emerson—she seemed to sense the ways her contemporaries and near-contemporaries would have wanted her primarily as mere moralist, as minister. She escaped many of the expectations of a woman of her time. And she was saved well enough for future readers of her poetry because they mainly saw her as incomplete rather than sweet, playful rather than wholly serious, a recluse rather than resourceful. She made her own kind of country.

Still, she seems to have sensed that her accomplishments made her something of an outcast in her own land, even something of a freak. That self-confession came from the recognition that she had almost no female precedents or models to assist her in believing in what she was or in discovering what she wanted to become. We therefore find out a great deal about Emily Dickinson's criticism of the role of intellectual women in America from the fact that the only women she found worth identifying with at all seriously were all foreigners: Elizabeth Barrett Browning, George Eliot, and the Brontës.

That does not mean that she was fully satisfied with these models; her awareness that she had few models to imitate and emulate was still ambivalent. George Eliot would not believe; the Brontës were a little nasty; they all had lives to gossip about. Still, they were intelligent women in the marketplace; Emily Dickinson had only the mirror of her own narcissism. Her society did not present the stimulus or encouragment of an audience. Were her full powers therefore never reached? Did it ever occur to her that she was not living in the right place and among the best people? For the most part, I guess we have to assume she found herself by not asking such questions. She could find herself by *not* finding such a world. She did not have

Melville's problem of conceiving of America as an inheritance, as a burden. America was not a problem she had to comprehend. It is still another sense in which she was a kangaroo among the beauty.

The usual indigenous poet, even when as much of an anomaly as Emily Dickinson was in many ways, participates in the given and the ongoing and helps make the course of things. This is Emily Dickinson, as I hope I have shown. But Emily Dickinson must be thought of as indigenous in still another sense: she is now strong enough as a writer in our literary history to transform our view of the culture itself. She makes *it* indigenous to *her*. We may understand much of it somewhat differently because of her.

INDEX TO POEMS
BY EMILY DICKINSON

335

GENERAL INDEX

Note: ED refers to Emily Dickinson

Library of Congress Cataloging in Publication Data

Keller, Karl, 1933–
    The only kangaroo among the beauty.

    Includes index.
    1.   Dickinson, Emily, 1830–1886—Criticism and
interpretation.   I. Title.
PS1541.Z5K4   811'.4   79–10462
ISBN 0–8018–2174–6 (hardcover)
ISBN 0–8018–2538–5 (paperback)